References for the Rest of Us!®

COMPUTER BOOK SERIES FROM IDG

Are you intimidated and confused by computers? Do you find that traditional manuals are overloaded with technical details you'll never use? Do your friends and family always call you to fix simple problems on their PCs? Then the *...For Dummies*® computer book series from IDG Books Worldwide is for you.

...For Dummies books are written for those frustrated computer users who know they aren't really dumb but find that PC hardware, software, and indeed the unique vocabulary of computing make them feel helpless. *...For Dummies* books use a lighthearted approach, a down-to-earth style, and even cartoons and humorous icons to diffuse computer novices' fears and build their confidence. Lighthearted but not lightweight, these books are a perfect survival guide for anyone forced to use a computer.

> *"I like my copy so much I told friends; now they bought copies."*
> — Irene C., Orwell, Ohio

> *"Quick, concise, nontechnical, and humorous."*
> — Jay A., Elburn, Illinois

> *"Thanks, I needed this book. Now I can sleep at night."*
> — Robin F., British Columbia, Canada

Already, millions of satisfied readers agree. They have made *...For Dummies* books the #1 introductory level computer book series and have written asking for more. So, if you're looking for the most fun and easy way to learn about computers, look to *...For Dummies* books to give you a helping hand.

5/97

by Cynthia L. Baron
and Renée LeWinter

IDG Books Worldwide, Inc.
An International Data Group Company

Foster City, CA ♦ Chicago, IL ♦ Indianapolis, IN ♦ Southlake, TX

Web Animation For Dummies®

Published by
IDG Books Worldwide, Inc.
An International Data Group Company
919 E. Hillsdale Blvd.
Suite 400
Foster City, CA 94404
www.idgbooks.com (IDG Books Worldwide Web site)
www.dummies.com (Dummies Press Web site)

Copyright © 1997 IDG Books Worldwide, Inc. All rights reserved. No part of this book, including interior design, cover design, and icons, may be reproduced or transmitted in any form, by any means (electronic, photocopying, recording, or otherwise) without the prior written permission of the publisher.

Library of Congress Catalog Card No.: 97-80225

ISBN: 0-7645-0195-X

Printed in the United States of America

10 9 8 7 6 5 4 3 2 1

1B/RW/QZ/ZX/IN

Distributed in the United States by IDG Books Worldwide, Inc.

Distributed by Macmillan Canada for Canada; by Transworld Publishers Limited in the United Kingdom; by IDG Norge Books for Norway; by IDG Sweden Books for Sweden; by Woodslane Pty. Ltd. for Australia; by Woodslane Enterprises Ltd. for New Zealand; by Longman Singapore Publishers Ltd. for Singapore, Malaysia, Thailand, and Indonesia; by Simron Pty. Ltd. for South Africa; by Toppan Company Ltd. for Japan; by Distribuidora Cuspide for Argentina; by Livraria Cultura for Brazil; by Ediciencia S.A. for Ecuador; by Addison-Wesley Publishing Company for Korea; by Ediciones ZETA S.C.R. Ltda. for Peru; by WS Computer Publishing Corporation, Inc., for the Philippines; by Unalis Corporation for Taiwan; by Contemporanea de Ediciones for Venezuela; by Computer Book & Magazine Store for Puerto Rico; by Express Computer Distributors for the Caribbean and West Indies. Authorized Sales Agent: Anthony Rudkin Associates for the Middle East and North Africa.

For general information on IDG Books Worldwide's books in the U.S., please call our Consumer Customer Service department at 800-762-2974. For reseller information, including discounts and premium sales, please call our Reseller Customer Service department at 800-434-3422.

For information on where to purchase IDG Books Worldwide's books outside the U.S., please contact our International Sales department at 415-655-3200 or fax 415-655-3295.

For information on foreign language translations, please contact our Foreign & Subsidiary Rights department at 415-655-3021 or fax 415-655-3281.

For sales inquiries and special prices for bulk quantities, please contact our Sales department at 415-655-3200 or write to the address above.

For information on using IDG Books Worldwide's books in the classroom or for ordering examination copies, please contact our Educational Sales department at 800-434-2086 or fax 817-251-8174.

For press review copies, author interviews, or other publicity information, please contact our Public Relations department at 415-655-3000 or fax 415-655-3299.

For authorization to photocopy items for corporate, personal, or educational use, please contact Copyright Clearance Center, 222 Rosewood Drive, Danvers, MA 01923, or fax 508-750-4470.

LIMIT OF LIABILITY/DISCLAIMER OF WARRANTY: AUTHOR AND PUBLISHER HAVE USED THEIR BEST EFFORTS IN PREPARING THIS BOOK. IDG BOOKS WORLDWIDE, INC., AND AUTHOR MAKE NO REPRESENTATIONS OR WARRANTIES WITH RESPECT TO THE ACCURACY OR COMPLETENESS OF THE CONTENTS OF THIS BOOK AND SPECIFICALLY DISCLAIM ANY IMPLIED WARRANTIES OF MERCHANTABILITY OR FITNESS FOR A PARTICULAR PURPOSE. THERE ARE NO WARRANTIES WHICH EXTEND BEYOND THE DESCRIPTIONS CONTAINED IN THIS PARAGRAPH. NO WARRANTY MAY BE CREATED OR EXTENDED BY SALES REPRESENTATIVES OR WRITTEN SALES MATERIALS. THE ACCURACY AND COMPLETENESS OF THE INFORMATION PROVIDED HEREIN AND THE OPINIONS STATED HEREIN ARE NOT GUARANTEED OR WARRANTED TO PRODUCE ANY PARTICULAR RESULTS, AND THE ADVICE AND STRATEGIES CONTAINED HEREIN MAY NOT BE SUITABLE FOR EVERY INDIVIDUAL. NEITHER IDG BOOKS WORLDWIDE, INC., NOR AUTHOR SHALL BE LIABLE FOR ANY LOSS OF PROFIT OR ANY OTHER COMMERCIAL DAMAGES, INCLUDING BUT NOT LIMITED TO SPECIAL, INCIDENTAL, CONSEQUENTIAL, OR OTHER DAMAGES.

Trademarks: All brand names and product names used in this book are trade names, service marks, trademarks, or registered trademarks of their respective owners. IDG Books Worldwide is not associated with any product or vendor mentioned in this book.

 is a trademark under exclusive license to IDG Books Worldwide, Inc., from International Data Group, Inc.

About the Authors

Cynthia Baron is the author of *Creating a Digital Portfolio*. She has been a contributing editor for *Computer Graphics World* and is currently a contributor to *Critique Magazine*. A designer and typographer, Cyndi is Technical Director of Computer Graphics for the Department of Art & Architecture at Northeastern University in Boston. She develops curriculum and teaches computer graphics courses for the undergraduate program in graphic design, for the new program in multimedia studies, and for University College, Northeastern's Continuing Education degree program.

Renée LeWinter is an artist, print/multimedia designer, and computer consultant based in Somerville, Massachusetts. She is the coauthor of *Photoshop Web Magic*. Her articles have appeared in publications such as *Computer Graphics World* (for which she was a contributing editor), *Computer Artist, U&lc, Siggraph Daily,* and *Electronic Publishing*. As the former head of an undergraduate visual and media design program at Northeastern University in Boston, Renée developed extensive curriculum to introduce design and computer graphics concepts to artists, designers, and business professionals. Her paintings can be seen online at the 9ll Gallery Web site — www.911gallery.org/911/renee.html.

ABOUT IDG BOOKS WORLDWIDE

Welcome to the world of IDG Books Worldwide.

IDG Books Worldwide, Inc., is a subsidiary of International Data Group, the world's largest publisher of computer-related information and the leading global provider of information services on information technology. IDG was founded more than 25 years ago and now employs more than 8,500 people worldwide. IDG publishes more than 275 computer publications in over 75 countries (see listing below). More than 60 million people read one or more IDG publications each month.

Launched in 1990, IDG Books Worldwide is today the #1 publisher of best-selling computer books in the United States. We are proud to have received eight awards from the Computer Press Association in recognition of editorial excellence and three from *Computer Currents*' First Annual Readers' Choice Awards. Our best-selling *...For Dummies*® series has more than 30 million copies in print with translations in 30 languages. IDG Books Worldwide, through a joint venture with IDG's Hi-Tech Beijing, became the first U.S. publisher to publish a computer book in the People's Republic of China. In record time, IDG Books Worldwide has become the first choice for millions of readers around the world who want to learn how to better manage their businesses.

Our mission is simple: Every one of our books is designed to bring extra value and skill-building instructions to the reader. Our books are written by experts who understand and care about our readers. The knowledge base of our editorial staff comes from years of experience in publishing, education, and journalism — experience we use to produce books for the '90s. In short, we care about books, so we attract the best people. We devote special attention to details such as audience, interior design, use of icons, and illustrations. And because we use an efficient process of authoring, editing, and desktop publishing our books electronically, we can spend more time ensuring superior content and spend less time on the technicalities of making books.

You can count on our commitment to deliver high-quality books at competitive prices on topics you want to read about. At IDG Books Worldwide, we continue in the IDG tradition of delivering quality for more than 25 years. You'll find no better book on a subject than one from IDG Books Worldwide.

John Kilcullen
CEO
IDG Books Worldwide, Inc.

Steven Berkowitz
President and Publisher
IDG Books Worldwide, Inc.

Eighth Annual
Computer Press
Awards ≥1992

Ninth Annual
Computer Press
Awards ≥1993

Tenth Annual
Computer Press
Awards ≥1994

Eleventh Annual
Computer Press
Awards ≥1995

IDG Books Worldwide, Inc., is a subsidiary of International Data Group, the world's largest publisher of computer-related information and the leading global provider of information services on information technology. International Data Group publishes over 275 computer publications in over 75 countries. Sixty million people read one or more International Data Group publications each month. International Data Group's publications include: **ARGENTINA:** Buyer's Guide, Computerworld Argentina, PC World Argentina; **AUSTRALIA:** Australian Macworld, Australian PC World, Australian Reseller News, Computerworld, IT Casebook, Network World, Publish, Webmaster; **AUSTRIA:** Computerwelt Osterreich, Networks Austria, PC Tip Austria; **BANGLADESH:** PC World Bangladesh; **BELARUS:** PC World Belarus; **BELGIUM:** Data News; **BRAZIL:** Annuário de Informática, Computerworld, Connections, Macworld, PC Player, PC World, Publish, Reseller News, Supergamepower; **BULGARIA:** Computerworld Bulgaria, Network World Bulgaria, PC & MacWorld Bulgaria; **CANADA:** CIO Canada, Client/Server World, ComputerWorld Canada, InfoWorld Canada, NetworkWorld Canada, WebWorld; **CHILE:** Computerworld Chile, PC World Chile; **COLOMBIA:** Computerworld Colombia, PC World Colombia; **COSTA RICA:** PC World Centro America; **THE CZECH AND SLOVAK REPUBLICS:** Computerworld Czechoslovakia, Macworld Czech Republic, PC World Czechoslovakia; **DENMARK:** Communications World Danmark, Computerworld Danmark, Macworld Danmark, PC World Danmark, Techworld Denmark; **DOMINICAN REPUBLIC:** PC World Republica Dominicana; **ECUADOR:** PC World Ecuador; **EGYPT:** Computerworld Middle East, PC World Middle East; **EL SALVADOR:** PC World Centro America; **FINLAND:** MikroPC, Tietoverkko, Tietoviikko; **FRANCE:** Distributique, Hebdo, Info PC, Le Monde Informatique, Macworld, Reseaux & Telecoms, WebMaster France; **GERMANY:** Computer Partner, Computerwoche, Computerwoche Extra, Computerwoche FOCUS, Global Online, Macwelt, PC Welt; **GREECE:** Amiga Computing, GamePro Greece, Multimedia World; **GUATEMALA:** PC World Centro America; **HONDURAS:** PC World Centro America; **HONG KONG:** Computerworld Hong Kong, PC World Hong Kong, Publish in Asia; **HUNGARY:** ABCD CD-ROM, Computerworld Szamitastechnika, Internetto online Magazine, PC World Hungary, PC-X Magazin Hungary; **ICELAND:** Tolvuheimur PC World Island; **INDIA:** Information Communications World, Information Systems Computerworld, PC World India, Publish in Asia; **INDONESIA:** InfoKomputer PC World, Komputek Computerworld, Publish in Asia; **IRELAND:** ComputerScope, PC Live!; **ISRAEL:** Macworld Israel, People & Computers/Computerworld; **ITALY:** Computerworld Italia, Macworld Italia, Networking Italia, PC World Italia; **JAPAN:** DTP World, Macworld Japan, Nikkei Personal Computing, OS/2 World Japan, SunWorld Japan, Windows NT World, Windows World Japan; **KENYA:** PC World East African; **KOREA:** Hi-Tech Information, Macworld Korea, PC World Korea; **MACEDONIA:** PC World Macedonia; **MALAYSIA:** Computerworld Malaysia, PC World Malaysia, Publish in Asia; **MALTA:** PC World Malta; **MEXICO:** Computerworld Mexico, PC World Mexico; **MYANMAR:** PC World Myanmar; **NETHERLANDS:** Computer! Totaal, LAN Internetworking Magazine, LAN World Buyers Guide, Macworld Netherlands, Net, WebWereld; **NEW ZEALAND:** Absolute Beginners Guide and Plain & Simple Series, Computer Buyer, Computer Industry Directory, Computerworld New Zealand, MTB, Network World, PC World New Zealand; **NICARAGUA:** PC World Centro America; **NORWAY:** Computerworld Norge, CW Rapport, Datamagasinet, Financial Rapport, Kursguide Norge, Macworld Norge, Multimediaworld Norge, PC World Ekspress Norge, PC World Nettverk, PC World Norge, PC World ProduktGuide Norge; **PAKISTAN:** Computerworld Pakistan; **PANAMA:** PC World Panama; **PEOPLE'S REPUBLIC OF CHINA:** China Computer Users, China Computerworld, China InfoWorld, China Telecom World Weekly, Computer & Communication, Electronic Design China, Electronics Today, Electronics Weekly, Game Software, PC World China, Popular Computer Week, Software Weekly, Software World, Telecom World; **PERU:** Computerworld Peru, PC World Profesional Peru, PC World SoHo Peru; **PHILIPPINES:** Click!, Computerworld Philippines, PC World Philippines, Publish in Asia; **POLAND:** Computerworld Poland, Computerworld Special Report Poland, Cyber, Macworld Poland, Networld Poland, PC World Komputer; **PORTUGAL:** Cerebro/PC World, Computerworld/Correio Informático, Dealer World Portugal, Mac*In/PC*In Portugal, Multimedia World; **PUERTO RICO:** PC World Puerto Rico; **ROMANIA:** Computerworld Romania, PC World Romania, Telecom Romania; **RUSSIA:** Computerworld Russia, Mir PK, Publish, Seti; **SINGAPORE:** Computerworld Singapore, PC World Singapore, Publish in Asia; **SLOVENIA:** Monitor; **SOUTH AFRICA:** Computing SA, Network World SA, Software World SA; **SPAIN:** Communicaciones World España, Computerworld España, Dealer World España, Macworld España, PC World España; **SRI LANKA:** Infolink PC World; **SWEDEN:** CAP&Design, Computer Sweden, Corporate Computing Sweden, Internetworld Sweden, it branschen, Macworld Sweden, MaxiData Sweden, MikroDatorn, Natverk & Kommunikation, PC World Sweden, PCaktiv, Windows World Sweden; **SWITZERLAND:** Computerworld Schweiz, Macworld Schweiz, PCtip; **TAIWAN:** Computerworld Taiwan, Macworld Taiwan, NEW ViSiON/Publish, PC World Taiwan, Windows World Taiwan; **THAILAND:** Publish in Asia, Thai Computerworld; **TURKEY:** Computerworld Turkiye, Macworld Turkiye, Network World Turkiye, PC World Turkiye; **UKRAINE:** Computerworld Kiev, Multimedia World Ukraine, PC World Ukraine; **UNITED KINGDOM:** Acorn User UK, Amiga Action UK, Amiga Computing UK, Apple Talk UK Computing, Macworld, Parents and Computers UK, PC Advisor, PC Home, PSX Pro, The WEB; **UNITED STATES:** Cable in the Classroom, CIO Magazine, Computerworld, DOS World, Federal Computer Week, GamePro Magazine, InfoWorld, I-Way, Macworld, Network World, PC Games, PC World, Publish, Video Event, THE WEB Magazine, and WebMaster; online webzines: JavaWorld, NetscapeWorld, and SunWorld Online; **URUGUAY:** InfoWorld Uruguay; **VENEZUELA:** Computerworld Venezuela, PC World Venezuela; and **VIETNAM:** PC World Vietnam. 3/24/97

Dedication

To Arlene, Jack, Judy, Larry, and Martin for all the shared memories. — Renée

To Shai for everything past, present, and future. — Cyndi

Authors' Acknowledgments

Thanks to Flo Scott and Scott Burgess at the Electronic Imaging Center in Boston and Norbert Florendo at Acme Digital Lab for taking time out from their busy schedules to lend us a hand.

Thanks to Douglas Mitchell for his continuing encouragement.

Thanks to Elizabeth Calitri for her invaluable help.

We would like to thank all the companies that generously supplied us with software, clip art, fonts, and photography.

Thanks are extended to our IDG Books Worldwide team: Jill Brummett, Freelance copy editor; Tammy Castleman, Senior Copy Editor; Chris Collins and Donna Love, Editorial Assistants; E. Shawn Aylsworth, Project Coordinator; Shelley Lea, Supervisor of Graphics and Design, and the rest of the Production team; and John Chastain, Technical Editor.

Special thanks to Senior Acquisitions Editor Jill Pisoni and Project Editor Robert Wallace for their advice, encouragement, and good humor.

Publisher's Acknowledgments

We're proud of this book; please send us your comments about it by using the IDG Books Worldwide Registration Card at the back of the book or by e-mailing us at feedback/dummies@idgbooks.com. Some of the people who helped bring this book to market include the following:

Acquisitions, Development, and Editorial

Project Editor: Robert H. Wallace

Senior Acquisitions Editor: Jill Pisoni

Media Development Manager: Joyce Pepple

Associate Permissions Editor: Heather H. Dismore

Copy Editors: Tamara S. Castleman, Jill Brummett

Technical Editor: John Chastain

Editorial Manager: Leah P. Cameron

Editorial Assistant: Donna Love

Production

Project Coordinator: E. Shawn Aylsworth

Layout and Graphics: Cameron Booker, Lou Boudreau, Linda M. Boyer, Angela F. Hunckler, Todd Klemme, Tom Missler, Heather N. Pearson, Brent Savage, Michael A. Sullivan

Proofreaders: Sharon Duffy, Christine Berman, Janet Withers

Indexer: Sharon Hilgenberg

Special Help

Mark Kory, Media Development Intern; Joell Smith, Associate Technical Editor; Diane L. Giangrossi, Associate Editor; Quality Control; Publication Services: Gwenette Gaddis, Copy Editor; Dwight Ramsey, Reprint Editor; Tamara Castleman, Senior Copy Editor; Elizabeth Netedu Kuball, Copy Editor; Tina Sims, Copy Editor

General and Administrative

IDG Books Worldwide, Inc.: John Kilcullen, CEO; Steven Berkowitz, President and Publisher

IDG Books Technology Publishing: Brenda McLaughlin, Senior Vice President and Group Publisher

Dummies Technology Press and Dummies Editorial: Diane Graves Steele, Vice President and Associate Publisher; Kristin A. Cocks, Editorial Director; Mary Bednarek, Acquisitions and Product Development Director

Dummies Trade Press: Kathleen A. Welton, Vice President and Publisher

IDG Books Production for Dummies Press: Beth Jenkins, Production Director; Cindy L. Phipps, Manager of Project Coordination, Production Proofreading, and Indexing; Kathie S. Schutte, Supervisor of Page Layout; Shelley Lea, Supervisor of Graphics and Design; Debbie J. Gates, Production Systems Specialist; Robert Springer, Supervisor of Proofreading; Debbie Stailey, Special Projects Coordinator; Tony Augsburger, Supervisor of Reprints and Bluelines; Leslie Popplewell, Media Archive Coordinator

Dummies Packaging and Book Design: Patti Sandez, Packaging Specialist; Lance Kayser, Packaging Assistant; Kavish + Kavish, Cover Design

♦

The publisher would like to give special thanks to Patrick J. McGovern, without whom this book would not have been possible.

♦

Contents at a Glance

Introduction 1

Part I: Room to Move: Animation Basics 7
Chapter 1: Surveying a Moving Landscape 9
Chapter 2: The Dream Theme — Telling a Visual Story 31
Chapter 3: Planning a Moving Experience 41
Chapter 4: Getting into Character 55

Part II: Tricks with Pix 83
Chapter 5: Color Me Simple 85
Chapter 6: Roll Over, Gutenberg, and Rock Your Type 107
Chapter 7: Art without Guilt: Using Clip Art 127
Chapter 8: Dynamic Photos 147
Chapter 9: Universal Graphic Widgets 167

Part III: Heavy Lifting: Making Technology Work for You 181
Chapter 10: The Skinny on Image Size 183
Chapter 11: Mondo Conversion: Rehabbing Your Files 195
Chapter 12: Getting Browser Ready 221

Part IV: Getting Moving: Animating GIFs & Plug-Ins on Parade 229
Chapter 13: Free Ride: Web Animation on a Shoestring 231
Chapter 14: Cheap Tricks: Inexpensive Web Animation Software 253
Chapter 15: You Pay, You Play: Commercial Web Animation Software ... 275
Chapter 16: Making the Final Cut 291

Part V: The Part of Tens 301
Chapter 17: The Checklist — Ten Software Gotta Haves 303
Chapter 18: Ten Commandments of Image Conversion 307
Chapter 19: Ten Ways to Make the Earth Move 311

Part VI: Appendixes 319
Appendix A: Places to Visit Online 321
Appendix B: About the CD 327

Glossary 335

Index 341

IDG Books Worldwide Registration Card .... Back of Book

Cartoons at a Glance

By Rich Tennant

Page 7

Page 229

Page 83

Page 319

Page 181

Page 301

Fax: 508-546-7747 • E-mail: the5wave@tiac.net

Table of Contents

Introduction 1
How to Use This Book 1
How This Book Is Organized 2
    Part I: Room to Move: Animation Basics 3
    Part II: Tricks with Pix 3
    Part III: Heavy Lifting: Making Technology Work for You 3
    Part IV: Getting Moving: Animating GIFs & Plug-Ins on Parade 3
    Part V: The Part of Tens 4
    Part VI: Appendixes 4
No Margin for Error: All About Those Icons 4
Moving Right Along 5

Part I: Room to Move: Animation Basics 7

Chapter 1: Surveying a Moving Landscape 9
The Many Faces of Web Animation 10
    Personal Web sites: Anything goes 10
    Business Web sites: Not quite button-down 11
    Animated advertising: A banner year 11
    Editorial animation 11
Split Levels: The Animation Continuum 12
    Easy threshold solutions 12
        GIF animation 12
        Repurposing presentation software 15
    Midrange solutions for more power 16
        Java applets 17
        Inline plug-ins 20
        Going inline 22
    Programmer's paradise 25
        VRML and animation 26
        CGI scripts 26
        ActiveX 28
Learning to Love Your Limitations 28

Chapter 2: The Dream Theme — Telling a Visual Story 31
What's the Big Idea? 31
    Web animation is not a daytime game show 32
    Brainstorming without galoshes 32
Cold Assessment: What Can You Really Do? 34

Make 'Em Laugh . . . Maybe 36
Connecting Ideas to Existing Sites 37
    Animating logos 37
    Animated buttons 38
    Animations as emphasis 39
Come Into My Parlor, Said the Spider to the Fly 40

Chapter 3: Planning a Moving Experience 41

Surf's Up: Making a Storyboard without Wiping Out 42
    Boy Scouts at the beach 42
    Preparing the storyboard template 44
    Location, location, location! Placing your characters 46
    "I've been framed!" — breaking out of the box 48
        Using imaginary 3-D 49
        Cropping to fit the action 51
        If you can't beat 'em . . . join 'em! 52
The Secret of Index Cards 53

Chapter 4: Getting into Character 55

Setting the Mood — Posing Your Characters 55
    Strike a pose: Making simple changes for good effect 56
    Asymmetry: Avoiding the perils of perfection 56
    Personality: Becoming a minor god 59
        Moody hues 60
        The eyes have it 62
        Body language 64
Dissecting the Moving Parts 65
Trading Technique for Technology 67
    Onion-skinning without tears 67
    Betwixt and in-between 68
Making Still Images Move: The Classic Techniques 69
    Studies in Arc-y-ology 69
    Making a mass with volume: Weight and gravity 73
        Anticipation: The weighting game 74
        Squash and stretch 75
        Overlapping action 77
        Speed up and slow down 77
        Going cyc-lotic 78
Timing — or, the Lowdown on Stand-Up 79

Part II: Tricks with Pix 83

Chapter 5: Color Me Simple 85

Color Is Not a Box of Chocolates 85
    Finding the Color Picker 87
    Deciphering the RGB numeric values 89

The Lean, Mean Palette for Fat-Free Color 90
Going Beyond Default Palettes 91
Making Your Custom Color Palette 93
Creating the Right Color Mix 94
    The Color Model Sketch 95
    Reading the color thermometer 96
        Warm colors 97
        Cool colors 98
        Neutral colors 99
After Mixing, Throw Out the Blender! 101
Putting a Positive Spin on Negative Space 103
High Contrast Avoids High Anxiety 105

Chapter 6: Roll Over, Gutenberg, and Rock Your Type 107

Designing Type 108
    Opening your type chest 108
    Building a font family 111
        Changing the proportional ratio 111
        Changing the stroke thickness 112
        Roman versus italic and script typefaces 113
Bagging the Right Typeface 114
Looking for Type Fonts? 116
Playing the Mix and Match Game 117
    Combining serif with sans serif fonts 118
    Opposites attract 120
Figuring Out When to Anti-Alias 122
Combining Titles and Text 123
Using Decorative Letters and Numbers Without Overkill 125
Flying Logos and Icons: How Not to Crash and Burn 126

Chapter 7: Art Without Guilt: Using Clip Art 127

Can't Draw? Don't Worry: Clip Art to the Rescue 127
Selecting Clip Art for Animation 128
    Moving your visitor 129
    Staying put 130
    Other animating experiences 130
    Escape from the endless edit 130
    Collections originally designed for print 132
        Buy their CD-ROM catalog sampler, or check out
            their Web site 132
Hints for Customizing Clip Art 136
    Changing clip art colors 139
    Modifying a silhouette to suggest action 140
Basic Training on Intellectual Property — Garlic for Legal Vampires 142
    First variation in our story 143
    Second variation in our story 144

Chapter 8: Dynamic Photos 147

Raiding Your Photo Album 147
Scanning Your Photos 151
Getting Digital Photos Ready for the Web 154
Millions You Can Choose 158
    Licensing and usage fees 158
    File formats and file sizes 159
    What's out there 160
Playing with Effects and Filters 161
    Feathering an edge in Photoshop 4.0 161
    Corel PHOTO-PAINT 6.0 artistic vignette effect 163
    Creating a cutout drawing 163
        Creating a cutout in Photoshop 4.0 164
        Creating a cutout using Microsoft Image Composer 1.0 165

Chapter 9: Universal Graphic Widgets 167

Building Frames: One Layer at a Time 167
Grid for Action 171
Transforming Multiple Objects from One Source 173
Lifting a Finger: Creating Isolated Action in Your Image Area 174
Metamorphosing Photos into Clip Art 179

Part III: Heavy Lifting: Making Technology Work for You 181

Chapter 10: The Skinny on Image Size 183

Lessons in Economy 183
    Image size 185
    Cropping 186
    Losing your resolution 188
    Unnecessary background detail 191
Simplify, Simplify, Simplify 192
    Virtual zit prevention made easy 193
    Anti-aliasing can be counterproductive 193

Chapter 11: Mondo Conversion: Rehabbing Your Files 195

Choosing a File Format 196
    GIF file format 196
    System picture-file formats 196
    TIFF file format 196
    Photoshop file format 197
    JPEG file format 197
    Other file formats 197
    What do we recommend? 197
How Do You Compress a File? 200
    Making a JPEG conversion 200
Convert One for the GIFfer 203

The Incredible Shrinking GIF 210
Vive la Différence! 214

Chapter 12: Getting Browser Ready 221

Planning Events 221
Appreciating the Value of Testing 221
Attaching Your Animation to Your HTML Page 224
Quo Vadis? Seeing Your Animation Through Browsing Eyes 226

Part IV: Getting Moving: Animating GIFs & Plug-Ins on Parade 229

Chapter 13: Free Ride: Web Animation on a Shoestring 231

Common Ground 231
   Position 234
   Delay 234
   Disposal 234
   Looping 235
Using GifBuilder — Moving in Place 236
   Bringing in the files 236
   Transparency obscura 237
   Setting universal animation options in GifBuilder 239
      Changing frame size 239
      The delights of delay 241
      A good disposal method 242
      Getting a little loopy 242
   Using the special features of GifBuilder 243
      Using transitioning effects 243
      Shrinking after we dissolve 245
Using Microsoft Gif Animator — Seeing Stars 245

Chapter 14: Cheap Tricks: Inexpensive Web Animation Software 253

Animating with GIFmation Special Features 254
   Opening multiple animations 254
   Making real-time edits 254
   Building global palettes automatically 255
   Controlling transparency 258
   Editing anti-aliased edges 259
   Onion-skinning 261
Using GIF Construction Set 263
   Using the Animation Wizard 264
   Making an LED sign 269
   Creating soft shadow banners 270
   Editing transitions 273

Chapter 15: You Pay, You Play: Commercial Web Animation Software 275

Java Applet of Our Eye: WebMotion 276
    Why use WebMotion? 276
    Drawbacks? 278
Flexing Animation Muscle: RubberWeb Composer 279
    Why use RubberWeb? 279
    Drawbacks? 280
Tripping the Light Fantastic: ObjectDancer 282
    Why use ObjectDancer? 282
    Drawbacks? 283
All in One Box: WebPainter 284
    Why use WebPainter? 285
    Drawbacks? 286
No Flash in the Pan: Macromedia Flash 2 287
    Why use Flash? 288
    Drawbacks? 288

Chapter 16: Making the Final Cut 291

The Wisdom to Tell the Difference 291
Major Problems — Can This Movie Be Saved? 292
Minor Headaches — Take Two Aspirin And 293
    The file is too big 293
        Animation as football field 293
        Animation deep as a well 294
    The file is too long 294
        Limiting yourself to one simple action 295
        Breaking up your animation 295
    The file is too slow 296
        Delaying reaction 296
        Eliminating frame creep 297
    The file runs rough 298
        The case of the missing frames 298
        The case of the incomplete edit 298
        The case of the mixed messages 299
Post-animation blues 299
    Please make it stop! 299
    The file worked fine on my system! 300

Part V: The Part of Tens 301

Chapter 17: The Checklist — Ten Software Gotta Haves 303

Gotta Have Layers 303
Gotta Have Scale, Skew, Rotate, Flip, and Flop 304
Gotta Have Transparent Background 304
Gotta Have Palette Optimization 304

Table of Contents

    Gotta Have Placing Coordinates 305
    Gotta Have Netscape and Microsoft Browser Compliance 305
    Gotta Have Editing for Text, Image, Header, and Comment Blocks 305
    Gotta Have a Viewer 306
    Gotta Have a Download Test 306
    Gotta Have Good Documentation 306

Chapter 18: Ten Commandments of Image Conversion 307

    Thou shalt consider bandwidth and keep it holy 308
    Thou shalt crop thy files to their minimum 308
    Thou shalt work at screen resolution 308
    Thou shalt scale files before indexing 309
    Thou shalt edit before JPEG conversion 309
    Thou shalt index to the Netscape palette 309
    Thou shalt optimize thy palette 309
    Thou shalt not dither flat art 310
    Thou shalt not anti-alias moving objects 310
    Thou shalt not interlace animation frames 310

Chapter 19: Ten Ways to Make the Earth Move 311

    Earth Turning 312
    Earth Closing In 312
    Earth Circling Sun 313
    Rock 'n' Roll Earth 313
    Earth Walk 314
    Earth: Soccer It to Me 315
    Earth Lifting 315
    Earth Express 316
    Earth Moving 317
    Earth Rising 318

Part VI: Appendixes 319

Appendix A: Places to Visit Online 321

    Global resources 321
        Searching Yahoo! 321
        Web sites that go somewhere 321
        All about GIF animation 322
        Freeware and shareware to download 322
    Resources 322
        Software and Filters 322
        Fonts 323
        Stock Photography Agencies 324
        Clip Art, Stock Photo, and Textures CD-ROM Collections 324
        Royalty-Free Sound and Music CD-ROMs 325
        Digital Cameras 325

Appendix B: About the CD 327
    System requirements 327
    How to use the CD using Microsoft Windows 328
    How to use the CD using a Mac OS computer 329
    What you find 330
        Animation tools and viewers 330
        Authoring and imaging tools 331
        Image and sound samplers 332
    If you have problems (of the CD kind) 333

Glossary *335*

Index *341*

IDG Books Worldwide Registration Card .... *Back of Book*

Introduction

Web animation is not for wimps. At least that's what any right-thinking person would assume by looking at the current crop of material available on the subject. We beg to differ. You don't have to be the Charles Atlas of the Internet to hold your own. Web animation is within your grasp — assuming, of course, that you're currently grasping this book.

We don't want to mislead you. Some animations at the high-end corporate sites are probably beyond your current reach. They require an ace programmer, an experienced designer, and a firm ready to bankroll these massive talents. Such animations also use a lot of cool and expensive stuff. "Get Shocked!" they admonish. "Drink in that Java!" they chortle. "If you aren't into VRML, you're no place!" (And if you had to look up VRML in the glossary in the back of this book, you know that they're talking to you.)

But we'll let you in on a secret: The real key to a good Web animation isn't how jazzy your software is. (Don't get us wrong, we like jazzy software, we use jazzy software, and lots of jazzy software is included on the CD that comes with this book.) What matters are good ideas, knowing how to make (or adapt) good materials, and an understanding of what grabs and holds attention. We cover all of these things in this book — as well as how to apply them successfully in some of those jazzy software programs.

Even better, we like to think we do so in a way that makes the whole package easy to swallow. This book is packed with step-by-step instructions and useful tips. We also supply occasional technical sidebars and tangential digressions that you're free to ignore or appreciate, as you wish.

And by the way, don't be fooled by the "For Dummies" in the title. This book is meant for people smart enough to know what they're not experts in, and that means people who are very smart indeed.

How to Use This Book

We assume right up front that you won't read this book in order. In fact, we assume that you won't read the whole book at all, that you'll just jump into the chapters that speak to your needs and interests. That's okay, although we humbly submit that this book is packed with great info, is well organized, and is even a great deal of fun. If we had it in our power to do so, we'd insist that you read everything, in chronological order, because we think you'd be a better person for it.

But we're realists. Because this book covers a lot of ground, we know that you'll probably find something in here that you already know. When you do, skip it. Just remember, the stuff you find too simple someone else will read avidly, and vice versa.

Speaking of assumptions, predicting what you, the reader, may have available is an impossible task. We've decided to err on the side of low-tech and tight pocketbooks. Except when we use a specific Web animation program (and we tell you this up front), we assume as little as possible about what tools you use. You'll find our instructions generic, and, within unavoidable minimum standards, adaptable to your software of choice.

You should be able to do almost everything in this book if you have image editing software (like Adobe Photoshop or CorelPHOTO-PAINT!), a plug-in for this program that creates GIF89a files or a separate file format converter, and a shareware GIF animation program. A few things are easier to do if you also have an illustration program (such as Adobe Illustrator, Freehand, or CorelDRAW!).

As for animation software, we've tried to keep our information as current as possible, and offer you a taste of the software smorgasbord. But wow! Talk about a moving target! There has been an explosion of Web animation tools recently. Creators of illustration and presentation software have jumped in too, by making transferring material into Web animation form much easier. So we may not hit your favorite batch of software this time out. Rest assured, that shouldn't get in the way. We're concentrating on transferable knowledge here, stuff that you should be able to apply constructively to whatever set of software cards you've been dealt.

How This Book Is Organized

This book is broken into individual parts by subject theme. The parts are organized in a more or less chronological fashion, starting with a survey of Web animation, moving to idea generation and development, through individual frame creation, and on into making the movie and putting it up on the Web. Each part of this book can be read as a separate entity, although we sometimes refer to useful information in other parts and chapters.

Those sections that need visuals to explain what you need to do have them, occasionally in abundance. Sometimes seeing is understanding. You'll find these things on the CD-ROM, referenced clearly so you can find them.

Part I: Room to Move: Animation Basics

We firmly believe that you can't create an awesome Web animation if you don't know anything about animating. This part orients you to what Web animation is about, and tells you how to get from your basic idea to the point that you're ready to make animation frames.

Chapter 1 is a whirlwind tour of Web animation options, with an eye toward helping you recognize the different categories and understand how much (or how little) technical expertise they require. Chapter 2 introduces you to idea generation, style, and integrating your animation with an existing site's look and feel. Chapters 3 and 4 go for the nitty-gritty. They're a rich and fully-packed how-to on basic animation techniques.

Part II: Tricks with Pix

An animation is a series of individual images seamlessly linked. That means you have to make them before you can use them! Part II discusses the process of creating, altering, and assembling the individual frame images of an animation sequence.

In Chapters 5 through 9, we cover all the usual suspects: color, type, clip art, and photos. You find out how to use them all effectively in building the frames for your Web animation. Chapter 9 focuses on some of the most popular programs for building your frames and how to get the most out of them.

Part III: Heavy Lifting: Making Technology Work for You

Unfortunately, it's not all fun and games. This part is where we concentrate on the nuts and bolts of preparing a sequence of images for the Web. Web-ification presents some unique challenges, which if not met up front, will grab you coming out the back door. We give you enough technical expertise to be dangerous without burdening you with the tedious stuff you don't need.

Part IV: Getting Moving: Animating GIFs & Plug-Ins on Parade

Here's what you've been waiting for. Using some of the best and most popular methods, we go through a step-by-step process of converting your individual frames or slides into an animation. Along the way, we expose you to more nifty animation tricks and techniques. Chapter 16 helps you look back on your animation, tighten it, and tie up the loose ends.

Part V: List Lovers Delight: The Part of Tens

It wouldn't be a ...*For Dummies* book without the beloved Part of Tens. At least that's what the folks at IDG say, and who are we to argue? Here you'll find a potpourri of carefully distilled tips on what you absolutely positively must know about Web animation.

Part VI: Appendixes

The last Part of this book contains two valuable appendixes. The first appendix is a list of resources for clip art, photos, software, and fonts available to you through the Web and the regular mail. We also include an appendix that covers the goodies you find on the CD-ROM that's included with this book.

No Margin for Error: All About Those Icons

When you leaf through the book, you can't help but notice those cute circular icons in the margin. That's the idea. These icons exist to point the way to particularly important material. Not that the whole book doesn't qualify, of course! But if we put them next to every paragraph, we'd be like the boy who cried wolf. Eventually, you'd simply ignore them, get into trouble, or miss some juicy tip, and probably sue us for pain and suffering.

We don't want you to suffer, even for an instant, so we'll use this opportunity to introduce you to the friendly little pictures and what they represent.

Sometimes we come across something so absolutely juicy it cries out to be passed around and appreciated. Whenever that happens, you see this Tip icon. It's your signal that something really tasty is waiting for you here.

Like Dorothy in the *Wizard of Oz,* if you stay on the path, you'll find your way home. Or at least to the home page, which may be just as good. This Warning icon is our way of letting you know that you're facing a potential poppy field.

Introduction 5

 If you're really nerd-averse, you can think of this Technical Stuff icon as a special kind of warning. It lets you know that, like it or not, we simply feel driven to pass along a hunk of specialized knowledge. We try not to burden you with more of this esoteric info than we think you can stand.

 We occasionally feel compelled to break our rule and point out something that may be really useful in another stage in the process, even if it's not in the same chapter. When that happens, we use this Remember icon as a quick heads-up.

 Every once in a while something occurs to us that we really want to mention, even though it isn't, strictly speaking, on the agenda. We recognize that this behavior is obsessive, but we can't always control it. If you hate digressions, this icon will put you on notice.

 We'd be hard-pressed to talk about color and movement in a black-and-white book. To help you visualize the topics and give you the opportunity to try the things we discuss, we loaded the CD-ROM that accompanies this book with a candy store full of software, clip art, photos, and sample animations, as well as files to work through step-by-step. Whenever you see this icon, we're sending up a goodie alert.

Moving Right Along

We love making things move, and we hope you do too. If you have suggestions or comments — or just want to show off the things this book helps you make — we'd like to hear from you. You'll find us at www.webcreature.com.

But enough of the introductions. We know that you're here to make Web animations. And we don't want to stand in your way for a moment longer. Come with us as we jump right in.

Yes, really. Turn the page already! We're ready to get moving.

Part I
Room to Move: Animation Basics

In this part...

The chapters in Part I put animation on the Web into perspective with a whirlwind tour of technology and applications. You can gain an understanding of the possibilities and limitations of creating all current forms of Web animation. After you're thoroughly oriented, we take you through the principles for success in animation: idea generation, idea development, and classic animation techniques.

Chapter 1
Surveying a Moving Landscape

In This Chapter
- ▶ Deciding when to use Web animations
- ▶ Understanding limitations and opportunities
- ▶ Recognizing types of Web animations
- ▶ Finding what you need at each level of animation

A few years ago, our next-door neighbors decided to build a two-car garage. This proposed architectural nightmare would have been right near our bedroom window — not so great for us, given that they owned two cars without mufflers and kept distinctly weird hours with high-decibel friends named Masher and Bobo. After trying to negotiate with no effect, we hired a surveyor to prove that they didn't own enough space on that side of their house to build a garage. The boundary between our house and the neighbor's place ran up a hill for only 50 feet, but it took the surveyors with all their equipment almost two hours to get the measurements we needed. Everything seemed to get in the way of a clean line of sight: trees, a fence, one car, and Bobo.

It was hard not to think of this experience when we started writing about Web animation. Every time the data seemed to be in place, something new jumped into our sights and changed the view. The landscape of Web animation curves, dips, changes direction, and pushes up new branches as we write — and as you read. In this chapter, we follow those twists and turns to provide a usable map of what this new area is all about, what your options are, and what information you need to get from the beginning to the end of the process. Without Bobo, that is.

The Many Faces of Web Animation

A fable we've heard is about a group of scholars, all of them so old and studious that they had lost their sight from poring over ancient texts. The scholars were taken to examine an elephant. The first one grabs the elephant's trunk. "An elephant is like a snake!" he claims. The second is holding one of the elephant's ears. "How could you misjudge the situation so badly! An elephant is like a giant bat!" The third gives a superior sniff as he stands by the elephant's leg. "Obviously your powers of analysis have dimmed through lack of use. An elephant is very like a tree!"

The World Wide Web is at least as big as an elephant, and even more impossible to get a handle on. Like the scholars, much of your impression depends on what you've experienced. You can just as easily think that Web animation is difficult or a waste of time as you can come to the conclusion that it's simple and fun. In this chapter, we try to make sure that you get to fit all the pieces of this virtual elephant into a clear, true picture of the beast.

We begin by defining what we mean by Web animation. *Animation* is a series of still frames meant to be shown in a sequence and at a fast-enough speed to give the illusion of motion. Animation isn't a slide show of unrelated pictures, and it isn't a cartoon with dialogue balloons. *Web animation* is a special form of animation. It is created in formats that are viewable on a Web page by people using a variety of computer systems. Unlike film animation, which can be feature-length and very sophisticated, Web animation is not usually created to stand on its own. It is a decorative, narrative, or navigational element meant to enhance the Web site that it lives in.

Personal Web sites: Anything goes

Personal Web sites are the great unchartable wilderness of the Web. Given how many people now offer their own site and how many others join them every day, it doesn't look like civilization is going to crowd in anytime soon. Personally, we think this wild unchecked growth is a good thing. It practically guarantees that the Web will keep that cutting edge of experimentation, which makes the Web such a fascinating place (not to mention the source of steady income for all of us who write books about it).

Depending on the technical and graphics skills of the individual, you can find animations that are wonderfully clever or incredibly useless. Lots of Web animations on personal sites are simply a decorative substitute for a static GIF illustration. Many personal Web sites often boast several tiny animations on a page. Here also, you find lots of off-the-shelf animations. We've compiled a list of online sites (some of which are free or shareware compilations created by people who want to share their work) and commercial suppliers in Appendix A.

Business Web sites: Not quite button-down

The use of animation for corporate Web sites is on a growth trajectory. Even banks and finance corporations are adding animation to their pages. Of course, the number and flavor of these animations are keyed to the type of business. The tendency on many corporate sites is to keep the animations small and silent. This trend is particularly true for those companies whose businesses are seen as more conservative. You see some flashing or rotating logos, but the most frequent use of animation is in moving typography, banners, and attention-grabbing "new" buttons on corporate pages. Some of the larger, national sites, particularly sellers of big-ticket items like automobiles, depend on JavaScripting (more on that later) to create more complex or physically larger animations.

Animated advertising: A banner year

Advertising banners are clickable images, which means that they are linked to the advertiser's site with HTML code that activates with a mouse click inside the live area. Whether the banner is a simple flashing series of words or a complex animated image, advertisers want you to notice their message. Because of this, you're guaranteed to find animation used in some way on the majority of advertising banners. These banners tend to be a predetermined size and shape, and you may come across the same message on several different sites. This tendency can make Web advertising feel like the fast food segment of Web animation. Advertising banners tend to be GIF animations, for reasons we talk about a little later in this chapter.

Editorial animation

Although most animation is used either as punctuation or advertising, magazine and newspaper sites, along with some personal sites devoted to a specific topic, also have created a Web animation that is content, not navigation or decoration. Okay, so some of that is more like a table of contents than real meat, but it's only the beginning. Magazine sites are beginning to accompany their feature stories with cycling illustrations — a loop of photos and drawings that act as a visual preview for the text content. Personal, magazine, and cult sites are using Web animations as eye candy, or to offer visual commentary. And of course, you can find animations that are similar in concept to film cartoons, with a complete plot, characterization, and clear sequence of events. Here is one place where Web animation growth is assured.

Split Levels: The Animation Continuum

Web animation can really be as easy or as difficult as you want it to be. You'll see this as we tour the animation supermarket for our Web ingredients.

Indeed, Web animation has more faces than a Jim Carrey movie. Most people just accept the Web animation they see without thinking of the different technological levels they're actually experiencing. Things spin, or flash, or move, or play music. Some are right on the page, others are in their own separate frames or windows, and still others must be downloaded and played in with a separate viewer. Some are clickable, some are not. Some look like they were drawn, some look like photos, and others look like real movie clips. These variations are often not just personal style. Different levels of technology let the Web animator do different things.

Not knowing how many different levels you can operate on can lead you to expect too much from your first animation, or to take a big, code-filled bite when all you need is a low-tech tidbit.

Easy threshold solutions

Some Web animation possibilities have a very low entry threshold, which means that you don't need much prior experience to handle them successfully. We have a personal preference for these kinds of technology. Many people live their lives on the bleeding edge of Web technology. We admire them, just as we admire those people who lose their toes conquering Mount Everest. But we don't think we want to encourage you to emulate them. Some things take time, and they need to be approached in stages. Why spend weeks learning the intricacies of 3-D animation and scripting when you can be garnishing your Web pages with motion in mere days?

GIF animation

A GIF image is a picture file that has been compressed as a special file format to make it use up very little disk space. The GIF file format is universally supported by Web browsers and HTML coding. A *GIF animation* is a group of individual GIF images with some coding that tells a browser what frames to display, how much time should elapse between each frame, and what to do with the frame after it's been shown. If you've ever made a flipbook in an art class, you've experienced the basic idea behind GIF animation.

GIF animations offer many pluses that make them the current technology of choice for Web sites:

- GIF animations are very easy to create. In fact, they need no programming skills at all. With a Web page layout program capable of dealing with GIF89a files, you may not even need to know basic HTML coding. (Don't recognize the term *GIF89a*? Check out the sidebar "GIF 87 versus GIF89a" later in this chapter.) Even without this kind of tool, the HTML coding required to add a GIF animation to your Web page is relatively simple. (But we talk about it in Chapter 12, so don't worry!)

- When making a GIF animation, the hardest and most time consuming part of the process is creating the frames themselves, not in setting them up for the Web. But really, the same goes for all forms of Web animation, even those that require computer programming skills.

- If done correctly, GIF animations are really very small in file size. This is critical on the Web, where normal adults suddenly display even less patience than a six-year-old with a deluxe cable package and a remote control.

- Most browsers support GIF animations. Unless your Web surfer is working with a really antique browser (some people are selling copies of Mosaic 1.0 along with Victorian furniture now), it will display your animation. Because you want as many people as possible to admire your work, this is no small thing, and it's not true for any other options, like Java applets or inline plug-ins — alternatives that we discuss later in this chapter.

- GIFs are very dependable. When you think of all the possibilities of browsers, systems, and servers available, it's nice to know that what you make has a good chance of actually working the way you planned. Other forms of Web animation are less stable, less universal, or less compact than the GIF. If your object is mass, not massive, entertainment, GIFs are definitely the way to go.

- GIF animations don't require a plug-in. *Plug-ins* (special add-on software to enhance what your browser can read) take up disk space and loading time. A significant amount of people will be happy to pass up your animated exploding galaxy if viewing it means having to download a 200KB plug-in.

- GIF animations are a cheap date. You can download freeware and shareware programs from the Web to create these animations. You don't need a big investment to jump in immediately.

GIF 87 versus GIF89a

By now, most everyone who has created a Web page has used a GIF file. Certainly, if you've surfed the Web, you've encountered them, even if you didn't realize it at the time. Essentially, a *GIF* is a picture file compressed for fast down- and up-loading on the Internet. It was developed by the pioneering online service CompuServe as a cross-platform method of displaying high-quality images.

You may have run into two versions of the GIF format: GIF 87 and GIF89a. The major difference between the two is that GIF89a, which is based on GIF 87, supports two very important elements we need for Web animation: transparency and multiple images.

Trivia lovers will note that the 87 and 89a in these names refer to the year each version of the format was instituted. Yes, it's true, the possibility of creating a Web animation existed as long ago as 1989, long before a Web as you know it existed. So, even though Netscape can't claim credit for inventing GIF animation, it wasn't until the launch of its Navigator 2.0 that a browser existed to support any of the 89a animation possibilities.

Because of the long lead time between creating the 89a spec and its full usefulness, most image creation software prior to 1996 only supported the standard GIF 87 version. So if you don't have fully-upgraded versions of Corel PHOTO-PAINT, Adobe Photoshop, or another painting program (or if you're still working with an old copy of PixelPaint or Microsoft Paintbrush), the CompuServe GIF format you're saving your files in is probably 87. You'll either need a separate plug-in or a piece of software to do this conversion for you. (We offer a list of possibilities in Appendix A.)

Some GIF animation programs can take a wide variety of source formats, so it's possible that you can make a GIF animation with older paint and image tools. However, you could discover that you have less control over your animations, and that you have to keep going back to your original images to make them work the way you'd planned.

Minimum tools: You probably already own almost everything you need to get started with animated GIFs except the GIF animation program itself. When we talk about minimum tools for creating Web animations, the following list is what we have in mind:

- **Image creation software:** Adobe Photoshop 4.0 or above, Adobe Illustrator 6.0.2 or above, CorelDRAW or Corel PHOTO-PAINT, Painter, or Dabbler — anything that lets your create a raster image and export it to a standard image format for your platform.

- **File format converter:** If you have a recent and fully upgraded painting or drawing program, chances are it has some method of saving a file as a GIF89a. But if not, you can find several dedicated GIF converters around, at various levels of capability. A list of possibilities is found in Appendix A.

- **GIF optimizer:** Optimizers may not meet the strict definition of minimum tool, because you can create a GIF animation without one. However, the animation will probably be too slow and large if you haven't optimized your files, so we strongly recommend owning one.

  Your options range from freeware IrfanView32 (for Windows NT and 95 only) to fully-featured programs like Equilibrium Debabelizer Toolbox or Debabelizer Pro (demo versions of which are on the CD-ROM that accompanies this book), to GIF animation programs that offer their own palette-optimizing features. Once again, check out Appendix B.

- **GIF animation program:** Of course, you still need something that lets you compile and preview your frames, assign their speed, loop them, and maybe add some simple bells and whistles. Programs that cost little or nothing exist on both platforms. We explain these issues when we examine GifBuilder (freeware for the Macintosh) and Microsoft GIF Animator (freeware for Windows) in Chapter 13. Gif Construction Set (shareware for Windows) and GIFmation (an inexpensive product for the Macintosh with some very useful additional tools) offer some very nifty additional possibilities, which we profile in Chapter 14.

  Some commercial GIF-based animation programs have image creation tools as part of their package. These generally don't offer all the art-making options that full-fledged imaging software does, but they do eliminate the issues of converting and optimizing your files. And we like that a lot. We deal with one of them, Totally Hip's WebPainter (for Windows 95 and Macintosh), in Chapter 14. We've chosen it because it operates on three levels: GIF animation for simple work, QuickTime plug-in if you want to add sound, or its own Sizzler proprietary plug-in for interactive multimedia.

- **Text editor:** You need something to attach your animation to your Web page. Because HTML is just a text coding language, not a programming one, anything that saves plain ASCII text (Microsoft Write, Macintosh Simple Text, or almost any word processing program) will do. In fact, you need a text editor (or, of course, a Web page layout program) for any Web animation.

Repurposing presentation software

You may already have a Web animation ready to roll and not know it. A growing number of presentation packages either have functions within them to export directly to Web pages, plug-in software to make the translation, or a separate module for adapting, creating, and customizing these presentations for immediate Web gratification — a process known as *repurposing*. In many cases, this process is so seamless that you barely know you've moved into Web animation.

Of course, not every presentation lends itself to repurposing on the Web. Additionally, this direction is meant to create full Web pages with some built-in motion effects, not to enhance existing pages or offer content tailored for the Web.

Adapting a presentation has some obvious benefits:

- **Minimal learning curve:** Hey, you already know this software! Transforming your slides into Web material is usually no more difficult than learning some new function in your program.
- **Software to make the translation is probably free or very inexpensive:** With very few exceptions, taking a presentation (or parts of it) into Web form is being offered by the original software company as an upgrade or plug-in. Those companies that have separate software for this purpose (like Astound's WebMotion) are offering more value and control over the process, at a very reasonable price.
- **Instant content:** Isn't it nice to know that you can bypass all the agony of creating something new and add motion to your pages practically overnight?

Minimum tools: To adapt a presentation to the Web, you need the following:

- **A presentation software package.** Of course, not all presentation software supports transfer to the Web. Microsoft PowerPoint and Astound are two that already do. Unless you own one of these packages, you need to check the current state of your software, because these are the kinds of options that are likely to change almost weekly.
- **A repurposing plug-in, upgrade, or specialized third-party software.**

Midrange solutions for more power

Here's where the biggest possibilities for growth exist. GIF animation is a wonderful thing, but a little self-limiting. GIFs were never intended as animation frames; they've simply been hijacked for this purpose. What do you do if you want an animation that's longer, bigger, louder, or more complex? You turn to one of the coming generation of Web animation tools.

Unlike GIF animation programs (which all use the same file format, thus making it easy to move your animation frames from one to another, even across platforms), each of these new Web animation tools has its own user interface, and some of these are a little quirky. Additionally, they offer an incredible variety of different solutions to the Web animation equation. As we write, no one program is available that does everything you may want to do.

Note: Even though these solutions don't require any programming by the user, they demand some other skills, not the least of which are patience and determination. These are full-featured programs, with the kinds of prices that such programs command.

Java applets

Java is (choose one):

- What goes into my double latte.
- An island where people drink coffee while surfing the Web.
- That big, ugly alien who had Han Solo encased in carbonite.
- The Holy Grail for Web programmers, usually filled with caffeine. (No, no, they fill the Grail with caffeine, not the . . . oh, never mind!)
- None of the above.

Whether you see Java as the Holy Grail or choose one of the other options probably depends on whether or not you're a programmer. For most of you, Java and the Holy Grail probably have a great deal in common. You don't know where or how to use it, haven't ever tried to find it, and may not even recognize it if it knocked on the door and invited itself to breakfast. Fortunately, even if you flunk the Java recognition test, you can still reap the benefits of its existence.

You can take advantage of Java applets by buying a Web animation program that makes them for you from your material. Yes, just like instant coffee, you don't have to do a thing except provide the right ingredients and mix them together.

Also like instant coffee, however, you can get a bitter taste in your mouth and a case of jitters if you're not careful. Not all the bugs have been swatted in the world of Java applets.

First thing, Java applets are bigger and slower than GIF animations, because they have to download not just the animation itself but all the code that lets that animation run. When you surf through a really cool site and watch the animation start up in jerky slo-mo while your disk drive churns, you know you're seeing Java in action. Speed may not be a consideration if you assume that everyone who'll be surfing through your site is on a fast connection with a current browser. If you hope to appeal to a less empowered audience, you may want to think twice.

Java, script, and applets: Muddy waters

The inspired naming of Java by Sun Microsystems has resulted in a slew of programs, plug-ins, and competitors eager to add a little virtual caffeine to their names. The original Java and its supporting children haven't made this any easier by plopping the word in front of several related but not identical things.

The idea behind Java itself is rather cool, because it comes from the idea that you shouldn't have to rewrite all your software code just because you're writing for a different hardware platform. The idea of not having to support several different platform flavors is very attractive to many people, from software companies who spend lots of money in cross development, to people like you who would like to see the same program work the same way no matter where you are.

Java is a specific kind of programming language called *object-oriented*. To be honest, you don't really need to know what that means, because the possibility that it will be important to your Web animation is about equal to that of your being hit by lightning while dodging a hungry Tyrannosaurus rex in Topeka. To a programmer, object-oriented means that it's one of a new type of programming language and that it bears some relationship to C++, except it's more streamlined. Lots of programs you use on a day-to-day basis on your PCs are written in C++, but you never interact with the language directly yourselves. You don't have to expect any more contact than that with Java itself.

On the other hand, you will definitely come into contact with two of Java's "children" — JavaScript and Java applets. JavaScript, unlike Java itself, is actually something called an *API* (Application Programming Interface). APIs are like negotiators in diplomacy. They provide a means for unruly applications to all play together in harmony. Netscape developed JavaScript specifically to allow people on different platforms to take advantage of their browser's capacity to deliver information.

JavaScript is much simpler than Java and is designed to allow programmers and non-programmers alike a relatively simple way to control the way users interact with a Web site. Anyone who has gotten beyond the basics of Hypercard scripting, Macromind Lingo, or AppleScript will have no real problem mastering JavaScript.

Most of you, however, will work with Java through Java applets. As you may guess from the cute name, *applets* are little applications. They enable people without programming skills, or even scripting skills, to create cross-platform, browser-ready material. Because they activate from the Web server, they don't require any more action from the surfing audience than a downloaded GIF does. This enables the average user to create really sophisticated content (like Web animations) just as they would with Adobe Photoshop or Microsoft PowerPoint.

Second, lots of people are not using Java-enabled browsers or are using older versions of them that may not take advantage of all your bells and whistles. Most Internet Service Providers (ISPs) that hand out browsers as part of their package do not include the latest and greatest releases, and most people new to the Web don't know the difference. At least if your GIF animation doesn't work, your viewers will see the first frame as a still image. Who knows what they'll get from the Java applet? This problem is one of the major reasons why many high-end but mass-market sites have stuck with GIF animations so far. Ditto for advertisers who want their product message seen by anyone with a modem.

Third, most Java applets have a learning curve that looks a lot more like the Rockies than the Adirondacks. If you're one of those "No Pain, No Gain" types, this won't stand in your way. But we assume that if you're reading this book, you'd much prefer a pleasant walk in the woods to clinging to a couple of handholds in the wind. Maybe next book, when Java's installed some virtual ski lifts.

If you find an applet with a comfortable slope, then Java animation has many obvious advantages:

- **No plug-ins to worry about:** As we said before, plug-ins require a committed audience. Anything that lets you deliver a quality animation without requiring your viewer to do anything special to earn it is good for you.

- **Can write your own HTML code to add an applet:** If you're comfortable with HTML, you can integrate an applet into your Web page as easily as adding a picture. This is not always the case with plug-ins.

- **Takes several different forms of files and formats:** Because you're working with a separate application and not a GIF attribute, you can integrate JPEGs, Midi sound, and a host of other file formats into your animation. This ability gets around the problem of having to convert photographs to low-resolution, minimized-palette images and opens up a world of interactive possibilities.

- **Allows much larger and more sophisticated animations:** A faucet drip is irritating when you want to make a splash. Java applets provide the best potential solution for multimedia envy. Sound, transitions, and even animations that react differently according to what kind of system the viewer is on or what they do on-screen are all part of the Java potential.

Minimum tools: To use Java, you need all the minimums for GIF animations, plus *Java applet creation software.* This category of software is just beginning to expand. The first options on the market were so programming-heavy or complex that they just weren't worth the effort. However, WebMotion by Astound takes advantage of Java and is a beautifully elegant and easy way to understand this piece of software. We explore it in Chapter 14.

Inline plug-ins

Rabbits are cute, fuzzy, fun creatures. They're no bigger than a large cat, and they don't claw the furniture. They make great pets. But if you put a couple of rabbits of the opposite persuasion in close contact, pretty soon your neighbors will organize a lynching party. Because rabbits breed like . . . well, like rabbits. This is the downside (or, perhaps, fur-side) of letting them into your life.

Why are we talking about furry rodents when the heading is "inline plug-ins"? Because if you download a plug-in every time your browser prompts you, in short order your browser directory will be even bigger than Windows 95.

If you go to the Netscape site, you find almost 30 plug-ins devoted to 3-D and animation alone. Add the Audio/Video, the Presentation, and a few of the Image Viewers, and you're talking serious overpopulation. No matter what you'd like, you'd need a massive hard drive and enough RAM to render a Jurassic dinosaur in order to have them all.

Plug-ins also vary radically in size. Face it, software that lets you do seriously cool stuff usually comes with serious programming overhead. That goes for the plug-in sizes, too. In some cases, the plug-in is close to a megabyte large. Of course, not all plug-ins are big bunnies. The QuickTime plug-in, for example, is so tiny (about 38K) that anyone could (and should) have it. But the average animation plug-in is a lot bigger than that.

The bad news continues. Think about what you have to do to add a plug-in to your browser's collection. You visit an interesting sight. You click on a link to an animation, and the dialog box comes up. "Nya, nya! You don't have this plug-in! Follow me, and I'll bring you to a place where you can pick it up right now! Hey, come on, it's free!" If you bite, you're led to a download site where you're expected to wait on a modem line for ten minutes while the plug-in downloads. Then you have to install it into the right folder and . . . that's right . . . restart your browser. By this time, you have to really want to see whatever was on that Web page. Oh, you didn't bookmark it before you went to restart? "Nya, nya!"

Working with animation plug-ins is great as long as *one* of two requirements are met:

- **Your work is so interesting that everyone will download whatever is needed to see it.** If you have a Web site to die for, anyone who can will download your animation software's plug-in, no matter what it is or how obscure the software company.

- **You've used a plug-in that's popular with other people making animation.** Your work can be one step above cow pats (oops! watch that step!), but if you've made it by using something that everyone else uses, chances are even that your site will be seen more than a good animation done with an obscure plug-in.

What are plug-ins, really?

Plug-ins are an enormously efficient way of adding possibilities to a piece of software without having to create infinite numbers of upgrades. In general, a plug-in is software that adds something functional to another program but can't stand alone as an application. Adobe pioneered the concept of plug-ins with its Photoshop filter add-ons. Quark Xpress has some plug-ins (called Xtensions) that are so Xtensive some could qualify as real programs.

In the world of browsers, plug-ins are another word for "readers." After they're in place within your larger application, they enable your computer's browser to identify and read Internet files with special formats. These range from simply making Excel spreadsheets accessible on a Web page, to adding interpreters for animation and multimedia applications.

How are plug-ins different from Java? Java is a cross-platform programming language that works directly within your browser's HTML reading functions. A current browser that is Java-enabled treats your Java applets pretty much the way it treats everything else on a standard page. It looks for the place on the server that the applet sends it to and downloads the information on demand to your Web page.

Plug-ins, on the other hand, are proprietary programs that are external to your browser's own code. They are written by the companies who produce individual software programs and, like all other programs, are platform-dependent. In theory, that means that you can create a piece of software to run on only one platform, but you can create several plug-ins that make the results of the software readable on many platforms.

And in case you were wondering, an *"inline" plug-in* is not the opposite of an outline plug-in. It's one that displays the work inside the browser rather than in a separate viewer window.

These two reasons are why companies with new programs are so interested in having people download their trial software and use it.

If you want the power of working with plug-ins, you have to expect some resistance and work around it. That work-around can take several forms. The easiest method is just to warn your visitors on your home page that you're using a specific plug-in and to offer them a direct link from your page for the download.

The more difficult (but probably most effective) approach is to make a simple GIF animation version of your animation for the plug-in deprived. Doing so isn't necessarily that hard. Many plug-in software manufacturers now export their animations in both GIF and the plug-in versions. Of course, you'll lose the high-end capabilities you probably wanted the plug-in software for, but at least you won't send your visitors away hungry.

Because you're too smart to have a raft of rabbits in your backyard, you're probably clever enough to have figured out that plug-ins travel with some serious baggage — most of it too big to fit in your overhead compartment. So what are the advantages of plug-ins?

- **Easy to integrate music and other sounds:** Like Java applets, plug-ins offer you more than the sounds of silence. Some animations just cry out for music or sound effects. Inline plug-ins can make answering that cry a possibility. Many companies offer royalty-free sound files to integrate with your motion. See Appendix A to find out who they are.

- **Interactivity with stability:** Java is still evolving. You still have relatively few animation applets to choose from, and stability on all platforms and browsers leaves something to be desired. Inline plug-ins, on the other hand, are tested by the software company that created them. This testing doesn't mean that there can't be bugs in the marmalade, but at least they are fixable by one source after they're found. A problem with a Java implementation can be as hard to track as a lost contact lens on a shiny floor.

- **Plug-in files are often smaller than Java animations:** Yes, the plug-ins can be massive, but after they live on a hard drive, the animation files themselves can be wonderfully small. Assuming you can get past the initial download issue, you can deliver a great deal of animation on very little bandwidth.

- **Plug-in animations can serve many purposes:** Good plug-in software often allows you to save your animation in non-Web formats also. A good example, although not the only one, involves plug-ins that rely on Apple's QuickTime technology. These animations are not accessible only through a browser. You can use them within Windows and the Mac OS. They work on CDs, inside presentation programs, and within a host of other programs. Or you can go in the other direction: take an existing QuickTime movie, for example, and bring it up to the Web by using the QuickTime plug-in.

Going inline

To try to cover every animation-related inline plug-in would probably be worth a whole chapter by itself. We won't even try to do that. Doing so would be an exercise in futility anyway, because by the time you read this book, the information would probably be obsolete. But some established plug-ins do exist that may work with software you already own or that are somewhat necessary additions to really appreciate Web animation.

- **QuickTime:** The QuickTime plug-in is probably one of the must-haves in the Web world, especially now that Apple has released its new "fast-start" version, which puts animations directly on the Web page, sound and all. Several of the new generation of Web animation tools support this format. It's cheaper than MPEG (the high-quality format that most professional digital video artists prefer) because it doesn't require special hardware, it's better at synching sound and image than the Windows-only .AVI format, and it's totally cross-platform. It also is provided as part of Netscape Navigator 3.0 and is extremely small, so chances are fairly good that your audience will have it. If the trend continues, QuickTime may well become the most popular method of delivering motion on the Web.

✔ **Shockwave:** If you know how to use Macromedia Director or Authorware, Shockwave is your ticket to Web animation. If you're visiting the most sophisticated sites (and we mean graphically as well as technically), you've seen it in action. And the Macromedia Web site (www.macromedia.com) is a place you can get lost in for hours.

But then, if you know how to use Director, you're not a newbie in the animation game, and what are you doing reading this book anyway? If you are new to animation and unfamiliar with Director, this is probably not the place to start. Director is not a cheap date. It's expensive to purchase, time consuming to really master, and probably overkill for those who just want to add some zip to their Web pages. It is also the mother of all plug-ins. Compressed, it's over a megabyte in size. Additionally, if you want to add a little interactivity to your animation, you need to master at least the basics of Lingo. *Lingo* is the Macromedia scripting language, and it's not terribly intuitive.

The latest addition to the Shockwave family, Shockwave Flash (in a previous lifetime, FutureSplash) is much smaller and more accessible. It's notable for being a vector-based animation tool that makes small interactive files. It does not require a Director movie as a base, but it allows you to create your animations from scratch within the program. We discuss Flash and some of its animation plug-in competitors like ObjectDANCER in Chapter 15.

✔ **Sound plug-ins:** Some of the plug-ins we mention have their own audio capability included, like QuickTime. Many do not. Java animations also require additional sound plug-ins to deliver audio.

Sound plug-ins basically come in three general categories: voice-only, Midi, and digital audio. Voice is mostly used for video-conferencing or Web phone applications, not animation. Both Midi and digital audio, however, are connected to moving images. *Midi* is basically a form of artificial sound generation. You make Midi sound and music completely in the computer, or with complicated connections between digital instruments and the computer. Digital audio is what you get when you take analog (taped or recorded) sound and digitize it. Music CDs are an example of digital audio.

Unlike video formats, sound plug-ins are not necessarily limited to supporting one piece of software. Most Midi plug-ins, for example, will recognize and play Midi sound when they find it on the Web.

All I wanna do is stream

Until recently, if you wanted to put a large media file — a musical piece, a live-motion video, or a full-screen animation — out onto the Web, you had a problem. The only way to do so was to compress the file and make it downloadable. Then, by using some form of player, the user could watch your work offline, with a complete copy of your video sitting on his hard drive.

Practically speaking, this was a joke. Video and high-quality audio create monstrously large files. Waiting for a download didn't just mean taking a coffee break. A leisurely lunch was more like it. And consider the delight and rapture when people played the video — only to discover that they had downloaded the wrong thing. After all, you couldn't tell if you were interested in the piece until you already had it. This problem tended to limit such situations to those where the download was prearranged (a sales presentation or a training video that needed to be delivered from one site to another) or where the video clips were very short.

Today, several technologies offer solutions to this dilemma. All of them use *streaming,* which acts pretty much the way it sounds. The figure diagrams the process of creating and delivering a streamed file. A Web server is contacted and locates a large file that has been compressed by using one of a number of the current formats. This file begins to send a stream of data to the Web surfer's machine. Instead of waiting for the entire file to show up, a plug-in that understands the format begins to collect the streaming information into a *buffer* — kind

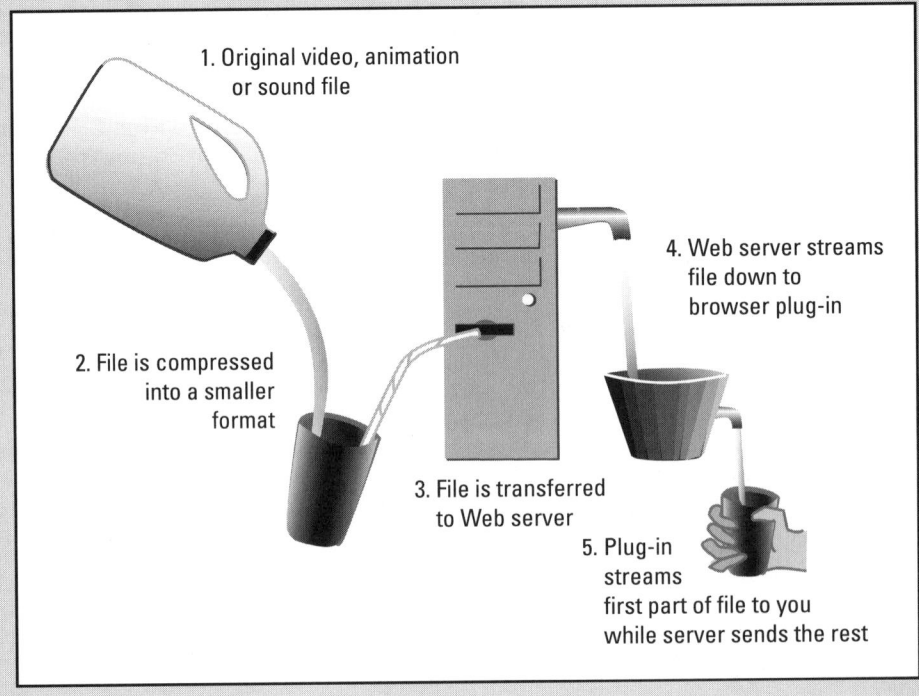

1. Original video, animation or sound file
2. File is compressed into a smaller format
3. File is transferred to Web server
4. Web server streams file down to browser plug-in
5. Plug-in streams first part of file to you while server sends the rest

of like a virtual bucket with a pour spout. As the buffer begins to fill, the plug-in starts playing the file, pouring it out of the buffer "spout" onto the screen, and collecting more at the same time. Once played, the streamed video is dumped out of the computer memory.

Streaming has opened up a number of possibilities on the Web. Not only can sites now deliver real-time video and audio, but sound and image can by synched together for a combination of the two. People can now embed these files right into their Web pages and have them play on demand.

Streaming isn't perfect yet. It takes a great deal of processor time and energy. If you try to do more than just accept the streaming data (like open another file or start a second application), you'll experience distortions or breaks. Or your audio and video tracks will fall out of synch, making your high-end masterpiece look like a low-budget dubbed film. Additionally, streaming often requires that your Web provider make changes in the server — or purchase additional server software — to support your plug-in type.

Minimum tools: Minimal tools for plug-in animation are too varied to mention. In some cases, you can bring files in from image creation software. In other cases, you must create your files directly in the plug-in program. Some software will accept both. If you want to work with plug-ins for your animation, the least expensive and easiest to handle is probably a QuickTime-based software package.

Programmer's paradise

As the old maps used to say, "Here be dragons!" — unless you're a programmer, in which case these are big, cuddly, friendly dragons. If you want to explore these programming technologies for your Web animation, we encourage you to put this book down as soon as you finish reading Part I (which talks about how to go about animating in general) and the color and type chapters in Part II, and run right out and purchase the appropriate *...For Dummies* book specifically geared for your needs and interests. Then you can come back to this book, picking and choosing the other chapters that still connect with your technological needs.

On the other hand, you'll find a big difference between wanting to actually walk on the wild side and wanting to sound knowledgeable when you talk to the dragon-tamers of the world. What follows is a brief explanation of what you'll find when you visit the edge of the known animation world.

VRML and animation

VRML (pronounced *ver*'mel by those in the know . . . aren't you glad you asked?) is short for Virtual Reality Modeling Language. If the initials look suspiciously like HTML, that isn't a total coincidence. VRML is to 3-D graphics what HTML is to text. VRML's possible applications are exciting: 3-D environments you can visit, walk around and do things in, 3-D animations that you can change at will, chat rooms and conferences where you become a 3-D "avatar" and interact with others, or move through a variety of 3-D worlds where abstract data becomes an accessible 3-D object. Sounds like fun, right?

Unfortunately, building a 3-D graphic is considerably more complicated than displaying a paragraph. That makes VRML much harder to learn and use than HTML ever was. In fact, unlike HTML, which isn't programming or even scripting, only a coding method with a lot of tags, VRML is a complex programming language specifically designed for its 3-D purpose. That makes its current entry threshold high. We mean really high. And wide. And deep.

VRML is also suffering from growing pains. You'll hear much discussion about its promise, but there are no user applications yet to bring its power to non-programmers. Because VRML takes so much time and energy to implement, it's a very expensive technology to support on a Web site. Will it be powered by Java, or will Microsoft succeed in its bid for an alternative? If different "standards" exist, then how will those nifty animated avatars move from world to world?

Examples of VRML 1.0 usage on the Internet are fairly limited. Full VRML 2.0 implementation — with interactivity, sound, and texture — is even more rare. And if you're a Macintosh user, your VRML 2.0 plug-in choices are limited to WorldView for Netscape Navigator (www.intervista.com), which at this writing is still beta software.

CGI scripts

All of you who've heard of CGI scripts raise your hands. Um-hum. Now, all of you who've ever written or used one, raise your hands. What? So few? If you've ever made a clickable image map out of a graphic, you've used a little CGI program to do it. Of course, you didn't have to write that script. It was already part of your Web server's capabilities.

CGI (Common Gateway Interface) scripting has been around for a long time in Internet terms. When a Web user's computer (the client) contacts a server by typing in a URL, the server must respond in a standard way. That means that all servers must share a common language. If you can communicate with the server in that common language, it will let you run programs or offer access to images or information that are not part of its own programming. CGI is the way of gaining this control.

What is server push?

No, *server push* isn't the waiter asking you to pay up and get out. CGI scripting is an example of server push. This concept can be a little hard to visualize, but we'll try to explain it.

What usually happens when a client computer contacts a server? The interaction is a little like calling an automated information line. "Push number 1 for information about flesh eating bacteria. Push number 2 for alien invasions. Push number 3 for Year 2000 computer crashes." You call, the machine responds. You push a button, the machine responds. Finally you're shunted to some general information on flying saucers.

Now imagine that, when you call into this information service, you're actually being observed by a real person at the other end of the line. She watches you thread your way through the menus, and she decides that you could use more information than you've requested. So she silently takes over from the automated program and follows the recorded message with a string of related information on green-eyed Martian sightings. You don't even realize that anything unusual has happened.

Your silent watcher has not waited for you to try to pull that extra information bit by bit out of the machine. She has pushed it down the phone line to you. Substitute a CGI script for the mysterious watcher, and you have server push in action.

Before browsers were capable of displaying GIF89a multiple image files (see the sidebar "GIF 87 versus GIF89a" for more information), CGI scripting was the only way to show a simple animation on the Web. It is still very versatile, and useful if you want to create a flipbook animation with non-GIF files, because it's not limited by the GIF89a spec. You can add interactive elements to create animated games, or even generate simple images and forms based on client input.

Before you decide to become a CGI guru, you may want to find out what your ISP's policy is about user-created CGI scripts. Besides the usual threshold involved in discovering how to script or program, using a CGI script to animate your Web pages involves getting access to your Web server's cgi-bin directory. Now, if you're your own Webmaster, doing so is easy. If you use a large ISP, or even a small ISP with a Webmaster concerned about security, this task may be impossible. Because CGI scripting is a way of altering the normal way a server acts and responds to requests from users, it is, by definition, a security risk. It could allow an unscrupulous cracker the access needed to cause chaos. Or if it's benign but sloppily written, it could cause server processes to back up, eventually leading to slow-downs or server crashes.

ActiveX

Last, but not least, on the list of animation-related programmer's goodies is ActiveX. Essentially, ActiveX is Microsoft's response to Java, although it is not exactly the same. Because ActiveX is designed to work by using Microsoft's OLE (Object Linking and Embedding) Controls, it's not a cross-platform tool. It works on and with Windows 95 and Windows NT systems only. And at least as of this writing, it is not supported by Netscape.

ActiveX Controls are like Java applets — little programs to do something specific. Because ActiveX applications can be written with Visual Basic and other long-standing development tools, it has a strong appeal for anyone who does not want to learn a new language (like Java) and sees no reason to worry about non-Windows users. In particular, this ability to trade on existing programming knowledge makes ActiveX a strong contender for animation on intranets.

Not surprisingly, Microsoft has been using ActiveX to port data from its non-Internet applications (like Excel and PowerPoint) to Internet Explorer. Chances are very good that you will soon see animation programs based in ActiveX Controls just as you have seen an increase in Java applets.

Learning to Love Your Limitations

If you're a little overwhelmed by the range of choices you have to make, relax. Yes, you'll find some show-stopping solutions out there. But Web animation is a little like fashion. It's fun to look at the parade on the runway, even if you can't imagine actually wearing that stuff to work.

In fact, we are really into limitations. It's great to think of great big gobs of interactivity oozing from your Web pages, but you can get stuck in all those features. When you're taking your first steps down the animation path, your ideas and how well you translate them to your frames are most important.

What does that mean in practical terms? Well, if you came here looking for how to program Java applets or create 3-D worlds, we suggest that you read *Java For Dummies,* by Aaron E. Walsh, or *VRML & 3D On The Web For Dummies,* by David Kay and Douglas Muder, both published by IDG Books Worldwide, Inc. We concentrate on animation options that give the most control with the least grief. This means that we really jump into GIF-based animation tools, with a dip into some good plug-in software and a little feet-wetting in a Java-based applet. Although haute technology is certainly out there, we can be comfortable and get everything we need right off the rack.

We think this approach has several benefits. In fact, even some of the seeming downsides of staying simple can be turned to your advantage. For example:

- **Simple means small:** Whoever said "Good things come in small packages" must have been anticipating the Internet. The more bells and whistles you add to any animation, the bigger it will be. And big is terrible in a Web animation. Most people agree that 30K is about the limit for a total Web page. Sure, this number can be much higher for people with ISDN or T1 lines, or on an intranet. But if you're fielding a garden-variety Web page to the average 28.8 modem user, a big animation can get old fast. And if it needs a plug-in or downloaded Java code too, it helps if your name is Disney.

- **Simple means modular:** Many times you don't want to redesign an entire Web site. You just want to add something temporarily. A simple animation is easy to move around on a page. That means that you have an easier time reworking a Web site to highlight new features, add temporary links, or squeeze in a new navigation button.

- **Simple means flavor freshness:** The Web is a place where the Cool Site of the Day can become Yesterday's Bread without regular updates. If you spend weeks creating an animation, how fast are you going to jump to throw it away and make a new one? Short and simple animations, on the other hand, encourage you to experiment and change. Once you get the hang of it, a GIF animation from clip art can be done in an afternoon.

- **Simple means easy to upgrade:** Eventually, you'll gain confidence and decide that you're ready to take on something more complex. One of the best ways to learn a new animation program is to take a previous idea and enlarge on it. If you start with simple frames, they can be re-imported into a wide variety of other software. Then you can concentrate on adding interactivity, improving your action by adding more frames, or breaking into music.

- **Simple means peace and quiet:** Music and sounds are powerful tools to hold a visitor's attention. On the other hand, how much do you know about music? The search for an appropriate, royalty-free tune can take time, and the use of the wrong material — like a heavy metal riff with a rotating fan — can be unintentionally funny. In addition, synching sound to image is not just a technical issue, any more than creating graphics is. To do it right takes additional time and effort.

  Sound may also be inappropriate for some Web sites. Imagine the average cubicle worker broadcasting a Midi rendition of the *Gilligan's Island* theme throughout the room. It's not only an intrusion on the other workers, it's like hanging out a big sign saying, "Hi Boss! I surf the Web for fun." If you're running a serious site, you may want to think very hard before you turn up the volume.

- **Simple means no alternates and no apologies:** If you're working with plug-in software and creating a commercial site, then you'll have to create alternate pages for those people who are still surfing with older browsers or for people who don't have the space and time to waste on a download. This fact can mean substantial additional work and more possibilities for things to go wrong because of hastily added HTML code or a moved link.

Convinced? Then you're ready to move on to putting that simplicity to good use.

Chapter 2

The Dream Theme — Telling a Visual Story

In This Chapter

▶ Why you need a story line for your animation
▶ The hows and whys of brainstorming
▶ Consider your audience and your goals
▶ Connect your ideas to an existing Web site
▶ Different types of Web animations

*B*irds gotta fly, fish gotta swim, animations gotta tell a story. You may not think these things are in the same league. "Plots in Web animations? Right. Think I'll skip this chapter!" We understand how you feel. Stephen King has yet to pen a Web animation (*Malloween*: once you download, it sticks in your drive forever). But if he did decide to take up the challenge, you can bet it wouldn't be boring. King understands how important storytelling is.

If you've ever tried storytelling, you probably know how hard it is to come up with an idea that everyone doesn't already know. That's why so many movies are made out of books, or are rubber-stamped sequels. But it can be done. In this chapter, we look at what makes a good idea, some hints on how to generate one, and how to develop your idea as a Web animation.

What's the Big Idea?

It may be small and short, but even a GIF animation has to have a reason for existence — a mini story to tell — or making the animation is a waste of time. In graphics lingo, that reason for existence is a *concept*. A concept really consists of two tightly related things: an idea or direction, and the visual expression of that idea. You can have a really great idea and then, like

Dr. Frankenstein with his monster, do a not-so-great job of bringing it to life. You can also do something visually glitzy and completely idea-free — think *Waterworld*. We're great believers in disaster avoidance instead of damage control, so we dedicate this chapter to keeping you above water. Chapters 3 and 4 will help keep the townsfolk from torching your castle.

How do you get a concept? A place of honor is waiting for you at some of the hottest advertising agencies in the world if you can answer that one. No surefire way exists. What is available is a process that most creative types use to generate lots of possibilities.

Web animation is not a daytime game show

Ever watch *Family Feud*? Pretend for a moment that it's your turn to play. Complete this phrase, "_____ ball". Come up with your best three guesses. If you're like most people, you probably started with "base" and then moved to "foot" or "basket." That's good if you're on *Family Feud,* where winning depends on how good you are at thinking like everyone else. But this reasoning just doesn't work when you're trying to make something new and different. You'd want to go further than your first three guesses. What else fits the phrase? Think "Nerf" or "beach" or "high" or "have a" . . . and that's just the beginning. You can fill that blank in dozens of ways.

Now this example was pretty simple, but it illustrates the first stages of the process of brainstorming. *Brainstorming* is basically a method for helping you spark your creativity and move beyond the game show. It has a few stages, and each one is critical to the success of the one that follows.

Brainstorming without galoshes

Say you want to develop a Web animation for your home page on cats. (This part isn't much of an exercise in brainstorming. The Alta Vista search engine lists 600,000 references to cats on the Web, and yours could be one of them.) But assume that you're on your own. Brainstorming is easier and more fun if you can do it with others, but this is probably a solo effort.

Okay, here you are, sitting back in your chair with only your personal feline for company and a pad of paper and pen. "What might be a neat thing to animate?" you ask. "Hey, I'll make a picture of Fluffy chasing a ball!" Done, right? If so, you haven't yet realized that dozens — no, probably hundreds . . . no, maybe *thousands* — of people are thinking the same thing. Their cats chase balls, or yarn, or mice, or jump around the screen without a toy. Now, this fact doesn't mean that you can't do a better job than they did.

But a little brainstorming may take you someplace new. Even if you end up with something close to your original idea, it will be fresher and more clever if you go through the brainstorming process before locking yourself in.

A brainstorming bash has six basic rules:

- **Strive for multiplicity.** Your first thoughts are usually based in knee-jerk reactions that many people share. You want to delve further. You'll probably come up with variations on your original idea first. How many ways can your cat chase an object? How many different objects?

- **More is better.** You can never have too many ideas. Hopefully, even though you started with just one possibility, pushing that idea around will make some other options occur to you. Maybe you'll wonder what other things cats do with objects, and start listing them, too. Perhaps you'll go beyond that, and think about other cat poses, or ways to portray the idea of cats without showing a cat itself.

- **Do some simple research.** After you think you've exhausted every possibility, find out what other people have done. Here's where you check out other Web sites. Don't just look at sites with subjects similar to yours. Surf around and notice what falls flat as well as what grabs you. You can learn from other people's mistakes and their successes.

Don't do this step first! Really. It's like always eating dessert instead of a real meal. Eventually your mental teeth will fall out, and you won't be able to chew on the good stuff. Instead of breaking new ground, you'll find yourself always limited to what other people have done.

If you see a good idea, work through all the variations. How can you do it differently, or better? Seeing other animations helps you figure out what doesn't work. It also gives you a reality check on your own first ideas. If every idea that you've come up with has been done elsewhere, you haven't pushed yourself quite far enough and need to try again, but this time try the following:

- **Use idea-generating tools.** Anything can be a good source for concepts if you look at it the right way. Sometimes clip-art catalogs are good resources even if you plan on making your artwork from scratch, because the catalogs often organize images by subject. Old movies or old silent movie stills are good too, because they often show exaggerated movement and broad comedy.

    Some easily available and surefire materials are word resources, like a dictionary or a thesaurus. These can be a great source of visual puns. Look up a key word related to your subject and look for words surrounding it that may help with an image. For example, a walk through the dictionary for the word *cat* brings: catty-corner, catsup, caterwaul, categorize, catbird seat, catastrophe, catacomb, and, one of our favorite visual pun words, catapult.

Figure 2-1 shows the "catapult" pun in its first stages of visual development. Imagine hordes of little cats being sling-shot over castle walls defended by cowering canines. Or malevolent mice.

Figure 2-1: Puns can be great generators of visual ideas that you can use as a basis for animations.

- **Write everything down that you come up with.** Nothing kills a brainstorming session deader than trying to edit your ideas while you're generating them. Don't judge yourself and the quality of what you're coming up with. Don't tell yourself the ideas are silly, or try to figure out how to make them work, or worry about what other people will think. Some of the best concepts come out of "dumb ideas," which turn out to have great possibilities.
- **Don't brainstorm when you're tired or distracted.** Brainstorming should be exciting and fun, but it demands your full attention. If you're tired, depressed, or distracted, go to an escapist movie instead. Who knows, the back of your mind may just keep working while the front is thinking about eating popcorn.

Cold Assessment: What Can You Really Do?

Mentally speaking, brainstorming is kind of like a wild party with Mr. Hyde. You have ideas strewn all over the place, your original concept is a mess, and you may have some apologizing to do to your housemates. A cold assessment means that it's time to let Dr. Jekyll back in to clean up the mess. Dr. Jekyll is the logical, sensible side of the brain, and he's been locked away during the wild brainstorming ride.

Chapter 2: The Dream Theme — Telling a Visual Story

What does the doctor recommend? Put your list from the brainstorming session under Jekyll's logical stethoscope.

- ✔ **Is this idea clear to you?** If you can't figure out what you had in mind when you wrote something down, no one else will figure it out, either. Fuzzy ideas that just won't come into focus are the first ones to go under the knife.

- ✔ **Will this idea be clear to others?** Maybe you know exactly what you had in mind, but when you explain it to someone else, she looks at you like you have marbles in your mouth. If you feel strongly that you have a great idea, look for a way to translate it for your audience. If you can't, put it aside for a follow-up visit later. Taking a rest from the idea often gives your subconscious time to solve the problem. If it doesn't, don't despair. Maybe the problem is that your idea is too far away from your subject. Revisiting it for a new project can help you approach the concept from a different angle.

- ✔ **Can this idea be shown visually?** Some ideas are just wonderful, but they're more verbal than they are visual. It's okay to use a little bit of type — a headline for an ad, or a bit of animated type with a key word — to get an idea across or tie it to other elements on your Web page. But beware of an idea that needs a paragraph of explanation — or even a one-line caption. Remember that a picture is supposed to be worth a thousand words. If you need ten more to make it clear, maybe this concept belongs on the discount rack.

- ✔ **Is this idea beyond your graphic skills?** This decision is sometimes a tough assessment, so don't be too quick to answer. You have clip art, photography, and the magic of scanning. You also may discover in Chapter 4 that your graphic skills, primitive though you may think them, are more than adequate for what you have in mind. On the other hand, any idea which depends on 3-D realism when you can barely doodle is an obvious mismatch. Save the idea for an artistic friend, or sell it to Disney for hefty royalties.

- ✔ **Is this idea too technically difficult?** If you do have a solid background in art or design, you can be tempted to create the Taj Mahal. Imagine how frustrated you may be if you discover that your technical know-how limits you to creating a Taj Mahal-level animation armed only with a virtual scissors and some virtual Styrofoam. If your idea is really strong, we suggest that you hold it aside until you've read through this book. You may discover that one of the new Web animation tools will do the heavy lifting for you. If your idea is still technically out of reach, try to scale it down to simple bungalow size.

Make 'Em Laugh . . . Maybe

After you do your basic checkup, you should still have a few ideas with a clean bill of health. Deciding among them can be a little tricky, because what works in one situation may fall flat as a cold soufflé in another. The next question you ask is fairly basic: For whom am I doing this?

Many types of Web sites are around. Some of them attract the general Web-surfing public, others are directed toward a specialized group. You'll also find purely personal efforts, visual portfolios or virtual art galleries, corporate service, advertising or sales sites . . . you name it and it's probably there. (And if it isn't, go for it fast!)

The bottom line is, unless this Web site is a personal one, and you simply don't care if anyone visits it (or what they may think about it when they do), you're creating your animation for an audience. What message do you want to send them about you or your site? Examine your concept ideas against the following checklist:

- ✔ **Is your idea humorous?** Being funny has its pitfalls and benefits. Not only do people laugh at different things, but some ideas that are perfectly acceptable in some groups can be considered insulting or insensitive in others. Humor comes with enough negatives that many corporate sites avoid it completely. On the other hand, some sites can benefit from gentle humor and visual puns. Try out your idea with others after you make your animation sketches and see if they "get it." If not, that's what all those other ideas were made for.

- ✔ **Will your animation have an international audience?** We know everyone tells you the Internet is global, so anyone from anywhere can visit your site and see your animation. Yes, well, this is true in theory. Practically speaking, will this international audience visit your site? Many sites exist for local, geographical, or internal company use (intranets). You have much more freedom in subject matter and development if you don't have to research cross-cultural symbols.

If you really anticipate visitors from Germany to Ghana, it's much safer to animate your site using type, the company logo, or a neutral graphic device (such as a traffic light, a desk accessory, or photos from the company annual report that have already passed legal and cultural hurdles).

- ✔ **Does your idea depend on insider knowledge?** Pleasing a crowd of friends is easier than pleasing a group of strangers. You can take a chance with popular references and inside jokes. For example, a wide enough range of people are familiar with *Star Trek* so that you can use its terminology in a site devoted to dog breeders. (For dog breeders, "Beam me up, Scotty" may take on a whole new meaning.) The same reference applied to a company supplying medical lasers may be seen as juvenile or overdone. You need to measure your list of ideas against your intended audience, and eliminate (well, perhaps keep in your idea file) those that just don't fit.

Connecting Ideas to Existing Sites

By now, you're down to one or two really solid concepts. How can you make them fit into your Web site? Remember, unlike Disney cartoons, your work won't be seen by itself. Your animation idea has to be integrated into the Web site as a whole. This fact is not worth considering during the initial brainstorming process because doing so leads you away from a free-wheeling, creative approach. As you get closer to making the idea take visible form, however, forging good conceptual links between what already exists and what you plan to do is very important.

Warning! Shameless marketing plug alert! We're making an assumption here that your Web site has a style. Good ones do. We hope that you've used the same basic look (background, color for linking text, frames or tables for info organization, and navigation buttons) throughout. If not, you ought to run out and get *Web Design & Desktop Publishing For Dummies*, 2nd Edition, before your spiffy animations embarrass the regular Web page content.

Look at your Web page very carefully. Are you adding an animation "just because"? You've seen sites where that has happened, although you may not have thought about it at the time. You go to the site looking for a good time, and all you get for your trouble is the sound of your disk drive grinding. If the animation is really interesting and well-integrated, you won't resent its presence nearly as much. In fact, a really well-integrated animation enhances the content and gives the viewer the impression that it belongs on the page.

No one wants to see his animations flushed from the browser cache at the earliest opportunity. Avoid the sound of water coursing down the pipes by examining your idea with an eye toward how it fits into one of three site-related animation categories: logos, buttons and other navigation aids, and content emphasis. Each has its own requirements and demands varying degrees of creative connection to the rest of the site.

Animating logos

We doubt that anyone will encourage you to redesign the corporate logo for the Web site (even if you think it looks like a six-year-old went crazy with a box of crayons and some construction paper). This means that you're limited in what you can do with the logo. So, while this sentiment doesn't mean "Hands off!" it does mean that you have to be careful and clever. Look for neutral ways to change the design:

- **Variations in size:** Logos can zoom up or down without compromising their integrity. If a logo is made up of several elements, these can be scaled separately for variety, as long as the logo comes back together as a recognizable unit.

- **Variations in position:** Logos that consist of a single, self-contained item — like the Apple Computer rainbow apple or the Mercedes-Benz circle — often lend themselves to motion across a banner or around another piece, such as the corporate name.

- **Building the logo from its individual elements:** Some logos are easy to break down into separate elements, like the Adobe A, which can either be seen as white connected bars on a red field, or red triangles and bars. You can animate the individual pieces to "rebuild" the logo from them. We show an example of this in Figure 2-2.

- **Making the logo three-dimensional:** Using a 3-D program or Adobe Dimensions, you can take a flat logo and create a solid-looking 3-D object. If you save "snapshots" of the piece at different rotations, you can create a simple but effective animation by stringing the shots together in sequence.

- **Enhancing the original logo idea:** A good logo has its own concept. Using that concept to drive your animation is always safe and effective. Think of the Nike logo. The famous "swoosh" mark is meant to show speed graphically. It takes very little effort to imagine the ways this logo could move on a Web page.

Animated buttons

Any animated buttons that you use must be tightly connected to the original look and feel of your Web site design, especially if your site already exists. Buttons also must be very short, simple, and extremely clear. Remember that buttons are vehicles for navigation, not the centerpiece of a Web site. The most important thing about animated buttons is that they be functional.

Color is particularly important. You want to match the color scheme of the rest of the Web site very carefully when animating buttons. Not only will doing so make the buttons feel more like they were part of the original design of the Web page, but you gain economies of download scale when your Web page is limited to a palette with very few individual colors. (For more on economical use of color for fast downloading, turn to Chapter 10.)

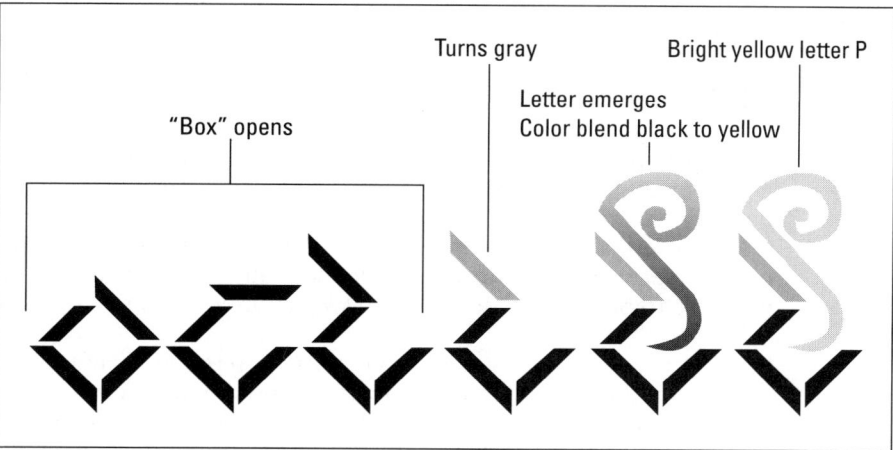

Figure 2-2: One idea for animating an existing logo is a piece-by-piece animated "build" approach.

Animations as emphasis

A Web animation is a terrific way to say, "Pay attention, look right here, this is new!" If this is your purpose, you have a little more slack between your original site and this new element. Unfortunately, like the cliché warns, this approach also gives you more opportunity to hang yourself.

We are morally opposed to Web animation as career suicide. Not to mention the fact that it gets in the way of repeat sales of this book. So as you develop your idea for an eye-catching feature animation, bear the following things in mind:

- Multiple animations on the page distract from your primary purpose. If you want to emphasize something special, put the rest of your site on an eye-candy diet. Either temporarily disable other animations or redesign the page to highlight your new material.

- Choose your new animation's place carefully. If you place it too far down the page or too far to the right, people surfing on low-resolution or smaller monitors may miss the animation when they initially access your page. That's like putting out a fast-food commercial saying, "Tastes like fertilizer and makes you fat." You get the deficit of the churning disk without the benefit of the eye candy.

- Avoid the "whazzat?" syndrome. Make sure that, if you really have something worth drawing attention to, you're not overshadowing it with the animation itself. How many times have you watched a great commercial on TV and been unable to remember later what the product had been? This method may be great for winning awards, but not so great for your content.

Come Into My Parlor, Said the Spider to the Fly

The most enjoyable Web animations to create (and the most challenging) are those that are actual content — not icons, decorative additions, or banners. These animations are not only longer than the usual Web animation, they are also more technically and graphically complex. They still require a strong thematic site connection, although that connection does not have to be stylistic. It should, however, be related to the site's purpose.

One of the coolest ways of using animation on the Web is to take the idea of the story line to its logical conclusion and create a series of related pieces, linked over space or time. This way, your Web animation becomes a means of generating repeat traffic or inducing visitors to move beyond your home page.

You can serialize your concept in many ways. The first is through variations in one simple idea, occupying different areas of your Web space. (Aren't you glad you explored variations when you brainstormed?) A cat at play can change from orange tabby to Siamese as the viewer moves from page to page, or portray different actions in different areas of your Web site, keyed to your topics. Another idea is to have a story play itself out as the viewer explores your Web site. In order to find out how the story ends, the viewer needs to travel through your site in depth.

Of course, the continuing soap opera concept works for animation, too. Create a mascot and involve your viewers in its exploits. Animate a product or bring a piece of artwork to life. One of the best examples we've seen of a site that really leverages its animation in this fashion is the Silicon Graphics VRML address: `vrml.sgi.com`. They have created a special character whose animated adventures are serialized, with old episodes available for reviewing online.

The Silicon Graphics site is a groundbreaking implementation of VRML. You'll need a special VRML plug-in to view it, but trust us — it's worth the effort!

Of course, you probably don't have the technical capability yet to animate your site using 3-D, but that's not necessary. What really keeps people coming back is the quality of the story line concept and the believability of your animation.

Chapter 3
Planning a Moving Experience

In This Chapter
▶ Surf's up: Making a storyboard without wiping out
▶ Location, location, location! Placing your characters
▶ "I've been framed!" — breaking out of the box
▶ The secret of index cards

Some people like planning. They're the ones who cross things off to-do lists. They carry organizers. Their closets are color-coded and they never run out of milk at midnight after they've made brownies. Planners recognize that this is an important chapter and jump right to it from the table of contents.

Everyone else is reading this chapter for the same reason we eat low-fat yogurt instead of a hot fudge sundae with whipped cream — because it's Good For You. This bothers us authors tremendously. We don't want you to feel coerced. Don't let the fact that this is a critical, incredibly important chapter that can make or break your future as a Web animation wizard influence your decision.

Somehow we thought you'd still be here. You're about to be well-rewarded for making the right decision. By the time we finish, you'll have a basic understanding of the primary tricks and techniques professional animators have developed to make everything from the simplest flip book to the most amazing feature films.

Of course, that doesn't mean you'll be an instant professional. That takes talent, years of study, painstaking work, and more caffeine than you'd probably want to ingest. But many key — and relatively easy — principles can really make your efforts pass the believability test. Along the way, we'll show you how to develop the clever idea brainstormed in Chapter 2 into the visual feast you'd like it to be.

Surf's Up: Making a Storyboard without Wiping Out

After you come up with an animation idea, it's really tempting to dive right in. But just as even the most insanely daring surfers check the weather and wax their boards, you need to do more than just open your paint program. All good animators begin by transferring their verbal idea into a series of sequential sketches called a *storyboard*. This is your opportunity to develop your idea, eliminate things that are too difficult or don't work, or add new things to refine the original concept.

Boy Scouts at the beach

Besides being clean, honest, cheerful, and helping little old ladies across busy streets, Boy Scouts have a great motto, "Sell those cookies!"

Oops. That's the Girl Scouts, isn't it? Boy Scouts were ordered to "Be Prepared." In practice, this phrase often meant remembering to bring enough marshmallows for the annual camping trip. But the underlying idea contains words to live by, particularly if you're about to embark on your first storyboarding adventure. Walk down the checklist below to make sure that you're packed and ready.

- **Retro tools:** Despite the fact that we use the computer for many of our examples in this chapter, don't think that we went straight from concept to computer with nothing in between. Every animation in this book started life as a series of quick sketches on paper. If you go right to the computer and skip the sketching, your work will look that way: unreal and mechanical. Besides, you'll waste a lot of time making complex objects over and over and over again.

  So if you want that scouting badge in animation, be prepared with real-life materials. No one but you is going to see these storyboards unless you choose to pass them around, and the time and flexibility you gain by storyboarding off the computer are priceless. Unless you really can't draw a box without a mouse in your hand, you should come armed with

  - Regular unlined paper
  - Tracing paper
  - A pencil with an eraser
  - A ruler

- A pair of scissors
- A stack of index cards
- Some glue or scotch tape

As for how much material you need, that's hard to predict. If you've never animated anything before, you should probably have more paper and index cards than you think you'll use. For CD-ROM or most other digitally-based film animations, you need about 15 frames for every second of action (double that for real-time, movie-quality), but Web animation is both more forgiving and more flexible. You'll generally need more sketches if you're contemplating lots of movement, or more realistic movement, and fewer if you only plan on simple flashing, blinking or cycling through a series of logos or images.

✔ **Dimensions, not dementia:** Animations come in a variety of sizes and shapes. You should already know about what amount of screen real estate you intend to build on.

Be prepared with a rough size. If you are making a large animation that people will download and run later, you can sketch fairly big. But if you are making a GIF animation (see Chapter 1 for a discussion of the difference between GIF animations and other flavors) to ornament and bring life to your Web pages, sketching *too* big is a very serious tactical error. It could lead you to expend energy on stuff that no one will notice.

What is a storyboard?

Back in the Golden Age of animation, when almost every cartoon was a groundbreaking event, animators operated like gag writers on Letterman. Each one would come up with a funny idea, and would kick it around with other animators in a meeting. The group then decided which gags should appear in which order. After that, they went off individually and drew their piece of the cartoon. They would exchange first and last frames with whomever had pieces before or after them. Sometimes this method worked out fine. Many times it resulted in ideas that didn't match, or animations that sounded funny when described but never worked visually.

It seems obvious to us now that someone was bound to ask, "Why not show me a picture, dude?" Eventually, they did just that. Quick sketches of their ideas allowed others to more easily see what they had in mind. At first they just drew a few frames — the key ones — to get their point across. Soon they were drawing everything, because doing so made meetings so much easier. But pinning so many little pieces of paper on the wall took a great deal of time. Little pieces of paper were replaced with large stiff boards with the frames mounted on them. Because the sketches told the story, these presentations came to be known as storyboards.

Be prepared with the right *aspect ratio* (the proportion of length to width of your image area). Will this animation be a banner? If so, your sketches will be long, skinny rectangles. Maybe you plan to run this animation as a little square in a frame on your home page. If that's your plan, then make sure that you draw your storyboard sketches in squares, not rectangles. The same idea looks and functions very differently depending on the space it's occupying. (See Figure 3-1.)

✔ **The devil is in the details, so call an exorcist:** You want to concentrate on your characters and how they move, not on whether they wear plaid ties. (Unless the plaid tie is your animated character!)

Be prepared to ignore the background. If you're handling this animation right, the background is a fixed element throughout. Roughly sketch the background once to help you orient your characters, and ignore it after that.

Be prepared to rough it. If you're one of those people who obsesses over getting something right the first time, get over it. These are sketches, tools to save you time on the computer. If your objects look rough and lumpy, don't waste time cleaning them up now. You want to concentrate on the big picture: how things move and change, and whether they do so in a way that will be clear to your viewers.

Preparing the storyboard template

Before you can sketch the action, you have to create the frame for your animation window. Doing so means creating a template that you'll use for every frame.

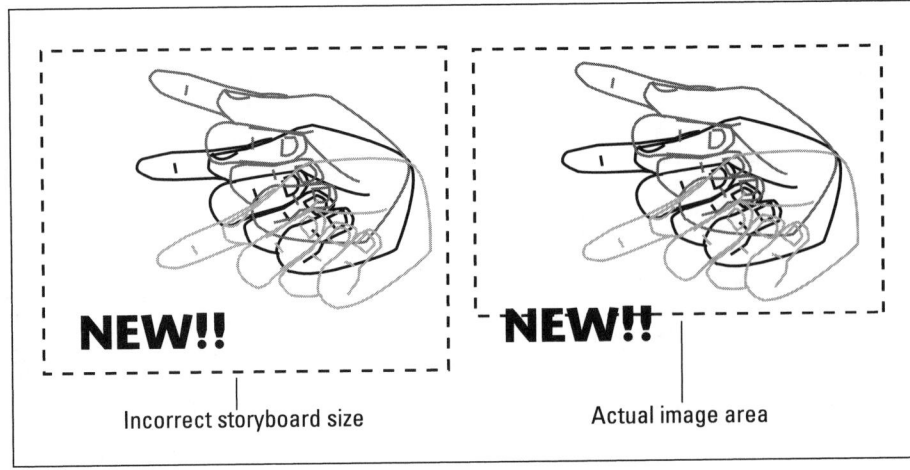

Figure 3-1: One idea, two aspect ratios. Obviously one was designed with storyboard frames and the other was not.

Incorrect storyboard size   Actual image area

Chapter 3: Planning a Moving Experience

1. **Print the Web page your animation will occupy.**

   Doing so gives you a realistic sense of how much space you actually have to work with. If you haven't created a Web page yet, we strongly advise that you do so before you tackle your animation. Improvisation may work for stand-up comedy, but if you try it in Web design, your self-esteem can suffer.

2. **Draw a box on this printout to define the space for your animation.**

3. **Measure the dimensions of this box.**

   The box is probably too small to work in comfortably, so you'll want to scale it up for your storyboard. Usually doubling the dimensions works, unless the space is really very tiny.

   Check to make sure that your working dimensions will fit on some standard size of index card (index cards come as large as 5" x 8"). You'll use these cards later to check your storyboard before you transfer it to the computer. See "Timing — or, the Lowdown on Stand-Up" in Chapter 4 for more information.

   Don't throw this printout away!!! It's your reality check. Forgetting that you are working bigger than your ultimate goal is all too easy. Pin the paper up on the wall, or tape it to your computer monitor. Whenever you get tempted to add some detail to your original idea, look at this sheet and ask yourself "Will anyone be able to recognize it on-screen?"

4. **Go to a drawing program that gives you rulers and a snap grid. Draw an outline box with the pixel dimensions of your animation's planned image area.**

5. **Copy and paste the box several times in a row with a consistent amount of white space between each box.**

   An inch between each is good. (See Figure 3-2 for an example of a page of frame boxes.) Because this sheet will be your template for all your animation frames, you'll want to print out several copies.

6. **Number your storyboards just to the left or right of the frame, and then neatly cut them apart from each other, leaving an equal amount of white space around each frame.**

   This step will make aligning the frames on one edge an easier task later. Numbering will also help you keep track of your sequence and prevent you from shuffling frames out of order when you test your animation later for timing and consistency.

Figure 3-2: A typical page of storyboards, four on a page. Your mileage may vary.

Location, location, location! Placing your characters

Now that you've built your template, you probably figure you just start drawing in the boxes. Well, that's true, but *where* you start drawing inside the box can have a big effect on almost everything about your animation, from how your character moves to how many frames your animation uses. Don't get off on the wrong foot by positioning your action poorly to begin with.

To understand how character placing works, we'll begin with a simple frame and one object. Look at Figure 3-3. Notice the solid circle in the center of the frame. The image created by the circle and frame is balanced and symmetrical and about as exciting as a boiled potato. The eye has nowhere to go because it's already looking at the dead center of the image.

Chapter 3: Planning a Moving Experience 47

Figure 3-3: A boring perfect circle taking up page space.

Now look at Figure 3-4. Notice that this is the same circle, but it feels very different on the page. Doesn't it feel as if it's about to drop? You experience this circle as an object with the potential of motion. Even if you don't plan to move the circle, anything you do decide to do with it will feel stronger and more active in a position above the center of the frame.

Figure 3-4: The same circle, ready to roll.

Notice also that you have the feeling that the circle is in a bigger frame. That's because the space surrounding the circle is no longer evenly distributed around it. Moving the circle away from the center also helps you give a sense of openness and space to the area.

You can try this technique out for yourself on the computer. For the rest of this section, we'll work digitally because our object is very simple — and everyone likes immediate gratification.

1. **Draw a square frame with a circle in it (use a program that lets you easily pick up and move an object).**

2. **Pick up the circle by using your mouse and move it to the lower right of the frame.**

   You still have the sense of space, but you should also have a completely different feeling about where the circle may move next.

3. **Experiment with moving the circle to different places inside the frame. Each time you move the ball around, save the file and print it out.**

   Do so until you have saved and printed at least six different positions. Now look at your group of frames. If you've put several on one sheet, cut them apart so you can move them around.

Lay the frames out on a table or on the floor where you can see them all. Can you arrange them in more than one way? If you change the order around, how many additional frames do you have to add to make it obvious to someone else where your ball is traveling?

In Figure 3-5, we placed six positions in a sequence from left to right. Many things still need to be done to this sequence to make it believable and interesting, but we have here a first pass at a storyboard.

"I've been framed!" — breaking out of the box

Deciding how to place your animation elements to begin your sequence is the first step in mastering the storyboard. But the frame is more like an enchanted forest than it is a city grid. The frame is alive and an active player in your animation. In fact, the magic of the animation frame has hidden traps for the unwary.

Chances are that you've heard of a magician named Houdini. His specialty was creating life-threatening situations — locked boxes, chained coffins, massive safes — and somehow escaping from them. He never found a box that could hold him, and neither should you. Building yourself a frame and then being trapped without realizing what's happened is a really easy thing to do. The trap of the frame won't threaten your life, of course, but it can make your animation roll over and die if you're not careful.

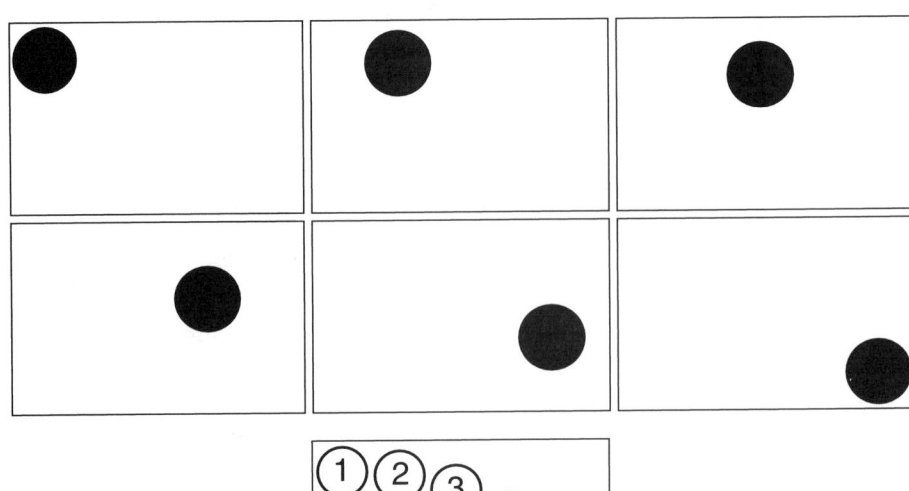

Figure 3-5: Reading top to bottom and left to right, a storyboard, with six key frames drawn.

Chapter 3: Planning a Moving Experience

> ### Content and a sense of direction
>
> Sometimes the subject of an animation lays some limitations on where you can put it on the Web page, or the sequence of its movements. This fact is true when you are making changes in color or size, not position, and especially so when type is involved.
>
> The majority of current inhabitants in the wonderful world of Internet read from left to right, or at least have to consider the reflex reactions of Western World viewers who do so. (It will be fun to see if this changes when more people from Asia and the Middle East start doing Web animation, don't you think? One of your authors is married to someone who, after 20 years in the States, still reflexively opens a book from the back cover.) Therefore, if you are creating an animated banner and want to bring the wonders of motion to it, you'll probably need to go with the left-to-right flow.
>
> Don't let this left-right issue prevent you from thinking creatively about movements — typographic and otherwise. Other options besides the horizontal line exist. The animated element can have top-to-bottom color sequencing. Type in a banner can take an active (animated) or passive (background) role, or be a mixture of these things. In some cases, type can flash on (or off) in order of importance, not pure reading sequence, as long as the critical information is strongly conveyed. We discuss some of these type issues in Chapter 6.

Using imaginary 3-D

Especially in banners, objects in Web animations tend to move in a straight line, as if an invisible string were pulling them. Some of this is content-driven, as we mention in the sidebar "Content and a sense of direction." But that's not always the case. Beginners in the animation game often forget that they live in three dimensions. Many situations exist where using the space allotted to an animation in a different way is perfectly reasonable.

Go back to your simple series of circles. This time, start your circle in the lower left of its frame. Create a sequence of circles that move up and down, like those in Figure 3-6. Making the eye bounce up and down as it travels from left to right is a little more interesting, right? But you still get the feeling that the ball doesn't have enough space to move through.

You can fix that. Watch what happens in Figure 3-7, simply by shrinking the circle as it rises and enlarging it as it drops. Your whole sense of how big the frame is changes.

Return to your bouncing sequence and try changing it so you get two bounces as you move the ball from left to right. You'll have to add a few more frames to get this sequence to work, because you've just expanded the action. Notice that when we did this example ourselves, the percentages the ball shrinks and expands are not exactly the same amount from frame to frame. We talk about why we did that in more detail in the section called "Speed up and slow down" in Chapter 4.

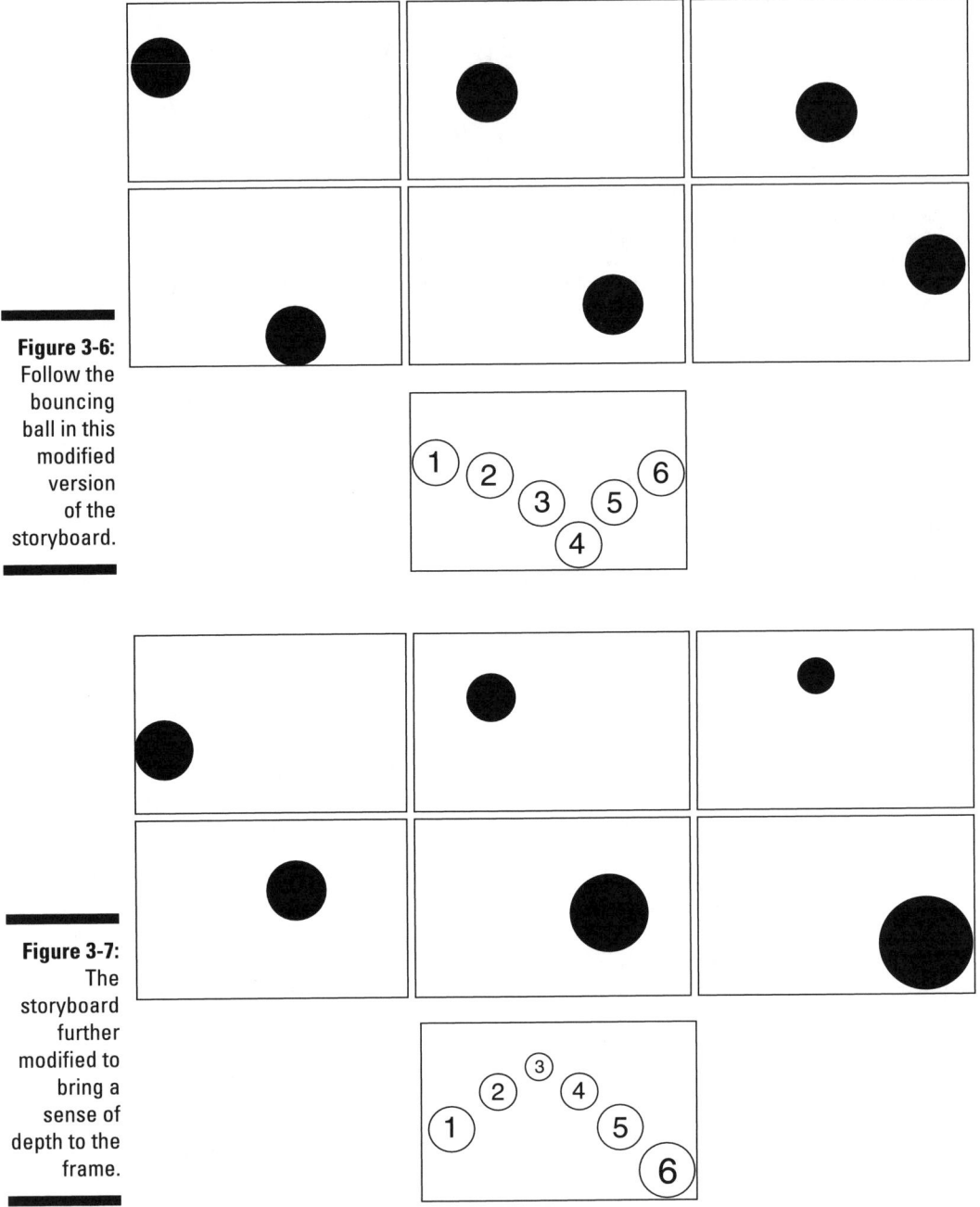

Figure 3-6: Follow the bouncing ball in this modified version of the storyboard.

Figure 3-7: The storyboard further modified to bring a sense of depth to the frame.

Chapter 3: Planning a Moving Experience

Cropping to fit the action

With a few additional tricks, you can really take advantage of all the possible dimensions. Look at the new bouncing ball in Figure 3-8. What's different? Yes, the ball is bouncing into the distance instead of up in the air. But hopefully you noticed that the last frame doesn't show the whole ball. The technical term for what we've done in this last frame is called *cropping* — trimming portions of an object with the boundary frame.

We're taking advantage of the entire imaginary space by letting our object leave the confining box completely. You can make this illusion even stronger by changing where the bouncing circle starts moving from and how much of it gets cropped away by the frame. Spend some time experimenting with this illusion. It's useful for more than bouncing balls. You can see this effect by watching almost any action or science fiction movie. (What an assignment! "I have to go rent a movie so I can finish the Web page! The authors said so!") The first *Star Wars* film uses it in many ways, including the opening sequence of Darth Vader's ship. Through the camera's stationary placement and through the massive star cruiser's flight above and through the screen so that it's never seen without being cropped, we're given a vision of overwhelming size and might.

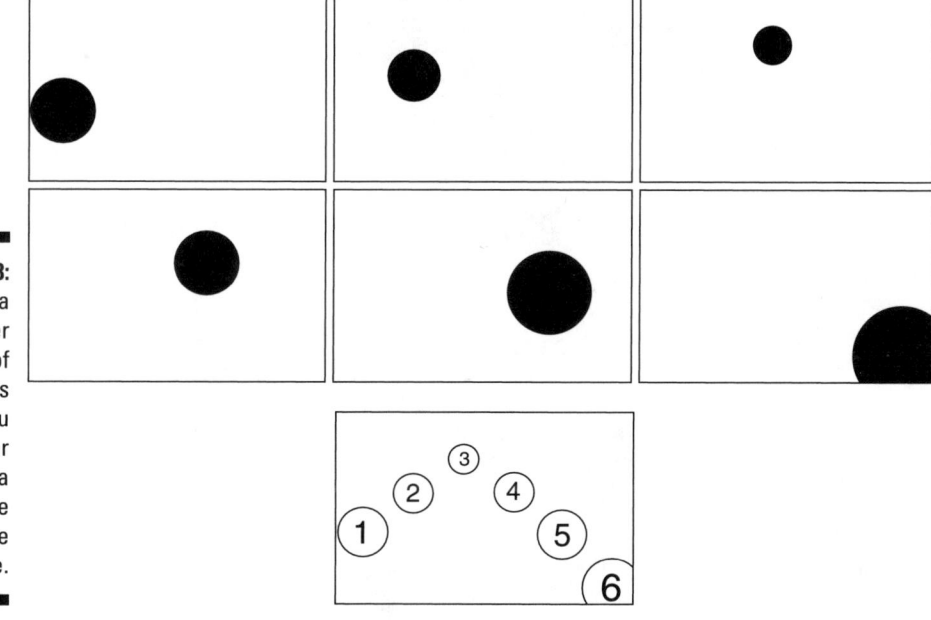

Figure 3-8: Adding a further sense of space is easy if you consider the area outside your frame fair game.

Cropping is also used to keep the viewers' attention oriented on the important element or elements. White space for air around an object is nice, but sometimes it's just too much. Look at Figure 3-9. You're looking at the same animal in both frames, but the effect is very different. In the first picture, the bat feels lost in the ozone. (We asked him about it. He quoted Jean-Paul Sartre on alienation until we cried.) In the second picture, you see only as much background space as you need to define his shape. The bat is closer, more active, and much more interesting to look at. (Not to mention much closer to the jugular vein.) You can take this concept one step further by cropping in for a detail of his head after you establish what his body looks like, and concentrate on the easier-to-animate head, fang, and eye motions.

If you can't beat 'em . . . join 'em!

Until this point, we've treated the frame as if it were the boundary of a TV or movie screen. Our objective was to make the frame as transparent and unnoticeable as possible. But you can also break the tyranny of the border by turning the frame into part of the animation itself.

Figure 3-9: Filling the frame can make you more involved in the action.

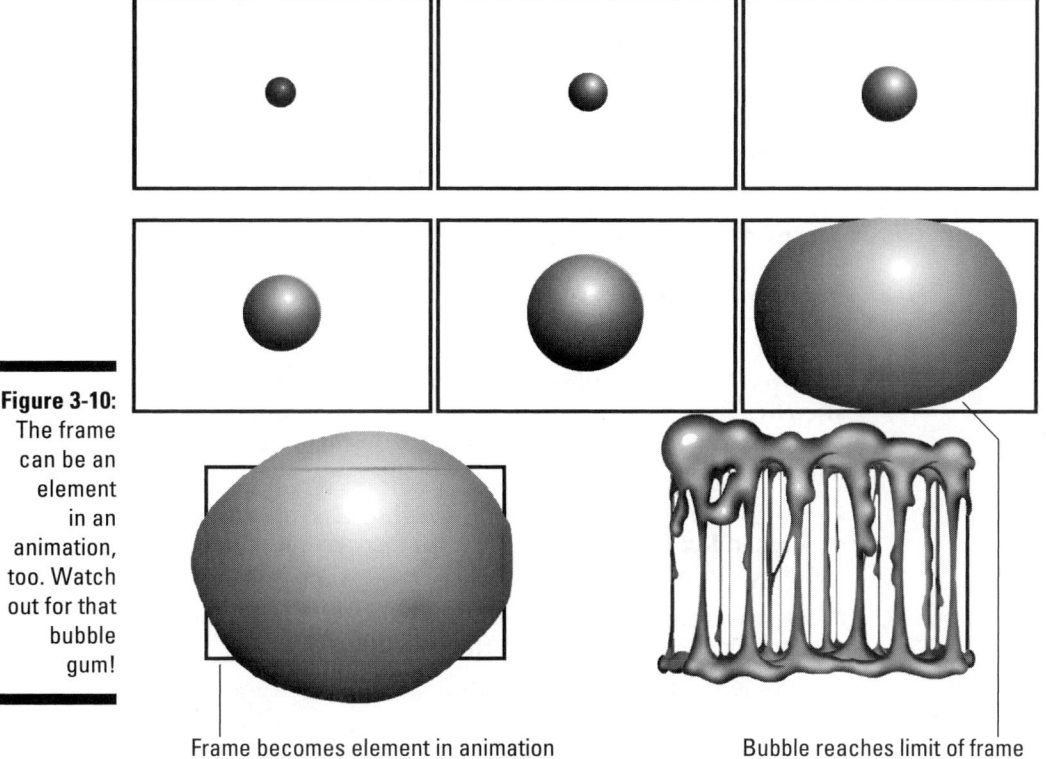

Figure 3-10: The frame can be an element in an animation, too. Watch out for that bubble gum!

Frame becomes element in animation

Bubble reaches limit of frame

Return to the bouncing ball. In Figure 3-10, we've taken the sequence from Figure 3-8, but instead of cropping the circle to imply that it's leaving our field of vision, we've done something new. Turning the frame into part of the animation lets us do several cool things:

- Say more about what the circle was made of
- Surprise the viewer — and maybe . . .
- Make someone laugh (which sets your animation apart from lots of other Web animations, and makes it and your site more memorable)

The Secret of Index Cards

If you read this chapter from the beginning to here, you're probably wondering why we asked you in the chapter's introduction to buy index cards. Note taking? Small paper dolls? Origami? Good guesses, but . . . no. We encourage you to do your sketches on paper because it's the most efficient way of trying out your ideas. First, you just draw the most important scenes. Then you begin to fill in the gaps. You will end up going back to change frames as you become more experienced. You'll alter the order of some actions, eliminate others, and add more pieces to smooth out transitions.

As you work, you'll begin to have lots of pieces of paper, many of them the product of erasing, folding, and redrawing. Eventually, you'll want to test them to see how your animation is developing, as well as your timing. The best way to do so is pretty low-tech; just do the following:

1. **Put all your storyboard sketches in numbered order.**

   Trim off the bottom to the edge of the frame.

2. **Take out a pack of index cards that's the next size larger than your sketches, number the cards on the lined side to match the number of sketches you've made, and match the cards' numbers to those of the storyboard sketches.**

3. **Using glue or tape, attach each storyboard frame to the unlined side of your index card, making sure that the trimmed frame is squared up to one edge (side and bottom), but not hanging over it.**

   Make sure that you have at least half an inch (a full inch is even better) space on the left side beyond the edge of your frame.

4. **Put the cards in numbered order, with the first one on top.**

   Add at least three or four blank index cards to the bottom of the pile.

5. **Square up the pile of cards so that all the edges match.**

   Congratulations, you're now the proud owner of a flipbook!

6. **Holding the edge of the squared-up pack of cards tightly in one hand, quickly flip through the sequence from top to bottom.**

   Doing so should give you a good sense of whether your animation is ready for production. If the animation seems to move too slowly or too quickly, or the action seems to jump in places, read through "Timing — or, the Lowdown on Stand-Up" in Chapter 4 for more information.

You don't actually have to wait until the end of your storyboarding to try this process. Anytime you have at least ten frames in a sequence, you can stop and test yourself this way. Because the cards are not attached in any way, they are a very flexible tool. As you learn how to create believable movement, you can use the cards to help you figure out what you're doing wrong and correct the problem more quickly. You also find these cards to be very important in Chapter 4. In that chapter, we take the tools of storyboarding and apply them to developing characters that stand, move, and act in smooth and believable ways.

Chapter 4
Getting into Character

In This Chapter

▶ Setting the mood — posing your characters
▶ Dissecting the moving parts
▶ Trading technique for technology
▶ Making still images move: classic techniques
▶ Timing — or, the lowdown on stand-up

*I*n Chapter 3, we deal with where to place things in an animation frame. Now in this chapter, however, we concentrate on *what* you place in that frame. First we examine believability in posing characters. No, we do not mean that you have to listen to politicians explain how they raise campaign funds. Unlike a good animation, that would be painful to observe, difficult to understand, and boring to watch over and over. Not to mention highly incredible.

Like voguing in the '80s, a good pose is only half the story. After you've given your character personality and a frozen position to start from, you'll want your character to move smoothly from position to position. The speed with which these actions take place will affect the result as well. Get your drawing fingers ready as we cover all these issues!

Setting the Mood — Posing Your Characters

A *pose* is a key position in an action. If you look at the moving circles in Chapter 3, you notice that you can pull out a few key frames that are more critical to understanding what's going on in the animation than others. The other frames are really just transitions between these key poses. Right now, these poses tell us very little about the circles themselves other than where they are in relation to the frame. That's because you haven't yet attempted to give the circles any character of their own.

> ### Characters for the drawing-impaired
>
> What if you want to skip the anatomy lesson? One of the nice things about simple objects (like pencils, computer monitors, or toasters) is that they're easy to draw or adapt. No joints, no muscles, no worries. All you need is a stock photo or illustration (See Chapter 7 for a discussion of clip art) and a program with a masking function, and you're in business. We discuss the special pleasures and pitfalls of animating from a photograph in Chapter 8.

A good pose should impart information about the character. Although posing may involve a character in motion, it doesn't have to. Think of a portrait: either a painting or a photo. The good ones tell you a great deal about the individual — how old he is, whether he's strong or weak, proud or shy, happy or sad. This kind of information can involve the face, but a good pose tells you as much (if not more) from the character's stance as its face.

When you animate, it's particularly important that your poses telegraph to the user as much initial information as possible. On the Web, your animation will be short and probably be repeated over and over while your page is being viewed. Although anything that moves initially grabs attention, holding that attention takes a good understanding of posing.

Strike a pose: Making simple changes for good effect

How can you tell a good pose from a bad one? The answer is deceptively simple: If the pose looks right to you, then it's good. You really can tell the difference, even without training. Look at the two stick characters waiting for a bus in Figure 4-1. They're the same size and shape, and neither one has a face. Which one feels more real to you? We hope the one on the left does. Of course, the hard part is knowing why, and then being able to create characters that feel more like the one on the left than the one on the right.

So what is the difference between the two stick figures? The one on the left illustrates two important posing principles: *asymmetry* and *personality*.

Asymmetry: Avoiding the perils of perfection

In Chapter 3, we cover how boring a perfect circle centered inside a frame can be. Take a look at that chapter. In Figure 4-2, we've drawn a straight line right down the middle of the frame. If you took a mirror and put it right on

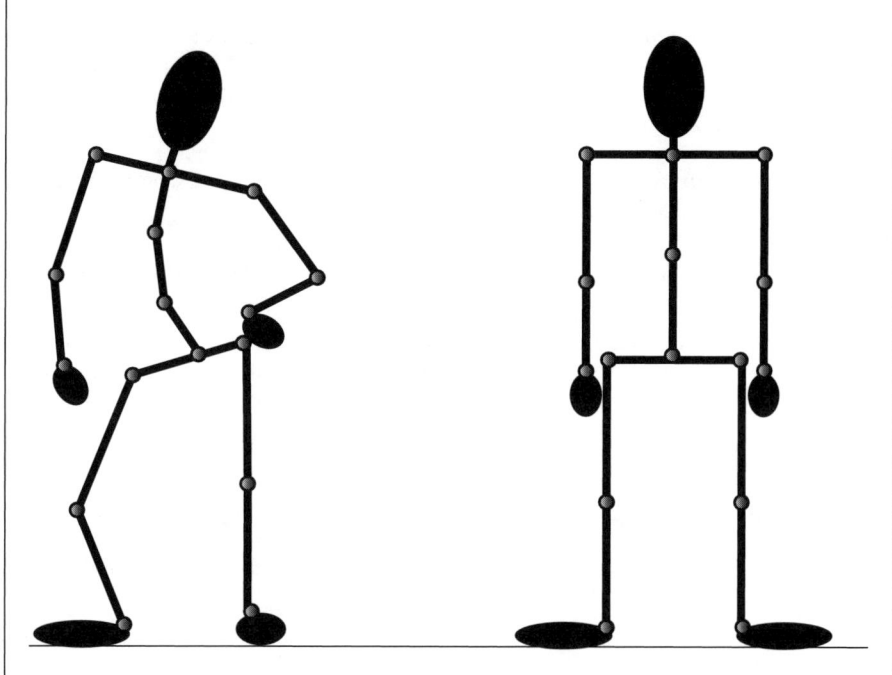

Figure 4-1: Two stick figures hanging out on the corner illustrate how important a good pose can be.

that line, you'd see that the left and right sides of the image are identical. This mirror effect is called *symmetry*.

Symmetry is perfection. Philosophically speaking, perfection is the ideal. Deep thinkers pursued perfection over the centuries, imagining what it might be like to attain it. We tell you today, "Call off the search and get a life." Perfection does not exist in organic things, only in mechanical objects. Animating a mechanical object, as we discuss later, is only interesting if you pretend it's not inanimate and give it life and personality. (Think about the enchanted furniture in Disney's *Beauty and The Beast*.)

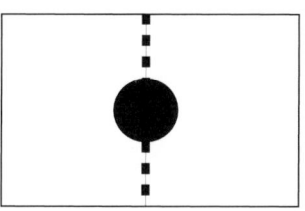

Figure 4-2: The dashed line cuts the image in half, illustrating the pitfalls of too much symmetry.

People are not symmetrical either, although they have even numbers of limbs, eyes, and so on. And no living being stands up as straight and stiff as the stick figure on the right in Figure 4-1. What he needs is a heavy dose of asymmetry, that nice off-center effect that tells you an object has the potential of life.

You can bring asymmetry to a character's pose, using your powers of observation and a little practice.

 1. **Open the file** puppet.pcx **in the** Chap04 **folder on the CD that accompanies this book.**

    Unlike the stick figures that you used to draw as children, this template character is more like a wooden puppet, with little knobs where major bends in the body exist, as well as identifiable shoulders and hips.

 2. **Print this file out at 200%, and then copy or trace it onto a piece of paper.**

    Leave plenty of room on one side of the paper for your own drawing.

 3. **Position yourself in front of a full-length mirror with paper and pencil handy.**

    Stand up artificially straight, as if you were at attention in the army. Doing so will make you look a little like the template.

 4. **Watch the mirror as you relax into a comfortable position.**

    What are you looking for? You need to know where a character can bend, and under what circumstances it does. The most important things to notice are the positions of the head, shoulders, and hips. When you stand at ease, your spine isn't stiff as a stick — it does a gentle S-curve. Which way do you lean? When you relax, which foot comes forward and which hip comes up?

 5. **Sketch a stick figure in this position.**

    Don't try to give it a face, or worry about hands and feet. Just translate what you see and feel to the stick figure. Even though you may be tempted, use the same straight lines we did so that you can concentrate on which major pieces move.

 6. **Compare your sketch, your image in the mirror, and the original stick figure.**

    Do you think you've managed to see and draw the change? Don't worry if you think you've missed something. Relax into a different position, and repeat the process. Learning how to see basic movement can be difficult at first, but gets easier with practice.

Chapter 4: Getting into Character 59

> ### Asymmetrical art appreciation
>
> One of the breakthroughs in the art of the Renaissance was the rediscovery of how to draw the human body. Pictures in the Middle Ages frequently show flat, symmetrical characters, sized according to how important they were to the picture's story rather than how near or far away they were from the viewer. Sculpture of the same period was flat, too, when compared to statues from the Classical or Renaissance eras. Saints tended to stare straight into space with one hand stiffly raised, their feet planted firmly and identically on the imaginary ground.
>
> Slowly but surely, the art of drawing from observation that made the Roman and Greek statues seem so alive was rediscovered in Renaissance art. With it came the rediscovery of *contrapposto,* an elegant Italian word that means "counterpoise." This word was coined specifically to describe the way all people stand when at ease, with one hip out and raised while the other hip drops and pulls in. In this way, the weight of the body is distributed unevenly between the two legs. That's why you tend to shift position if you have to stand in line for a long time — you're redistributing the weight to give one foot a rest. You recognized contrapposto when you looked at the two stick figures in Figure 4-1. Now that you know about it, you can use contrapposto when posing your characters to make a standing figure feel more lifelike and believable.

Personality: Becoming a minor god

Even if all you want to do is add some glitz to an "under construction" notice, your work may be more effective if your things don't act like things. That means you have to bring them to life. Just like Dr. Frankenstein, you want your little monsters to have personality.

Think about how you'd animate a ringing phone. Face it: Real ringing phones look just like quiet phones. That doesn't mean animation can't be done (and done well!); just that the animation isn't obvious and you can't create the animation by simple observation. Andy Warhol once made a 12-hour film — you can't really call it a movie — of the Empire State Building. We doubt that you'll find any clips from it on the Web. If you don't want your site to get the reputation as a hot stop for insomniacs searching for a miracle, you have to take liberties with reality.

On the other hand, you can be believable without being real, especially if you apply the rules of living creatures to mechanical ones. John Lassiter (the creator of *Toy Story*) first gained attention with a short computer animation called *Luxo Jr.* Its only characters were a large Luxo lamp and a smaller Luxo lamp. Its single prop was a beach ball. It was not boring at all.

Part I: Room to Move: Animation Basics

Moody hues

Think about the bouncing ball from Chapter 3. It has as much personality as a telemarketing script. Many cures exist for this problem, starting with color and shape.

1. **In a program that allows you to transform objects by fixed amounts (like CorelDRAW!, Adobe Illustrator, or a Web animation program like Totally Hip Web Painter), make a perfect circle.**

   Most programs let you transform objects by selecting the oval drawing tool and modifying it (with the shift key on most Macintosh programs and a variety of keys in Windows, depending on the program) so you can draw a perfect circle.

2. **Make a duplicate of the circle, move it away from the first one so that you have room to maneuver, and then distort the second circle into a flat oval.**

   Most draw programs have a scaling tool that lets you set different percentages of scaling for the horizontal and vertical dimensions of an object. In some programs, you can do this step all at once by setting up the scaling distortion and asking the program to make a copy, rather than changing the original circle.

3. **Using the blend tool, set four steps between the perfect circle and the distorted oval.**

   You now have a total of 6 objects, ranging from the perfect circle you started with to the squat oval from your original distortion.

   The blend tool icon takes different forms. Don't confuse it with the gradient tool, which sets color blends only. Look for an icon that implies a change between two shapes.

4. **If your program supports RGB colors, load your Netscape palette.**

   When we specify colors in this book, we identify them by their combinations of red (R), green (G), and blue (B). Most paint programs offer you the option of making a color by specifying these numbers on a scale from 0 to 255. In this book, all of the color combinations we make this way are members of the Netscape non-dithering palette.

   Unfamiliar with these terms? Check out Chapter 5. Not only do we define color terms there, but we help you unleash the power of color in animation. Don't miss it!

   If your program only supports CMYK colors, you should save this file in an image format (like .PCX, JPEG, or a generic Postscript file) and transfer it to an imaging program like Adobe Photoshop. (Check out Chapter 10 for a discussion of different file formats and animation.) If you're not already working in animation software, you'll very likely need to do this step eventually. Most Web animation programs without their own drawing and transform tools need an image format like GIF to work. Check your software for updates, though. Many programs, like Adobe Illustrator, now offer the Netscape palette and a GIF converter.

5. **Choose a color and its range of shades from light to dark.**

   We chose to start with a pale, warm blue-green (R=204, G=255, B=255) in the circle. We put black (R=0, G=0, B=0) in the flat oval at the end. Now apply the transitional shades of blue in order: #2 gets R=153, G=204, B=204; #3 gets R=102, G=153, B=153; #4 gets R=51, G=102, B=102; and #5 gets R=0, G=51, B=51. Voilà! As you can see in Figure 4-3, we just made a simple transition from happy and active to miserable and flat.

To use transitional shades in a different hue, check out Chapter 5 for a handy grouping of the Netscape palette by color and shade.

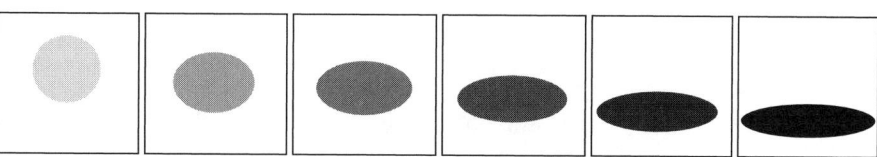

Figure 4-3: A simple transition in color and shape is sometimes all you need to create an animation.

Although you may be awfully tempted, don't try to use what may seem to be the nifty shortcut of just blending between the first color and the last when you do the shape blend above. You won't end up with reliable Web-safe colors this way! Visit the frequently mentioned Chapter 5 for a deep and meaningful discussion of Netscape non-dithering, Web-safe colors and how to get them.

This process can be even more effective if you have plug-ins or filters that let you make your object edges more jagged and irregular, like Filters⇨ Roughen Filter in Distort in Illustrator. See Figure 4-4 for this same transition with this filter applied to see how much more effective it makes the process.

Figure 4-4:
You can use simple tools and filters to add more visual interest to a shape.

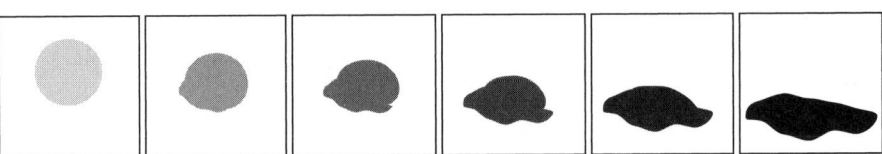

The eyes have it

Manipulating a shape is easy. How about trying something more challenging, like facial expressions? Although eyes are only one component of the face, they unquestionably telegraph the most information. If you can master the basics of eye-code, you can always communicate your character's mood. Combine personality with action, and you're well on your way to a great Web animation.

Examine Figure 4-5. It's our circle character with three different sets of eyes. Imagine these are three people watching your animation. Which one is most likely to tell her friends about it? Probably number 3, the one with the big eyes, although number 1 is paying attention. Larger eyes seem more wide awake. Very large eyes, particularly those with small pupils, look surprised.

Figure 4-5:
One simple character, three different ways of adding eyes.

Now look at Figure 4-6. These eyes are all the same size, but the pupils are different. Generally, eyes with small pupils make the character seem weak, dazed, or afraid. Larger pupils tell us the character is awake, focused, and in control.

Chapter 4: Getting into Character 63

Figure 4-6: Different pupil sizes give you clues about personality and story line.

The last example of eyeballs is in Figure 4-7. Notice that we've varied the eye shape. Now, instead of roughly circular, the eyes are ovals. Simply varying the angle of the oval and the placement of the pupil in the eye gives you not just a sense of the character, but also a sense of what it's thinking.

Figure 4-7: Circular eyes are somewhat limiting. Simply playing with ovals in different positions can convey a wider range of emotions.

Eyebrows can be very useful additions to your facial expressions. They add more depth and complexity to a face. But beware not to separate them from the eyes — they should work together, as they do in a real face. When in doubt, use the professional animator's reality check: Look in the mirror and draw what you see yourself doing.

Make a copy of Figure 4-7. (You can use a photocopier to make this quick and easy, or simply use your tracing paper.) Now that the eyes are in place, make them more expressive with the addition of eyebrows. You can work on including the other facial features: mouth, nose, even ears and hair. We played around with our circle character in Figure 4-8 to demonstrate the range of personalities and expressions you can create as you begin to feel more confident with your experiments.

You can and should combine these basic visual cues to combine motion and emotion in your storyboard. In Chapter 3, we create a storyboard (Figure 3-8) in which the bouncing ball character ricochets off the frame, then zooms off the screen toward the viewer in the final frame. In Figure 4-9, you can see how the same ball looks with some changes in expression.

Body language

In addition to facial expression, you can use body posing to get personality and mood across. Pull up the file `puppet.pcx` in the `Chap04` folder on the CD-ROM that comes with this book. What would you have to do to make this figure look sad or stubborn?

Follow the same process as outlined in the asymmetry study earlier in this chapter. Remember not to worry about facial expression; just think about the way your body rearranges to communicate a new emotion.

After you try these poses, take a look at files `puppet2.pcx` and `puppet3.pcx` to compare your efforts to possible solutions. See how little you need to do to translate an emotion to your character? The sad figure depends only on head, neck, and shoulder changes. The changes to create a stubborn look depend on shoulders and arms.

Figure 4-8: Anyone can create a character with personality, even starting with a simple circle. Shown is a range of examples.

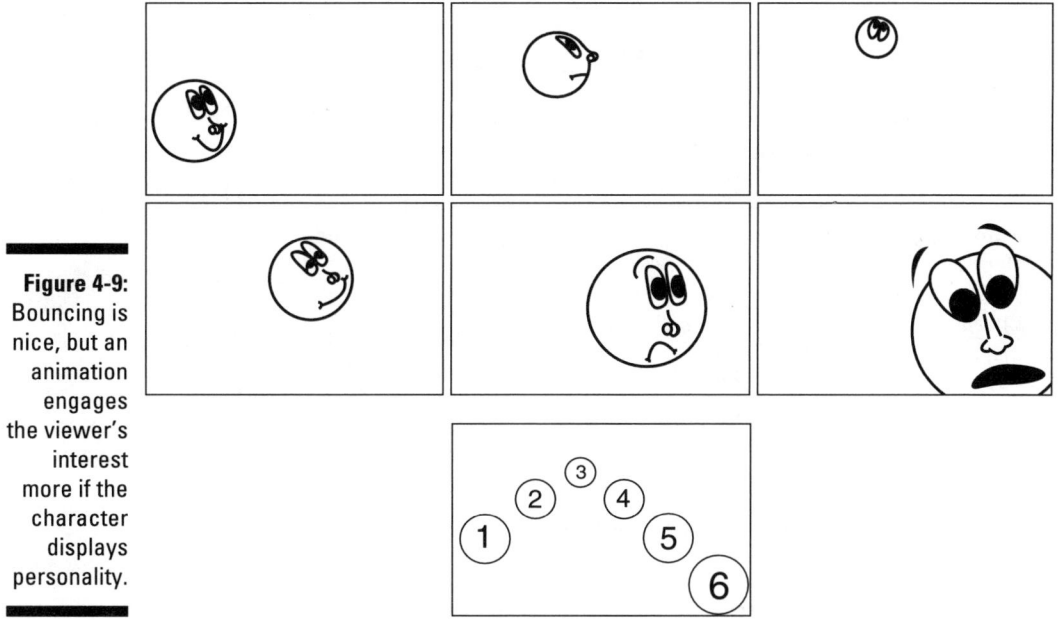

Figure 4-9: Bouncing is nice, but an animation engages the viewer's interest more if the character displays personality.

Don't stop here! Think about what you're planning on showing in your Web animation. If the animation involves a human character, act out your basic poses and observe them in a mirror as you did to conquer asymmetry. Your storyboard sketches will be more realistic, as will your actual animation.

Dissecting the Moving Parts

Because bandwidth is a critical issue for all Web graphics, you need to work as efficiently as possible in creating your animations, while still making your motions believable. Sometimes you're doing a really small GIF animation and don't have enough frames (or bandwidth) to be truly believable. Or you're still getting used to observing how arms move and what do to with them. If that's the case, you're better off cropping your action down to the body parts that you really need.

If you're working with an existing piece of photographic artwork or creating a simple animation like a bouncing ball, your animating will mostly involve simple move, rotate, or distort functions. Make your animation a close-up of the parts you can handle and let your viewers' imaginations fill in the rest. The real trick is at the beginning, when you decide what you want to do and what you actually need to do it.

> ### Constructive laziness
>
> Professional animators use many techniques to move a complex creature. You can observe the two most significant styles by comparing a Disney or Warner Brothers cartoon (*The Lion King,* Bugs Bunny cartoons) with one by Hanna-Barbera (*The Flintstones, The Jetsons*). The first approach is very fluid and realistic. Characters move through active landscapes, mimicking living motion with fluidity and grace. Look at *The Flintstones* carefully, however, and you'll notice that the characters are primitive in more ways than one. If Barney is talking, only his mouth moves. The rest of his body is stationary, unless some part of it is doing something specific, like his legs if he's walking and talking at the same time.
>
> Disney-type cartoons are very expressive, and very expensive. You'll probably want to emulate the down-and-dirty Hanna-Barbera techniques instead. You can call this *constructive laziness:* moving only what you need.
>
> After you create a character and give it its first pose, you should try to limit your redrawing from scratch. If you're working away from the computer, use tracing paper to "lift" as much of the character into the next frame or frames as you can. If you're on the computer, you use as many of the computer's copying and duplicating functions as you can.

A real-life example is the best way to help you understand how working with simple actions and object close-ups is done. Look at `caesar.pcx` in the `Chap04` folder on the accompanying CD-ROM. This photo is of a hand that was once part of a massive Roman statue with a pointing index finger. The photo is typical of the kind of picture that lends itself to a Web animation: simple lines, easy-to-recognize object, and it would translate fairly successfully to GIF format if needed. (See Chapter 11 for a discussion of file conversion.)

Some of your animation choices here are easier than others. The entire hand can move, with or without its base. If that's the case, you're dissecting the image into only two basic elements. The pointing index finger is another possibility. It could move back and forth, rotate, or bend.

If you decided to only move the hand back and forth or rotate the finger, you'll need to break the image into two parts again — hand and finger. However, to rotate effectively, you'll have to move the finger a little out from under the thumb, which means some work with an imaging program to flesh out the base of the finger.

If you decide to bend the finger as if it were beckoning, you're dealing with more dissecting and artwork. The finger needs to be broken in three parts at the joints, and the middle finger needs to be broken into two elements — the bent knuckle and the top joint with the nail — to create the flip side of the index finger.

If you want to bone up on the step-by-step process of animating an isolated element in a photo, we show you how to wiggle Caesar's finger in Chapter 9.

Even though you're working with an existing computer image, you'll still be better off if you create sketches to work from before you attack the image itself. After you choose your photo and eliminate its unnecessary background, print it out, trace it, and figure out your motions just as you would with an animation you're drawing from scratch. Nothing is so frustrating as working on the fly, and discovering that you need to make a change that will require you to edit the original image — and redo all the frames you've already created to match the change!

Trading Technique for Technology

In the next section, "Making Still Images Move: The Classic Techniques," we concentrate on those animation techniques that help you translate motion to the screen. The techniques are meant to help you break a sequence down into bite-size pieces. Such classic techniques are the most creative part of making animations — coming up with the ideas and characters, positioning elements, and telling a story. Not surprisingly, they represent the skills that acclaimed professionals developed for themselves.

However, two techniques have found very nontraditional and delightfully labor-saving analogues on the computer. We cover these techniques in this section. Use them to help you concentrate on your ideas and spare you the agony of traditional cel production.

Onion-skinning without tears

You've used the basic principles of onion-skinning each time you've traced one frame, moved something slightly on the trace, and then traced the next one. (See the sidebar "Cel animation cheat sheet" for an explanation of traditional onion-skinning.) This practice works fine when you're still at the storyboard stage, but what happens when you want to make that digital jump?

Some Web animation programs, such as GIFmation by BoxTop Software and WebPainter by Totally Hip, provide onion-skinning functions. But you can create your own on-screen onion-skinning in any illustration program, or an image editing program like Adobe Photoshop that supports layers. We go into depth on how to do this in Photoshop in Chapter 9.

Betwixt and in-between

If you've followed all the steps in this book from the front cover to this point, you've been making or working with storyboards all along.

Storyboards deal with *key frames* — the frames that explain visually the most important steps in your animation. But eventually the time comes when you need to fill in the gaps in between.

In-betweening is the creation of transitional frames to fill in these gaps between the key frames in your storyboard. If you've ever made a color gradient in a paint program or played with morphing by using Kai's Power Goo, Morph, or a similar package, you've experienced the concept of in-betweening without being aware of it. In a gradient, you give the computer a starting and an ending color. These are the equivalent of two key frames in an animation. You also help to define how many "frames" the transition should take, either by filling in a number of steps through a dialog box or defining an area for the gradient to use. The computer then does the calculating grunt-work.

In-betweening is something in which no one should ever have to emulate the tedium of a traditional animator's production cycle. Fortunately, many commercial animation packages now support some form of in-betweening. However, depending on how sophisticated their implementation of this critical function is, you may find that you have more control if you have an illustration package. As we demonstrated in the simple example in Figure 4-3, such a program can very easily handle the morphing stages, or evenly distribute a movement across a frame. Even better, through arcing, slow in and speed out, and squashing, you can control those changes by adjusting the computer's in-betweening to suit, and thus you can avoid the stiff, mechanical look that many beginner's Web animations have. This ability is often not possible in the simpler animation packages.

Beware trusting the computer too much in the in-betweening phase. It's only as good at in-betweening as you make it. You probably know that pictures can develop banding in blends where not enough steps are taken to complete the color change. Not providing enough key frames, or trying to stretch a motion out artificially, will create animation "banding" too. Your in-between steps will be too fast or slow, and your motion will appear jagged and uneven. Check out the section called "Timing — or, the Lowdown on Stand-Up" for more on this.

Making Still Images Move: The Classic Techniques

Look at the series of moving ball sketches in Chapter 3. Although they became progressively better and more interesting as they evolved, you can notice that the sketches are not quite right yet. Things are very precise because we've taken advantage of how easily the computer can duplicate shapes and change them in exact, mathematically even steps. Animating in this way is kind of like creating a movie from a series of photographs, rather than a video or film camera. You get the idea, but the action feels stiff. In this section, we bring the traditional methods of observing and portraying motion to our posed and placed characters.

We are assuming that you have at least the lowest common denominator of technology in this section: a program to open files and draw things in, and a simple shareware application to compile the individual frames.

Many commercial Web animation programs will handle some (but not all) of these traditional functions for you. For example, most object-oriented animation programs, such as Astound WebMotion, Paceworks Object Dancer, and Totally Hip Web Painter, have rotation, scaling, and distortion tools. However, each program implements these functions differently and offers different combinations and levels of animation tools. As a general rule, the more complicated and creative the function, the less likely it is to be available ready-made. Check your chosen Web animation software and compare its features to the techniques we discuss in this chapter to see which ones your software provides versus those techniques you'll need to master yourself.

Studies in Arc-y-ology

Did you ever see a TV program from the '60s called *Lost in Space*? One of its characters, the robot, was most memorable for rocking side to side and windmilling its arms while yelling, "Danger! Danger!" (This antic made Robbie the robot the most entertaining "star" in the program, which is probably why Hollywood took so long to revive *Lost in Space* as a movie.) The robot was a perfect mechanical creature — inflexible, with almost nowhere to bend at all.

One of the things that defines a good animation is when the character's movements show different parts of the body responding in sequence to the movements of other parts. Think about how hard throwing a ball would be if you didn't use anything but your wrist and hand. Yet lots of animations that use this motion just position an arm in the air and move the hand back and forth. When the ball whizzes away across the page, you don't believe it. You have to remember to bend the elbow joint, to rotate the forearm back, and then to snap the whole arm forward. That way, the snap of the wrist is the release of a complete series of related motions.

When you move, all your joints take turns bending and rotating to create a visible line of action. You are probably so accustomed to seeing this string of motion that you don't usually notice it, but it really jumps out if you look for it. On the other hand, the fact that people take these actions for granted can work to your benefit. Because everyone shares these expectations, we can apply the line of action principle even to objects that don't have joints, like the bouncing ball example.

Tall tales and big lies

If you were like most children, you probably had an active imagination. You'd see a tall stranger walking down the street, and by the time you got home with the story, he'd have become as big as a house and grown fangs. Your mother, somehow recognizing that reality had been bent, probably told you, "Don't exaggerate!" This was good motherly advice, and probably made you a better, more truthful adult. Following it now, however, will cramp your animation style.

In fact, our best advice to you is, "Lie like a rug." Okay, maybe that's a little strong. "Build creatively on the truth" sounds nicer. But like all good liars know, making up things that sound too far-fetched doesn't work. Embellishing on things that seem reasonable is simply good common sense when animating.

In the section, "Personality: Becoming a minor god," we asked, "How would you animate a ringing phone?" to illustrate how hard it can be to give personality to an inanimate object. But just because something looks hard doesn't mean that it needs to be, if you're willing to stretch reality a tad. We offer three would-be animators — Mr. Reality, Mr. Practicality, and Mr. Exaggerator — as examples.

Mr. Reality says, "Phones don't move when they ring. Therefore, a ringing phone just sits there. I need a sound clip, or I can't do it."

Mr. Reality goes in search of a sound file and attaches it to his line art with a button urging people to download his sound. Most people don't bother, especially because they have to download a plug-in first. Those who do are distracted from the content of the Web site by the feeling that someone's trying to reach them.

Mr. Practicality says, "Well, I've got to do it. But I don't have enough bandwidth for a sound clip. So I'll put the words 'Ring! Ring!' in a cartoon balloon and use some bright color for the type."

Mr. Practicality does exactly what he plans. He wants something to move, so he makes the type flash on and off, just like the ringing of a phone. All the ten-year-olds who've seen this ploy on *Sesame Street* surf past, giggling.

Mr. Exaggerator says, "Well, if phones don't move, why do we say a phone is 'Ringing off the hook' when it's really busy? To heck with Reality and Practicality. I'm going to show what that ought to look like!"

Mr. Exaggerator takes a photo of an antique phone, knocks out the background and makes the mouth and ear pieces do the Macarena in double time. Mr. Exaggerator's site wins Cool Site of the Day.

Have *we* exaggerated just a little here? Maybe. But the idea works. If you want to show motion and you don't have streaming video capabilities, you need to exaggerate that motion enough to make what you're trying to say clear. If you're animating a fast moving car, its wheels should angle forward into the motion. If you want a beating heart, it should expand to double the normal size on the beat. Watch how the powers of exaggeration are used in all the traditional animation techniques.

One of the easiest ways to show realistic motion was discovered by the earliest animators, when they noticed that things don't move in a straight line. Oh, some machines and machine parts do, but to animate believably, you need to work on a curve. Look at Figure 4-10. It compares two paths of motion for a ball. The first is a straight line. The ball doesn't really look as if it's moving in the air. It looks as if it's on an invisible wire strung from one side of the frame to the other. On the other hand, the second example looks more natural. That's because the ball moves in an arc: It rises into the air, and then falls as gravity takes over.

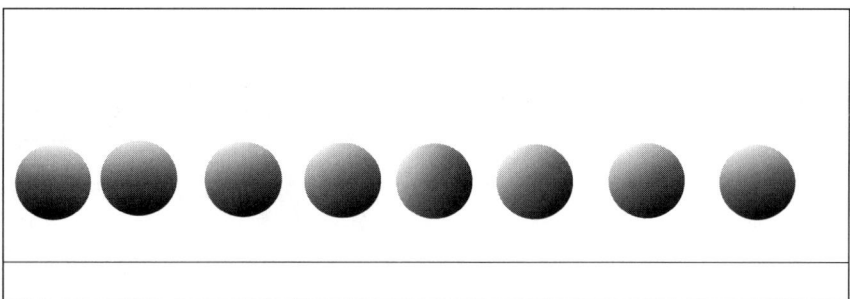
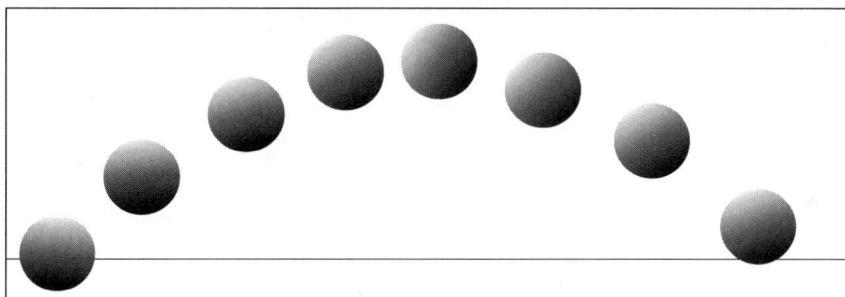

Figure 4-10: Mechanical versus realistic paths of a ball thrown from one end of the frame to the other.

You always need to take gravity into account when you animate.

Arcs are also critical when you animate living creatures. To understand how critical, we're going to send you back to the mirror. Stand with your arms at your sides. Now, very quickly, but without moving the rest of your body if you can help it, flap your arms up and down as if you were trying to fly. Watch the ends of your fingers as you do this. If you're moving fast enough, your hand will blur, and you'll see your motion describe an arc in the air. In fact, you'll see this arc with every movement you make. Extend your arm all the way out from your body and bend it at the elbow until you touch your shoulder. Do so quickly and watch the look of the fan you create.

How is this motion different from the way machines operate? If a machine has to move from one place to the next, it will always be designed to move in a straight line if possible. Figure 4-11 illustrates the difference between a natural and a mechanical design. If you were a machine, perhaps your arm would be designed like an elevator, running on an extendable track along your side so you could always reach something the same distance away from your body without having to move anything else.

In the storyboard found in Figure 4-9, we added personality to our moving ball. Note the section where our character turns his head to look at where he's going next. How would you animate this character by using the arc principle? Create a five-frame storyboard of just this sequence, but simplify it a little by assuming that your character is not also moving in space. Doing so will make it easier for you to see how arcing affects the viewer's sense of believability.

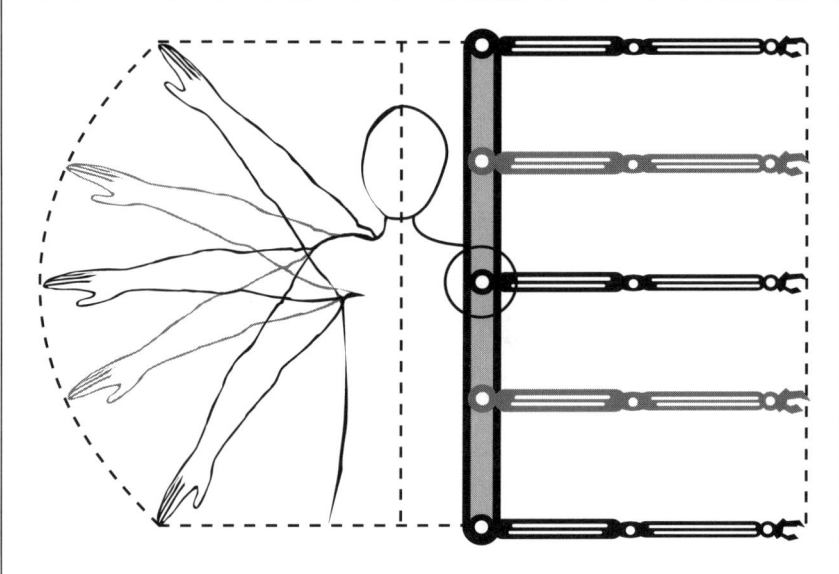

Figure 4-11: The human arm pivots so that its maximum horizontal reach only occurs at one point in the arc. A "more efficient" mechanical version would assure that the arm can reach the same distance at any height.

1. **Draw five identical boxes in a row.**

   Make these quick, simple sketches. Use one sheet of paper so you can see all the key frames at once.

2. **In box number one, draw the character shown in Figure 4-12, facing to the left.**

Figure 4-12: The first step in turning a character's head.

Chapter 4: Getting into Character   73

3. In box number five, draw the same character, but flipped to look to the right.

How do you get from the first to the last?

4. Draw the center frame, number three, next.

Doing so makes finding the positions in between an easier task.

Finished? If so, you probably have a series that looks much like Figure 4-13. Notice how everything lines up very perfectly. But a real head doesn't move this way. Ask a friend to act out this action for you. Unless he's moving very fast, you'll probably notice that his head actually drops slightly as it moves through the center. You need to add this arcing into your storyboard.

Animating becomes easier if you draw an arc to describe the motion you're trying to show before you draw the action. Figure 4-14 shows this arc superimposed on the path the head should follow. Redraw your five stages to follow this path, and see how much more alive your sequence becomes.

Figure 4-13: Head turning without an arc results in a stiff, assembly-line look.

Figure 4-14: Use arcing to take a mechanical motion and breathe life into it.

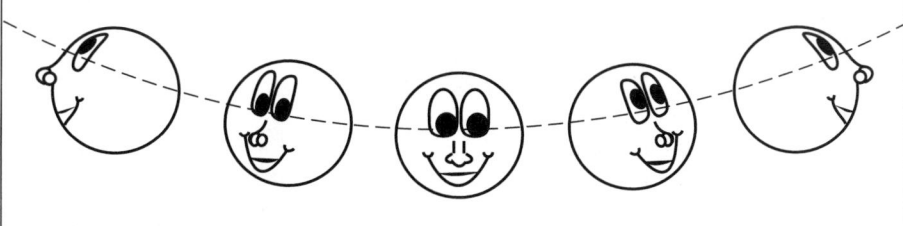

Making a mass with volume: Weight and gravity

As a refugee from the '70s might say, "Animation is heavy." In fact, you could argue that gravity is the single most important element in understanding how to make things move for you.

Right now, you're probably sitting in a chair. Try to visualize yourself standing up, but don't do the action yet. Once you think that you have the image in your mind, put this book down and stand up, paying attention to the process. Now sit down again, and make a list of all the little actions you went through to go from sitting to standing. Don't leave anything out or skip any steps.

Anticipation: The weighting game

What was the first thing on your list? **Hint:** It wasn't leaning forward. If you paid very close attention to your actions, you may have noticed that you rocked back quickly against the chair and braced yourself before standing. You were gathering momentum for the action, to counteract the pull of gravity. That process is called *anticipation,* and it's another important animation element.

You can see exaggerated anticipation at work in almost any cartoon. With the possible exception of the Road Runner, cartoon characters about to run tend to rear way back on one leg with the other bent and raised, arms bent like a taut bowstring.

Factoring anticipation into your work is important if your subject is going to move through space, unless you plan a continuous cycle of one simple action. Without it, characters look like they're trying to fake weightlessness in a third-rate space opera.

To see how you may apply this technique, look at Figure 4-15. Instead of starting our ball character with a gentle drop, we're going to have him take off under his own steam. See how he leans back against the frame, changing his shape and building momentum?

You can see this storyboard as we animated it by viewing the GIF animation `bounce` in the folder `Chap04\Bounce` on the accompanying CD.

Applying anticipation comes with a few simple hints. All you have to remember is to add that critical opposite lead-in.

- If your subject is moving in a clockwise circle, start the first few frames moving counterclockwise instead, hesitate slightly, and reverse direction. An up elevator always begins with a slight drop down.

- Although you should always exaggerate for effect, how much anticipation you show should balance how much energy your character will expend in breaking free of gravity. A windmill would probably show a very gentle effect. A tiger, on the other hand, needs lots of anticipation. If you have a cat, watch how he tenses his body, head down and back up, before exploding forward.

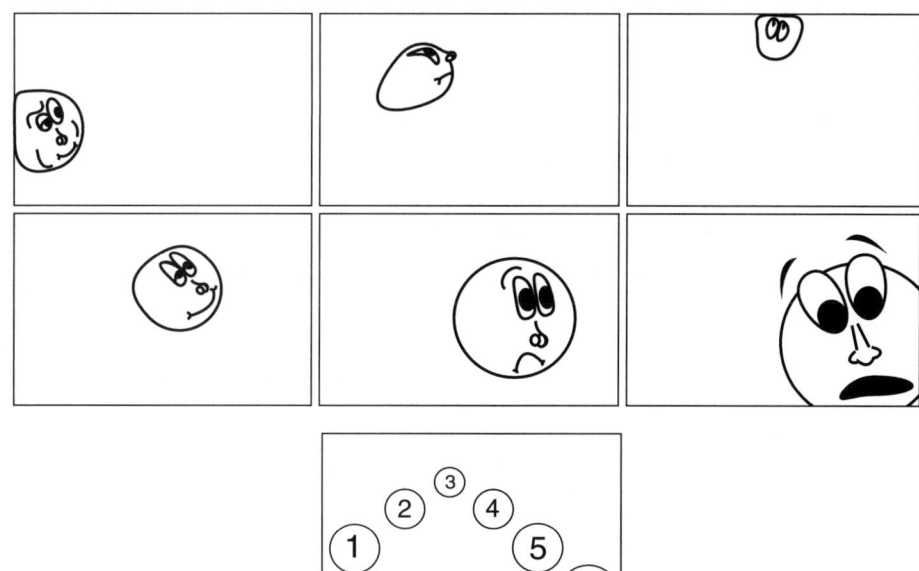

Figure 4-15: Our final storyboard, adding the effects of gravity and anticipation.

 ✔ Anticipation works for expressions, too. The famous double take is really just a special kind of anticipation. It's most effective when the character's face goes open and blank and the body tenses before the explosion.

Squash and stretch

If anticipation is the idea, *squash and stretch* is one classic way you show it. Squash builds energy, stretch releases it. Every time you tense a muscle, you're squashing. After you finish an action, you've stretched and released the muscle. Running, pressing weights, typing on the computer, chewing on a pizza with extra cheese — well, maybe extra cheese and pepperoni — all demand these two opposites. Think back to your "getting up from the chair" list. Our own list begins like this:

 ✔ Lean back hard against the chair.

 ✔ Lean forward from the waist slightly and move right leg back.

 ✔ Move arms to the edge of the chair seat and bend them slightly, putting weight on palms.

 ✔ Scrunch down shoulders. Bend one leg back toward chair.

Take a good look at this list. Notice that you scrunch down your arms and shoulders and shift weight on your legs before you push up. In animation terms, that motion is a *squash*.

Here's the rest of our list:

- ✔ Lean forward and push up with legs and arms.
- ✔ Straighten up quickly. Here's where you make your stretch. You rear up to your full length when you stand to use up the energy from your squash.
- ✔ Shift position to stand at ease.

Note that every squash and stretch has to end with the body coming back to its normal state.

When you squash, your character's size doesn't change, it just shifts volume. Where it shifts to depends on what the character is doing or is about to do. The body gets shorter in the direction of the movement and wider perpendicular to it. When you stretch, the body initially is a little longer and thinner than it was at rest, and then settles down.

You'll squash and stretch your character in differing amounts, depending on how heavy or fast your character is. It's fun to experiment with this effect. On the CD that accompanies this book, we've provided just the right kind of character for some initial explorations.

1. **On the CD, open the folder called** Chap04\Snowman.

   In it, we've provided you with two versions of a file (snowtmp1.gif and snowtmp2.gif) to get you started on the squash court.

   When you pull up snowtmp2.gif, you'll notice that the character is not put together, but all the individual elements are there. With each piece separately drawn, you can select each one individually and transfer it to separate layers in a program that supports one of these options (or use it as template objects in a vector drawing program like Adobe Illustrator or CorelDRAW!). We highly recommend one of these routes if they are available to you, because you'll discover that you have more control and more realistic motion if you can have a little variety in your squash and stretch distortions. However, snowtmp1.gif offers the beginning snowman as a completely attached character if the program you're working in doesn't support these possibilities.

2. **Transfer your chosen template file to your favorite software package.**

   If you're using the file with separate elements, arrange them as you like.

3. **First, make the completely squashed snowman frame.**

   The most efficient way of doing so is to group those elements that will distort about the same amount (like the three snowball segments) and use a scale tool to distort the horizontal and vertical dimensions. Note that some pieces, like the scarf, need to be handled separately, because they will not squash.

Chapter 4: Getting into Character 77

Your character needs to maintain the same apparent volume when you distort it. If it doesn't, it will look as if the snowman has grown or shrunk in size instead of scrunching up for the jump. That means that if you scale the vertical dimension to 50%, you'll have to scale the horizontal to 200% at the same time.

Always start at the most distorted frame first, on the principle that you can use a computer program's in-betweening function to help create the missing frames.

4. **Returning to the original snowman, create the stretched frame.**

5. **Using a total of nine frames, do three sets of in-betweening:**

   a. **from the original snowman to the squash step**

   b. **from the squash to the stretch**

   c. **from the stretch to the original snowman**

We've created a little group of animation frames (`squash1.gif` through `squash9.gif`) in `Chap04\Squash` on the CD to show squash and stretch in action.

Overlapping action

Pay attention to the snowman's scarf in our squash animation (`Chap04\Squash\squash.html`) on the CD. Notice how it seems to lag behind the snowman's actions slightly? As our engineer friends would say, this is not a bug, it's a feature. You're seeing one of gravity's domino effects. The scarf doesn't have any ability to move on its own, so any actions it may make must be based on whatever it's attached to.

When two sets of actions are linked in this way, with one playing follow the leader with the other, you're seeing *overlapping action*. Overlapping action is one of the reasons that isolating your elements so that you can move them individually can be so useful. If you simply squashed and stretched the scarf in time with the snowman, the scarf would look like it was a board, stuck to the snowman with crazy glue.

Speed up and slow down

If you take another look at the squash animation series we've created, you'll notice something very important. Although we've used nine frames to tell this story, the most squashed frame is not number five (the one in the middle). We've used more frames to get into the squashing, and fewer to show the stretch phase.

This practice illustrates another important way that gravity affects how you need to animate. One of the few lines that stuck with us from high school science class was, "An object in motion tends to stay in motion. An object at rest tends to stay at rest." For those of you who slept through science class, this statement is not an explanation of why you're wide awake at a midnight party and unable to even hit the snooze button the next day. It's a description of how the pull of gravity interacts with energy, and it's called *inertia*.

Inertia explains the unequal division of squash and stretch. Actions take time to build up energy, which means that the anticipation side of the equation needs more time to develop than the release, which can happen very quickly and should therefore take up fewer frames.

Now that you have a better idea of what to look for, go back to your template snowman. Correct the amount of frames you're using. Adjust the scarf. Your animation should now pass the believability test.

Going cyc-lotic

Some actions have a beginning, a middle, and an end. Others can comfortably be placed in an endless, seamless loop. Any action that can begin at the same place and the same frame that it starts from creates an *animation cycle*. These can be as simple as a chromatic run from one end of the rainbow to the other to the classic animation walk cycle. A waving hand, rotating propellers on a plane, or a dog's tail wag are cycles that fall somewhere in the middle in complexity. These actions are particularly suited for the Internet, where it is becoming common to set an animation in motion and let it repeat an infinite amount of times.

If you want to show a walking character, you'll need a certain amount of technical precision, as well as good timing. However, creating the character is not really that hard, once you know what to look for. As with other things, self-observation can help. Try walking a few paces. If you use the "one-one-thousand" count to mark a second of time passing, you'll discover that you can take about two normal-paced steps in about a second's time. This knowledge should help you figure out how many frames you'll need.

In Figure 4-16, we step through (yes, pun intended) the critical walk positions. Note that our old friend arcing comes into play here. Unless they're on skates, people don't roll along the ground. They rise up as they push off, and drop down again at the point where their feet are furthest apart.

When you divide up your character's walk in your storyboard, try to avoid an uneven number of frames. Although they'll look fine if your animation is slow, on a speedy computer your walk may speed up, and your character's walk will begin to look too mechanical, like a door opening and closing.

Cel animation cheat sheet

When discovering how to do something new on the computer, knowing how it was done before computers were there to pick up the slack can be useful. Not only do your chances of scoring big in *Jeopardy!* increase, but it also helps put many unfamiliar concepts into perspective.

Most professional studio animation used a process called *cel animation* to turn out our best-loved cartoons and films. The *cel* was a clear acetate sheet with one character (or a part of one character) inked on it. Cels were drilled with holes so they could be locked down on a board and overlaid on each other to create the completed frame. You might have one cel for the background, another for one character, and two more for another character (if she was in the process of moving just a portion of her body like an arm). After the cels were inked and locked, they would be shot, one frame at a time, onto film.

This process was tedious, so the different tasks were split up. First, one set of animators imagined and sketched the scene on paper. They started with only the key frames that broadly described the action. After these were in place, they passed the sheets to a group of assistant animators, who would put one key frame on a light table and attach it there. Then they would place very thin tracing paper (called *onion skin* because of how much it resembled it) over the frame and draw the next frame in the sequence. The onion skin could be flipped back and forth, and acted as a ghost guide for the next frame. This operation continued until they reached the key frame that followed. Because they only drew the frames that came in-between the key frames, these animators became known as in-betweeners.

After a series of frames had been drawn, it would be shot sequentially on black and white film. The result was called a *pencil test,* and was the equivalent of our flipbook. If something didn't work at this stage, it was redrawn and reshot until everyone was satisfied. Only then would the frames be transferred to acetates for the real filming.

Timing — or, the Lowdown on Stand-Up

Have you ever noticed how some people can tell a joke and you practically roll on the floor with laughter, but others just don't seem to have the knack? They back up and repeat. Even worse, they'll suddenly say things like, "Did I tell you that the dog's owner was a Patriots fan?" that give the joke away. Or worst of all, they get to the punch line and *forget* it. Or they take ten minutes to tell a joke, and then say, "Did you get it? Bird brain! Bird brain! Isn't that funny?!" Well, no. But because you're much too polite to say that, you mutter something about needing to get your car inspected and run away.

These people tend to be bad animators because they haven't mastered the art of timing. And we know where all bad animators go, right? Of course, this won't happen to you, because you'll have learned to: Beware the seven deadly sins of timing!

- **Running in slo-mo:** This timing error is the one most frequently committed by beginners. You can get so concerned that the motion isn't fluid that you add more and more in-between frames to smooth things out. Unfortunately, the result is an animation with all the energy of poured concrete. This sin is especially heinous on the Web, where normally reasonable people get frustrated if they have to wait an extra two seconds for something to happen.

- **Speed demons:** You don't want to be guilty of sins of omission — omitting too many frames, that is. An animation that forces someone to watch it six times before it's clear is like a fly buzzing around a Web screen. "What was that?" can be too quickly followed by "Squish it!" Get someone who doesn't know what you're trying to do to view your animation, and then tell you in her own words (no prompting!) what she saw. If she says that she's not sure because it went by kind of fast, be prepared to either add frames or slow the delivery down.

- **Missing the punchline:** Variety in timing can be critically necessary to help the viewer appreciate the scene. For example, imagine you want to show someone being stung by a bee while out walking. Without enough difference between the before and after sting frames, the viewer can take too long to realize that something important has happened. To avoid this problem, remember to subtly vary the pace whenever you can. Doing so keeps your animations from looking like they were designed on an assembly line.

- **Jerking the viewer around:** Quick starts and stops, movement without anticipation, characters and objects that mysteriously appear and disappear can all happen because you don't have transitions between frames. Missing a key frame in your original storyboard is the most likely culprit. Avoid an animation that looks like stop-motion photography. Remember to use the flipbook concept to test your transitions for timing errors.

- **Uneven pacing:** A cousin to jerking the viewer around, uneven pacing often happens, ironically, as you begin to improve your storyboarding. The beginning (when you were still grasping the concepts) will be too fast or slow. When the pacing is corrected later in the animation, it's like listening to a tape on a player that needs batteries and abruptly changing them in the middle of the song. Suddenly the baritone is a soprano, which could be extremely disorienting for all concerned. Avoid this sin by redoing your flipbook test after you make changes.

Chapter 4: Getting into Character *81*

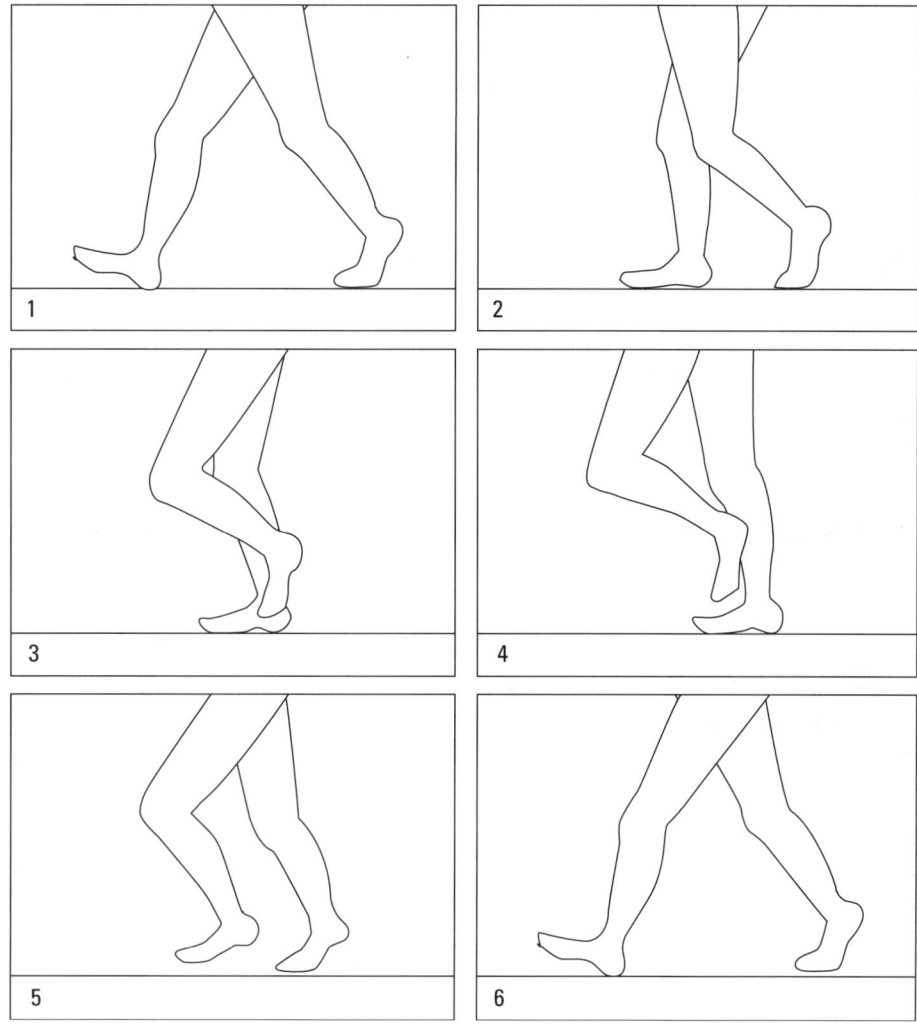

Figure 4-16: Breaking down the critical stages of the walk cycle.

- ✔ **The scale to speed equation:** Timing that's technically "right" can be effectively wrong, particularly when animating is done directly on the computer. This problem is most likely to happen when an animation has more than one character in it. Moving all characters the same amount in each frame is very tempting, because it's so much easier that way. You can avoid this sin by animating each character according to its own set of rules. In general, heavy things move slower than light things, particularly when they initially begin to move. Big things cover more ground, but usually don't move as quickly as small things.

- ✔ **Well, honestly, we thought we had seven. Really.**

So how do you avoid these sins? Alas, with practice. The first two are the easiest to fix on the computer, where all Web animation programs allow you to set the overall speed (and sometimes the frame-by-frame speed) of the finished clips. Many forms of uneven pacing respond to a purely technical solution, too. (We discuss timing cleanup and troubleshooting in Chapter 16.)

One helpful procedure is to create a chart of approximate in-between frames based on your key frames (the ones you drew before in-betweening). Try to visualize the action as it takes place, and count the seconds between each key frame. Even better, try to physically walk through the scene with a stopwatch in hand. You don't have to become an actor, but you'll have a much better idea of how long something takes if you can see it operate in the real world.

Part II
Tricks with Pix

In this part . . .

Every animation begins with a collection of images, objects, and ideas that eventually come together as a sequence of frames. In this part, we concentrate on creating, altering, and assembling these individual frames. No matter what material you plan to start with — clip art, old photos, quick sketches, illustrations — we concentrate on using that material most effectively, attractively, and painlessly.

Chapter 5
Color Me Simple

In This Chapter
▶ Understanding computer color
▶ Going beyond default palettes
▶ Planning a lean, mean palette
▶ Making your own custom color palette
▶ Creating the right color mix
▶ Forgetting everything you know about blends
▶ Putting a positive spin on negative space
▶ Applying color contrasts

*Y*ou don't really need color to give the sense of motion. After all, dogs seem to have no problem chasing a Frisbee of any shade despite the fact that they are essentially color-blind. A dog follows the motion of your arm, the blur of the disk, and the slight "whoosh" a Frisbee makes as it travels through the air.

Despite how color is not a requirement, using color in your animation is supported by three good arguments. First, color is your most effective tool in gaining and holding attention. Second, like Mount Everest, it's there. Color on the Web costs nothing, unlike the escalated price for color printing. Third and most importantly, very few dogs surf the Web.

But wait! Before you create any paisley Frisbees, you need to understand a little about how to make your colors, what combinations are particularly effective, and why a little color goes a long way.

Color Is Not a Box of Chocolates

When you were young, you probably had a box of crayons or watercolors. Some of those colors — red, yellow, and blue — were referred to as *primary colors* because you couldn't make them by combining any other colors. You may also remember that if you colored the same area many times with different crayons, eventually you got a muddy brown-black mess. If you changed your mind and wanted to return the area to white, you had to find a way to erase all those colors. That's why any color scheme with these characteristics is called *subtractive color,* because we have to subtract to reach white.

All paints, dyes, and printing inks fall into this category. Until the invention of color computer monitors and painting software, subtractive color was basically all you had to work with. Any other forms of color organization were merely theoretical, at least as far as most applications were concerned.

When computers reached a level where they could reproduce color on screen, artists discovered that the subtractive rules didn't apply. That's because computers display color by projecting light on screen. And as good old Isaac Newton discovered by watching light pass through prisms and break up into a rainbow, light is not subtractive, it's *additive.* But what does that term mean and why should it matter to you?

Additive color is a way to describe how colors are made and mixed by using different wavelengths of light. As you may expect from its name, the more colors you mix together, the lighter your result. So if you want a pure, untainted white, you need to add as much color as you can. This is what we do in Figure 5-1.

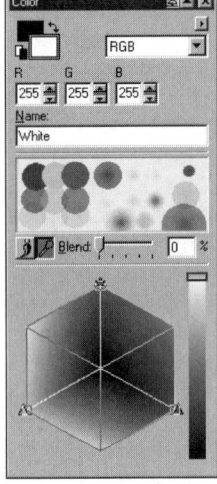

Figure 5-1: Adding red, green, and blue to make white.

The best way to do so is to combine the additive primary colors — red, green, and blue (RGB) — in equal amounts so that no one color gains the upper hand. (Refer to "Deciphering the RGB numeric values" later in this chapter for more information on this topic.) Alternatively, if you subtract as much color as you can, you will eventually wind up with black (as we did in Figure 5-2), which makes good intuitive sense. If you decrease the brightness on your monitor, you can watch the screen dim and all the colors tone down. Your white background fades from gray to black.

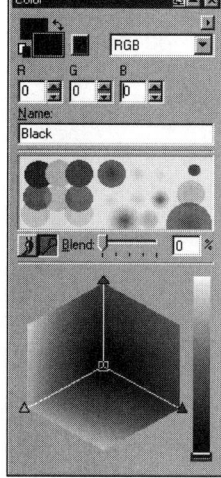

Figure 5-2: Subtracting red, green, and blue to make black.

Finding the Color Picker

You do your mixing and choosing of colors in an image-creation program in a place called the *Color Picker*. Finding the Color Picker in a new program can be a treasure hunt. Each software program handles these functions differently. The following is a selection of instructions for displaying the Color Picker dialog box for some of the graphics programs commonly used for creating Web-ready graphics. For your graphics program's detailed instructions, check the software manual.

- **Corel PHOTO-PAINT 6.0:** Choose View➪Roll-Ups➪Color. See the Color Picker dialog box displaying color selection window and RGB settings (numeric entry available). The keyboard shortcut is Ctrl+F2.

- **Photoshop 4.0:** To display the Color Picker dialog box, click on the Foreground or Background color icon (see Figure 5-3). The icons (two colored squares) are located near the bottom of the toolbar. What a screen real-estate hog! Be production savvy, press F6, and open the Color/Swatches/Brushes palette dialog box. Drag the swatches tab (left) to create two palette windows — color and swatches.

- **Microsoft Image Composer 1.0:** You can create a custom palette (8-bit color) of up to 256 separate colors. To do so, click the Color Swatch icon at the bottom of the tool bar. The Color Picker dialog box appears. Select the RGB Color Space option to use the Red/Green/Blue sliders and edit boxes.

Part II: Tricks with Pix

TECHNICAL STUFF

CMYK: A close second-ary

If you've been playing with computer illustrations or desktop applications, you're probably more familiar with CMYK color. CMYK is actually an acronym for *C*yan, *M*agenta, *Y*ellow, Blac*k* — the four "primary colors" of traditional four-color process printing.

CMYK and RGB have an interesting relationship. We show it with a *color wheel* — a diagram used to illustrate color relationships. The diagram is in the form of a wheel to emphasize that colors at opposite "ends" of the spectrum can still be mixed with each other. The color wheel on the left diagrams the subtractive color wheel. It shows the primary colors of blue, red, and yellow and their secondary colors — purple, orange, and green. Secondary colors are the result of mixing two primary colors in equal amounts. This color wheel is the one that most people recognize.

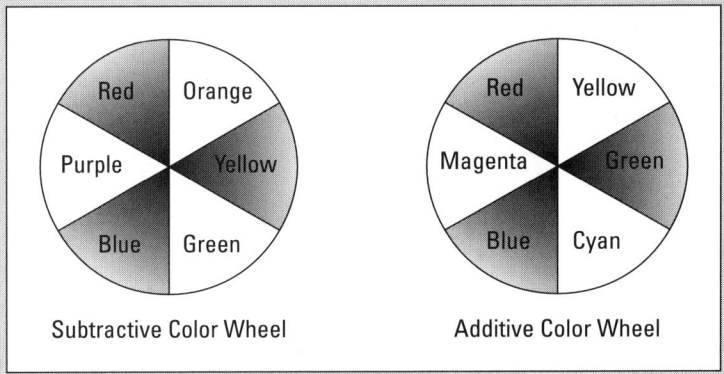

The color wheel on the right is a similar diagram of the additive color wheel. Notice the secondary colors that are created by mixing the red, green, and blue primaries. That's right, they're yellow, cyan, and magenta! You may be puzzled for a moment that all the secondary colors are lighter than the primaries. Remember that additive colors get closer to pure white the more you add them together.

This relationship explains why you shouldn't use CMYK color to build Web illustrations or why you'll need to adapt CMYK illustrations if you have. Because CMYK is created from secondary colors, that process can't be used to make many of the RGB colors we need for Web design, any more than you can make the color yellow by using a box of crayons that's missing the yellow crayon.

Chapter 5: Color Me Simple

Figure 5-3: The Foreground and Background color icons.

Deciphering the RGB numeric values

If you're making graphics for the Web, you're working with the additive primary colors red, green, and blue (RGB) — that acronym you've seen in paint programs. If you mix these primary colors in varying amounts, you create a new color. On a computer capable of displaying 24-bit color, that means you get to play with 255 different levels per each primary color.

On many occasions in this chapter (and some others), we want you to play with a specific color. When we want you to use white, for example, we use this notation in the text: White (R=255, G=255, B=255). Don't worry, this isn't a mathematical equation! We're just telling you that white is made up of 255 levels of red + 255 levels of green + 255 levels of blue. When you see this kind of notation, we're asking you to enter the value that appears after the equal sign into your Color Picker's RGB numeric entry boxes.

Using this notation, you can make some basic RGB combinations. If you want, you can work with your Color Picker RGB numeric entry and insert a color value number as the following examples show:

- We show you how to make white in the preceding paragraphs, so black is next. We write it this way: Black (R=0, G=0, B=0). The numeric entry box shows a 0 next to the R (Red) label, 0 next to the G (Green) label, and 0 next to the B (Blue) label.
- Now make the three primaries, Red (R=255, G=0, B=0), and then Green (R=0, G=255, B=0), and finish with Blue (R=0, G=0, B=255).
- Say, for example, that you'd rather create yellow. You'd need to combine red and green, right? (R=255, G=255, B=000).

Part II: Tricks with Pix

- Don't want yellow? Then how about magenta? Keep R=255, but change G to 000, and B to 255.

- To complete the set of additive secondary colors (see the sidebar "CMYK: A close second-ary" if you're unfamiliar with this term), change the setting for R to 000 and G to 255. That's how you create cyan.

If you followed along with the preceding examples, you just made the additive primary and secondary colors, plus black and white. These eight colors are your basic additive color palette.

Ever wonder how many different colors you can make on a computer? With a display capable of seeing 255 different levels of the three additive primary colors, you get 255×255×255. This equals 16,581,375 different color combinations.

The Lean, Mean Palette for Fat-Free Color

If you've already created a Web site or have read anything about creating graphics for the Web, then you may already know about color limitations and the 216-color browser-safe palette. If so, you can probably skip this section. On the other hand, if you don't immediately know what we're talking about, this is one of the most important sections in this book.

It's an unfortunate fact of life that different operating systems also have different ways of displaying color on a monitor screen. And you never know what combination of computer, monitor, or browser someone may be viewing your animation on. The clever people at Netscape thought about this problem when they created the first versions of Navigator.

The Netscape people noticed two things. First, more people were likely to surf the Web from a Windows operating system with a standard 8-bit video card than any other option. Not being asleep at the wheel, the Netscape people decided to base their browsers' universal palette on what the majority of people would be able to see. This decision limited them to a maximum of 256 colors. But the second thing they realized was that they really didn't have any combination of 256 colors. Microsoft had locked up the first 20 colors of that palette for Windows itself. That left only 236 colors. Because writing a browser is a little like writing an operating system, Netscape took some colors for itself, too. What remained for all of us to play with was 216 colors. (When Microsoft wrote its own browser, it simply matched this existing color scheme.)

If you use any colors in your animation that aren't in this "safe" palette, the colors will look like two-tone Swiss cheese to anyone with a system with specs different from what you built your design on. Only those magic 216 colors are guaranteed to show up on PC and MAC systems as solid, flat color, with no nasty distracting patterns.

If you're looking for more technical information, here are three URLs to add to your Bookmarks list. These Web sites provide a listing of the browser-safe colors and links to other pages to whet your appetite about Web color issues.

- **Color Computer Displays for the World Wide Web:** This site includes fun-to-use JavaScript interactive color cubes showing *hexadecimal values* for different color sets. Hexadecimal values describe in HTML coding the selected Web page colors. Go to http://www.alphabet.com:80/color/.

- **An Illustrated Index of Web Colors:** This page shows hexadecimal values with their RGB equivalents. Wander through the site and check out all the links. Refer to "Deciphering the RGB numeric values" earlier in this chapter for more information about this topic. Point your browser at http://raven.ubalt.edu:80/students/lichtenstein/design/color/color6.html.

- **Lynda Weinman's Web site:** Lynda offers tidbits on Web color and Web page design. Take a look at http://www.lynda.com.

Many other Web sites, too numerous to list, devote pages to safe palettes. Go to your favorite search engine and type **Netscape safe color palette** in the search parameter box.

Going Beyond Default Palettes

Inside your paint or imaging software program, you want to build your custom Netscape palette or choose the custom Web color palette option. Some companies like Corel (PHOTO-PAINT 7 PLUS), Microsoft (Image Composer 1.5), Adobe (Illustrator 7), Equilibrium (Debabelizer Pro), and JASC (Paint Shop Pro) distribute a ready-made browser-safe palette as a *color look-up table* (CLUT) or *custom palette swatch* to use with their software. Such palettes make things easy for creating Web graphics. Check out these companies' Web sites; we list the URLs in Appendix A.

Your program should have a function that lets you save a custom palette and input RGB values or should come supplied with industry-standard Web browser color palettes. If your paint program doesn't have these options, now would be a really good time to upgrade.

92 Part II: Tricks with Pix

Check out the software folder on the CD-ROM. We include demo versions of graphics and imaging programs. Try them out and compare their features for creating Web color and graphics.

If you're an Adobe Photoshop 4.0 user, you can create a Web CLUT and Swatch by following these steps:

1. **Launch Photoshop and create File⇨New with Mode: RGB color and Resolution: 72 dpi.**

   You need to have a file open to continue this process, but any file dimensions are okay.

2. **Convert the file from RGB to Indexed color by selecting Image⇨Mode⇨Indexed Color; as seen in Figure 5-4, click on the Palette arrow key and scroll down to select Web color.**

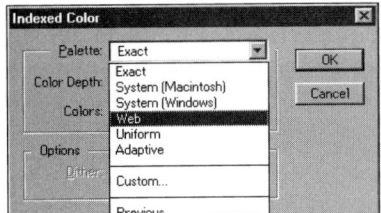

Figure 5-4: Picking Web color as your Indexed Color palette.

3. **Go to the menu and select Image⇨Mode⇨Color Table.**

   You see the Color Table dialog box.

4. **Click the Save button to convert the Indexed color image file into a CLUT table, name the file** Web, **and place the saved CLUT table in the Photoshop Color Palettes folder.**

   Look at Figure 5-5 to see the Color Table dialog box. For Windows users, please note that CLUTs are saved as .ACT files. Mac users see the word CLUT in the File list Kind description or in the file icon.

5. **Choose Window⇨Show Swatches.**

   The Swatches window appears, as shown in Figure 5-6.

6. **In the Swatches window, click on the arrow in the upper-right corner and scroll down to select Replace Swatches.**

   When you swap your Web palette with the default palette, make sure that you only select the Replace command. Otherwise you'll end up with more than the 216 Netscape colors in your palette.

Chapter 5: Color Me Simple *93*

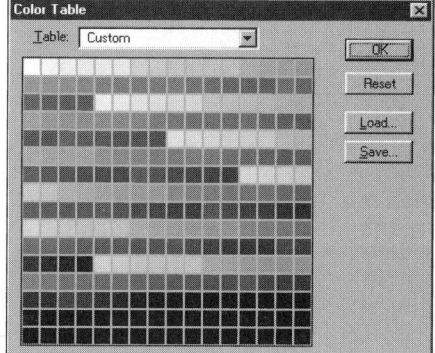

Figure 5-5: The Adobe Photoshop Color Table dialog box.

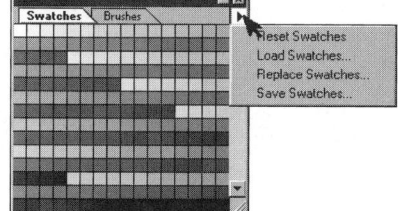

Figure 5-6: The Adobe Photoshop Swatches window.

7. **From the Photoshop Color Palettes folder, open your newly saved Web CLUT (Windows users look for** `Web.ACT`**).**

    You now view your Swatches window with the 216 Netscape colors.

    Windows users should note that in the Load window, the Files of type window displays the Swatches (*.ACO) file extension. Click on the Files of type right arrow to show the Color Table (*.ACT) file extension. Otherwise you will not find your Web.ACT file in the palette folder file list.

    You can now save your CLUT file as a Swatches (.ACO) file by clicking on the Swatches window arrow and selecting Save Swatches.

Making Your Custom Color Palette

Your animation may only have a few colors, or you may want to use a special custom palette in more than one animation. If so, you're ready to customize the 216-color Web palette. After you open the Color Picker of your graphics program, load your Web palette. Following the instructions in your software manual, remove any unused colors from your color palette swatch. Remember to save your customized palette with a different file name than your 216-color Web palette.

Here are other considerations with regard to custom palettes:

- You can make a new palette by entering RGB values or by using the eyedropper tool.
  - Do numeric entry of RGB values at the appropriate dialog box. The maximum number you can enter is 255. The smallest value is 0. (See the section "Color Is Not a Box of Chocolates" earlier in this chapter if you're unfamiliar with RGB values.)
  - Using the eyedropper tool, select a color from a sample Netscape color palette page that you can download from the Web or from your Color Model Sketch (discussed later in this chapter).
- Transfer each color one at a time to the custom palette that you are building. Unless you transfer the new color to the swatch, the palette change will *not* be permanent.
- Confirm that all your colors in the new palette are Web "safe." Click on each color in the palette and check the RGB numeric values.

All Web browser–safe palette colors are made up of a combination of three of the following numbers: 0, 51, 102, 153, 204, and 255. If you see any other RGB number value, the color is not "safe."

- Save your palette under a new name, with your program's file extension for color palettes. Locate the file in the palette folder that comes with your software.
- If you want to share your palette, save it as a .GIF file. This file can be opened by any graphics program. (If you're fuzzy about file format issues, go to Chapter 11.)

Creating the Right Color Mix

Begin by taking a look at professional animation. If you visit your local video store, check out one of the Disney classics. *The Little Mermaid* is a good example. Notice how few colors the Disney animators used to create the main character, Ariel: red hair and lips, a green tail, blue eyes and bra, skin tone, some white for the eyes and teeth, and a black outline. All of the other characters are equally straightforward. The complexity is in the combination of these moving characters against a rich background.
Your goal is to emulate the masters: Keep it simple and pay attention to combinations.

The Color Model Sketch

Professional animators begin by developing a Color Model Sketch, which is made up of two elements. The first is the foreground art which is usually made up of objects in the animation that will move or change. The second is the background, which can either be a single color or an unchanging image. See Figure 5-7.

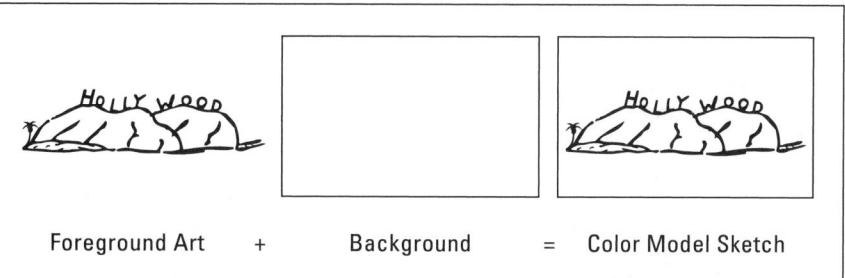

Figure 5-7: The parts of a Color Model Sketch.

Foreground Art   +   Background   =   Color Model Sketch

A completed Color Model Sketch for Web animation assigns color name descriptions and their RGB values. Figure 5-8 is an example of a single-frame Color Model Sketch. This sketch shows the colors assigned to the foreground art and the background.

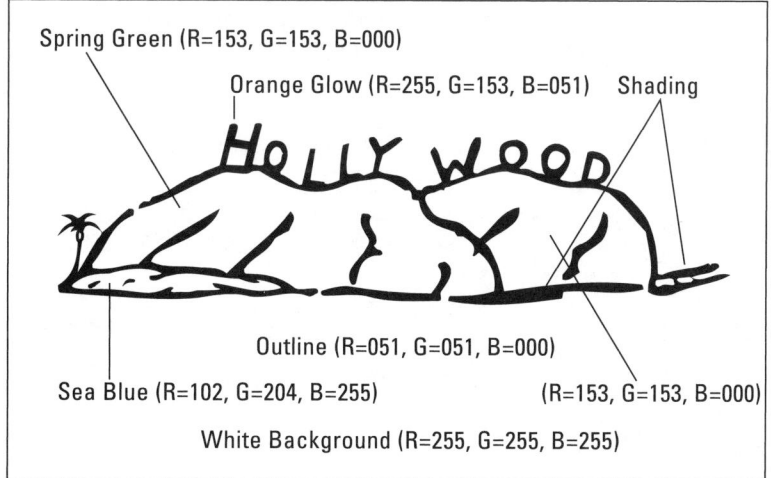

Figure 5-8: Coloring your master frame — the Color Model Sketch.

Spring Green (R=153, G=153, B=000)
Orange Glow (R=255, G=153, B=051)   Shading
Outline (R=051, G=051, B=000)
Sea Blue (R=102, G=204, B=255)   (R=153, G=153, B=000)
White Background (R=255, G=255, B=255)

Animators do not choose their colors arbitrarily. They make their decisions based on the mood they want to convey, the animation's theme or, if dealing with type and logos, the corporate colors. Legibility plays a part, too. You also should consider these issues before you fill your paint bucket from your Web-safe color palette.

We're going to introduce some basic concepts that can help you make color decisions to enhance your animation. Your palette colors can be broken into different categories. The ways you use or combine these categories can make a big difference between cool and confusing, or hypnotic and ho-hum.

Reading the color thermometer

Not surprisingly, peoples' reaction to colors is pretty deeply ingrained. Although individual cultures and countries have color associations that are very specific, many color identifications are remarkably consistent for all human beings. Everyone is aware of these gut reactions, but most of the time, you don't actually think about them. But when you work with visual elements, bringing these assumptions to the front of your conscious mind is a useful tool.

A full understanding of how to combine colors is something an artist or designer usually takes a semester — or longer — to learn. We just hit the basics that you need to make some intelligent color choices for your animation, and we emphasize experimenting and observing. Using the file `Chap05\mount.gif` from the CD that accompanies this book, you can create several color schemes from the Netscape palette and apply them to the objects in this file. (See Figure 5-9.)

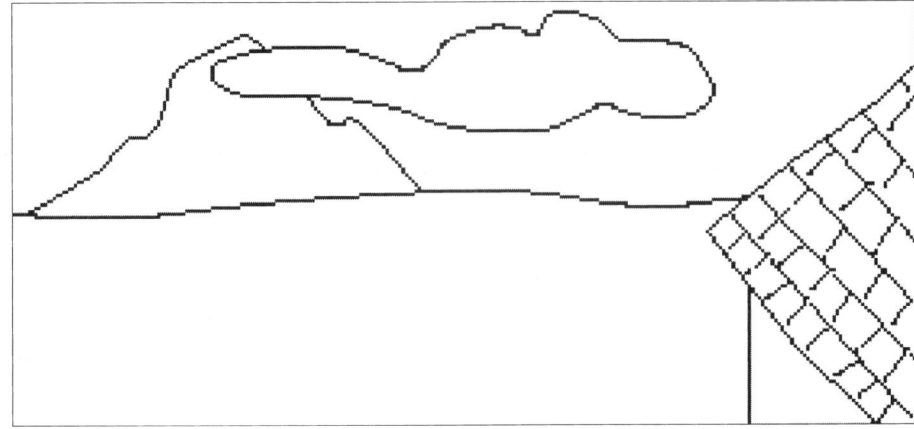

Figure 5-9: The template file mount.gif.

Open `mount.gif` in your paint program and then save it as a new file on your drive. We refer to this template file several times during the course of this chapter.

One of the most basic connections we can exploit is the idea that colors have temperatures. Essentially, colors fall into three basic groups: warm, cool, and neutral.

Warm colors

Warm colors are attention-grabbers: the vivid reds, oranges, and yellows of a blazing fire or a tropical sunset. Like most egotists, they hate competition. Generally speaking, unless your animation is really "on fire," you have to be careful about how many colors you use at a time and how close together they are.

Assign some warm colors to the objects in the practice file `mount.gif`.

1. **Begin by filling in the background sky with a bright orange-yellow.**

   The color values for the orange sky are R=255, G=204, B=000.

2. **Put lemon yellow in the cloud and paint the mountain with a deep orange.**

   The cloud's values are R=204, G=255, B=000, and the mountain gets R=204, G=255, B=000.

3. **Fill the large area of the ground with an electric yellow-green.**

   Our choice of green is R=204, G=255, B=051.

4. **End by filling the roof with red and the wall with orange.**

   Color values for the roof are R=255, G=051, B=000, and the wall is R=255, G=102, B=000.

Wild, right? The colors really jump out at you. But notice, this image is very hard to look at for any length of time. Determining what's an object to watch and what's merely meant to be background is also difficult. One of the reasons for this confusion is that all these warm colors are very pure and intense. And the closer to pure a color is (the less black or white that has been added to it), the nearer it will seem to you. So all our elements are fighting for the limelight, like a group of actors all trying to upstage each other.

Open up `Chap05/mntwarm.gif` on the CD and put it on your screen at the same time as the file you've been working in. All the colors are still members of the warm family, but varying amounts of lightness have been added to some of them. Notice how these background elements suddenly seem to recede into the distance. That's because we've played a trick based on

Mother Nature. In real life, things that are far away get hazy-looking and less brilliantly-colored, because we have to see them through the thickness of our atmosphere. Check this out sometime when you have a far-away object (a mountain or tall building) on the horizon.

The opposite is true of the tiled roof in the foreground. Because it's such pure, extroverted color, it grabs the focal point without having to fight a color duel to the death. Experiment with other combinations of these colors, choosing related warm colors from the Netscape palette to make the cloud the focal point, or the house wall instead of the roof.

Cool colors

Now think cool. On a really hot, steamy day, people seek out deep blue waters and shady forests. The colors we associate with these refreshing sensations radically change the landscape of mount.gif, filling it with greens, blues, and violets.

Bring up the blank template file Chap05\mount.gif and do the following:

1. **Leave the cloud white (R=255, G=255, B=255) for now but fill the sky with a pale blue (R=153, G=255, B=255), and the mountain with a deeper blue (R=000, G=153, B=204).**

2. **Fill the ground with a grassy shade of green (R=051, G=204, B=102).**

3. **Make a deep teal roof (R=051, G=155, B=155) and a strong blue-violet wall (R=051, G=051, B=204) to finish the picture.**

Examine this version, putting it next to the two previous ones. You used a deep, strong blue for the mountain, yet it still feels comfortably far away, while the cloud seems a little closer. That's because of some other cues from nature. You used a shade of blue for the mountain that is basically a darker, slightly bluer version of the sky color. From our experiments with warm colors, we know that things tend to blur and lose color intensity as they become distant.

But you find another visual hint as well. Because our atmosphere contains gases, dust, and moisture, it bounces and scatters some of the wavelengths of light, mostly the short blue and violet ones. That gives the impression that distant objects have a bluish tint. People are so used to this relationship that they automatically accept many blues and blue-grays as natural backgrounds.

So far, you've discovered that cool colors are like introverted people at a party — they tend to move toward the walls. Unlike a warm and intense palette, a group of cool colors behaves very nicely, never making a fuss or trying to upstage. In fact, sometimes they behave too nicely. Like the host at a cocktail party, you want enough variety to keep conversation going. To see what happens when you cool things down even more, go to the CD and open the `mntcoolr.gif` file (`Chap05\mntcoolr.gif`). Put it next to the image that you just finished.

We added gray to the colors in this file by decreasing the *saturation* (amount) of all the colors except white. (Pick up the new colors with the eyedropper tool, look at their RGB values, and compare them to the ones you've used to see how it's done.) Notice how much colder the scenery feels and how prominent the white cloud becomes.

Go to your Web-safe palette and change that white cloud to a pale gray (R=204, G=204, B=204). Look how much flatter and duller the image is.

Make sure that you always have some colors that are clearly warmer or at least considerably lighter to help you define boundaries between cool colors.

Note: You can have warm blues, greens, and violets, just as you can have a cool red. Take a look at `Chap05\mntwmcl.gif` on the CD. As you can see, if you add enough black to a warm shade, or light to a cool hue, you can reverse the normal order of things. In this image, you can see that the attention is drawn to what would normally be considered the background. This kind of ploy can be very useful if you want to imply that the foreground is in shadow, or simply to force the view to focus toward the horizon line if you are going to animate an object that will first appear small and far away.

What happens when cool colors and warm colors share an image? Warm colors generally appear to come forward while cool ones tend to recede into the background; you can use this fact to your benefit. Pull up your template file again. Pick up the red and orange house from your warm palette, and the grass, mountain, and sky colors from the first cool palette on the CD. The house is even more prominent in this version than it was in the alternate warm one, and it may even appear slightly larger to you. Do something similar in a two-color animation and watch your moving character pop out from the screen.

Neutral colors

If you continue farther away from pure color in both the warm and cool families, you eventually find neutral. This color grouping is less clearly defined than the previous two. Any color can become a neutral color by the addition of enough black, white, or gray. Of course, every hue in the gray scale (the 255 different levels of value between pure white and complete black) is a neutral color. But for your purposes, so are hues with enough gray in them so that they appear on screen to be a shade of gray with a color tint.

Comparatively few neutral colors are available in the Netscape 216-color browser-safe palette. (Very few good neutrals have RGB values evenly divisible by 51.) Go ahead and make a neutral alternative of the mountain scene from some of the options that you do have.

Only four true grays are found between white and black on the Netscape palette, and you'll use three of them here — the lighter (R=204, G=204, B=204) for the sky, the midtone (R=153, G=153, B=153) for the cloud, and a darker one (R=102, G=102, B=102) for the mountain. Do the following:

1. **Fill the ground with a pale olive color (R=204, G=204, B=153).**
2. **Add a rose (R=204, G=153, B=153) for the wall.**
3. **Finally, add a deep green (R=000, G=051, B=051) for the roof.**

Very effective instant depression, right? Neutral colors are very popular with designers in print applications because they are elegant and understated. Unfortunately, these positive characteristics tend to make them useless for anything other than shadow or background effects in Web animation. On the other hand, they play both of those roles well. Neutral colors are a terrific foil for a warm color, or for a cool color aching to look warm in comparison. Remember the blue that you used for the mountain in the more colorful cool scene? Try filling the wall with it. That blue triangle shape jumps out of the screen as if it were a luminous red.

If you've followed the steps in this chapter so far, you've been working with variations of an image to discover how to adapt a color scheme to a mood. But right now, you'd have to hunt and peck through your Netscape Web-safe color palette to find the colors that are different tones of the same high intensity here. Here's how you'd make a group of related colors with varying amounts of gray:

1. **Open the file** `grayscal.gif` **from the CD.**

    You see five levels of value: white plus four grays (minus black).

2. **Starting with this template file, build a color scale from magenta to dark purple.**

    Do this by substituting a new color in each of the five gray rectangles.

3. **With the eyedropper tool, pick a gray and read its RGB value in the numeric entry boxes.**

4. **Make the new colors by changing all the green values to 000.**

    - Box 1: Magenta (R=255, G=000, B=255)
    - Box 2: (R=204, G=000, B=204)

Chapter 5: Color Me Simple

- Box 3: (R=153, G=000, B=153)
- Box 4: (R=102, G=000, B=102)
- Box 5: Dark Purple (R=051, G=000, B=051)

As an alternative, try changing yellow. The numeric entry is the same, but remember that you make yellow with red and green. The color shifts from yellow to yellow-greens to finally an olive green.

After Mixing, Throw Out the Blender!

After you choose your color strategy, you have to apply it. One of the favorite ways for people who are new at the animation game to apply color is through blends. A *blend* is a series of color steps, each slightly different from the next. When used properly, these graduated fills are a wonderful graphic element to add pizzazz to a printed document. Blends are made with a *gradient tool* in a graphics program by filling an area with a gradual transition between one or more colors. Unfortunately, blends are frequently overused because they're so easy to create. In the case of Web animation, however, easy come definitely means no go!

Blends cause such a problem when you animate because, as you transition from one animation frame to the next, the pieces that make up the animated character change shape, position, and viewer orientation in the scene. Imagine that you've used a blend to give the impression of light and shadow on a curved shape, like a ball. Then try to consider how difficult it would be to make your blend shift position to account for changes as your ball spins across the page. This difficulty is one of the reasons why, except for the biggest budget, 3-D animation productions created with the most powerful software and hardware, animators stick with flat colors. Instead, most animators create the effect of shading by combining a color with variations in value and by then applying those variations in well-defined bands.

To better understand this concept, complete the following steps. Your goal is to create one vase, colorized by using gradient blends, along with a second variation painted with flat colors of different values.

1. **To create the gradient-filled vase, go to the CD and open files** `vase01.pcx`, `vase03.gif`, **and** `yelscale.gif`.
2. **Save the files to your hard drive.**

   You can remove them later if you like. Using the brightest and darkest colors in `yelscale.gif`, fill `vase01.pcx` with a gradient blend. The file `vase03.gif` is your guide.

   Filling an image with a gradient blend is easy.

3. **Grab your magic wand tool and select the exterior of the vase.**

4. **Go to the toolbar and click on the gradient blend tool icon.**

5. **Move your cursor to either the left or right side of the active image area.**

6. **Click-drag your mouse and click again on the opposite side of the active area.**

   Voilà! Looks fine, right? If not, then undo and repeat the steps. If it does, deselect your active area. The interior shape at the top of the vase is next.

7. **Repeat the steps again to fill the top interior shape with a gradient blend.**

   Notice the gradient inside the top of the model vase. It blends in the opposite direction from the gradient filling the exterior of the vase. Set your second blend to fill in the opposite direction from your first blend in your vase.

8. **Complete your vase by filling in the lip and base with your paintbrush tool.**

   Use a small brush size (such as 2 pixels) to easily fit into the corners of the lip and base.

   For detailed brush work, zoom in to 250% or more to enlarge your image. Painting is easier at the higher magnification, and you reduce the strain on your eyes, as well.

9. **Save the file in your program's native format and then convert the file to GIF format.**

   If you're unclear about converting files to GIF format, go to Chapter 11.

   With the gradient filled vase completed, you're ready to create the flat color filled variation.

10. **Open file** `vase02.pcx` **and** `vase04.gif`.

    Like working with a coloring book, file `vase04.gif` shows you where to place your colors. (The `yelscale.gif` color strip has all the required colors, too.)

11. **Select a color from** `vase04.gif` **with the eyedropper tool.**

12. **Change windows and use this color to fill in an area in your template file.**

    You can color fast by using the fill tool. Pick your color and then go back to the toolbar to click on the fill icon. Bring your cursor to the center of the area you want to fill. Click the mouse button to dump all that color in. Repeat the process until you're done. Finish up with the brush (1 or 2 pixels) for the small areas like the lip of the vase.

Chapter 5: Color Me Simple

13. **Save your second vase in your program's native format and convert this file to GIF format.**

    Place the four versions of your vase side-by-side and compare. (Zoom in 300% to 400%.)

Remember that Web animations seldom take up much real estate on the page. Even if you manage to conquer the moving blend, it probably takes up such a small area that your audience will not appreciate what you've done. At their worst, blends can add noise, vibrating patterns, and make your animation totally unrecognizable. And remember that your beautiful gradient disappears when you export the native format file version to GIF format. The color mode changing from RGB to Indexed color destroys the subtle transition of color and leaves you with uneven stripes.

Putting a Positive Spin on Negative Space

While you're considering color selection for foreground objects, don't forget your background. The background is alive. It's not a negative afterthought — "Oh well, I can't wait to get this animation done. This background works just fine." Neglect your background and don't be surprised if it doesn't sneak up and grab you. After all, changing a background to a foreground object or vice versa is so easy to do. Take a look at Figure 5-10 and see what we mean. This animation is a visual puzzle — take a guess. Is white or black the background color? Not sure. Try turning this book upside down. Mmm . . . ? Okay, there's no right or wrong answer. It's an optical illusion. To build an optical illusion, allocate an equal amount of image area to your foreground and background colors and maximize the color contrast between the two halves.

This illusion can be fun, but it's not generally something that you want in your animation. Your animation is a lot more fun to watch if your foreground action pops out from the less important background.

In the following series of examples, you can experiment with color combinations to enable you to see what happens when you use different colors together. (Refer also to the section "Reading the color thermometer" in this chapter.)

Go to the CD and open the Visual Teaser image from the \Chap05 directory (file vistease.pcx). Save the file to your hard drive. (Delete the files later if you need the disk space.)

Figure 5-10: Visual teasers can be great fun.

Now, if you want to try these techniques, snatch up your paint bucket. Here's how it works:

- **Make sure that your foreground and background are not equal in importance.** Go to your Netscape palette and change all the black areas to a pale gray (R=204, G=204, B=204) or medium gray (R=153, G=153, B=153). Notice how the white comes forward. Or try this technique — keep the black but change the white to a cream yellow (R=255, G=255, B=204). This time the black looks closer to you. The cream yellow says, "I'm background." (Check out the CD to find a sampler of different color combinations for you to look at and compare.)

But if you must use two colors of equal value and intensity, assign more image area to one color. Take a peek and open `vistea13.pcx` and `vistea14.pcx` on the CD. Notice how we removed the light gray rectangle from `vistea14.pcx`. The cream yellow in this version shouts, "I'm foreground!"

- **Avoid overemphasizing the background by selecting colors that are vivid or highly saturated.** Just as if you are driving west facing the setting sun on a homebound commute, the vibrating glow hinders your ability to focus on anything else.

Many a Web site uses a bright yellow background with black type for the animated button bars. Duplicate this example yourself by adding vivid yellow (R=255, G=255, B=0) to `vistease.pcx` — first as a replacement for white, and then for black. Now compare the two. White and yellow, not a chance. Put on those sunglasses. Black and yellow is better, but look at the black rule line. If you're not sure, then add some black type to the image in front of a yellow area. Any letters will do. Stare at the image. Blink, blink, blink. Here comes eyestrain. What do you do then? Keep your sizzling saturated colors cooling on ice in the virtual refrigerator. Defrost them when you need something special like animating a hot "NEW" bullet.

- **Background busyness detracts from viewing pleasure.** If you want to use a background pattern, keep it simple. To make your pattern, choose two colors from the color wheel that are very close together, or use one color with variable amounts of light and darkness. Our examples from the CD are `vistea01.pcx`, `vistea11.pcx`, and `vistea13.pcx`. Try some other color combinations such as two lighter blues or greens.

Alternatively, take whatever pattern you want to use and gray it down. *Graying down* a pattern keeps it in the back of the scene and not up front where it can compete with the action. You can use several strategies for graying down. If your software offers the option, simply make the image more transparent. If it doesn't, a light tint of white or black can have the same effect.

The graphics company D'pix graciously provided us with texture photos, so check out that section of the CD. Also, if you like to experiment with pattern making, take a look at the software demos on the CD.

You may admire the elaborate backgrounds of a Disney animation, but remember that these feature-length cartoons are designed to be projected on a large movie screen. The viewing screen for Web animation is at the other end of the scale — very small.

High Contrast Avoids High Anxiety

Some colors, such as yellow, orange, light reds, and other pastels, fade away and appear smaller against large white spaces. One way to help these colors stand out is to outline them with black. The same concept applies in reverse if you place dark blues, dark greens, dark reds, or browns against a black background. In this case, you outline with white.

Outlining works nicely for some styles of animation, but what can you do if you want the effect of objects created from torn paper or want to give a more realistic impression? Fortunately, other options for creating contrast between foreground action and background are available.

Beware of imitations! The general rule is to avoid combining colors that are so dark that they almost look like black, or are all very close to white. On a great many monitors, users will have a hard time telling the difference.

In your graphics program, pull up the template file `Chap05\mount.gif` from the CD and do the following:

1. **Leave the sky white but fill the ground with black (R=0, G=0, B=0).**
2. **Use pale pink (R=255, G=204, B=204) for the mountain and pale yellow (R=255, G=255, B=204) for the cloud.**
3. **Fill the wall with deep magenta (R=51, G=0, B=51) and the roof with brown (R=51, G=0, B=0).**

Notice how well the house disappears into the bottom half of the screen, and how beautifully the cloud becomes an off-color smudge on the white. These are delicate, subtle combinations. Subtlety is *not* the name of the game for Web graphics.

So what are your options? Start with the cloud. You can't very well outline it. Anything more than the one-point guidelines you used to fill the object will make it look like a ghost. Essentially you have three choices:

- **Decrease the brightness of the cloud.** Try filling the cloud shape with the next darkest version of the color, in this case R=204, G=204, B=155. Looks too dirty? Move to the next choice.
- **Decrease the brightness of the background.** Try changing the white to the lightest gray (R=204, G=204, B=204). Lose that nice contrast with the black? Then try the next technique.
- **Change the color.** If you're using a flat white or black as your background, you'll want to take advantage of its strong statement by using colors that stand out well in front of them.

Open `Chap05\mntcon.gif` on the CD and see how much more visible the elements of the image are when darker colors are placed against white and lighter or brighter colors are used with black. Also notice how well the red roof works visually with both the black ground and the white sky. Red has as much intensity as either black or white, while having the eye-catching powers of a very warm color.

Chapter 6
Roll Over, Gutenberg, and Rock Your Type

In This Chapter
- Designing type
- Bagging the right typeface
- Finding type fonts
- Playing the mix and match game
- Figuring out when to anti-alias
- Combining titles and text
- Using decorative letters and numbers without overkill
- Flying logos and icons: How not to crash and burn

*T*hey're there. Click on a link, and they appear. It's the usual suspects — that cast of characters known as the ABC gang. You know their aliases. Call them "text," or maybe "font," or even by their nickname "heads." Don't worry; you'll have no problem arranging a lineup. But you'd better move quickly if you want to nab them. Remember to keep a sharp lookout as you travel the Web's highways and byways. Text flashes in; it flashes out. If you blink, you just may miss them.

Viewing all those wiggling, flashing, dancing letters on your monitor can be entertaining. Figuring out how they got that way is another matter. Okay, take a deep breath and pause. Before your heart starts to flutter and your palms begin to sweat at the thought of designing with type, consider the following:

- You are a longtime user of the ABCs.
- Using a graphics program, you can write or type a letter of the alphabet.
- You know the difference between Helvetica Bold (also known as Arial Bold) and Times Roman. And you should have no problem picking that old familiar typewriter face, Courier, out of a crowd.

Then have no fear. You can orchestrate text into visually pleasing animated type effects and add value to your Web site.

Designing Type

Before you begin designing with type, create a level playing field for yourself. Expand your selection of available typefaces or *fonts* (another name for a single typeface version) beyond the basic set that's standard with your computer. But before you go on your shopping spree, here are some concepts to consider.

You don't have an urgent need to turn on your computer. All you need is a pad of paper (at least 8.5" x 11"), some black markers with thin, medium, and wide tips, and a red marker. (Actually, any color other than black will do.)

Don't worry; you're not creating anything you haven't made before. You're putting a new spin on the writing basics you learned as a child. Regardless of the hand tool — pen, crayon, marker, or chisel — anything that makes a mark can be the foundation of a typeface. Johannes Gutenberg, the man from Mainz, used *calligraphic letters* (formal writing) as his models to create the first moveable type cast in metal. If you compared the Gutenberg printed Latin Bible with a Bible handwritten by monks of the same time period (mid-1400s), you'd notice that you can hardly tell them apart. (If you're curious, the Library of Congress in Washington, D.C., has a copy of both Bibles.)

Opening your type chest

From Johannes Gutenberg's time to our time, type designers have shared their little secrets with each other. Your mission, should you choose to accept it, is to unlock the lid of the font treasure chest and extract the secrets for designing beautiful type.

 1. Using a medium-tip marker, loosen up by filling one sheet of paper with circles, ovals, and arcs; a second sheet of paper with horizontal and vertical line segments; and a third sheet with diagonal *strokes* (another name for line segments).

    Modify the height, width, and thickness of the lines to create a large number of variations.

    Okay, this task was easy. Now, look at your three sheets filled with lots of different lines. You've made the basic components of all typefaces — type's primordial soup.

2. **At the top of a clean sheet of paper, draw a circle, a square, and a triangle.**

   They don't need to be exactly the same size; you can approximate. Fit the three geometric shapes in about ½ the width of the page.

   Here you used line segments to build the three basic shapes: a square or rectangle (lines perpendicular or parallel to an invisible baseline), a circle or oval, and a triangle (pointing up or down).

3. **Write the capital H underneath the square, the capital O underneath the circle, and the capital A beneath the triangle, as shown in Figure 6-1.**

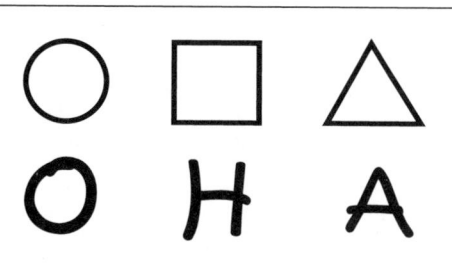

Figure 6-1: Translating shapes into characters.

   Look at your characters. Notice how the three basic geometric shapes you made translate into a letter form (character). This concept is important. Later in this chapter, you build on this idea when you mix and match typefaces. It's also a key point to remember in logo or icon design. Put this sheet aside for the moment.

4. **On a new sheet of paper, write the word** WEB **in all caps.**

   Make the letters fairly large.

5. **Using your second color marker, fill in the interior shapes of each letter.**

   The capital *W* is built by overlapping your two triangles, both pointing down. The capital *E* is, of course, two rectangles stacked vertically. The capital *B* is more complex. It's two rectangles with one end rounded, also stacked vertically. The interior shape is a merging of your rectangle with an oval.

6. **Get the sheet that looks like Figure 6-1, and add to the top of your page a square + circle symbol and a square + triangle symbol, as shown in Figure 6-2.**

7. **Follow the concept of the "WEB" word you just designed by listing on your sheet of paper, below each geometric symbol shape, the letter of the alphabet that looks most like that shape.**

   Do all 26 capital letters, as shown in Figure 6-2.

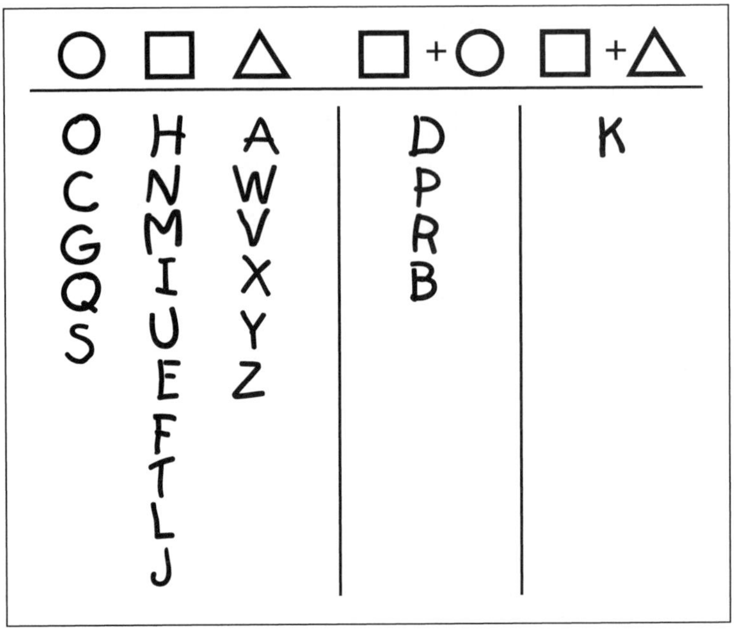

Figure 6-2: Organizing the capital letters by geometric shape.

○	□	△	□+○	□+△
O	H	A	D	K
C	N	W	P	
G	M	V	R	
Q	I	X	B	
S	U	Y		
	E	Z		
	F			
	T			
	L			
	J			

Psst . . . Psst . . . want some hints? Single stroke characters like the capital *I* or *J* fall under the square. That's because their stroke is perpendicular to the baseline. The capital *Z* is a rectangle with two sides removed and a diagonal line drawn from the upper-right corner down to the lower-left corner. Because the diagonal stroke is the dominant focus, place the *Z* with the capital *W*.

8. **On a fresh sheet of paper, repeat Step 7 again, but this time use all the lowercase characters.**

   Figure 6-3 shows how to do so.

Compare both alphabet lists. Find the capital *E* and lowercase *e*. Notice how the capital letter is a rectangle and the lowercase letter is circular. Move on to another pair, the capital *Q* and lowercase *q*. The lowercase *q* becomes a merged shape built like the lowercase *p, b,* and *d*. The capital *G* and lowercase *g* follow this same formula. Note that the capital *R* changes into the much simpler lowercase *r*, which resembles the lowercase *n* and *m*. And to complete the set, the capital *A* triangular shape shifts in lowercase form to resemble the lowercase *d*. (To view a typeface that looks like your sketch, check out Futura or ITC Avant Garde.)

Congratulations! You've successfully completed your task. In your hands you hold the Type Designer's Master Plan. As a reward, you've earned the key to unlocking the secret to thousands of fonts. By repeating elements of one letter form in another, designers create characters that work together as a group.

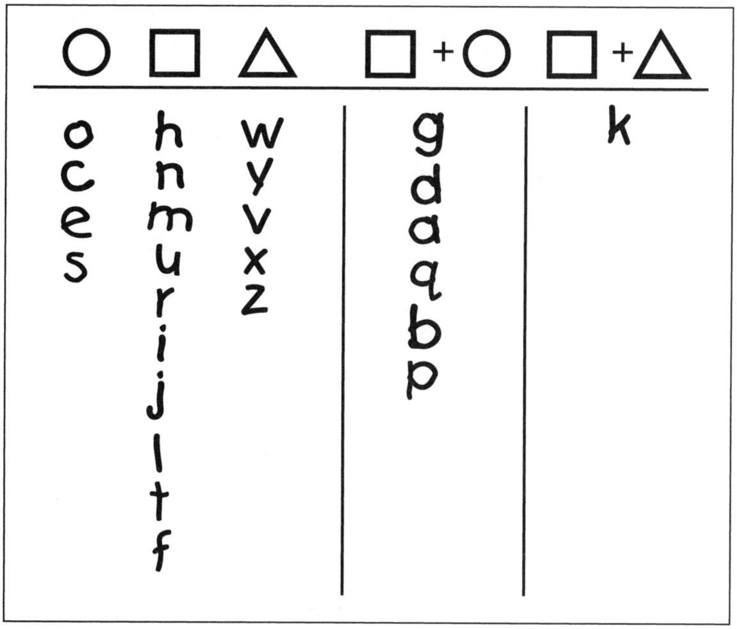

Figure 6-3: Organizing the lowercase letters by geometric shape.

○	□	△	□+○	□+△
o c e s	h n m u r i j l t f	w y v x z	g d a q b p	k

Building a font family

No self-respecting font wants to live alone. You're ready to add members to the font family tree. Show your support for the cause by expanding the single font into a larger family group. You have three options:

- Change the proportional ratio of character height to character width.
- Change the thickness or weight of the stroke.
- Change the angle of the stroke to the baseline.

Changing the proportional ratio

When you're modifying a letter's proportional ratio, you're changing the relationship of the letter's height to its width. Here's an analogy to help clarify this concept. Instead of thinking characters or letters, think puppies. As puppies grow taller and wider, their silhouettes change. They look different; we apply this information to help identify their breed. It's the same idea for typefaces.

1. **From the left center of a clean sheet of paper, draw a square, an oval of about the same width, and a triangle with a base that's the same width as the square.**

2. **Above this first set of geometric shapes, create a group that is narrower in width by about 25 percent.**

    The height measurement stays the same.

 3. **Now make a third row, but this time expand the width by 25 percent.**

    The height again stays constant.

 4. **Using each row's geometric shape as a proportional guideline, write three different versions of the capital O, H, and A.**

If you look at Figure 6-4, you can see how these proportional changes can be interpreted as a new font. In the third column, you have three variations of the typeface Univers: Univers Condensed (top row), Univers Roman (middle row), and Univers Expanded (bottom row). The fourth column represents three unrelated typefaces (Woodtype, Tekton, and Americana) whose proportional ratio influenced the look and feel of the design.

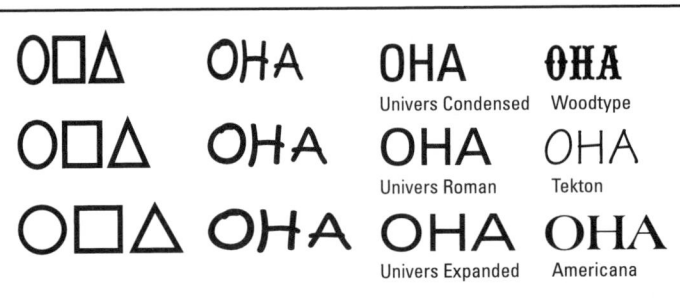

Figure 6-4: Changing proportions to make new fonts.

Changing the stroke thickness

To get an idea about what stroke thickness does to a letter, go back to our dog analogy in the preceding section. This time visualize a greyhound changing into a Labrador retriever and then into a Newfoundland. As your virtual dog gets wider and the legs thicken, your perception changes. You rethink what job you'd assign them.

 1. **Select three different markers: thin point, medium nib, and a wide nib. Draw the three sets of geometric shapes, making each group a different pen width.**

 2. **Below each circle, square, and triangle, match the same line thickness to write your O, H, and A.**

    The character width increases as you add weight. Otherwise, the interior white space fills in. Each variation in weight must appear to have the same look and feel — just like dogs who share the same DNA.

Look at Figure 6-5 to see how this concept is applied. This figure shows the three typefaces, Univers, Times Roman, and Time-Script, in three different weight variations. Notice that no constant naming convention exists. Standardization across typeface families for weight doesn't exist. An Extra Bold in one font may be called Heavy, Ultra, or Black in another. Watch out for this minefield when specifying type for your Web site.

Figure 6-5: Changing line thickness to make new fonts.

Roman versus italic and script typefaces

A typeface font is called *Roman* or *Upright* if its stroke is perpendicular to its baseline. The typeface that you're reading now is upstanding, Mr. Hardworking, Cheltenham. Italic, on the other hand, is the Leaning Tower of Type. Actually, italics are a group of Romans who tilted to grab your attention. You have to admire them, standing there with nary a peep at a 15° to 20° angle to the baseline. But italics don't hold the prize for bravura. Script typefaces are the showoffs of the neighborhood. Flourishing here, there, and everywhere, script typefaces have a personality all their very own. You'd never find them crowding into a submenu list like those Helveticas. See Figure 6-6.

Figure 6-6: Changing angles to make new fonts.

Web Animation
Franklin Gothic Bold

Web Animation
Franklin Gothic Bold Italic

Web Animation
Stone Serif Semibold

Web Animation
Stone Serif Semibold Italic

Web Animation
Brush 445

Web Animation
Allegro

Web Animation
Formal Script 421

Bagging the Right Typeface

Adding new typefaces to your font list is like visiting a supermall to do your holiday shopping. The wealth of choices and the number of outlets can be overwhelming and tiring. Whether you're picking out your new wardrobe for casual Fridays at the office or fonts for your Web graphics, it pays to plan first. Here are some helpful hints to think about before you hand over the cash.

- ✔ Which fonts do you currently have? Pull out a pad of paper to take notes and launch your graphics program if it's not already in use. Next, go to the tool bar and choose the Type Tool icon. Your font selection window appears. To see your font menu list, place your cursor on the scroll arrow next to the font name box, click, and then drag your mouse toward you. As you scroll down your graphic program's font menu list, write down each font name, such as Times Roman, Times Italic, Times Bold, and so on. Don't forget to add to your list any fonts not loaded on your computer or network.

Chapter 6: Roll Over, Gutenberg, and Rock Your Type **115**

Do you want to slow down one of those fancy 200 MHz computers? Load every font suitcase you can find into your system folder. If there's one job your computer hates to do, it's keeping track of all those bitmapped fonts located in your system folder. Keep your font list small and use only what you need for current projects.

Create a large-print version of your font library. Finding that special font is easier if you can see the details that make it unique. In your word processing program, pick 72 point as your font size and type the capital and lowercase letters, numbers 1–0, punctuation (.,;:!*()?'/), and special characters like $, %, and &. Leave enough white space for your handwritten notes. Place your new font book close to your computer for easy reference.

✔ Organize your font list. Begin by looking for fonts with words in their name like Bold, Extrabold, Heavy, Ultra, Black, Italic, Oblique, or Script. Count up how many you have in each category. You're not being rude, but ignore any typeface called Light or Medium. More about this in the following paragraphs.

✔ Evaluate your font list. What do your numbers say? Do you have many more Bold than Extrabold or Heavy fonts, for example? That's not surprising. The computer marketing gurus assumed that you'd be spending most of your time generating word processing documents rather than large Web page headlines.

Web animation presents a different set of production problems. When designing with type for monitor viewing, find your big brass band. Otherwise, your message will get lost in the din on the Web. Those lighter-weight typefaces (the ones you ignored in your earlier font count) are too thin for screen resolution. Lightweight typefaces don't have enough pixels in their stroke for your eye to focus on, especially against a textured background. Leave delicate looking typefaces in reserve for your glossy paper brochures, where your artistic creation can be seen for appreciation's sake.

Provide a home for those Extrabold, Heavy, Ultra, or Black designated typefaces. For those tight-fitting headlines, add at least one condensed version to your font list, such as Helvetica Compressed, Futura Extrablack Condensed, or Extrablack Condensed Italic. They're solid, workhorse fonts, and they deserve a place at the top of your shopping list.

If you're thinking of splurging for a few more fonts, then consider adding the heavier weights of your existing font families. You get a better dollar value here because you'll find that those heavyweights are also great for your printed document covers or product marketing handouts. Complete your purchases by including bolder versions of script or decorative fonts to provide that extra spice to your site.

Avoid decorative faces filled with fussy little details like those Victorian wood-block typefaces. If you want to advertise your traveling circus, antique railroad, or minstrel show, then that's fine; order some decorative faces. Otherwise, stick to fonts that are quirky or have oddly-shaped characters like Neuland, ITC Rennie Mackintosh, or OCR. See Figure 6-7.

Web Animation
Helvetica Compressed

Web Animation
Futura Extrablack Condensed

Web Animation
Futura Extrablack Condensed Italic

WEB ANIMATION
Neuland

WEB ANIMATION
ITC Rennie Mackintosh Bold

Web Animation
OCR

Figure 6-7: A font sampler.

Looking for Type Fonts?

Just about anyone sells fonts these days. With stiff competition among type manufacturers, finding a good deal on fonts is not difficult. You can pick and choose one font at a time from an à la carte menu, buy a complete font family, or purchase fonts by the pound. Here's a list of options. (Look in Appendix A for a listing of addressees and telephone numbers.)

- **Value-added bundles:** To further induce you to buy their CD clip art collections, companies like Corel and Nova Development package thousands of fonts on the disc. These fonts are supplied by type manufacturers such as Bitstream and URW. You can economically add both fonts and clip art to your library this way.

Chapter 6: Roll Over, Gutenberg, and Rock Your Type **117**

- **CD-ROM collections:** Several CD-ROM options are available. The first is the unlocked CD-ROM collections from companies like URW and Bitstream. For one flat fee, you license several thousand typefaces ready to load to your system font folder. The second option is the on-call strategy. Here you purchase a CD-ROM for a nominal fee from Adobe, Agfa (a division of Bayer Corp.), Monotype, and so on. Adobe also distributes the CD with its popular software packages. When you register the disc, the company sets up an account and payment plan for you. After you're registered, you call the company at its toll-free number to place an order from the catalog. The customer service representative provides you with a code to unlock the fonts that you purchased. From time to time, the companies announce special deals to encourage you to buy this moment's featured font collection or join forces to find new ways to sell fonts, like the Agfa-Monotype Creative Alliance CD.

- **Boutique font manufacturers:** Besides resources like Adobe and Agfa, you can find other innovative companies like Émigré, ITC, and The Font Bureau. Here's where you find some of the newest designs that are the favorites of award-winning graphic designers. Get on their mailing lists to keep track of the trends in typeface fads and fashion.

- **World Wide Web:** All the aforementioned companies and others like Image Club Graphics, a division of Adobe Systems, Inc., and The Publishers Toolbox have Web sites from which you can now view their catalogs. If you do a search to find these sites, limit your search parameters to **typeface suppliers or manufacturers**. Otherwise, the resulting list will include lots and lots of useless stuff.

Playing the Mix and Match Game

When you're designing a Web page or adding elements to it, consider these two factors:

- How do you create focal points on the page? If everything looks too similar, then it's hard to tell at a quick glance what's the most important or time-sensitive information.

- How do you fit an animated headline into its allocated space on the page? This may not seem like a problem, but what if the copy is too long, you can't change it, and you don't want to make it any shorter in height?

To resolve these situations, you can mix and match different fonts. To show you how this works, play the mix and match game by applying concepts we discuss in the section "Designing Type." If you're a type-design novice and haven't read those pages yet, then now may be a good time to go to that section.

Continue to use your pad of paper (at least 8½" x 11"), some black markers with thin, medium, and wide tips, and a red marker (actually, any color other than black will do).

Combining serif with sans serif fonts

A *serif* is a short line crossing the open end of a stroke. *Sans serif* means a font without serifs. Adding or removing serifs is one of the easiest ways to change a type design. To see what we mean, do the following:

1. **Pull out the sheet that matches Figure 6-1, translating shapes into characters.**

   If you don't have a sheet like the one in Figure 6-1, go to the section "Opening your type chest" earlier in this chapter and create one. You work with the letters you've written on this sheet.

2. **Create a third row by duplicating your O, H, and A.**

   You're going to modify these duplicate letters by adding serifs to the strokes. Start with the *H*.

3. **Draw a very short horizontal line at the top and bottom of your two vertical strokes.**

4. **Now, add the short line to the open base end of the *A*'s diagonal strokes.**

   You've designed a new typeface, a serif version of your original design. It's that simple. Because font characters are based on simple geometric shapes, you don't have to do much to create a new look. See Figure 6-8. Figure 6-9 shows how you can modify all your other capitals by adding serifs. Notice that letters like the cap *E* and *T* also have vertical short lines added to their horizontal crossbar strokes.

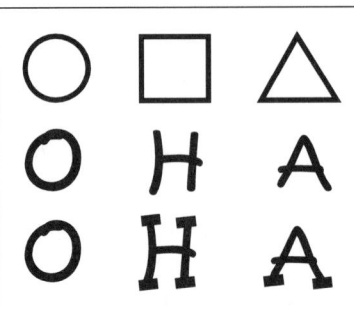

Figure 6-8: Changing a sans serif font into its serif version.

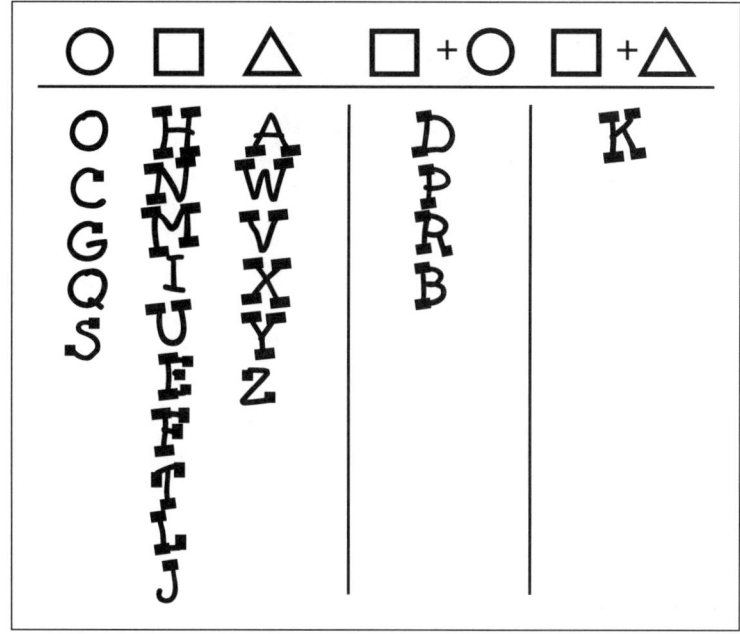

Figure 6-9: Applying serifs to the full alphabet.

If you look at Figure 6-10, you see two examples of the words *Web animation* set in the ITC Stone typeface family. Type designer Summer Stone developed three different subfamilies — Serif, Sans, and Informal — for a total of 18 typefaces based on one design idea. Another stylistic grouping that makes mixing and matching an easy task are ITC Avant Garde (sans serif) and ITC Lubalin Graph (serif).

All these fonts work together because they are based upon the following:

- Same capital-letter heights.
- Same lowercase *x-heights* (top of the *x* to its base). If you change the proportional relationship of the lower case *x-height* to the height of the capital, the typeface design or style will change. Compare Futura and ITC Avant Garde or the script typefaces Coronet and Snell to see what we mean. (If you don't have these typefaces, go to the Web sites of font manufacturers to see a sample showing of these and other fonts. Manufacturers are listed in Appendix A.)
- Same stem weights.
- Same proportions.

Apply these four factors when you're mixing different typefaces not in the same family group. Doing so will assist you in finding the best fonts to mix and match for your Web site.

Figure 6-10: Mixing and matching within a font family group.

Opposites attract

Sometimes homogenization is not a good thing. If you're looking for that dramatic effect to pop your graphic off the page, then consider playing opposites attract. It's great for developing a major focal point on your page, and it's a good candidate for animation. Here are five practical ways to create the effect:

- Extremes of textures (very smooth versus very rough or coarse)
- Free-flowing curves of a script face versus hard-edged angular geometry
- Extremes of scale (one element is double the size of the other)
- Outline shapes versus filled in shapes
- All caps versus all lowercase

You see two applications of this idea in Figures 6-11 and 6-12. The first example, "game room," mixes extremes of drawing style and scale. Notice how the *g* descends below the baseline to make a pocket to tuck in the all-caps word *ROOM*. Take advantage of words like "word" where one end character extends above or below all the others in the line. This technique is frequently used in logo design.

Chapter 6: Roll Over, Gutenberg, and Rock Your Type

Figure 6-11: Mixing Kids with Univers.

Figure 6-12: Twice freebies The second F put on weight.

"Freebies" is the second example in the figures, and here's a Phyllis Swash *F* typeset at twice the size as the other letters set in Helvetica Compressed. Note the two versions. Phyllis Swash comes in only one weight (top), which may be too light for screen use. The second *F* is a modification that we made in Adobe Photoshop.

To easily add weight to a typeface in Photoshop, follow these steps:

1. **Use the Type Tool to enter the text.**
2. **Select the character you want to change with the Magic Wand Tool.**
3. **Choose Edit➪Stroke.**

   The Stroke dialog box appears.

4. **Set stroke width to 3 pixels, center alignment with transparency option off.**

5. **Click OK.**

   Voilà! The typeface is bolder and Web-ready.

Figuring Out When to Anti-Alias

You probably heard the term anti-aliasing at your last computer convention. What does it mean, and why would it be of concern to you, a budding Web animator? *Anti-aliasing* adds pixels to the edge to minimize the jagged look of bitmapped text. To see what we mean, use the following series of steps to guide you.

1. **Launch your graphics program and then create a new file.**

   Set the file resolution to 72 dpi and the color mode to RGB.

2. **Click on the Type Tool icon to open the Type Tool dialog box.**

   In the dialog box now on view, you can pick font style, set size and alignment (and in some programs leading and tracking), choose to activate the anti-aliasing option, enter text, and see the text previewed in the selected font style and point size.

3. **In the Type Tool dialog box, pick Times Roman or a font that's similar in appearance.**

4. **Set type size to 60 point.**

5. **Type** BbYy.

   Don't select the anti-aliasing option. The text now appears in your image file.

6. **Repeat the process again, but this time select the anti-aliasing option by clicking on the empty box next to the label.**

7. **View the text you just entered on-screen at 100%, Actual Pixels.**

   See how in the second version, the anti-aliased type edge appears smoother and less jagged than in the first version?

8. **Change View: Zoom In to 600%.**

   Look at the curved edge of the *B* or the diagonal stroke of the *Y*. In your first version, you see a sharp contrast between the foreground character and the background. You can see each pixel and the resulting jagged, saw-toothed edge. Now squint your eyes as you look at your first example. What happened? The edge blurred, and the curves and diagonals appeared smoother. That's what those extra gray pixels are doing in your second example.

Chapter 6: Roll Over, Gutenberg, and Rock Your Type

Anti-aliasing does pose a trap! Repeat the above Steps 1 through 7, but this time set your point size to 12 points, the standard for body copy. Zoom In all the way up to 1600% view. Where'd the text go? Its type turned to mush (see Figure 6-13). Because the character's lines weren't wide enough, you said bye-bye to your black (100% value) pixels. For screen viewing, anti-aliasing is a no-no for fine line drawings, small text sizes, or thin-weight typefaces.

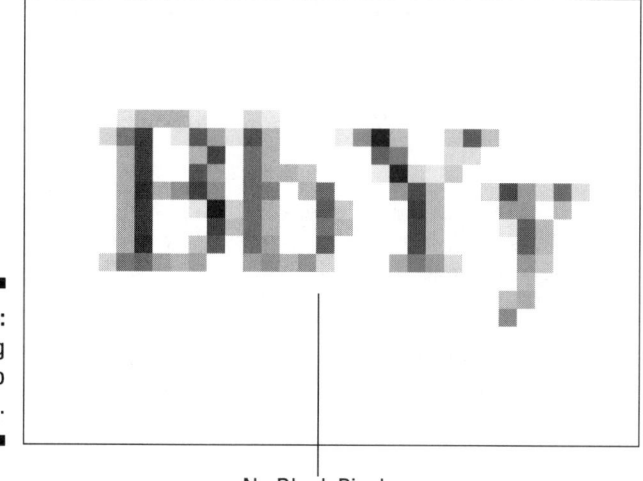

Figure 6-13: Turning type to mush.

Hold on a minute, we're not quite finished with the bad news department. This book is about animation — right? So here's a couple of $64,000 questions: What happens if your text moves? If anti-aliasing adds pixels to the edge by using color information from its background, then what happens if the background changes? Your answer is — dandruff! Those extra pixels become annoying flecks on-screen that you'd love to brush away. So here's a general rule: If the text stays put, consider anti-aliasing the edge. If it moves, don't.

Combining Titles and Text

Successfully combining titles and text requires a clearly formulated plan for your Web site. We're not talking just about Web page layout and design here. It's more than that. At the heart of any site is its personality and what it's communicating about its contents.

Consider this analogy. If you walk through the streets (even via an old movie, TV show, or travel poster) of London, Milan, Boston, San Francisco, Barcelona, or Tokyo, you experience a sense of place and a recognizable state of being that you can describe. And for better or worse, the same is true about most every place where people gather. The scale, color, and architectural style of the buildings, the clothing of the local citizenry, the cars parked on the streets, the poster in the bookstore window, the flashing neon at the local nightspot, the metallic cut letters at the office building, the chiseled letters above the courthouse steps. . . . The *signage* is the label you place on things to remind you of where you've been and point you to where you plan to go. Building on this architectural metaphor, think of titles as place markers, too — the signage of your Web site pointing the visitor to the contents.

Now, try this question on for size: What makes a good title become a memorable place marker?

Well, the title "fits in." You find a consistency of style or look and feel. It's repeating a shape, a curve of line, color, or texture from other objects on the page. (You may want to refer to the sections "Designing Type" and "Playing the Mix and Match Game" earlier in this chapter.)

But in playing the mix and match game, you see that opposites can attract, too. For everything? No, but maybe once or twice to create a focal point. Otherwise, you lose that consistency of style.

This information is a good place to start, but you need to go further. Here's a checklist to help you plan the consistency of your site.

- **The body copy.** Which typeface is it? The repeating characters of this font create the dominant texture or pattern on the page. It's the wallpaper on the wall that wraps everything else. All the other objects on the page interact with this font.

- **Frames and menu lists.** Does your site support frames? Which font did you use for your menu list? These are good places to apply the opposites-can-attract principle. Try a serif typeface for the body copy text and a sans serif boldface for the menu list or vice versa.

- **Headlines and subheads.** Here are two options to try: a bolder weight in the same typeface family as the body text, or the menu list typeface in a larger point size. You're repeating good things from other page elements. Too many unrelated typefaces can distract your eye and cause it to jump from place to place. Ask yourself which idea you want to communicate first, to follow up with, and then to move on to next. Heads and subheads are the street signs guiding the way to the information that you want your visitor to absorb.

- **Main titles.** Is this element the corporate identity logo, or is it the corporate slogan? Which font(s) are you using? How much space does the font take up on the page, and is it built into a menu bar? Main titles are an all-important grouping. Main titles are a key placemarker for the site and the graphics that your visitors will most likely remember (assuming they downloaded all of it).

Web surfers are impatient folks — consider how you can layer this grouping to download in smaller pieces as frames of an animated event. You can complete the process by rewarding the visitor with another small animation pointing the way to your special event of the day or the hot news that you don't want them to miss. More on this topic is in Chapter 12.

✔ **Advertising banners.** Any flashing screens here? Are the banners at the top of the page or at the bottom? Wherever it is, place your animation at the opposite end. You've been to that famous three-ring circus; remember how your eyes couldn't keep still, trying to follow everything all at once. If you're going to spend the time creating an animated title, give it breathing room and keep the visual noise to a minimum. No one likes listening to more than one piece of music at a time, even if both won a Grammy for best song. Playing two animations in the same space can have a similar sensory effect.

Using Decorative Letters and Numbers Without Overkill

Ah, those delightful visuals that catch your eye and become a visual feast are just like ice cream sundaes for the eyes. But that's the catch. How many sundaes can you eat in one meal?

Instead of one scoop each of vanilla, chocolate, and strawberry piled high with whipped cream and a cherry, go with one scoop of vanilla, pass on the whipped cream, but keep the cherry. Digestible and enjoyable, right? But that strawberry still looks tempting. You wouldn't mind trying some of that, too. Hmm . . . wait a little bit, give that first sundae time to be digested, and then give the strawberry a try.

When working with decorative letters and numbers, think about this little sundae story. If each paragraph leads off with a decorative element, how effective or enjoyable would those elements be? It's the same old problem of too much competition for your visitor's attention.

Try limiting your decorative letter or number to the beginning of each new large section of information. Allow your reader time to scroll on or to move to another page before introducing another visual delight. These decorative elements can be good candidates for animating, if they're not too close to an animated head. Again, the idea is to avoid placing too much razzle-dazzle on the same page at the same time. Just like planning out your animation, using decorative type is a matter of timing and placement in the frame.

Flying Logos and Icons: How Not to Crash and Burn

Using another person's or company's logos or trademarks in your animation usually means three things: permissions, permissions, permissions. Beware the legal eagles and the committee that enforces corporate identity standards! Here are some general rules for keeping your animated logo soaring.

- **Sign-off.** This can take two forms:
  - **Right to use.** Unless you own the rights, you need written permission to use any registered or trademarked logo and icon, even if your intent for the logo is your own personal use. Remember that the Web is a public forum. A corporation will want to know how you plan to use its logo. Be prepared to submit detailed documentation with your request. Don't be surprised if your request is denied. If corporation representatives say no, move on and think of something else to use on your site.
  - **Design standards.** Ask whether corporate identity guidelines exist and how closely you must follow them if they do. Don't change something as simple as color without permission. You know the expression *Big Blue;* no need to say that the company in question is IBM. If the company guidelines are too vague, then prepare a proposal that offers suggestions for improving the guidelines and includes your animation ideas. Be prepared to do more legwork on the front end of your project to avoid a major migraine later.

- **Converting a flat 2-D logo or icon into a 3-D animated logo.** Making 2-D into 3-D is a matter of creating sides where none existed before. Adding this third dimension to the mix is not as straightforward as hitting the extrude button and hoping for the best. Some things to look for:
  - **How tight or narrow are the interior white spaces in your logo or icon?** If they're too narrow, they'll fill in when you convert to 3-D. Be prepared to create a new expanded version of your 2-D logo. It may look weird, but the final 3-D result is what counts.
  - **What's the depth of the sides?** Link this dimension to your animation sequence. If the sides are too narrow, you run the risk that your logo will momentarily disappear as it rotates around. Too wide, and you'll slow down the action.
  - **What's happened to the file size?** 3-D objects contain more data than their 2-D cousins. Will converting to 3-D push your file size out of the realm of viewing pleasure for your intended audience? Or will your audience have to find and download a special plug-in? Web surfers are the cousins of TV channel surfers — they're never in one place very long. Keep this fact in mind before you invest your time building a 3-D animated version of your logo.

Chapter 7
Art Without Guilt: Using Clip Art

In This Chapter
- Finding clip art resources
- Making good choices
- Fine-tuning your selections
- Getting permission to use copyrighted material

Remember grade school, and the day your teacher told you to pull out a sheet of paper, a pencil, and a ruler? "Draw," she said like a coxswain barking out orders to her crew. Your hand probably still cramps when you think about that day. Now is the time to wiggle your fingers and remember that drawing isn't about making straight lines. It's the willingness to trust your hand and your imagination. If you're still convinced after our little pep talk that you're terminally art-impaired, however, clip art can be your life preserver.

In this chapter, we tell you where you can find clip art collections, how to take advantage of what you find, and provide simple rules of thumb for staying out of the usage-rights quagmire.

Can't Draw? Don't Worry: Clip Art to the Rescue

Talk about collections, and more collections! The choices of clip art collections are mind-boggling. No matter what your taste, interest, or topic, a bevy of clip art awaits you. Here are some of the resources available. (See Appendix A for a listing of resource addresses and telephone numbers.)

If you want to find the latest, hot new artist collection, or mega-deal, consider getting yourself on the mailing lists of these companies:

- **Dynamic Graphics ArtWorks:** Dynamic Graphics features the Showcase series, a collection of contemporary clip art styles from top illustrators. The company commissions work from its pool of talent, such as Lonnie Springer, creator of *On The Go*, a series of clay photos. Included in their catalog are Web-ready illustrations in a variety of image looks and subjects. The Dynamic Graphics Web site is at www.dgusa.com.

- **Image Club Graphics:** This division of Adobe Systems Inc. offers collections of classic and contemporary art, and ARTROOM, a series of clip art volumes. The volumes include thousands of images representing a large assortment of illustrators and themes. Visit the Image Club Graphics Web site at www.imageclub.com.

- **Publisher's Toolbox:** The catalog for this company lists CD-ROM collections from multimedia and software companies. A host of titles, from mega-collections to specialty topics such as medical illustrations, are here for you to consider. Point your browser at www.pubtool.com to visit the Publisher's Toolbox Web site.

If you need even more sources for graphics, take a look at the following:

- **It's in the box:** In the highly competitive drawing and paint programs market, bundling art collections with software is the name of the game. Products like Deneba Canvas and CorelDRAW! include thousands of clip art images on their software CD-ROMs. Corel, like Nova Development, distributes clip art CD-ROMs via computer retailers and mail order catalogs. You can visit those companies' Web sites, too, for more about their products. Corel Web site: corel.com; Deneba Software Web site: deneba.com; Nova Development Web site: www.novadevcorp.com.

- **Browse the Web:** Many clip art catalogs are posted on the Web, and searching can reveal a treasure trove of images. Before downloading and using freeware artwork, don't forget to read our basic training on intellectual property. Protect yourself with virtual garlic, and keep legal vampires at bay.

Selecting Clip Art for Animation

Before selecting a clip art collection, develop the design master plan for your Web site. The plan is your compass, guiding you through the forest of options. Setting clear style standards and subject themes help you to meet production goals and budget projections. You can learn the ins and outs of Web design by reading *Organic Web Design Studio Secrets* or *Web Design & Desktop Publishing For Dummies,* 2nd Edition, both published by IDG Books Worldwide, Inc.

Chapter 7: Art Without Guilt: Using Clip Art 129

After you develop your design plan, apply what you know about how the reader will move through your site to your first-pass, rough-cut selection of your clip art for both illustration and animation needs. Clip art collections represent a wealth of professional art talent, and their drawing styles. If you take the time to become familiar with the different collections (where to find them is covered in the previous section), you can find artwork that reflects your sense of style and personality. Make these visual morsels the reward that you give to your guest for visiting and staying at your site.

Moving your visitor

As you scroll through your site, the animated elements can be visual cues that help move your visitor along to the next item you want them to notice. Use your animation to give your Web site a kind of tour guide; as you evaluate clip art possibilities, keep this concept in mind.

For example, if you want your visitor to scroll across your Web page as well as down, you may want to pick clip art that can move believably in a long horizontal line of action and that has an easily recognizable shape. To see what we mean, open file 059TGL01.eps in the Dynamic Graphics clip art folder on the CD-ROM that accompanies this book. (You can find all the examples that we cite in this section in this folder.) You could easily send this sailboat moving along using a few frames of animation.

Moving a sailboat in an animation is a great idea, but what if the clip-art sailboat is headed toward the right, and what you need on your Web site is a boat that's moving left? That restriction is not a major headache or reason for disqualification of the right-pointing sailboat. Open the graphic file in your graphics program to flip it. (We give hints for customizing later in this chapter.)

As another example, you may want to encourage your visitor to move down a menu list. Think of what falls naturally, like the droplet of water in file 024DNE02.eps. Remember that your animated object has to fit into the margins without crowding out your menu list text and still be interesting to look at. A small, odd-shaped object can be just what the doctor ordered.

You don't need to use everything you find in a piece of clip art. It's okay to select only one part and save the rest for another day.

Staying put

What if you want your visitor to stay in one place for a bit? You may want to find clip art that features something that hovers. The small hummingbird in file `085SSC02.eps` could fit the bill. With the hummingbird, you can even add a little visual pun. The loose drawing style that in one frame already suggests motion could easily be translated into several frames of action.

Consider how certain drawing elements lend themselves to the different animation techniques that we discuss in Chapters 3 and 4. Take particular note of the Chapter 4 section "Strike a pose: Making simple changes for good effect." Consider the point made in that section about how a pose is good if it looks right to you. The clip art you're selecting will turn into one animation frame. Can your potential candidate take on that role? Or will your choice make it hard to suggest the anticipated next move?

Other animating experiences

Anticipation about what comes next drives a developing story. Some clip art, such as the rooster welcoming the rising sun in file `062HIL01.eps`, can tie directly to the text on your Web site. Animated clip art can be more than a pointer in the story of your site; such clip art can be used to illustrate an article or piece of fiction that you post to the Web. The rooster can become the opening element of a children's story that takes place on a farm. Or if you're thinking about a story for adults, file `075BZC01.eps` can be an example of an animated informational graphic for a business site. Animating the arrows with a color cycle highlights ideas shown in the clip art and adds punch to the information that you want the viewer to learn.

Lots of clip art is available for you to choose from, so be clear about what role you want your animation to play in your Web site. You'll find it much easier to narrow down your choices and find the one you want at a clip art supplier's Web site.

Escape from the endless edit

Ever hear of Sisyphus, that character from Greek mythology whose punishment in Hades was to roll a stone up a slope, watch the stone slip down the slope, and then roll it up the hill again — in an endless loop? That's how you'll probably feel if you try editing some of the clip art on the market. It's delete this point here, delete that line segment there, and so on. Value your production time, and save money in the process, by checking out the new Web-ready clip art collections. When ordering Web-ready images, look for these technical specs:

Chapter 7: Art Without Guilt: Using Clip Art 131

- **Ready-to-use GIF or JPEG files:** These files don't require conversion, unlike the standard high-resolution RGB or CMYK clip art for print documents. All you need to do is drop them into your favorite animation program. Depending upon content, consider using the images as backgrounds or isolating an element in one image to animate. Read the Chapter 9 section titled "Lifting a Finger: Creating Isolated Action in Your Image Area" for more details.

- **RGB, indexed color images:** These images' color palettes are Web safe. You don't need to convert CMYK images to RGB or indexed color. We talk about color palette basics in Chapters 5 and 11.

- **Transparent backgrounds:** Some animation programs like GIF Construction Set (see Chapter 14) can't import files with transparent backgrounds. But for those that can, this feature can be a blessing for creating composite image frames or for animations that appear to float on your Web page's background. Watch out for stray pixels if the edges of the clip art are anti-aliased and your Web page background is not white (generally the default clip art background color).

- **Very small file sizes:** Graphics files should be less than 10K, though, in very rare instances (such as those situations in which only two or three elements are on the entire Web page), files between 10 and 20K are okay. Never exceed 20K, regardless. The smaller the better — bullets are usually 2K. The goal is to have all the elements on your Web page not exceed 30–40K, or you could slow the download of your Web site to a crawl. See Chapter 11 for "The Incredible Shrinking GIF."

- **Average dimensions:** Size varies from as small as 19x19 pixels for a bullet to 464 pixels wide x 128 pixels high for a banner. Horizontal rules equal the width of your Web page: about 512 pixels. Picture elements size from about 77 pixels square to about 144 pixels x 216 pixels.

- **Black and white or color options:** Don't discount the usefulness of black and white for layouts in which the animation has tiny dimensions and you require high contrast against a textured Web page background.

- **A browser:** This is a real time-saver. You need one of these for viewing thumbnails at a size larger than the standard file picture icon (to differentiate similar images). But best of all, the graphic browser is a research assistant who's there to help you find images by subject, content, or theme.

GIF and JPEG files require special care when you edit them. If this isn't your forte, visit Chapter 11 for more details on file management and conversion.

Collections originally designed for print

Time to sound the alarm. Buyer beware! A clip art file reproduced in a print catalog may be sized down and may look okay, but remember that the file is a high-resolution file. Parts barely visible in print disappear on screen at the same size. Also, what looks like a solid gray-toned background may actually be a *Benday* screen (a screen made by a pattern of dots). If you size down a figure that has a Benday dot screen, the screen becomes a blotchy pattern when viewed on your computer monitor. Your monitor just doesn't have enough pixels to show all those dots correctly in the space alloted. You wouldn't buy a new car without test-driving it first, so you probably don't want to order a clip art collection without checking out a few sample files first.

Buy their CD-ROM catalog sampler, or check out their Web site

Order their catalog sampler, or download sample images from their Web site. Find out if you're barking up the wrong tree. Open sample files in your favorite drawing or paint program to evaluate them. The question is not one of quality, drawing style, or beauty. Pure and simple — you're judging file specifications and adaptability. Here's a checklist of things to consider while you're evaluating files:

- **The file format:** If the format is EPS (Encapsulated Postscript), all sorts of totally useless CMYK (4-color printing process colors — cyan, magenta, yellow, and black) information is embedded in the file. That information fattens up your file size. You need to strip out that data and resave the file in a new format. It begs the question: Is all this extra work worth my time? Read on.

- **The file dimensions:** There's a good possibility the clip art was sized to fit an 8 $\frac{1}{2}$" x 11" print document page. That's way too big for Web usage. In your graphics program, resize your intended image to 25 percent of the original dimensions. Is the illustration still attractive to you? Are parts filling in, losing key details? If you answer no to the first question and/or yes to the second, it's a washout.

- **The reproduction criteria used:** Sometimes the artist who created the image used print reproduction criteria, which doesn't work for the Web. Look at Figure 7-1 to see an example of an illustration created for print, from the Dynamic Graphics clip art collection (file number: 035X0697). Figure 7-2 shows the image's Photoshop Image Size dialog box, which reveals the reason why this illustration is not a good candidate for Web animation. The color image file size is 4.53MB, its dimensions are 872 pixels wide x 1,363 pixels high, and its resolution is 170 pixels/inch. If you attempted to adapt this figure for Web specifications, you'd lose the airbrushed detail and the scattering of confetti and dots, and the gradients would band. The end result would eliminate the drawing qualities that made the image attractive in the first place.

Figure 7-1: Dynamic Graphics clip art created for print and not for the Web.

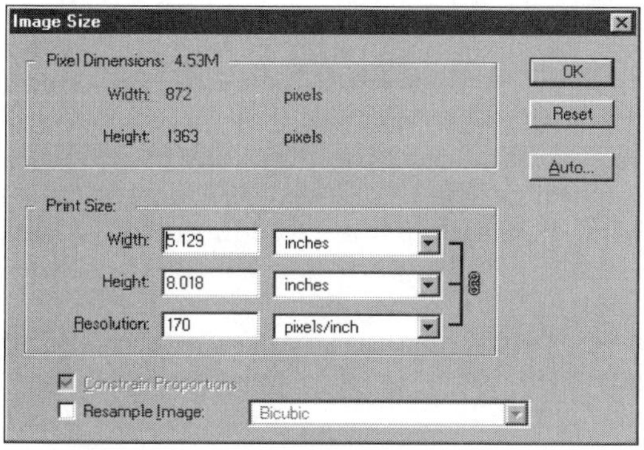

Figure 7-2: The Photoshop Image Size dialog box showing specifications for the Dynamic Graphics timid man image.

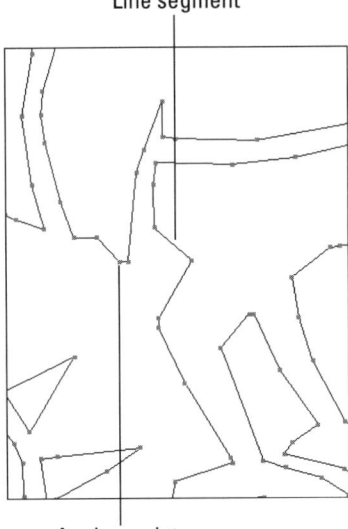

Figure 7-3: The anchor points and line segments that make up a vector-based drawing.

- **How many points:** Vector-based drawings (created in programs such as Adobe Illustrator, CorelDRAW! or Macromedia Freehand and scaled to fit a full letter-sized page) can be too elaborate in detail. The fewer the anchor points and number of line segments, the easier it will be to adapt; see Figure 7-3 to see what we mean by *anchor point* and *line segment*. Trying to eliminate anchor points (which define the start and stop points of a line segment or multiple line segments) returns us to our old friend Sisyphus. If it seems like you could go on forever editing those points, you probably feel like you've joined Sisyphus in his endless loop through time. Remember to be production savvy and choose a file that can be modified quickly and easily. Don't create extra production headaches for yourself. As an alternative you may consider exporting the vector-based clip art into a paint program, but remember that you're reducing size dimensions, too. These are the same problems we discuss in the previous bullet.

- **Value-added assets:** If stock photography companies are in a really good mood, they include clipping paths or built-in alpha channels for artwork saved as a Photoshop file (PSD). For an example, refer to Figure 7-4, which is a stock photo from the MetaCreations PowerPhotos Bugs and Butterflies series. The photo can be found in the Chap07 folder on the CD-ROM as the file named 0080030.tif. Figure 7-5 shows the alpha channel mask included with this photo. These ready-made clipping paths or alpha channels can be used to create clip art silhouettes. (We explain what alpha channel masks are and how to do this conversion in Chapter 9.)

Figure 7-4: A two-bugs photo from the MetaCreations PowerPhoto series.

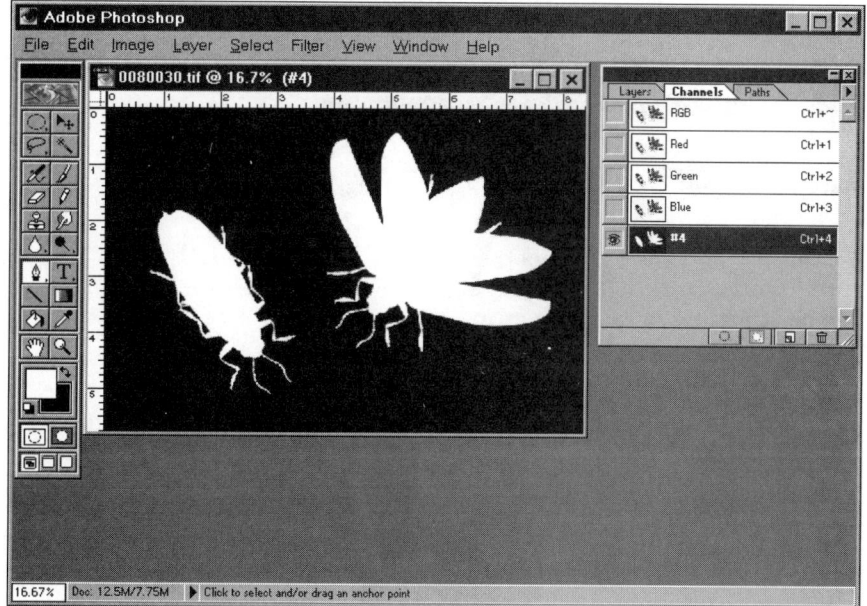

Figure 7-5: The channel makes a silhouette.

Hints for Customizing Clip Art

Playing with clip art can be lots of fun. In the following section we show three examples of playing with clip art that are easy to do. Our first example helps out those of you who may not have purchased any clip art collections. The artwork's actually from Zapf Dingbats, a typeface font. Dingbats, decorative typeface elements, are typed out using your program's Type or Text tool. Here's how you layer two Zapf Dingbats to create clip art.

1. **In your graphics program create a new file and set the screen resolution to 72 dpi and the color mode to RGB.**
2. **Click on the Type tool icon to see the Type dialog box.**

   Select Zapf Dingbats as your font, and then set your type size to 72 point (about 1 inch) or larger. The example shown in Figure 7-6 is 200 point.

Figure 7-6: Dingbats can help in a pinch.

3. **To make the star dingbat, press the hyphen (for both Macintosh and Windows users).**

   The dingbat appears in your file.

4. **Use the Stroke tool to modify the star dingbat by creating a 5-pixel black outline.**
5. **Fill the star with a bright yellow (R = 255, G = 255, B = 0).**

   See Figures 7-6, 7-7, and 7-8 for examples of this entire process.

Figure 7-7: Artwork outlined using Stroke tool.

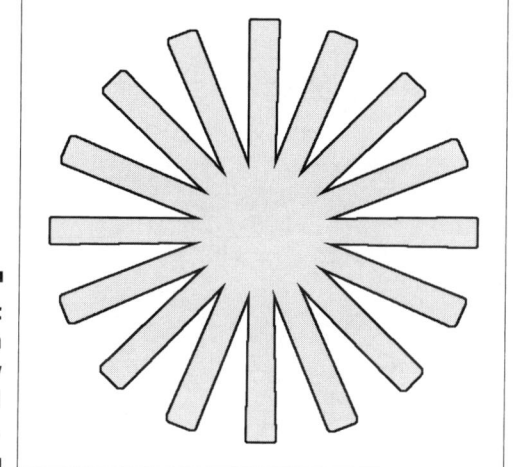

Figure 7-8: Filling in with yellow to build a halo.

6. **Repeat Steps 2 and 3 to add the second dingbat.**

    The second dingbat is the hand holding the pencil. For this dingbat set, change the type size to 175 point, and then press Shift+Z to see the character. The Photoshop Type tool adds a new layer. If your program doesn't do this, first create a new layer, and then use the Type tool to add the second dingbat. See Figure 7-19.

7. **With the Magic Wand tool, select each part of the hand one at a time.**

Part II: Tricks with Pix

   8. Fill each area with the Paint Bucket tool, as shown in Figure 7-10.

   Remember to pick your color before filling in the area.

   9. Save your new clip art and export to GIF.

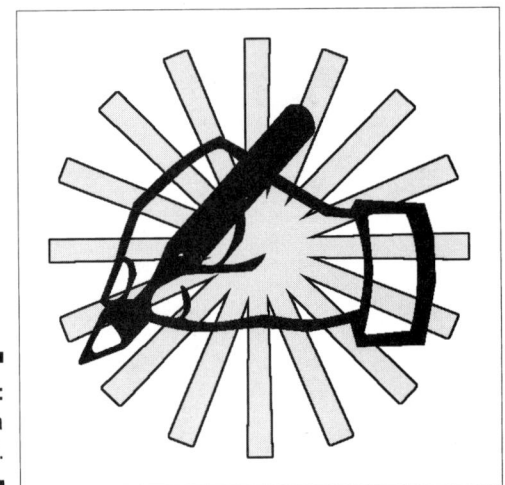

Figure 7-9: Lending a hand.

Figure 7-10: A new piece of clip art.

Zapf Dingbats isn't the only decorative font on the market that substitutes icons or pictures for alphabet letters. The artwork we use in Chapter 5 to illustrate a Color Model Sketch (Figure 5-6) comes from ITC's Design Font collection. Samples of ITC's font collection are on the CD-ROM. You can also visit the ITC Web site: `www.esselte.com/itc/index.html`.

Chapter 7: Art Without Guilt: Using Clip Art   139

Changing clip art colors

A great way to create new clip art is to modify the color scheme of existing clip art. You don't need a lot of art talent to try this. (For more information about selecting color combinations, check out Chapter 5.) The following bulleted list explains some considerations to weigh when making such modifications:

- Take a look at the Dynamic Graphics clip art sampler folder on the CD-ROM and open file 023HIL01.eps. The art is a black-and-white pumpkin from the Iconografs I collection. (In Chapter 14 we use a photograph of a pumpkin in our sample animation. You can use this clip art to create a variation of the animation.) When we opened the file, we resized the dimensions smaller to 1.028" x 1.222". The resolution was set to 72 dpi and anti-aliasing was not selected.

- If you look at Figure 7-11, you can see how the lines on the pumpkin filled in when we resized the file. When you resize file resolution and dimensions, fine lines will often disappear.

- View Figure 7-12. In this figure you see the lines we added to the image using a 1-pixel-width Pencil tool. We added lines to the pumpkin's face, at the base of the stem, and between the pumpkin and the background shape. By dividing each piece of your image into a separate part, you'll find it easier to colorize your image. This process eliminates the need to create a mask for each color.

Figure 7-11:
An unretouched, resized pumpkin.

Part II: Tricks with Pix

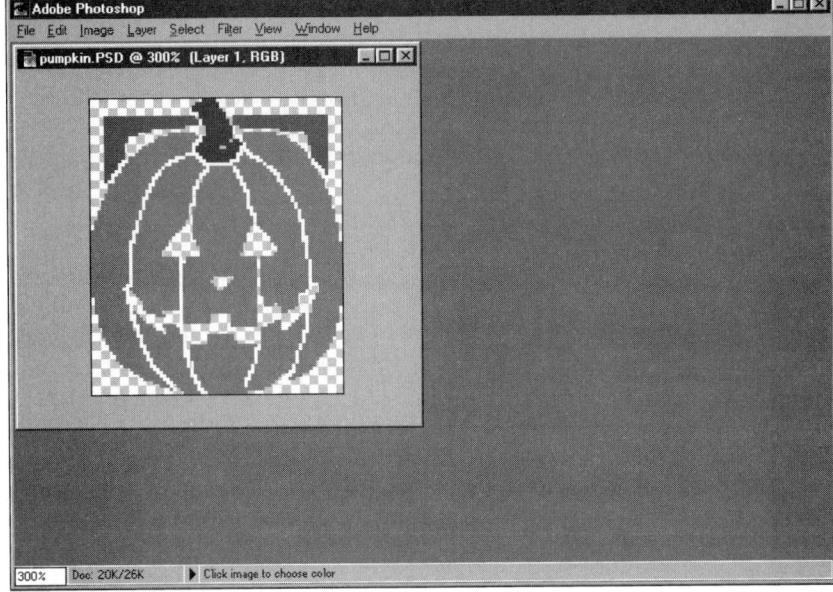

Figure 7-12: The retouched pumpkin, in which we put back lines lost because of resizing.

✔ If you want to colorize your image, just select an area with the Magic wand tool and fill with the color of your choice. Remember to choose a Web-safe color. (In Chapters 5 and 11 we review Web color palettes.)

Modifying a silhouette to suggest action

Using a one-color silhouette can offer advantages when file sizes need to be small. But this has drawbacks when you want to suggest fast action or movement across the screen.

If you create contrast between the two sides of an object, you can suggest motion. Although filters can make files larger (yellow caution sign!), the Photoshop Wind and Fragment filters have minimal impact on file size, and will definitely speed things up. The original image is shown in Figure 7-13 — a bicycle racer from the Corel clip art collection that is packaged with CorelDRAW!

1. **From the menu, select Filter⇨Stylize⇨Wind to open the dialog box.**

2. **In the dialog box, use the scroll-down menus to set Method: Blast, and Direction: From the right.**

   We used Blast because the Method: Wind effect is too subtle for Web graphics.

Chapter 7: Art Without Guilt: Using Clip Art **141**

Figure 7-13: A cycling silhouette from Corel.

Look at Figure 7-14 and see how one side of the racer has a smooth edge, and the other is jagged. The rough edge is always farther from the direction you are moving towards.

Figure 7-14: The cycling silhouette modified using the Photoshop Wind filter to suggest motion.

3. For our second version, select Filter⇨Pixelate⇨Fragment.

No dialog box appears. The filter is automatically applied. You can modify the filter effect by changing screen resolution. Figure 7-15 has a screen resolution of 266 dpi, and Figure 7-16 has a screen resolution of 72 dpi. Compare the figures. The filter effect is greater for the 72 dpi version because you're working with bigger pixels. Keep this in mind whenever you use filters: Adjust filter settings lower when you decrease screen resolution.

142 Part II: Tricks with Pix

Figure 7-15: Applying the Photoshop Fragment filter to a 266 dpi image.

Figure 7-16: The 72 dpi version showing the increased effect of the Fragment filter.

Basic Training on Intellectual Property — Garlic for Legal Vampires

Visualize this scenario: You're browsing the Web, and you've discovered a site that's a treasure trove of freebie clip art and photographs. They're FTP (File Transfer Protocol) files ready to download, and you can't believe your luck. This is just what the doctor ordered to finish both your animation and Web site. But is this a cure for what ails you? We're not lawyers, but here are some tips to consider. When in doubt, always consult your attorney.

First variation in our story

You're visiting a homegrown Web site that is offering lots of freeware to download. Not a bad haul for an hour's worth of browsing — three pictures fit the bill as starting points for your animation. A trap door that takes you to the dungeon is here, however. Consider this before rushing ahead with the latest cure.

- **Whose copyright is it anyway?** Have you determined whether or not the homegrown site's Webmaster or designer had permission to use those great images or animations? The Web is a public domain, and you can easily get caught using someone else's work without permission. Before posting any artwork — still, animated, or musical — to your Web site, find out who holds the copyright. Write down the information and save it, because you'll always need to have this information on file. Then contact that person or company and obtain written permission — "Sign here on the dotted line, and don't forget the date, please." Refer to the logos and trademarks issue covered in Chapter 6. Ignorance of the original source is not an excuse. You can still be held liable for violation of copyright and of stealing someone else's intellectual property.

- **Use of a clip art portrait or picture filled with humans requires a model release form.** You need an okay from everyone in the picture to use their likeness on your Web page. You may want to play it safe and get written permission from any family members or friends who volunteer as subjects. If a minor is involved, parental permission is required. Keep in mind that you can't use the likeness of a famous person to market your Web site or product. This is considered an endorsement, so find your nearest lawyer to negotiate a license agreement.

Also, to protect yourself, register *your* content with the U.S. Copyright Office. Visit the Web site, where you can find FAQs (Frequently Asked Questions) and other copyright information resources. The URL is lcweb.loc.gov/copyright.

Exercise your own good judgment. Pornographic, defamatory, libelous, or otherwise unlawful use of images is prohibited (and is more stuff for the lawyers to argue over).

Copyright versus Right to use versus Royalty-free: An exercise in confusion

Copyrights are held by whoever owns the rights to the CD-ROM, if your purchase came on a CD-ROM or floppy disk, and the artwork or intellectual property contained therein.

When you order the CD-ROM or artwork, the *intellectual property*, the copyright owner grants you a personal license, nontransferable, nonexclusive right to use and copy those files onto your computer hard drive. The conditions under which you can use these files are specified in the licensing agreement that comes with the CD-ROM or artwork. Although you may not be signing any documents, your opening the package, or downloading from the Web site, signifies your acceptance of the terms of the license. No standard license exists. What's okay for one company or person may get you a nasty letter from another party's lawyer. Don't assume anything. Read the small print.

Make sure that you don't equate the term royalty-free with the transference of copyright ownership, because they're not the same. *Royalty-free* refers to a fee payment arrangement for the license to use the intellectual property (how you hand over the cash). Rather than paying a fee each time you use the artwork, like fees for film exhibitions or music use, you pay once, up front, to use the stuff. The company gives you the better deal because they're saving on administrative costs.

If you'd like to find out more information on this topic, check with your lawyer. Before your consult, here are three Web sites to visit. They can help you to focus your questions.

The Copyright FAQ:

```
ftp://rtf.mit.edu/pub/usenet/
    law/copyright/
```

Copyright Myths FAQ:

```
http://www.faqs.org/faqs/law/
    copyright/
```

Ivan Hoffman, B.A., J.D. Attorney At Law (posts articles on legal topics):

```
http://home.earthlink.net/
    ~ivanlove
```

Second variation in our story

Imagine that the site you visit is an online catalog for clip art and stock photography collections. As a marketing teaser, they allow you to try some of their product. Free stuff! This is great! But what's the catch? Time to pull out your glasses again to read the small print.

First of all, the demo clip art or photos are for your personal use. What does *personal* mean? Here's the yarn: Your family's getting together for a reunion. You've decided to be a good sport, and have created a Web site to share genealogy, organizing information, and historical tidbits like Great Aunt Sarah's trek along the Oregon Trail. This is fine, you're publishing information — no profit motive is involved.

As the days pass, however, your expenses mount, and you decide to sell mugs and T-shirts to help defray costs. Uh-oh! Watch out for the legal vampire. Your garlic has dried up. Because you're selling products from your Web site, it has become a commercial site — personal use transformed into a business application. How do you get fresh legal garlic? Order the artwork, and then pay the fee to use it.

Okay, that's taken care of, but everyone loved your animation so much that you decided to use a frame of the animation artwork to decorate those mugs and T-shirts. Garlic's drying up again. You need a second license, this time for resale. See Table 7-1 for a breakout of some usage applications such as brochures, Web design, and greeting cards. Remember that this is only a general summary. Always read the licensing agreement for details (we hate to remind you again, but we don't want you to forget this piece of advice). Protect yourself with a good dose of common sense.

Table 7-1	A Licensing Summary
Comping	A *comp* is a preliminary version of a design that is shown to a client for concept approval — it isn't final art and design ready for the printer, or for posting to the Web. Although they're Web resolution, catalog CD-ROM images (72 dpi, low resolution) may not be used at your Web site. The files are for comping and previewing only.
Royalty-free	Artwork and photography used for advertising, promotional, and editorial purposes in which the images are not resold, such as Web design, brochures, and advertising and promotion.
Resale Uses	You need to negotiate a second license for these. Some examples that can apply: clothing items such as T-shirts and hats; hard goods — it's duffel bags and mugs this time; greeting cards and postcards; computer fine art; non-disposable packaging; products produced for resale.

Another red flag: Don't save any artwork (intellectual property) that's not your own (for which you don't hold the copyright) as FTP files. You can't offer anyone else's work for download. Unless you have a signed contract stating that you can do so, don't do this. Keep your garlic fresh.

Chapter 8
Dynamic Photos

In This Chapter
- Choosing your photos
- Capturing your images
- Preparing photos for the Web
- Searching stock photo collections
- Working with filters

The Web is as much a collection of pictures as it is of text. When the Mosaic browser was introduced — seems like eons ago but it's only been a few short years — the Internet visually metamorphosed like a caterpillar to a butterfly from boring text screens to a rich graphic-based environment. Check a Web site's source code, and you'll find many more Web designers are using HTML commands like transforming graphics and graphics on graphics to position artwork on their pages. By adding animated GIFs, Netscape plug-ins, and Java applets to the mix, the Web has taken on a life of its own to rival the visual complexity of television.

This chapter is about working with photographs — whether they started out as a piece of film or were digitally captured, if they're yours or from a photo collection — and how you can adapt them for animations.

Raiding Your Photo Album

Before you rush out to buy the latest clip photo collection, take your photo albums off the shelf and go prospecting. Remember that you're working in a small size, the picture will be moving, and you're at screen (low) resolution of 72 dots per inch (dpi). Photos that you wouldn't consider for print (the latter of which are usually output at 300 dpi and higher) may fit the bill. Because it's harder to see fine detail at 72 dpi, minor photography mishaps like small scratches or dust on the negative (visible in your photo print) can't be seen when viewed on a computer monitor.

WARNING! Before you pick out any family portraits, refer to Chapter 7. Anyone appearing in a photo will have to sign a model-release form, which is a signed permission form saying you can use their likeness in your animation.

The following five figures came from one of the author's scrapbooks. The figures are examples of the good, the bad, and the not-quite-ready-for-prime-time. Look at the grazing cows of Figure 8-1. On the whole the photo works, but very little detail exists in the highlights, such as the rump of the foreground cow. With minor editing, the photo is usable. All you need to do is add a light transparent wash of color to the highlights to remove that bleached-out look.

TIP Now look at the sailing ship in Figure 8-2. Very little detail exists in the whole picture, and it looks washed out and fuzzy. In an interview that we conducted for the February 1990 issue of *Computer Graphics World*, expert photographer and digital imaging specialist John Harcourt gave us this rule: "A good print for scanning will display a lot of detail, although it may look flat compared to a transparency." Harcourt continued with a reminder to use "very flat, low contrast originals, because you can always add contrast successfully later. It is very hard to restore what you didn't get." This means that having detail in highlights, or deep blacks, helps your picture to look better.

Figure 8-1: Two moos from the family album.

Figure 8-2: Sailing into history.

If you now look at Figure 8-3 you'll see another factor for discarding a picture from consideration. Although the exposure looks okay, the angle at which the photo was shot doesn't work. The spouting whale is a tempting possibility because it's humorous, but the angle is wrong. Too much of what makes the whale attractive will be lost if you crop out its background. Ask yourself this question: Will your audience comprehend what they're seeing if visual cues are removed? If you answer no or maybe, then choose another photograph from your album.

Figure 8-4 poses an interesting question: Why consider this picture if it's a good example of a bad photo? You may discover extreme contrast offers a winning hand. Look at the edge contour of the castle. You can clearly see the ins and outs of the tower — it works as a silhouette. Scan and export the image to a paint program. In the paint program, remove the background, and save the castle as a channel selection mask. Use the mask to create a filled or outlined 2-D shape. See Chapter 9 for details on how to do so.

Our final example, as seen in Figure 8-5, is a photo of Caesar's hand from a statue in Rome. Everything comes together: The exposure works, the contrast is crisp, and the angle is right on target. In Chapter 9 we show you how to adapt this photograph to make an animation.

Figure 8-3: Spouting off at odd angles.

Figure 8-4: What lurks behind these dark walls?

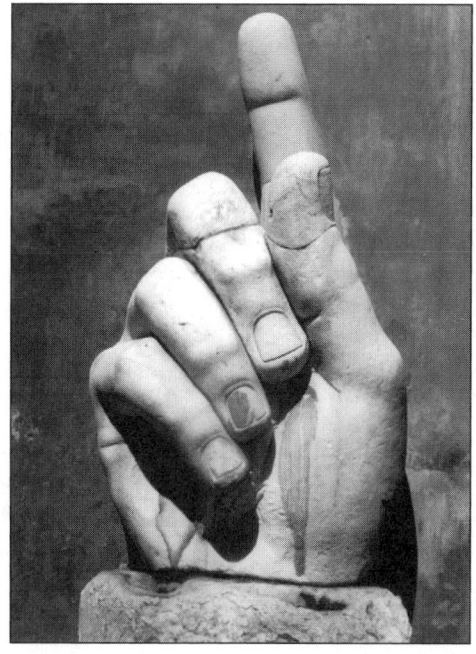

Figure 8-5:
Fingering a famous Roman.

Scanning Your Photos

Scanners can be lots of fun, and they're not as forbidding as they may seem. They're versatile tools that can be used to capture things such as

- Color photos in 24-bit true color or 8-bit 256 colors
- Black-and-white photos
- Color halftones
- Color or black-and-white drawings
- Black-and-white halftones
- Line art
- OCR (Optical Character Recognition)

Halftone screens are used in printing to convert a continuous-tone photograph to thousands of tiny dots. Each dot becomes a place to lay ink on paper. As you increase the number of dots per inch and make the dot pattern even finer (the elemental dot decreases in size), the halftone becomes closer in appearance to the original continuous-tone photograph.

To see what we mean, scan in a photograph from a newspaper or magazine, and then zoom in the file to 600 percent. You can see the halftone dot grid. If you scan a printed photograph from a book or magazine, use your scanner's software (if available as a feature) to do dot removal. The software does this by adding *noise*, irregular dot patterns, to the image, thereby reducing the effect of the obvious halftone grid pattern. Other options to remove halftone dots are Filter⇨Noise⇨Dust & Scratches (Adobe Photo-shop 4.0) or Effects⇨Noise⇨Dust and Scratch (Corel PHOTO-PAINT 6.0).

Another problem that occurs when scanning is *moiré*, or unacceptable patterning or image distortions, made by selecting the wrong screen angles for your halftone scan. For a more detailed discussion on this topic, check out books that are prepress printing resources.

Many desktop scanners can capture images from 50 to 4,800 *dots per inch* (dpi) resolution, depending on the final file destination: screen, printer, OCR, or fax. By designating your image source, screen resolution, and final destination of the scan, you lock in the auto exposure controls for setting the exposure values to your specifications.

Sound the trumpets! Because you're scanning at a low resolution (72 dpi), many of the bugaboos that worry print designers and prepress specialists don't apply here. As long as you follow the hints we previously discussed in the section "Raiding Your Photo Album," you can stay out of trouble and keep your files from needing minimal retouching. Before you begin scanning, read through our list of helpful hints:

- **Calibrate your scanner to your monitor.** You'll be less likely to create scans that are underexposed or oversaturated.
- **Clean the scanner glass before each scan.** Wipe off the surface with a lint-free cloth to remove any solvent residue.
- **Handle your photos or artwork by the edges.** The scanner's CCD array (the hardware part that reads your image) can see fingerprints at 20 paces. If you keep hair or sweater fuzz off the scanner's glass, you'll see a dramatic decrease in retouching. Otherwise, you may spend time in zoom mode removing hair and fuzz from the image.
- **Position the photo facedown on the scanner.** Place the original facedown on the scanner glass, using the ruler guides to line both sides square to the edge (see Figure 8-6). Keeping your photo perpendicular and parallel to the scanner window eliminates another retouching job. If your photo is slightly out of position, don't worry. Many image editors have a tool to automatically correct slightly skewed photographs.
- **Specify the scan parameters for source, resolution, and destination.** Picking the correct source (photo instead of line art, for example) is critical for configuring your scanner exposure controls correctly. So is setting the right destination. Set the resolution to 72 dpi, which is the Web standard. See Figures 8-7 and 8-8.

Chapter 8: Dynamic Photos   153

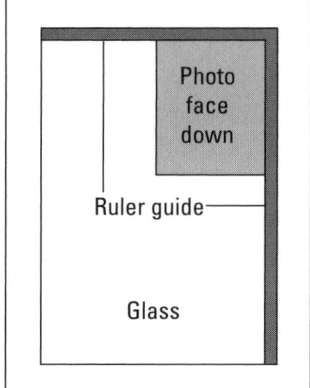

Figure 8-6: Positioning your photo facedown on the scanner glass.

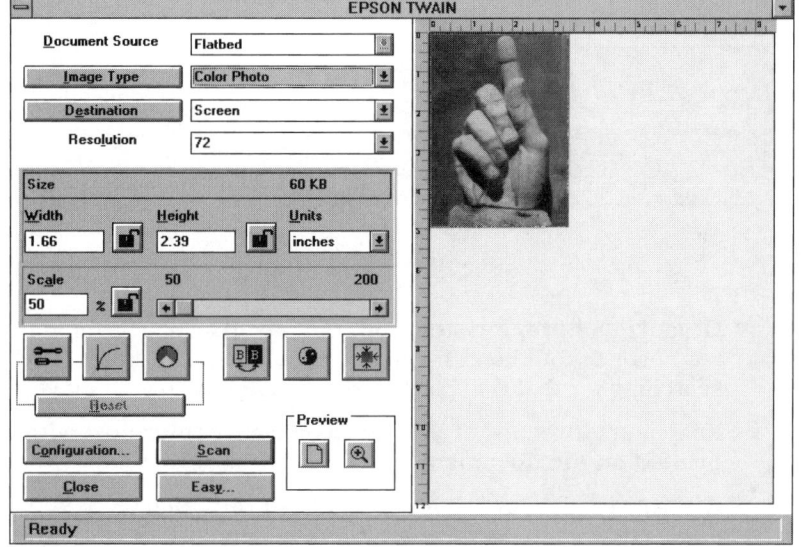

Figure 8-7: An example of the scanner twain driver dialog box.

- ✓ **Set scale percentages.** Look at Figure 8-9 for an example of this. You want the file height and width to match the final image specifications. Resize your file dimensions larger or smaller here. If you postpone this process until you export to your graphics program, the resized result may appear fuzzy, no matter how well you apply Unsharp mask or Sharpen filter settings. Resizing when you're scanning is always better.

- ✓ **Make a preview scan, and select the correct scan area.** Do your hard drive a favor by eliminating from the image any portions that you don't need. If you're not sure what to select, scan a full version and then a cropped variation. Doing so is a good thing if the original source print will not be on file in your area or is on loan for a short time. You may also want to scan a high-resolution version, too, just for your records.

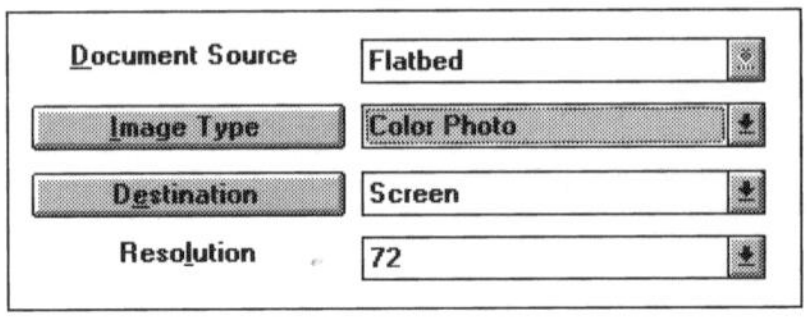

Figure 8-8:
A detail of the scanner twain dialog box showing Image Type, Destination, and Resolution scrolling menu lists.

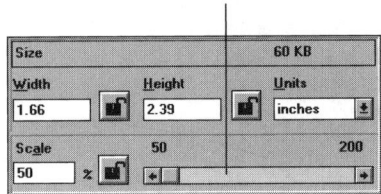

Figure 8-9: Scale slider for adjusting file width, height, and file size.

- ✔ **Organize a library system for your saved scans.** Scanning takes only a few seconds, but good file management can save hours often lost when searching for that one picture you absolutely have to have.
- ✔ **Keep a print record of your scans for easy reference with filenames printed on the document.**
- ✔ **Always respect copyrights.** Don't scan work that's not your own unless you have written permission. Maintain a record of all copyright images, trademarks, and logos that appear in your image. Give credit where credit is due, and you'll avoid those nasty letters from attorneys.

Getting Digital Photos Ready for the Web

The future is here. Digital cameras capture images that compete with traditional film processes. The photographs you see in many of the major national newspapers such as *USA Today* are shot with digital cameras. Digital photography enables a photographer on assignment to shoot pictures and then transmit them to editors via computer notebook or cellular hookup. Gone are the days when you will see photographers rushing to the airport to get a flight back to the office.

Chapter 8: Dynamic Photos   155

Three levels of digital cameras exist: point-and-click, mid-range, and high-end for advertising and annual report assignments. The low-end point-and-click variety is priced from about $500 to $1,200. Although the low-end variety is considered more suitable for insurance investigation, real estate marketing, and amateur photography, these cameras are great for capturing pictures for the Web. We list the Web sites of various digital camera companies in Appendix A.

In Figure 8-10 you can see an example of a *digital contact sheet,* or thumbnail versions of photographs that are stored in the camera's memory or on a PC storage card system (accessory). This contact sheet shows studio portrait and landscape photos shot by Flo Scott with the Agfa ActionCam, a professional mid-range camera. Figure 8-11 is a black-and-white reproduction of a color photo (which has not been retouched) from that contact sheet.

Digital cameras can capture in low (screen) and high resolutions (300 dpi and higher depending on the camera). If you plan to use a digital camera to capture pictures for your Web site, shoot in low resolution. Doing so saves time later because you don't have to resize your image's resolution to the lower screen setting of 72 dpi. You can also save more files to the camera's internal storage system if you shoot in low resolution.

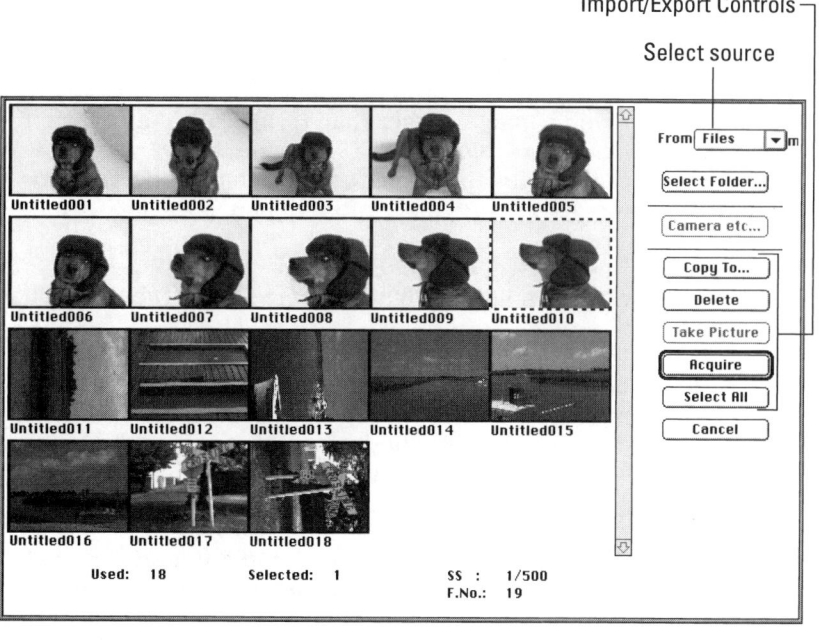

Figure 8-10: Contact sheet screen of Agfa ActionCam, a professional mid-range digital camera.

Figure 8-11: Dog with Hat, a digital photograph courtesy of Flo Scott at the Electronic Imaging Center in Boston.

Do shoot in both high and low resolution, if you may possibly have a print application for the pictures. You get a much better result when you reduce the resolution of an image, rather than trying to make a 72 dpi file work at 300 dpi. To increase resolution, your graphics software adds pixels to the image file, but the software cannot add the sharper detail that a true 300 dpi photo contains. As a result, more often than not you create an unusable, out-of-focus picture.

To prepare a high-resolution digital camera file for the Web, follow these suggestions:

- **Save a copy of the file.** Keep the original on file in a safe place, and consider making a CD-ROM backup for storage in a safe-deposit box. Think of all the 1996–97 flooding disasters along the Mississippi and Ohio Rivers. Removable media can be damaged by flood waters.
- **Before you resize the image, crop it and then do color correction.**
- **Convert the image from 300 dpi to 150 dpi, and then to 72 dpi.** You get a better result if you take two smaller steps to reduce resolution than one big step.

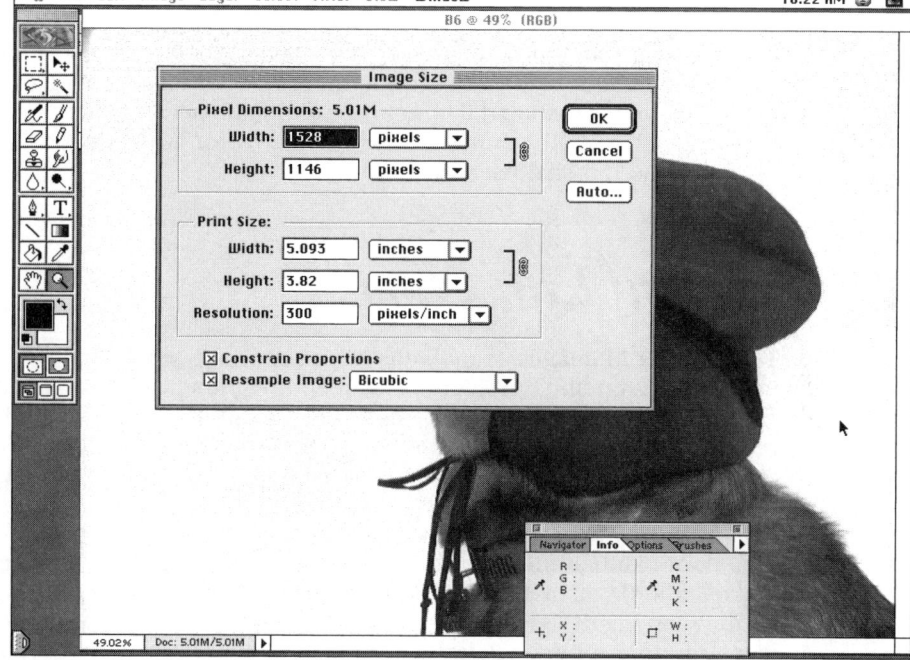

Figure 8-12: The file size of the ActionCam photo is 5.01MB. megabytes. Too large in size and resolution for the Web, but great for print.

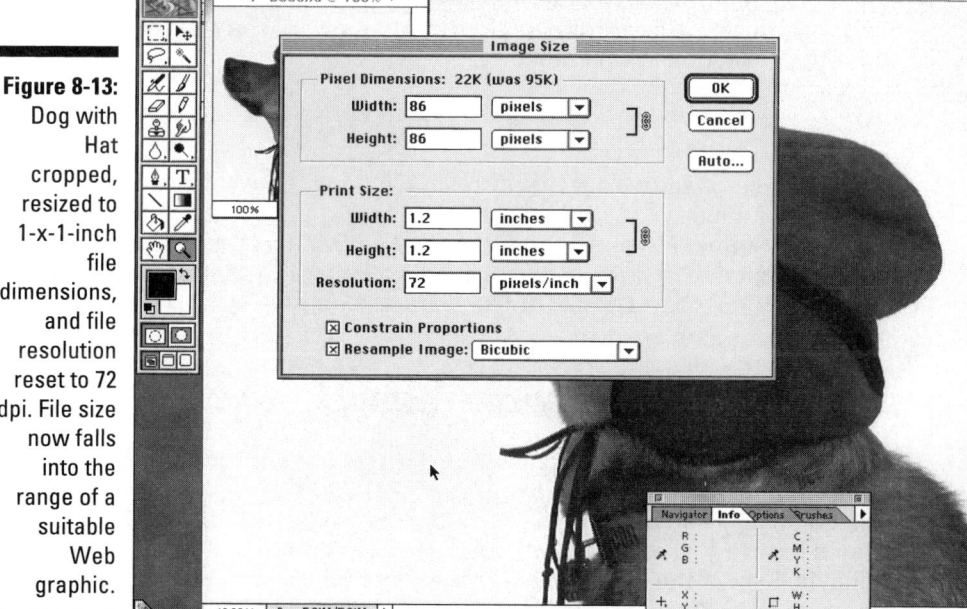

Figure 8-13: Dog with Hat cropped, resized to 1-x-1-inch file dimensions, and file resolution reset to 72 dpi. File size now falls into the range of a suitable Web graphic.

✔ **After you resize the image, apply Unsharp mask to sharpen the image.** (For this step we reference Adobe Photoshop 4.0.) Use the settings 100, 1, 1 in the Image Size dialog box. Remember that we're talking about screen resolution here. Look at Figures 8-12 and 8-13. Here are two Photoshop 4.0 Image Size dialog boxes showing how small the original image becomes when we resize it for Web use (cropped, reduced dimensions and resolution).

Millions You Can Choose

The number of images available is awesome, and we mean *awesome!* Even if you set up your slide projector and keep it running 24 hours a day for 7 days a week — projecting every photograph you can find — you would never reach the light at the end of the imaginary tunnel. Easy access to millions and millions of film-based images stored in photographic and picture archives is quickly becoming a reality.

Type font manufacturers and clip art suppliers led the way, showing how to make a bundle of cash distributing and repackaging their library of products digitally on CD-ROMs. Stock photography agencies, internationally recognized photographers, magazine publishers, and news services jumped on the bandwagon and began the enormous task of converting their existing film-based images into digital image database libraries. How big is this market? Just ask Bill Gates. He added the Bettmann Collection, the largest commercial historical and news photo archive with more than 16 million images, to Corbis, the editorial archive that he owns. You can read more about the collection at this URL:

```
www.corbis.com/corbis/image_catalog/bettmann/
```

Image providers realize that the system of loaning their film negatives and positives for a fee is a dying standard. The new standard is digital! As more and more graphic designers and other communication industry players move to a total digital workflow — converting an idea to a final printed piece or for posting on the Web — the use of film transparencies is fast becoming old hat.

Licensing and usage fees

Companies who produce stock photo CD-ROMs are in an intense rivalry with each other for shelf space in computer stores and catalog listings. Because each company is attempting to gain a leg on its competition, no clearly defined industry rules for royalty fees, copyright notifications, or pricing are available. Expect the price you pay for a CD-ROM to vary from company to company. A CD-ROM disc can cost as little as $39.95 to license 100 images,

Chapter 8: Dynamic Photos

or as much as $800 for a 4-volume set. Because the Web is a whole new arena for these companies, Web photo usage fees will continue to fluctuate until the market develops pricing standards.

Stock photo companies, whose markets were in the graphic arts, advertising, and design, are still developing their pricing and policy structures for Web usage. They are trying to strike a balance between the needs of the photographers they represent and the demands of Web developers for sensible pricing and licensing agreements.

Tony Stone Images, as an example, provides royalty-free, low-resolution image files for use in preliminary layouts and in-house presentations. For final artwork, the company provides a high resolution file and a *license to use* contract with fees priced according to the extent of usage. This system has been the standard practice established by the members of the Picture Agency Council of America. The Web has thrown a monkey wrench into the works, however. Low resolution is the standard for the Web, so things have become much more complicated. Ultimately, you benefit from shopping around to find the best deal.

Images in collections may be royalty-free, but this status does not mean that ownership of the images is transferred to the end user at the time of purchase. Refer to Chapter 7 for more information on this topic.

File formats and file sizes

The features of photographic archives vary from company to company. Images per CD-ROM volume can be as few as 45 or as many as 400. The number of images that appear on a CD-ROM depends on these factors:

- Color and grayscale file formats
- Image sizes
- Default resolutions
- Compression methods
- Number of files and resolutions

For example, in the Digital Stock collection (samples of which are on the accompanying CD-ROM), each disc contains 100 images from a specific category. All discs are Mac, PC, and Unix compatible. The images are drum-scanned and stored in Photo CD format in five different resolutions ranging from 72K to 24MB.

The file sizes provided for each image are as follows:

128 x 192 pixels	72K
256 x 384 pixels	288K
512 x 768 pixels	1.13MB
1,024 x 1,536 pixels	4.5MB
2,048 x 3,072 pixels	18MB RGB or 24MB CMYK

Although other companies may support Kodak's Photo CD-ROM formats or offer photographs saved as TIFF or JPEG file formats using the RGB color system (see Chapter 5 for more on RGB), make sure that you request technical specifications before you purchase a CD-ROM. Otherwise, the image parameters may not accommodate your software application, hardware configuration, or project specifications.

If you purchase files in the Kodak Photo CD-ROM format, make sure that the original photos were drum-scanned to make the image file. *Drum-scanning* creates higher-quality digital image files than the standard Kodak Photo CD-ROM scanning methods. The drum-scanned images have better color fidelity to the original source print, transparency, or slide, and are sharper in detail.

Download time for a high resolution picture from the Web to your hard drive varies. Download time is impacted by the usual Web pipeline problems. An average time for a 10MB (compressed) image, using a 28.8Kbps modem, is 15 minutes. Using a T1 line reduces download time to less than a minute.

What's out there

Software developers such as Corel and MetaCreations find that the distribution of digital image collections is a natural extension to their software product lines. MetaCreations features MetaPhotos, thousands of high resolution, royalty-free CD-ROM photographs. MetaPhotos covers such subjects as textures, holidays, hot rods, professions, religious icons, and everyday objects. The files

- Feature built-in alpha channel masks and clipping paths (Alpha channel masks and clipping paths are discussed in Chapter 9).
- Have transparent backgrounds for see-through effects when you overlay photo object images on your chosen background.
- Are fully retouched.

Chapter 8: Dynamic Photos   161

These features are a real production time-saver. Look for them in the object photo collections you buy. In Chapter 9 we describe how you can use these ready-to-use channels and clipping paths to convert a photo image into flat 2-D clip art.

Because new titles are coming onto the market in greater frequency, check regularly with publishers and with the catalog companies listed in Chapter 7. We also list companies that offer stock and clip photography collections in Appendix A. You can find samples from companies such as Digital Stock and D'pix on the CD-ROM, so check this out, too.

Playing with Effects and Filters

Graphics and imaging programs offer a wealth of effects and filter options for customizing your photographs. Because you want to keep your Web graphics and animation file sizes as small as possible, use these options with caution. Each time you reprocess your image file by applying an effect or filter, you add a little more information to your file's coding, which your computer follows for displaying your file on screen. The more filtering you do, the bigger the file grows, and the longer it takes to download. Also, some effects that work well in high-resolution printed documents can't be seen at screen resolution. It's all in the details; can you really see them?

That said, here are two for you to try, Feather and Cutout. Applying these to your photos offers you stylistic alternatives to the standard rectangular realistic photographic look.

Feathering an edge in Photoshop 4.0

Sometimes that old hard-edged rectangle sticks out like a sore thumb. As an alternative, you can create a soft-edged vignette. Don't use this effect for your moving parts. Instead, apply this effect to a background, or to a close-up shot that contains an isolated area that's moving — like a portrait with moving eyelids. Here's how to set up a soft-edged vignette in Photoshop 4.0 by using the Feather and Marquee tools.

1. **Open file** Chap08\RmanFin1.PCX **from the CD-ROM.**

   You will use the Marquee tool — the elliptical shape — to select the area you need.

2. **In the toolbar, double-click on the Marquee tool icon, shown in Figure 8-14.**

Double-click here to open
Marquee Options dialog box

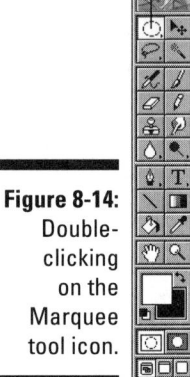

Figure 8-14: Double-clicking on the Marquee tool icon.

The Marquee Options dialog box appears, as shown in Figure 8-15.

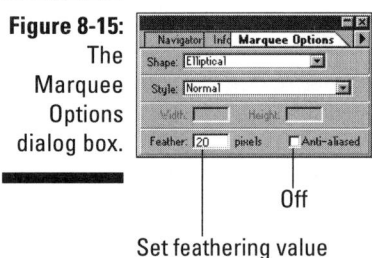

Figure 8-15: The Marquee Options dialog box.

Set feathering value   Off

3. **In the Marquee Options dialog box, set the Feather option to 20 pixels, and deselect the Anti-aliased check box.**

4. **Position the cursor on the image area and draw an oval selection.**

5. **Inverse your selection.**

6. **Create a new layer, and then fill your selection with white.**

   As you can see in Figure 8-16, the large feathering value creates a soft edge around the carved hand.

7. **Close the Marquee Options dialog box.**

   To close this dialog box, click on the box in the top right corner marked with an X (Windows) or top left corner (Macintosh).

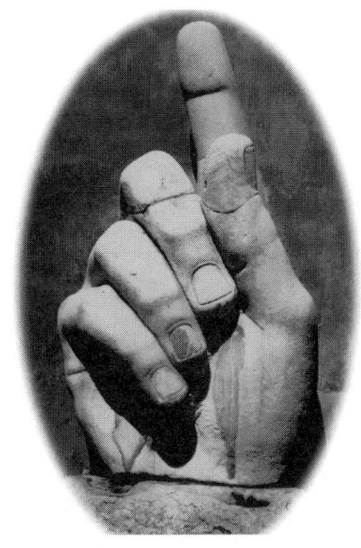

Figure 8-16: Caesar's hand in a vignette.

Corel PHOTO-PAINT 6.0 artistic vignette effect

If you're using Corel PHOTO-PAINT 6.0, creating a vignette is as easy as one, two, three. Select Effects⇨Artistic⇨Vignette from the menu. The Vignette dialog box opens, as shown in Figure 8-17. By moving the sliders, you can change the shape of your vignette. The higher the Offset number, the smaller the vignette becomes. The higher the fade number, the softer the edge effect becomes. If you want to use a color other than black or white, choose your color first and then open the Vignette dialog box.

Creating a cutout drawing

If you're tired of seeing soft-edged vignettes and would like to try another look, you can convert your photograph into a cutout drawing. Cutouts offer a simple flat-shape alternative to animating with a photograph. They're great when you need to use photos that have thumbnail-size dimensions. If you were creating a cutout drawing from scratch, you would worry about positioning and picking out the right color and shapes. The Cutout filter does all this for you by referencing the information in the photograph. Presto, chango — all those little shapes are positioned where they belong.

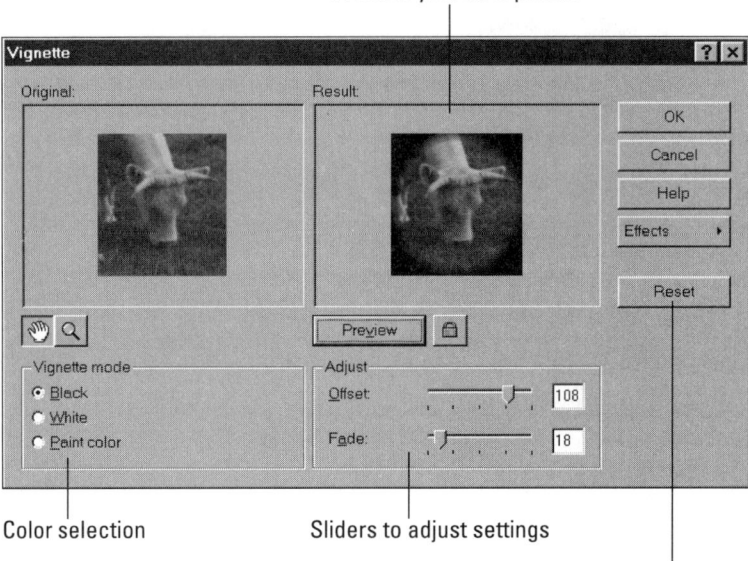

Figure 8-17: Corel PHOTO-PAINT 6.0 Vignette dialog box.

Creating a cutout in Photoshop 4.0

Here's how to create a cutout drawing in Photoshop 4.0:

1. **Choose Filter➪Artistic➪Cutout.**

   The Cutout dialog box appears. You can set your changes here, but the defaults work just fine. The preview window in the dialog box shows you what will happen (see Figure 8-18).

2. **Click OK to accept the changes.**

   The filter is now applied to your image.

For those who haven't upgraded to Photoshop 4.0, or for those who have a program that doesn't accept Photoshop filters, you can still try creating a cutout. Adobe Gallery Effects has Cutout as one of the filter options.

Creating a cutout using Microsoft Image Composer 1.0

Photoshop 4.0 is not the only program on the block to offer the Cutout filter. For those of you who use Microsoft Image Composer 1.0, try the following:

1. **Choose Tools➪Art Effects (Alt+7) from the menu.**

   The Art Effects dialog box opens.

Chapter 8: Dynamic Photos *165*

2. **From the Art Effects dialog box opens, select Graphic from the top left scroll-down menu.**

   In the same dialog box, the Graphic filter options appear in the menu list below the heading Graphic.

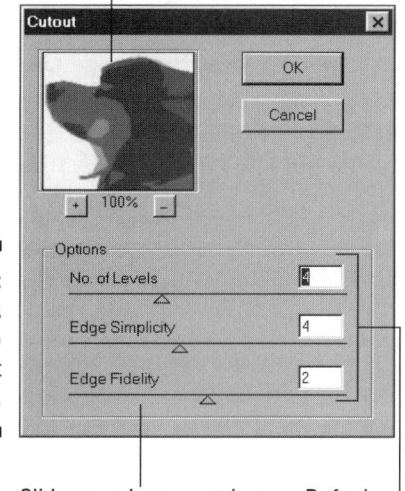

Preview window

Figure 8-18: A Photoshop 4.0 cutout dog.

Sliders to change settings   Defaults

3. **Scroll down until you see the word Cutout and then click to select it.**

   The Art Effects dialog box with the Cutout selection highlighted is shown in Figure 8-19.

Sliders to change settings

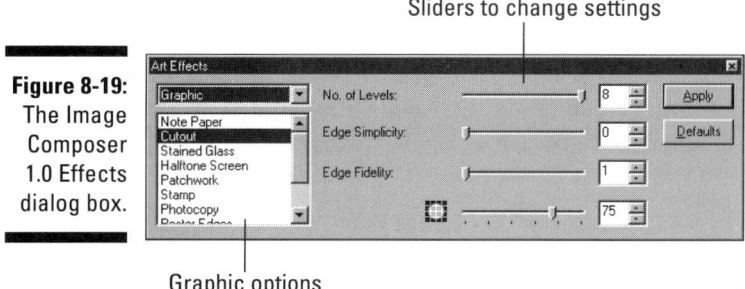

Figure 8-19: The Image Composer 1.0 Effects dialog box.

Graphic options

4. **Set the filter values by moving the sliders.**

   We found that the following settings gave us the best results for creating an abstract version of the dog photo shown in Figure 8-11:

   No. of Levels: 8

   Edge Simplicity: 0

   Edge Fidelity: 1

   Opacity: 75

5. **Click Apply to filter your image and to view the image changes.**

   If things don't look right, undo the changes (Ctrl+Z) first before trying another setting. Otherwise you'll be filtering on a previously filtered image. If you want to return to the default settings, select Default to reset.

Chapter 9
Universal Graphic Widgets

In This Chapter

▶ Using layers to create frames
▶ Working with grids to place objects
▶ Transforming your image
▶ Isolating action in an image
▶ Building clip art with channel masks

*I*f you compare the features of the most popular graphics and imaging programs, you'll find tools and command functions in common. In this chapter we highlight several features that we found universal to many, and very helpful for building the individual image frames of an animation.

On the CD-ROM that accompanies this book, you'll find demos of programs such as Adobe Photoshop and Corel PHOTO-PAINT. Take the time to try out those that you're not familiar with, and compare them all. You'll find out which program user interface and tool set best fits your style of working, and the projects you have to complete.

Building Frames: One Layer at a Time

The *layers* feature (some programs call this the *objects* feature) is a feature offered by many popular graphics and imaging programs. This feature is a cell animation tool par excellence that can save you umpteen hours of painstaking work. For this example we used Adobe Photoshop 4.0. Here's how the layers feature helped us create frames for the Windowshade animation (you can find these frames in Chapter 14, and on the CD-ROM in the \Chap14 folder).

The Windowshade animation shows an arm trying to pull down an uncooperative window shade. We used a simple but effective technique known as a *color cycle*, which keeps the action interesting. The background color in the room changes as the shade lowers, becoming cooler and darker. The entire action loop takes place in only ten frames.

Making these frames takes very little work if you plan carefully:

1. **Select <u>W</u>indow➪Show <u>L</u>ayers, or press F7.**

    Make sure that you keep the Photoshop Layers palette open as you work.

2. **Figure out what things are part of your background and what things need to move.**

    In our case, we need a different background for each color change. We also need an arm, a white window shade, a cord for the arm to pull the shade down, and enough of the window exterior to make what is happening clear. In Figure 9-1, we show the basic elements we use.

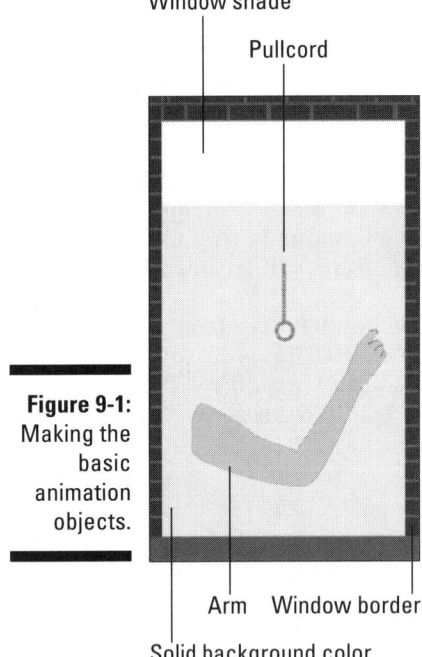

Figure 9-1: Making the basic animation objects.

3. **Create every basic element on a separate layer.**

    Merging two or more layers together if you want to composite an image is easy. *Compositing* is when you combine elements or objects from different files into one image. Separating elements is much harder after they're flattened. If you keep everything on a separate layer, you also make it easier to create alternates, or to make a change if you get a brainstorm while working.

Take the time to name your layers as you make them, or rename them if you make copies. The preview in the layers window is too small to show subtle differences and small objects. If you stop working for a few days, you may not remember the difference between *Layer 6, Layer 6 copy,* and *Layer 6 copy copy,* unless you have a sharper memory than we do, of course! In Figure 9-2, we describe our parts and how we plan to use them. Notice that we've also tried to visually group our alternates together, whenever possible.

Figure 9-2: Organizing the Layer window with individual elements grouped so that they can be found easily.

4. **Make alternate layers for major changes.**

   Some objects need to be scaled, rotated, or even redrawn to fit your action. Here's a general guideline: If it will take you more time to re-create a change than it will take to add the change to your Layer window, create a new layer. You can always delete extra layers when you're sure that you no longer need them, or export them to a new file for safekeeping, if your basic file is getting too large.

5. **Use layers to onion-skin correct new positions.** Refer to Chapter 4 for more information about this animation technique.

Setting up a new frame is easier if you can still see the old frame. Use layers like virtual tracing paper. Figure 9-3 shows Frame 2 and Frame 3 of the animation on the left. The image on the right shows how we used Frame 2 to help us position the arm for Frame 3. Find the *ghost*, a lighter version of Frame 2 in the frame on the right. A ghost of the previous or next frame is what you reference to onion-skin a new animation position. In the Layers palette, just click the eye icon off and on in the new layer to watch the motion between the two frames.

 6. **Use the Move tool to correctly position your objects or visual elements.**

    Work with View⇨Show Grid, or Show Guides, if you need help aligning things. Refer to the "Grid for Action" section in this chapter for more information.

 7. **Before saving a copy of individual layers as one frame of animation, turn off all elements that you don't need.**

    Do so by hiding an object's layer. Click on the Eye icon, the icon disappears, and the object no longer appears in the image window for this animation frame.

 8. **Save a copy as a new file.**

    Never use Save or Save As when making animation frames. As we mention in this chapter's gray-shaded sidebar, "The Save Hours of Time Photoshop command," use the Photoshop Save a Copy function to save all your animation's artwork. Figure 9-4 shows the Save a Copy dialog box. Notice that you can automatically eliminate channels and layers.

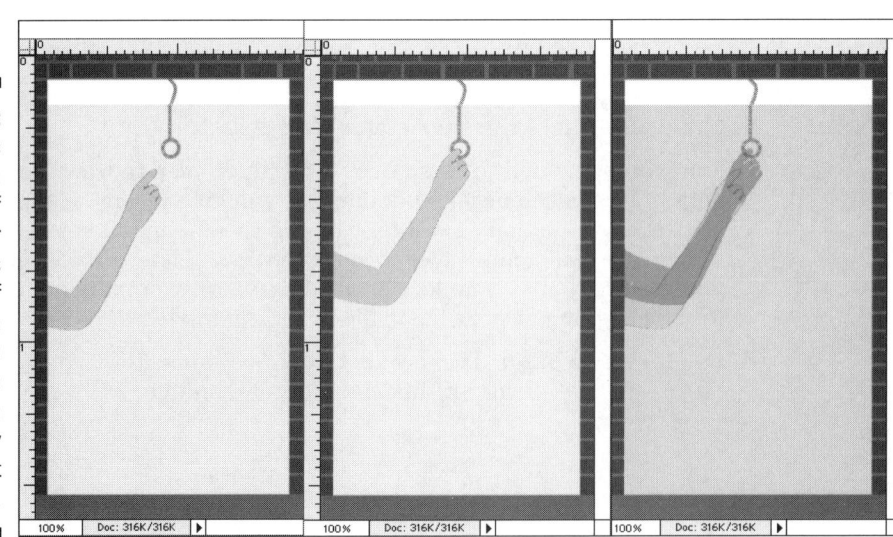

Figure 9-3: Using layers to turn a ghost of your previous frame off and on helps you position them correctly the first time.

Chapter 9: Universal Graphic Widgets 171

Figure 9-4: The super-versatile Save a Copy function makes creating animation frames fast and easy.

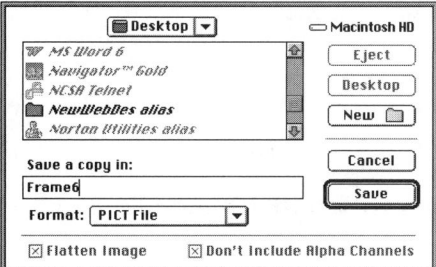

You won't be able to save your file in GIF format with the Save a Copy function, unless you've been working in Indexed Color Mode. Consider using BoxTop Software PhotoGIF to get around this difficulty. With this useful tool, you can use Save a Copy to index your file and save it in GIF format — in one step.

Grid for Action

Not every animation program supplies a Registration tool in its bags of tricks. The tool is used to set a common reference point for all the animation's frames or cels. If you're eager to build a smooth running 2-D animation, you need to work with a common x- and y-coordinate registration point. Even if your animation program has a Registration tool, show your graphics program grid function. Doing so makes it easier for you to scale your animated objects, position them along an accurate line of action, and lock into a single point of reference when the grid is turned on. Take a look at Figures 9-5 and 9-6. You can see how we use the Photoshop 4.0 grid function to align the moveable arm of the backhoe. You can find a sample copy of this image, created by Lonnie Springer, in the Dynamic Graphics folder on this book's CD-ROM.

After planning out your animation storyboard, customize your grid to fit your sequence of moves. Set grid guidelines and subdivisions in your graphics program Preferences dialog boxes. You also may find that marking out the layout positions on a temporary new layer to be helpful. This concept is similar to placing strips of tape on a stage to guide actors as they perform their scene.

172 Part II: Tricks with Pix

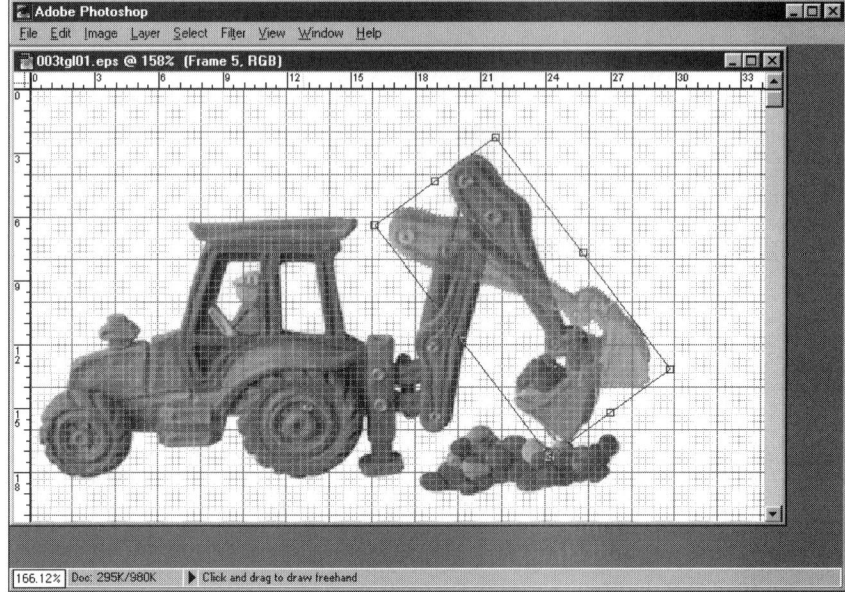

Figure 9-5:
Using a grid to help align rotated or other transformed selections.

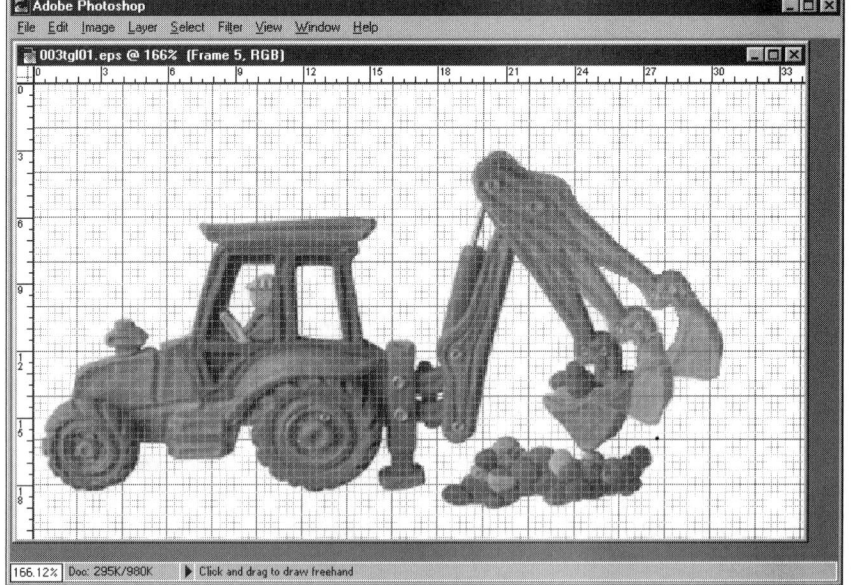

Figure 9-6:
Grid out the different stages of animated movement.

Transforming Multiple Objects from One Source

The Transform tools we describe here are an important part of your arsenal for building complex, dynamic, and more visually seductive animations. If you are not that well acquainted with these graphics program features, we suggest that you set aside time to experiment with them. Working with tools like Perspective and Distortion can be intimidating at first, but you'll discover that the more you try things, the more easily you can show flow, momentum, and anticipated action in your animation. As you read through Chapters 3 and 4, where we discuss animation fundamentals, think about how you can apply these transform tools to your advantage.

Here are the basic Transform tools you'll find in a graphics or imaging program:

- **Scale:** An image can be scaled vertically and horizontally (locking proportional ratio) or along either the x-axis (horizontal) or y-axis (vertical).
- **Skew:** This tool is also called *shear* in some programs. It slants an object along an axis you specify.
- **Rotate:** This tool changes the position of an object relative to a single point of reference that you choose.
- **Perspective:** This tool creates foreshortened objects. *Foreshortening* is a drawing technique used to suggest the illusion of 3-D in a 2-D image.
- **Flip and Flop:** This tool changes an image's orientation by using either its vertical or horizontal axis.
- **Applying Distortions:** Doing this to an object can suggest squash and stretch, a basic animation technique.

These transformations, except Flip and Flop, can be achieved by dragging a bounding box control point to a new position or by numeric entry in a dialog box. If you use Numeric Entry, you can keep track of your settings by saving a screen capture of the dialog box.

Remember to make a back-up copy before you modify anything. That way you're sure that you can return to the original, if you don't like any changes you've made.

Lifting a Finger: Creating Isolated Action in Your Image Area

Using photographs in an animation can be more than flipping back and forth between two pictures in an advertising banner. You may want to try to make only a small portion of your photograph animated, for starters. This animation technique is a real bonanza for those situations in which you want action, but are worried that your site visitor may be impatient and have a fast mouse-clicking finger. In the following steps, you combine one photograph with several very small moving parts. File sizes remain small, and you offer that quick hit of humor.

1. **On the CD-ROM, find file** `RmanFing.PCX` **in the** `\Chap09` **folder and then save it to your hard drive.**

2. **Open the file in your favorite paint or imaging program and save the file as a new name** `Romanf` **in your program's native file format.**

   You use this file to build your animation frames.

3. **Select and delete the background.**

   We've already removed the original background for you to make this process easier. As shown in Figure 9-7, you see the original photograph of Caesar's hand, and our version of the image with a solid color background.

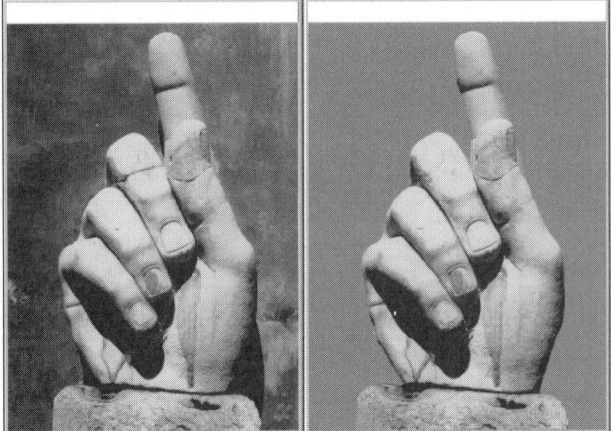

Figure 9-7: Caesar's hand, pointing the way.

4. **Select the background, and invert the selection so the whole hand is selected.**
 5. **Save this selection as channel mask #4, as shown in Figure 9-8.**
 6. **Trim this selection with your program's selection tools until only the index finger is still selected.**
 7. **Save this selection as channel mask #5.**

    You can see a channel mask in Figure 9-9.

 8. **Move the selected index finger to a new layer named Index, and shift the layer down below the rest of the hand.**
 9. **Copy the small pieces to the left and right of the thumb to the Index layer.**

    See Figure 9-10 to view small pieces selection, channel mask #9.

 10. **Using a Cloning or Rubber Stamp Tool, fill in the missing portion of the finger — the part that was once covered by the thumb.**

     See Figure 9-11, which shows which portions of the finger we cloned and the finished result.

 11. **Make a new selection of the edited index finger.**
 12. **Save the selection.**

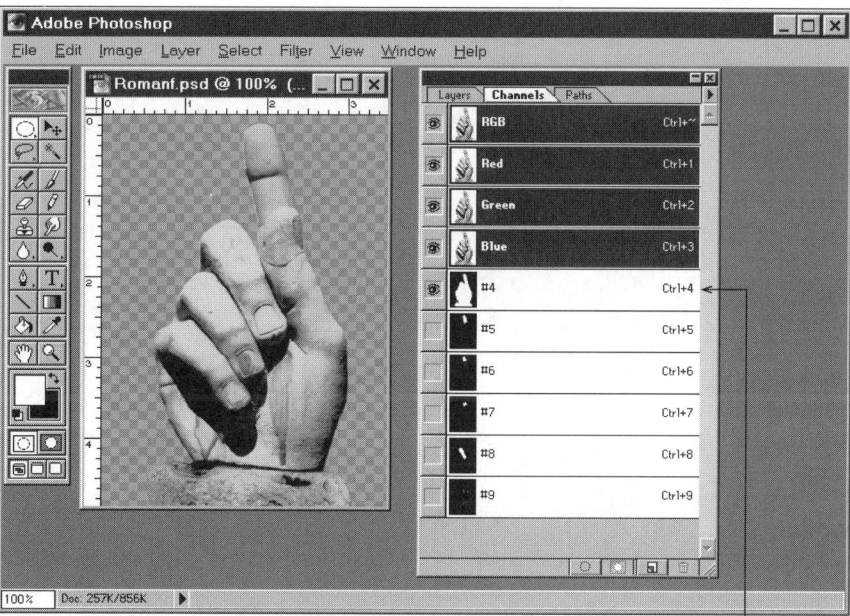

Figure 9-8: Putting the whole hand to work.

Channels showing masked areas

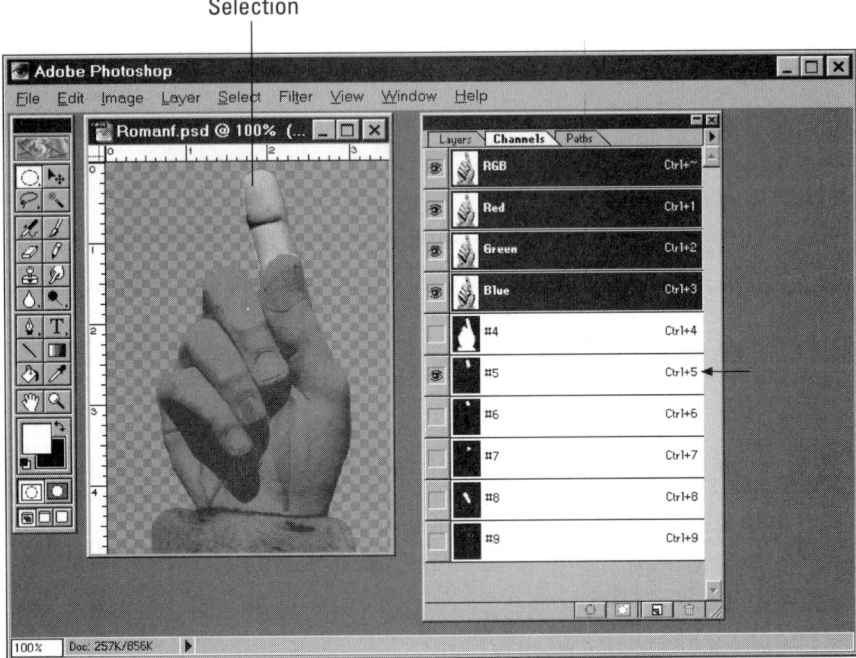

Figure 9-9: The index finger joins in.

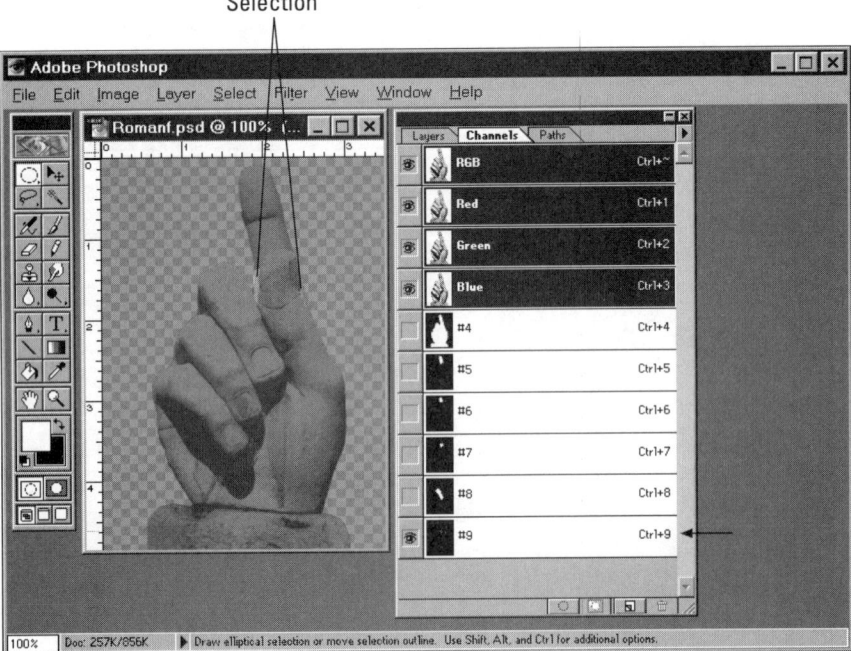

Figure 9-10: Picking up the pieces.

Chapter 9: Universal Graphic Widgets *177*

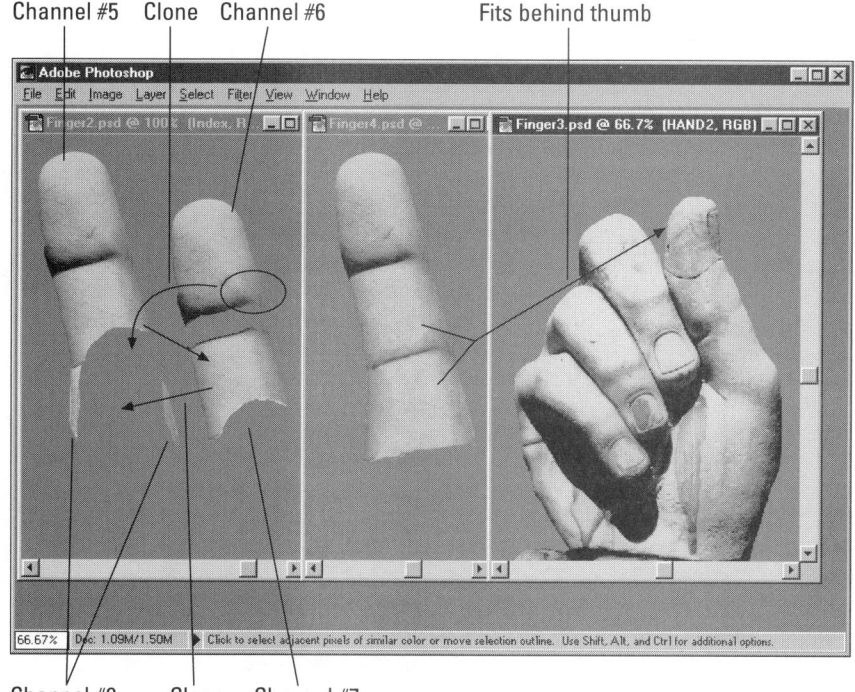

Figure 9-11: Cloning a whole finger.

13. **To add complexity to your animation, make the middle finger a selection.**

    As shown in Figure 9-12, the middle finger is saved as channel mask #8. Create the bent version of the index finger from the middle finger.

14. **Save what you have so far, and then print it.**

    If your program offers you the option, print the image with a 1-point border to make it easier to work with.

15. **Trace the starting position of the hand onto a separate piece of paper.**

    For more details on storyboarding and developing an animation, refer to Chapters 4 and 5.

16. **Using layers of tracing paper, draw your frames to make the index finger rotate in a circle.**

    Exaggerate the forward rotation of the finger slightly so that the animation actually looks like a rotating finger, not just one moving side to side.

178 Part II: Tricks with Pix

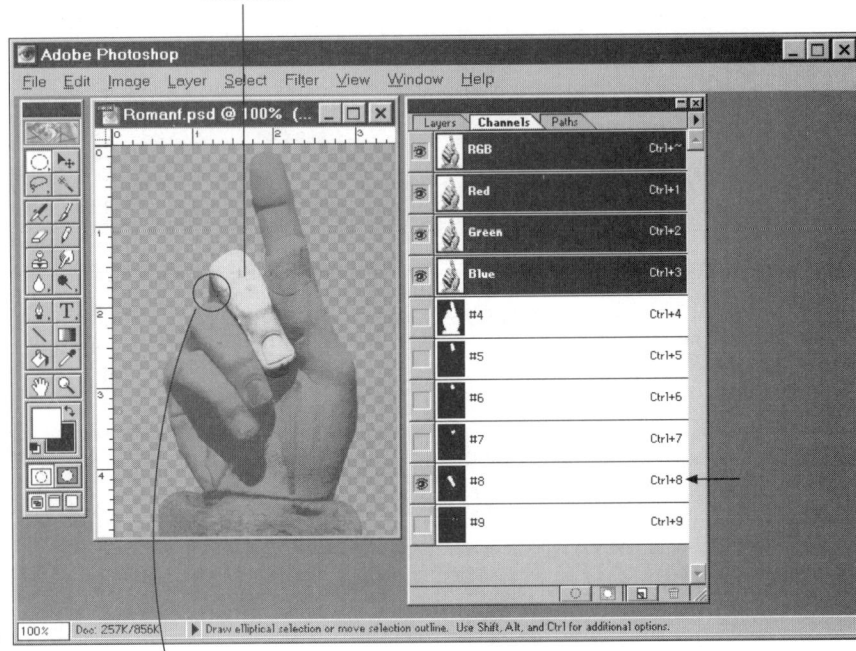

Figure 9-12:
It's all in the family. The middle finger to the rescue.

17. Return to the image on the computer and reload the index finger mask selection.

18. Make a copy of the finger and then place the copy on another layer.

19. Armed with your sketches, move the new finger to match your first sketch.

    Show a Grid, and apply the Transform tools to help you to lay out your animation frames. We review these topics earlier in this chapter.

20. Continue repeating Steps 18 and 19 until you have finger versions of all the different stages.

21. When you're satisfied with the finger versions, use the program's Save a Copy function to convert the individual layers to separate files of the motion.

22. Continue creating copies at different stages and then import them into your favorite animation program.

The Save Hours of Time Photoshop command

In Photoshop, besides the standard Save As command, you can also use a truly awesome command called Save a Copy, which should probably be called *Save Hours of Time*. This command lets you create a flattened, GIF89a-ready image without having to ever close or reopen an original layered file.

To *Save a Copy* of one layer, do the following:

1. **Hide all the other layers first.**
2. **Choose Save a Copy from the File menu.**
3. **As seen in Figure 9-4, in the dialog box, choose Flatten Image and Don't Include Alpha Channels.**
4. **Rename your file and click OK.**
5. **Open your new file and then choose File⇔Export⇔Export to GIF89a.**

Before you name your image files, check the animation program you'll use for special file naming or numbering conventions. You need to be able to import all the files at one time, and in the right order. Most animation programs have this option, but the precise way to word the files varies.

Metamorphosing Photos into Clip Art

In the previous section, you find out how to build *alpha channels,* the additional channels in an RGB color image for making and storing masks. An RGB image has three default channels; one for each color and a composite channel. These additional channels, starting with channel #4, are also a great source for creating 2-D clip art silhouettes. Create a new variation of your animation where your animated file's dimensions and size can be critical. For example, you can use the masks created in Figures 9-8, 9-11, and 9-12 to build another version of our wiggling index finger. Here's how you can convert the masks to new art files in these three graphics programs: Photoshop 4.0, PHOTO-PAINT 6.0, and Image Composer 1.0.

In Adobe Photoshop 4.0:

1. **Open a file that has an alpha-channel mask or clipping paths saved with the file.**
2. **Select Window⇔Show Channels.**

3. **In the Channel Window, select your channel mask (#4).**

   The channel mask is visible in the image window.

4. **Select and copy the channel mask to a new file.**

5. **In the new file, fill the selection with foreground color by choosing Edit⇨Fill.**

   You can also press Option+Backspace (Macintosh), or Alt+Backspace (Windows).

6. **Save the file again.**

In Corel PHOTO-PAINT 6.0:

1. **Open a file that has an alpha-channel mask or clipping paths saved with the file.**

2. **Select Mask⇨Save⇨Save to Disk.**

3. **In the Save to Disk dialog box, rename the file, choose your image file format, and then click OK.**

In Microsoft Image Composer 1.0:

1. **Open a file that has an alpha-channel mask or clipping paths saved with the file.**

2. **Select Edit⇨Copy Channel⇨Alpha.**

3. **Choose Edit⇨Paste into a new file.**

   You can also use Ctrl+V.

4. **To fill the mask-created object with color, choose Tools⇨Patterns and Fills.**

   You can also press Alt+5.

5. **Save file.**

Part III
Heavy Lifting: Making Technology Work for You

In this part . . .

No matter what material you're using to make your animation, it must be massaged into a form that browsers can understand and modems can handle. This part concentrates on the technical steps you must take to ensure that your frames are truly Web-ready: palette issues, file format converting, and strategies for browser compatibility-checking.

Chapter 10
The Skinny on Image Size

In This Chapter

▶ Understanding bandwidth
▶ Shrinking image size
▶ Cropping multiple image frames
▶ Losing resolution
▶ Avoiding unsafe colors

Today, we think nothing of scanning multi-megabyte pictures purely for fun. "Hand me another Zip disk and watch my dust," we chortle. Working on graphics for the Web is something like dropping into a time vortex. Go back to the days when Microsoft Excel was still trying to catch up with Lotus, when presidents were made of Teflon, and when we all worried about inflation. Return to a world where 256 was a lot of colors, and the only monitor bigger than a 14-inch was a TV. Go back — to our future animation.

It's true, Web animation is still limited by technology. Because of this limitation, a lot of emphasis is placed on making things small for Web consumption. Many miniaturization strategies focus on converting files for use in an animation program. We discuss this too, in Chapter 11. In this chapter, we start with things that you can do while you're still creating your frames.

Lessons in Economy

You may not pay much attention to politics, but you probably remember how much the media made of Bill Clinton's famous campaign mantra, "It's the economy, stupid!" Supposedly this line was pasted all over campaign headquarters to keep the troops focused on the number-one issue. We don't presume to compare Web animation to the finances of the United States — well, maybe we do. So we say to you, fellow Web site makers, "It's economy, animators!" Economy of size, that is. Anything you can do to make your animation frames download quickly and painlessly will make your Web site more successful, even if you never have coffee in the White House.

What's wrong with big?

Sometimes big is good. Big chocolate desserts, big pizzas with everything on them, big merit raises, big snowstorms when you haven't finished a term paper — the list is long. Unfortunately, big Web animations aren't on the list. The day may come when everyone accesses the Web via satellite or underground cable, and size restrictions will go the way of polyester pants. Today, however, we are constrained by bandwidth.

Bandwidth? Yes, we're sneaking in another technical term. This one is now thrown around in polite conversation, so we treat it gently and send it on its way. When people refer to *bandwidth*, they're talking about the Internet's capacity to handle user traffic: e-mail, Web sites, downloads, animations — everything that shares a common set of cables, wires, and computers.

The bandwidth equation has four basic components: your connection to the Internet, your target site's connection to the Internet, the gateways between you, and the amount of usage at the time you're attempting to connect. We illustrate this with a nontechnical analogy.

Imagine that your Internet connection is a ten-lane highway at rush hour. Ten lanes is a fairly large road, and its capacity for normal traffic is considered more than adequate. Imagine that you're on this road, traveling in your nice red Jaguar. You're passing every other car on the road, and you're feeling pretty good.

Then imagine a brand new mall near this highway is your target Web site. You, and thousands of other cars, want to visit it. To get off the highway, everyone has to negotiate a two-lane exit ramp, and at the end of the exit ramp is a traffic light. The ramp merges with another local road that is the only feeder to the mall itself.

When you get to the mall, you discover that you're competing for the scarce parking spaces. It seems like everyone wants to use this site! After circling madly, you park and head for the store that has what you want. Oh, no! At the gateway entrance are dozens of tall, elegantly dressed employees with long fingernails and spray bottles of expensive perfume. You know that you're going to have to run this obstacle course, even though all you need is two pairs of socks and a new sweater. Fortunately, besides owning a Jag, you are also the bouncer at an expensive nightclub and former marathon racer. You politely take all their samples, promise to check them out, and throw them in the trash as soon as you can.

What you've just experienced is what happens when any one of the four bandwidth variables is in trouble. Ultimately, your Web surfing experience is going to be affected by whatever is the lowest common denominator in the experience. You're better off with a fast connection, but once you hit a busy Web site, the speed of your connection isn't worth much. It comes down to the breadth of the band leading to and from your target site, and the number of incoming connections the site can accept. With so many obstacles between Web surfers and their goals, creating large, beautiful animations on your site is not a friendly thing to do.

Chapter 10: The Skinny on Image Size

As in any campaign, there are trade-offs. Anything you do to add zip to your animation is likely to result in cutting something else. Some of those cuts will be completely painless. No one will notice them, not even you. Others may force you to change your ideas slightly, but are probably worth the effort. Where will you have to make your cuts?

Image size

Wouldn't you rather see your work running on a full screen instead of in a tiny corner of a frame? This is every Web animator's unrealized fantasy. Web animations, to be small in bandwidth, must often be small in size, too.

Here's one little loophole: If you are only planning on showing one animation on a page, and the animation uses a small color palette with very few frames (six or seven) that simply loop back on themselves, you may be able to justify keeping your animation a bit larger. Bear in mind that the relationship between the number of frames and size of frames is an inverse relationship. More of one variable (colors, number of frames, size of frames) decreases the possible number for the others.

If you've been working on your animation at double, or more, of your finished frame size, use your image-creation program's capability to resize file dimensions to scale the animation down before conversion. Scaling is always necessary unless you are only creating objects for importing into a plug-in or Java applet animation. (These types of object-based programs allow you to scale individual or grouped objects, and don't require you to prepare your finished frames in advance.)

HTML enables you to set the window size for your animation at any horizontal or vertical combination, but this isn't the time to play with scaling on the fly. No matter what the apparent size, the computer downloading your animation opus will need to read every pixel at its real dimensions. Even with a fast connection, the download time on a large frame will make dripping molasses look like a running racehorse. Even worse, if your viewers don't have powerful computers, an animation that played smoothly for you may run unevenly for the viewers.

Be sure that you don't intentionally make your animation frames smaller with the plan of running them larger on the screen. Any increase in size of more than five percent will cause your animations to look jagged.

If you have a short animation, you can change the image size on all the frames, making sure that you have been absolutely consistent in each one. Consult the documentation for your image-creation software if you don't know how this is done. Don't try to scale the work down by 50 percent. If you are off by even one pixel, your animation will shake like Jell-O when it runs.

If you have a long animation, you need a program that will enable you to batch your changes. Image editing programs don't have this option. This is a job for a dedicated file manipulator, like Equilibrium's Debabelizer. We talk more about this program in Chapter 11, because we're tremendous fans of how easy Debabelizer makes image conversion.

Cropping

Cropping an image is not the same as resizing it. When you crop, you actually change the active area of the image by deleting parts of it. You'll want to crop if you have left too much white space around your action. Even if you are making your background transparent, any extra pixels in that background still stand up for a head count when file sizes are determined.

The cleanest way to crop a group of images is to drop them all into a program with layers, so that you can see where the pixel fat lies. Photoshop is perfect for doing this because it enables you to export each individual image as a layer. Some of the more complex animation programs also have multiple cropping functions. The following steps are the easiest and most satisfying way to crop, because you can see what you are doing at all times.

1. **Create a new file the same size as your current animation frames.**

    We've called our new file CropShop. Once you create this file, make sure that you keep it open so Photoshop can "see" it.

2. **Open all your animation frames in Photoshop.**

    Make sure that the frames are named with consecutive numbers; otherwise you may get confused and miss one frame or import one frame twice.

3. **With the first frame open, choose Duplicate Layer from the menu.**

    You can also do this by opening the Layer Window, clicking on the arrow for more choices, and choosing Duplicate. The Duplicate Layer dialog box in Figure 10-1 opens.

4. **In the Duplicate Layer dialog box, replace the words** `Background Copy` **with** `Frame`**, and add this image's identifying number to it.**

    Doing so enables you to keep track of which frame is on which layer. Because this is our first frame, our layer will be called Frame 1.

5. **In the Destination portion, go to the pull-down menu and choose CropShop (or whatever you have named your multi-layer file) and click the OK button.**

    Your frame has magically become the second layer of your master file.

    The first layer is always Background. You can delete the Background layer if you want to, after you create this new layer.

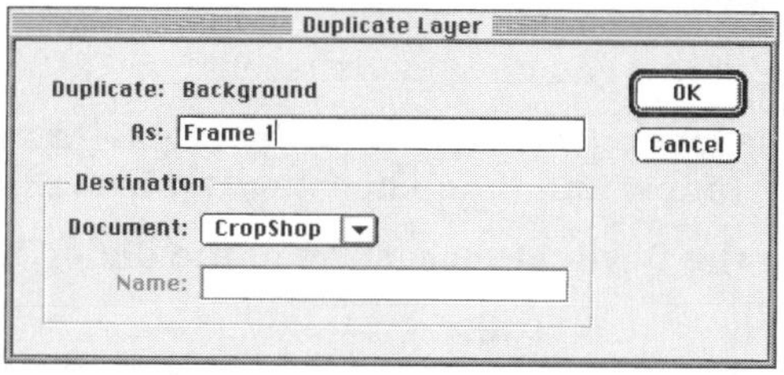

Figure 10-1:
The Duplicate Layer dialog box is about to create a clone of your frame number 1.

6. **Repeat Steps 1 through 5 for all of your frames.**

   After you finish, your Layer Window looks very much like Figure 10-2.

Figure 10-2:
The multi-layer file, with all frames overlaid and visible.

7. **Make sure that the Photoshop eye icon is next to all your frame layers, indicating that they are visible.**

   You don't want to miss a single pixel of actual image in this process!

8. **Zoom up to a size that enables you to see your multi-layer image without difficulty, but doesn't cut off the image.**

9. **Using the Crop tool, draw a box around everything you actually need in all the frames.**

   The Crop tool shown on the left is one of the multiple choices under the Marquee in the Tool Box. You can use the handle bars to adjust this selection.

10. **Once you're sure you've trimmed to exactly what you need, choose Image⇨Crop in the menu.**

    This may take a little time if you have many layers.

 11. **Now start playing the layer game in reverse by highlighting your first frame in the Layer Window and then choosing Duplicate Layer.**

 12. **Next, choose New in the Destination section of the dialog box, and then name the new file.**

 13. **Repeat Steps 11 and 12 until all the layers have been exported to files.**

Think twice before you use the same name for the altered frame as the original. Doing so replaces the old frame with the new one. If you miscalculate and crop out something you need, you lose the ability to repeat the process.

Losing your resolution

If you've done any work with printed graphics, clip art, or stock photography, or if you've been scanning and editing photos, you want to check your resolution settings on your animation frames. Chances are that you haven't changed your image-editing software's resolution since you scanned your other work. The software's preferences are probably defaulting to a resolution that's too high for your current Web publishing needs.

"So what?" you ask. Well, to answer that question, you need just a bit of information about resolution. *Resolution* measures the depth of visual information that the file contains. If too little resolution exists, your image will look jagged and grainy. If too much resolution exists, your image will look good — but it will swallow up megabytes of storage space without giving you anything in return. This phenomenon is kind of like a liberal arts major moving back home after graduation.

If you want to see how the difference in resolution can affect things, scan a photo at 72 dpi, and then scan it again at 150 dpi. Zoom the two files up to 200 percent and compare them. The low resolution image already begins to degenerate into pixel squares, whereas the high resolution image still looks like a continuous tone print.

Of course, if you're planning to print your images, they must be scanned and stored at a high resolution. That's because laser-printer output starts at 300 dpi and goes way up from there. We're going to assume that you've just backed up those big, beautiful files and put them away. Now it's time to head for the low-rent resolution district.

Chapter 10: The Skinny on Image Size 189

As you probably know if you've ever output an image downloaded from the Web, low resolution looks like a dog's dinner on a laser printout, even though it looks great on the screen. This happens because your monitor is more limited in what it can display than a printer is in what it can render. Given monitor limitations, there is no reason to hold extra information in Web graphics. So your Web graphics, be they flat art or photo images, should never be set at anything higher than screen resolution. This number varies between systems and monitors, but 100 dpi is the absolute best. Most work can be set to 72 dpi without any noticeable drop in quality on the screen.

Unlike most paint programs, Microsoft Image Composer takes its resolution directly from the most frequently used Windows monitor resolution of 96 dpi. This resolution is not changeable, which means that Image Composer is of limited use for printed output. Image Composer is a terrific time saver for Web work, however.

Fortunately for us, we can handle changing resolution in only so many ways. Most software reflects this by keeping size changes and resolution changes together in dialog boxes. For example, both Adobe Photoshop and Corel PHOTO-PAINT have an Image selection in the menu. This selection enables you to access both size and resolution changes at the same time. Here's how you alter resolution in Photoshop and PHOTO-PAINT:

1. **To change resolution in Photoshop, choose Image Size under the Image menu; in PHOTO-PAINT, choose Resample.**

   The Image Size dialog box features three separate variables: on-screen image size (measured in pixels), printed image size (measured in inches, or picas and points), and resolution. (See Figure 10-3.) You see a similar dialog box in the Corel PHOTO-PAINT Resample box.

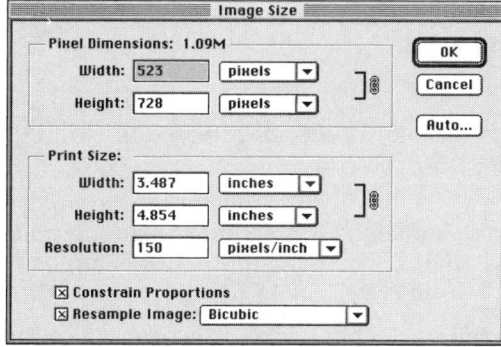

Figure 10-3: The Adobe Photoshop Image Size dialog box.

2. **Deselect the Resample Image check box at the bottom of the dialog box.**

   In PHOTO-PAINT, you select the Maintain Original Size instead.

3. **Take a good look at the two sets of dimensions for height and width (pixel dimensions and print size), change the resolution to 72 pixels/ inch, and click OK.**

   Yikes! Look at what happened to the print size in Figure 10-4. It's twice the size it was before, yet nothing has happened to the on-screen size. You want this to happen sometimes, but preparing frames for Web animation isn't one of them.

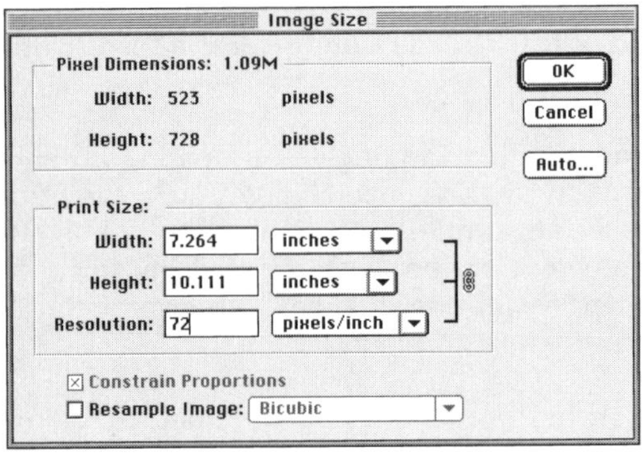

Figure 10-4: Image print dimensions after changing resolution without resampling.

Curious as to why this image growth took place? It's all in the Resample. When the software resamples the image, it looks at the image again. The software checks for and removes all the visual information that you don't really need to create the best new version of the image at a lower resolution. We prevented the Resample from happening. The software had to put all the extra information somewhere, so it spread the information out over a larger space.

We bet that you know what comes next.

4. **In Photoshop, choose Image⇨Image Size again; in PHOTO-PAINT, choose Resample.**

   The Image Size dialog box features three separate variables: on-screen image size (measured in pixels), printed image size (measured in inches, or picas and points), and resolution. (See Figure 10-4.) You see a similar dialog box in Corel PHOTO-PAINT.

5. **Enable the Resample Image check box at the bottom of the dialog box and click OK.**

   In PHOTO-PAINT, you select Maintain Original Size instead. The results appear in Figure 10-5.

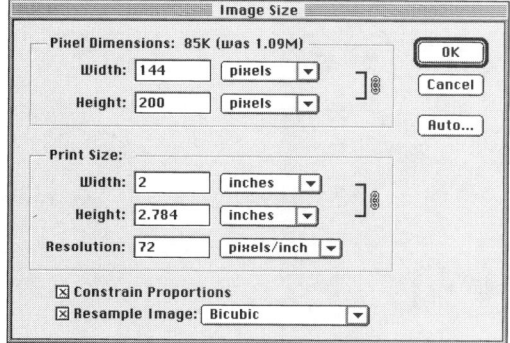

Figure 10-5: Image dimensions after resampling.

We maintain the print output size, but the file size and pixel dimensions reflect that the information is thrown out by lowering the resolution. The on-screen file is smaller because there's literally less to see.

Don't change the resolution on your files until you are sure that you've finished editing them, and that you've cropped or resized them as needed. Dropping the resolution means deleting information, whether you can see it or not. Without that information, your image-editing program may do a less-than-excellent job of resampling your file when it changes size. You'll get a distracting combination of fuzzy image and pixelation — those jagged, boxy edges we all hate. It is, however, okay to resize and *down-sample* — a fancy way to talk about decreasing the resolution — in the same step.

Unnecessary background detail

Many animations from photos are done by masking away all background material and focusing on a specific element. The background may be an important part of the animation sometimes, and can't be stripped away. If this is the case, look for opportunities to eliminate elements that distract from the animation and hinder image compression. These opportunities range from completely useless elements, like stray noise introduced by the scanner, to real background elements that add nothing to the overall image. We did this kind of judicious editing in Figure 10-6. This image, provided by Digital Stock, of an oil refinery has many details that look great in color print but will never be missed in a small Web animation. Even though your image size will stay the same, you'll have less variation in visual information. Your file sizes will ultimately squeeze down to make a zippy animation.

Figure 10-6: Photo before and after judicious editing.

Deleted rigging

Simplify, Simplify, Simplify

We haven't a clue about what Thoreau might have thought about the Internet. Probably he'd have hated the idea. Too much communication with people, too little time spent getting your hands callused, arms scratched by branches, and back stung by mosquitoes in the places you can't reach without help. On the other hand, he may not have been above giving good advice to animation frame makers: "Strip out the unnecessary. Get back to basics. Simplify!"

Have you already simplified your animations? Maybe you think so, or maybe while your right hand was doing spring cleaning, your left hand was visiting yard sales. When you're working away in an image-editing program, this is all too easy to do. Lurking within every tool, every filter, every simple alteration, is the possibility of a bloated, useless file.

Virtual zit prevention made easy

Ice cream, chocolate candy, and potato chips taste great, but treating them as a major food group isn't healthy. Your mom was probably always warning you that too much of these good-tasting things would lead to fat, flab, and a mountain of nasty pimples. So now that you live on yogurt and ration your splurges, you believe that those days are over.

Well, Mom's back to warn you about your animation files. We know that filters are tasty fun. Filters save time, they help you master effects you can never find time to do by hand, and they're handy. So you take your key frame and blur it a little, maybe throw in a little neon glow and other visual frosting. Before you know it, your little file has puffed up to twice its original size. "No problem!" you exclaim. "I'll just apply all those nifty shrinking strategies, and all will be well." Well, all isn't well. Your file refuses to shrink. You figure it will work out when you convert it in Chapter 11. Instead, your animation develops blotches in weird places. Colors shift. It's uuuuugleee.

The rule here is: Stay away from filters. Only use filters on photographic images, and never after you've already stripped down the image. Definitely don't use filters in separately drawn or scanned images that will need to be *in-betweened* (see Chapter 4) — unless you are creating a morph between the frames. Otherwise, your characters will appear to change colors, or develop distracting artifacts that appear and disappear.

If you work in Photoshop and are planning to create a simple GIF animation, change your Mode to Indexed Color and choose the Web palette option in the Indexed Color dialog box before changing an existing file. Indexed Color disables many tools and filters that create browser-unfriendly colors. We discuss browser-friendly color palettes in Chapter 5.

Anti-aliasing can be counterproductive

Filters aren't the only function that can balloon your file sizes, although they are the most blatant offenders. Many things that you may not consider to be special effects can lead to similar problems. In fact, anything that uses the principle of anti-aliasing can create problems for you down the road, especially if you're not aware of it while you're working.

In case you've always wondered but were afraid to ask, *aliasing* is the effect you get when two sharp edges of color or value collide on a diagonal or curve. You probably know them as the dreaded *jaggies*. Anti-aliasing diminishes or eliminates that effect by creating a buffer zone of transitional colors between the hard edges. Transitions are nice, but each additional color is added to the image's color palette. This isn't usually a problem, but when you've been working so hard to minimize that palette, you want your anti-aliasing to be part of a conscious decision.

 If you're working in Photoshop, be wary of unexpected anti-aliasing. Most of Photoshop's tools default to anti-aliased mode. Check each tool as you use it to make sure that anti-aliasing is disabled if you don't need it. For example, you may want to make a simple graphic with as few colors as possible. In Figure 10-7, we've done this two ways. The graphic on the left was created with these defaults turned off, and has only four colors in its palette: the background and three colors in the graphic itself. The one on the right uses the default settings, and has generated several additional colors — 64 to be precise — most of which are not on the Web-safe palette.

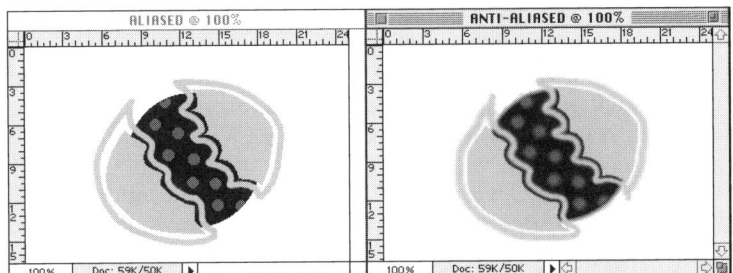

Figure 10-7: The beautifully anti-aliased image on the right has lots of extra colors to worry about.

Check out the Selection tool palette in Figure 10-8. The anti-aliasing check box is selected, and the tool is set to *feather*, which is a turbo-charged version of anti-aliasing. Deselect both anti-aliasing and feathering.

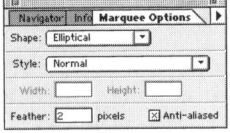

Figure 10-8: Deselect anti-aliasing and feathering in the Selection palette.

Some tools depend on being able to create new colors to make transitions. The Dodge and Burn tool, the Smudge tool, and the Spray Paint tool in Photoshop are examples. Use these tools if you must, but do so sparingly. You'll be surprised how much larger your finished files will be if you've started with a flat color and simply added a little spray paint for highlights. Remember that your files are likely to be small; the fact that they are moving means that little details will not add greatly to the viewers' experience.

Chapter 11
Mondo Conversion: Rehabbing Your Files

In This Chapter
- Figuring out which file format to use
- Understanding indexed color
- Converting files to GIF and JPEG
- Creating transparent backgrounds
- Shrinking strategies for individual and batched frames

Every once in a while, people get the urge for a makeover. Guys shave their beards or grow them, women get their hair dyed or restyled, and everyone responds to general fashion trends. Sometimes a makeover urge is sparked by the realization that you can't work in an office wearing torn jeans and a nose ring without being mistaken for the bicycle messenger. After a makeover, you still feel like yourself, but the rest of the world suddenly treats you differently. If files could talk, they'd probably tell you that format conversion is a little like a makeover for them.

We change file formats for different applications, because — just like fashion — you won't find any one *right* type. When we're talking image conversion, the major change involves decreasing a part of the file's information to make it small enough to use for Web animation. (As we explain in Chapter 10, Web animations must be very small in file size to conserve bandwidth.) This conversion is akin to stripping someone wearing layers of clothing down to a bathing suit. Files may end up looking good after the process, but others may end up with flaws or quirks you never would have guessed were there when they were dressed up. Our mission in this chapter is to make this process a little less painful for the poor files, and to leave them with enough coverage so that they can still show themselves on the Web.

Choosing a File Format

Choosing the right file format is like choosing the right bathing suit: If you've just started dieting, you don't want to force yourself into a *Baywatch* special. You don't need to throw a caftan over a perfectly developed body builder, either. Short of staying away from the beach entirely, you have to do something. This section discusses general guidelines to consider as you choose a file format.

Not all file formats can be used to create Web animations. The number of file-format options you have depends on the form your animation takes, whether your animation contains drawn art or photo-quality imaging, and what kind of program you plan on working in next. The next few sections take a quick tour of your options.

GIF file format

Almost every Web animation program accepts GIF files. Certain animation programs *only* accept GIFs, which makes GIF the hands-down preferred format for file conversion. The GIF format offers you the broadest range of choices for animation programs. It enables you to start your work in a shareware program and then, as your skills and ambitions grow, import your files into a program with more bells and whistles. You can even change your computer platform and GIF files remain recognizable and editable on your new computer without any major adjustment.

System picture-file formats

In the major PC operating systems, basic picture-file formats are importable or readable in all image software in that operating system. In the Windows operating system, these file formats are BMP, PCX, and PNG. In the Macintosh operating system, they're PICT files. Unless the animation software you're using is itself cross-platform, these files are probably specific to their source operating system. The formats are, however, the most likely file formats added to the software's import options as updates are released.

TIFF file format

A surprising number of animation programs accept TIFF files. Maybe we shouldn't be surprised, given that TIFF was the original cross-platform image format. The TIFF format is recognized by the major shareware animation and graphics programs and almost all of the new commercial entries.

Photoshop file format

The next most-popular image format is the Photoshop file (.PSD) or one of its layers or alpha color channels, depending on how the individual animation program processes information. Programs that accept Photoshop images usually have more features and are geared toward a more graphically sophisticated audience.

If you plan to use a Photoshop file, make sure that you save the file in Photoshop 2.5/3.0 version, because many Web animation programs can't deal with the extra goodies that Photoshop 4.0 offers. Don't worry about using any of the normal Photoshop-based saving and preferences strategies for making this file leaner. It's perfectly okay to have preview icons, or preview thumbnails, saved with your file. These are extras that any self-respecting Web animation program skillfully strips out when the program converts the file.

JPEG file format

Why is JPEG, which is a familiar option for static images, so far down the list of accepted animation formats? The answer to this question lies at the heart of the different ways to compress files for Web use. We discuss this in greater depth throughout this chapter. A growing number of Web animation programs accept the JPEG file format for conversion, but few — if any — keep them in this format for the final animation.

Other file formats

Individual animation programs add other options to their list of acceptable formats. These possibilities range from Kodak PhotoCD file formats to existing animations in QuickTime or AVI formats. These programs encompass certain types of sound files, too. Make sure that you always check the requirements of the program you plan to use.

What do we recommend?

We'd like to just suggest, "Use whatever you feel most comfortable using, as long as your program can import it." Doing so gets us off the hook and sounds like safe and neutral advice. If, on the other hand, you back us into a corner with a ferocious, red-eyed rabbit about to mistake us for roughage, we have an either/or answer. It goes like this:

> ## Do we have something against JPEG files?
>
> Er, well, nothing is *inherently* wrong with the JPEG file format. JPEG is a great format for showing individual photos on the Web. We use JPEG all the time. If you have a handle on compression, know exactly how you're going to work with the files, or are using a program like Alchemy Mindworks Animation Wizard — which recommends JPEG and handles its quirks fairly well — then JPEG is a great format. JPEG creates very nice-looking files, without any of the nasty things that can happen if you convert a photo into a GIF. JPEG files always make great background frames. They just have two teeny-weeny problems:
>
> - They can't be assigned a transparent color. Even if they could be assigned one, you probably wouldn't like the results! JPEG was meant to compress continuous tone images, so assigning a transparent color would probably create a file that looked like it had terminal zits.
>
> - If you save them at Low and sometimes Medium quality to make them small, you strip out lots of visual information.
>
> The latter limitation is absolutely okay if you only plan to move the files around in a path or have the files stay in one place as you apply a sequence of filters. This is not so great, however, if you want to zoom in on the JPEG images, distort them, or resize them (or pieces of them). Don't forget that if you're planning to make a GIF animation, your program remaps your JPEG information into GIF compression anyway. If this is your first time as a Web animator, avoid converting to JPEG before looking at your storyboards carefully and testing how a sample JPEG file converts in your animation program.

- If your program can output a GIF animation, convert your files to the GIF format. You'll probably have more control over the conversion process if you can make visual decisions on what stays and what goes. Most of the GIF animation programs that do this conversion automatically have limited user options for the conversion process.

- If your program creates a file that requires a proprietary plug-in to be viewable by a browser, it probably also has a proprietary compression system. Import flat art as GIF, import photos according to your program's recommendations.

- Don't use JPEGs for photos unless your program specifically suggests them, and then only if the JPEGs are already at the dimension and size at which they'll be presented on your Web page.

Image compression compressed

You have to change the file format to make your image readable on the Web, but why is this necessary? Why not just enlarge the Web standards so that you can show any file format? This question has two answers: The first answer is beyond the scope of this book and has to do with image-viewing standardization on every computer capable of attaching to the Internet; the second answer has to do with the issue of bandwidth that we discuss in Chapter 10.

Every bit of bandwidth is precious, because it turns into a wait time, and wait time is absolute poison. If you make people wait long enough, they don't wait at all — they leave your Web site. So every image you put on the Web has to strike a balance between size and quality.

Notice, however, the difference between what you can see and what a computer needs to process. Imagine that you have a full screen file with a white background and one tiny red dot in its center. Although you can see the whole page, the computer looks at it and thinks something like this: "Hmm, this is an RGB code. R = 255, G = 0, B = 0 at positions x = 320, y = 240. Everything else is R = 255, G = 255, B = 255. So I only have to send a two-color palette along with this image." The computer says this considerably faster than we typed it or you read it. Sending this information to another computer takes up very little bandwidth.

In a nutshell, that's how GIF compression works. Things become objects with positions, and anything that can be lumped together visually is lumped together. Once they're lumped, the colors are mapped to a limited palette for the next computer to read and display.

This works very well for drawn art with flat colors, but you can probably imagine how it can get tricky with a photograph. Every other pixel can be slightly different, and the poor computer can be reduced to describing each one individually. This can take a great deal of time, so the result will not be a file much smaller than the original one. A photo run through GIF compression often looks noisy or splotchy, because the computer has lumped similar colors together instead of keeping each one unique.

Here JPEG compression comes in to save the day. It starts out by breaking the file into a horizontal and vertical grid, looking for similar colors near each other. After lumping together the identical colors, it then describes the rest according to how much they change. When you choose to save a JPEG file in a high-quality compression, the program keeps track of smaller increments of change than it does if you choose low-quality compression. That's why a high-quality compression JPEG has a much larger file size than a low-quality one.

JPEG does have one little quirk that can cause problems in an animation, but not in a static photo: When keeping track of your file's changes, JPEG averages out slight changes in color and value that would be too complex to hold. This information, once examined and tossed, is gone forever. That's why JPEG compression is called "lossy," because it doesn't just convert information like GIFs do. JPEG eliminates the information in the name of efficiency.

Why does this matter in an animation? It depends on what you're animating and what you plan on doing with it. Many Web animation programs, particularly Java applets and in-line plug-in software, do their magic by treating imported files as if they were illustration objects. With less information in the JPEG files, scaled files get jagged more quickly. So do files that are rotated, stretched, or otherwise manipulated.

How Do You Compress a File?

In many cases, when it comes time for you to choose a file format to compress your file for your animation, you can rely on functions that come as features in your image-editing and creation program. All current image-editing programs have Export or Save As functions for both GIF and JPEG file formats. In fact, if you only want to create JPEG files and you use Adobe Photoshop 4.0, we recommend that you rely exclusively on the abilities of Photoshop.

If you don't have a program that exports GIF or JPEG formats, don't despair. Many Web animation programs simply take your files and handle conversion and compression automatically. One-size-fits-all compression formulas of tools such as these don't necessarily create the smallest possible results, but the tools do save a great deal of time and agony.

Making a JPEG conversion

A JPEG conversion in Photoshop 4.0 is relatively easy, as you can see in the procedure that follows.

1. **Open** `Chap11\wndmll.tif`**, which is on the CD-ROM that came with this book.**

   You see an old French windmill cropped from a larger photo. This image is fairly small, and it has already been reduced to 72 dpi. We actually made this image considerably larger than it would really be for a Web animation, but we want you to see the JPEG changes clearly.

2. **Choose File⇨Save a Copy from the menu.**

   The Save a Copy dialog box opens.

   Choosing Save a Copy is always a good move if you are making a different version of something — the same picture in a different file format or image size, for example — and want to keep the original image live on your screen.

3. **Choose JPEG from the Format options/Save file as Format Type in the Save a Copy dialog box, and then rename and save the file.**

   Because we plan to make a few versions of this file, we renamed it `WindMax.jpg`. After you save the file, the JPEG Options dialog box, shown in Figure 11-1, automatically appears.

4. **Choose Maximum from the drop-down list in the Image Options section of the JPEG Options dialog box.**

    Notice how the quality level moves to eight and the slider bar moves closer to large file. We're going to start with a very good quality JPEG image, but if we start at quality level ten we won't save much space. Choosing Maximum retains the most image information in the file, resulting in a high-quality image.

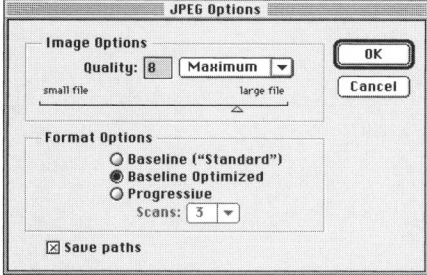

Figure 11-1:
Photoshop's JPEG Options dialog box.

 5. **Select Baseline Optimized in the Format Options section of the JPEG Options dialog box and then click OK.**

    Baseline Optimized improves the color quality of the file and makes a file that is slightly smaller than the standard option. By the way, notice that you have the option of making this file Progressive, which means the file would load in stages on the Web. This option is good for a static Web image, but a very bad one for an image that you want to use in an animation.

 6. **Repeat Steps 1-5 with your original file, but change the level of compression each time.**

    You change the level by making the next version High, the following Medium, and the last one Low.

    We made these changes so that you can see the results of the different levels of compression JPEG offers. Here are the file sizes of the different versions:

    - The original file, wndmll.tif, was about 172K.
    - In our copies on the CD, WindMax.jpg (created by choosing Maximum) is 42K.
    - WindLo.jpg (created by choosing Low) is only 23K.

    Obviously, the difference is very big, but all of these files are too big to use in a Web animation. The nice surprise, however, is that we're working with such small images that almost no difference exists, at 100 percent, between the original file and WindLo.jpg.

If your numbers don't match ours, you're probably being misled by what look like unusually large file sizes. If you are using a Macintosh, go to the Get Info dialog box for each file and look at the file size in parentheses. See Figure 11-2 for an example of this dialog box. This file size is the amount of space that the file is actually using. The other size changes depending on disk size. The apparent file size is bigger when the disk where the file resides is bigger. On the Web, the only thing that counts is the real amount of data.

Figure 11-2: The Macintosh Get Info dialog box, with `WindLo.jpg` info displayed.

The bigger your file is to begin with, the larger the percentage of shrinkage you can get on the file. The biggest jump in size always happens in the first level of compression, which is from an uncompressed file to one of maximum quality but minimum compression. The percentage becomes less dramatic in later compression levels.

When your file is small, the differences as you drop quality can be very small indeed. For example, if your file starts out at 100K in size, it may be 26K at high quality, but may only drop to 20K at low quality. You can check this out by redoing the preceding steps with a more realistic picture size. Try using `wndmllsm.tif` on the CD-ROM. It is only 71K before compressing.

Don't get too carried away with how good our sample image looks at high compression, or with how small it can get. We have chosen an image that has a lot of sky, partially because the contrast will make it very easy to separate the windmill blades for animation. Many other images look much worse at the same settings and take up more file space. Check out Chapter 8 for a discussion of how to choose your images for maximum animation potential.

Convert One for the GIFfer

JPEG conversion is so simple that launching into a discussion of GIF conversion almost doesn't seem fair. GIFs are more complex than JPEGs in that you have more options with GIFs, and thus more ways to get into trouble. In this section, we take converting GIFs one stage at a time:

1. Convert to GIF while indexing the file.
2. Make the image's background transparent.
3. Optimize the palette attached to this image.
4. Use this optimized palette to optimize the other frames of your animation.

We do most of these steps in PhotoGIF, a Photoshop plug-in by BoxTop Software. You can find a demo version on the CD-ROM; the demo will let you follow all our steps but won't allow you to save the result. For more information about indexing, see the gray-shaded sidebar "Understanding indexed color."

Understanding indexed color

What is indexed color and why do we need it? Unlike the JPEG format, which saves colors by choosing from the ones that the image has, the GIF format needs a color palette for reference. This palette has a maximum of 256 possible colors and is a part of the GIF-formatted file. These colors, which can be any subset of those that the computer can display, become a look-up table that all the pixels in an image are matched against. This matching process is called *indexing*. Unfortunately, on the Internet only 216 colors display as true flat colors. This collection of 216 hues is called the Netscape non-dithering palette. (We discuss this palette in Chapter 6.) Every other color needs to be made by dithering.

Dithering is a little like impressionist painting. It takes advantage of how small dots of color laid very close together give the impression of an entirely different color. When the computer dithers, it chooses the two colors from its existing palette that most closely match the missing color Then it fills that color area with a two-color pattern. Sometimes dithering is very successful. Most of the time, however, dithered colors look like barnyard leftovers.

Obviously, the ideal situation is to create all your artwork by using the Netscape palette so that nothing will dither. This technique doesn't work if you are doing a GIF animation from a photo, or from an illustration with shading and blending. In these cases, you either have to accept whatever color substitution the indexing process dishes out, or you have to go in by hand to optimize your image to the Netscape palette.

Part III: Heavy Lifting: Making Technology Work for You

Although doing so won't affect your indexed file, before you index you may want to go to File➪Preferences and change the Display & Cursors setting to Diffusion Dither. This setting ensures that what you're viewing on-screen matches what's happening to your files.

In the following steps, we index a pumpkin file that appears on the CD-ROM that comes with this book. Notice that we resize the graphic first, because the results, if we index first and resize second, will be less than stellar. Remember to change resolution and resize before indexing, and always keep a copy of the original file to edit, in case you're not satisfied with the results.

1. **In Photoshop, open the file** Pumpkin.pcx, **in the** \Chap11 **folder on the CD-ROM that accompanies this book.**

   We created this file by using the Netscape non-dithering palette, but we did it in RGB (see Chapter 6 for more on palettes and colors), which means that in some places we used blending as well as other tools that can mix and create new colors. We also worked on a larger version of the graphic than what we want its finished size to be, to save our eyesight and make it easier to work.

2. **Go to Image➪Image Size and change the pixel dimensions to 100 in width.**

   These dimensions are more manageable for the Web. Refer to Figure 11-3 to make sure that you've duplicated our settings.

Figure 11-3: Resizing our pumpkin to Web dimensions before indexing.

To index Pumpkin.pcx, you're going to use the PhotoGIF plug-in, because it allows finer control of the indexing process. But before you do, look at a file that was indexed using Photoshop only for comparison.

3. **Open the file** PumpStd.gif.

   This file is on the CD-ROM, in the \Chap11 folder. PumpStd.gif has been indexed and turned into a GIF using only the standard menus and dialog boxes in Photoshop.

   Look at PumpStd.gif at its current size. It should look basically the same as Pumpkin.pcx, although it's a little rougher.

4. **Use the Zoom tool to increase** PumpStd.gif **to 400 percent.**

   You can see the result clearly in Figure 11-4. Although most of the pumpkin is filled with solid color, the section lines and all of the transitional colors in the pumpkin face are created with solid-color pixels from the safe palette. This is Photoshop's standard dithering in action. Keep this image open while you do the rest of the steps.

Figure 11-4: A grayscale version of our dithered pumpkin, zoomed up for easy recognition.

5. **Choose File⇨Save as, type** Pumpkin.GIF **in the Filename text box of the Save dialog box, choose 00 PhotoGIF from the list of file format choices, and click OK.**

   The PhotoGIF color reduction dialog box appears on-screen, as shown in Figure 11-5. This dialog box deals with the indexing portion of the transformation.

We recommend that you put the GIF extension on your new files to distinguish them from older versions. You can also easily keep them together when the time comes to transfer them to your Web animation program.

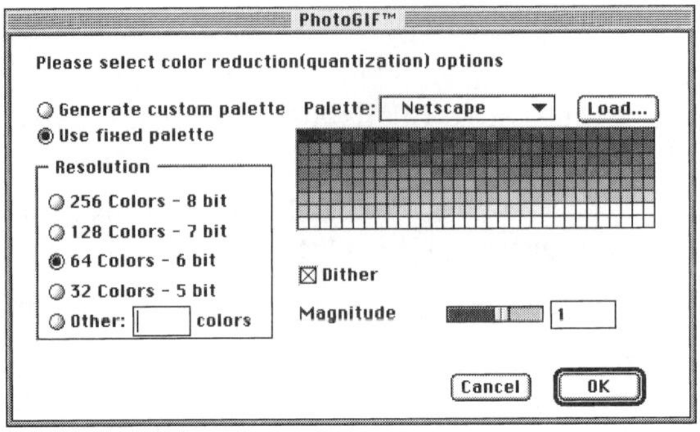

Figure 11-5: PhotoGIF's palette reduction options are clear and very visual.

6. **Choose Netscape from the Palette drop-down list, and select the Use fixed palette radio button.**

   These two elements work together. If you only selected Use fixed palette, whatever is in its default box is used, which is usually the System palette. If you choose the custom palette, you run the risk that your animation will only look good on systems that are the same as yours.

7. **Select the Resolution.**

   We've looked at `Pumpkin.GIF` and given an educated guess. In this case, PhotoGIF is referring to how many of the possible Netscape colors you want to use for this image. Each choice is a maximum. If you choose 64, for example, your palette could only need 50 colors.

   If you only have four colors in your file, for example, select Other and type **4**. Every color square that follows along with your image as part of the image palette takes up a little bit of space. These little bits accumulate.

8. **Select the Dither check box and choose how much dither you want applied.**

   This is one of the functions that makes PhotoGIF such a useful program. The Magnitude bar slides from - 5 to + 5. The negative numbers create slightly smaller files, but unless you go very far down the scale, we don't think the size trade is worth the damage to your files. We look wistfully at + 5, but usually end up at a setting of 0 or 1.

9. **Click OK.**

   The main PhotoGIF menu appears, as shown in Figure 11-6. Notice the palette on the right column. Above it are the dimensions of the file and an exact count of how many colors your image actually needed from the Netscape palette. If this number is significantly lower than the palette choice you made in the previous screen, you may want to go back and resave your image later without these extra place-holders taking up space. In this case, PhotoGIF tells us that 54 8-bit colors were used, so choosing the 64 Color radio button in the Resolution section of the first PhotoGIF dialog box is okay.

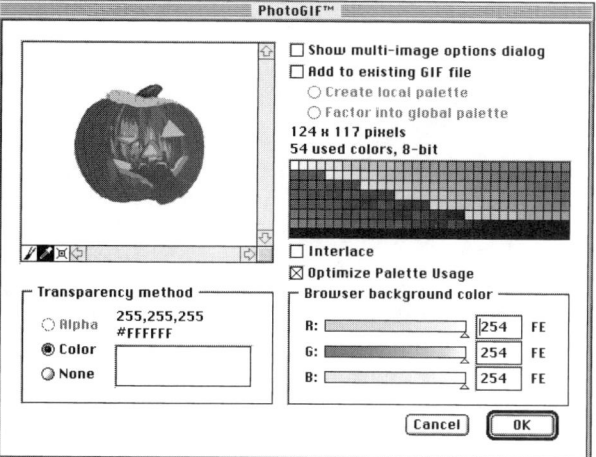

Figure 11-6:
The main dialog box in PhotoGIF is where the conversion decisions are made.

10. Deselect every check box from top to bottom right.

You ask, "Wait a minute! What am I doing here?" Well, the Show multi-image options dialog and Add to existing GIF file check boxes are only useful if we are working with several images at a time. Right now, we're only working with one.

Then you ask, "What about interlacing? I thought I wanted to interlace GIFs so they come up faster!" Unfortunately, this doesn't work in animations. Usually the second image is trying to load while the first image is still finishing its display. This leads to an interesting effect if you're into Deconstructivism — a philosophy that raises illegibility to art. It's not a lot of fun for the viewer, unless they're a Deconstructivist, too. So don't select the Interlace check box.

As for the Optimize Palette Usage check box, this box has a slightly misleading title. It really optimizes the palette size, usually by deoptimizing the look of your image. You may have to select this box later if your files are still too big to work with. Pretend that you're an eternal optimist and go without checking this box.

11. In the Browser background color section of the dialog box, adjust the RGB settings as appropriate for your needs.

Leave the Browser background color as the default browser gray (R=192, G=192, B=192) if you don't use a background color in your HTML for your Web page. Otherwise, change it to the RGB equivalent to your Background HTML tag for your page.

What do you do if your background is a texture or a pattern? If it's a subtle texture, choose the most prominent color in your background. If it's wild and crazy — well, are you sure that you want this animation to be transparent? Consider a complementary solid background in its own boxed frame or in a separate banner.

After you make this change, look at the window on the top left of the dialog box. This window previews your frame, showing the effect of indexing. Right now it's sitting in a bounding box in the middle of your browser color. We deal with transparency issues in the sidebar "Talking transparency" later in this chapter.

We really like PhotoGIF, and consider it hands down an elegant and cost-effective improvement to Photoshop's own indexing and conversion functions. PhotoGIF has one function, however, that isn't living up to its potential yet. That's the Touch-up Paintbrush for eliminating the anti-aliasing around an image. See the "Talking transparency" sidebar for more explanation of this issue. If you're making images for the Web (and who isn't!), by the time you make GIFs, your files are probably fairly small. Trying to touch up the one- or two-pixel halo around an image without a Zoom tool is a job for an action hero's X-ray vision. If you don't touch these up well, your image edge loses the anti-aliasing, but becomes very jagged. You're better off trying to clean up this problem in other ways.

12. **Click OK.**

    We zoomed our finished version up to 400 percent, shown in Figure 11-7, so it's the same size as `PumpStd.gif`. Compare Figure 11-7 with Figure 11-4.

    The image in Figure 11-7 is more dithered than the standard one in Figure 11-4. When seen at 100 percent, it looks like it has more detail. Yet, if you leave Photoshop and check the file sizes of these two files, you'll discover that `PumpStd.gif` is about 17.1K in size. On the CD-ROM is a file called `PumpPGIF.gif`. This file is the result of the process outlined in these steps, and is only 12K.

13. **Close the file in Photoshop.**

Note additional pixel detail compared to Figure 11-4

Figure 11-7: A more detailed, but less sizable, GIF through the PhotoGIF plug-in.

Talking transparency

Look at the windmill picture we converted into a JPEG file in the section "Making a JPEG conversion" in this chapter. To make an animated windmill that stands by itself on a Web page, we need to *silhouette* the image. Silhouetting means cutting away the background that surrounds the object we want. Using image-editing software like a virtual scissors, we can delete the sky and ground and crop the file so that only the windmill remains. However, our file will still have some "blank" space between the windmill and the edges of the file. To use the file on the Web, we want to make this blank background space appear transparent so that the windmill stands by itself.

Currently, if you want to transparentize, you must convert your image into a GIF file. That's because the only sensible way to work this magic is to define one color in the palette as transparent. That way, any pixel with the chosen color definition drops out of the picture. Of the file formats that can be read by all browsers on the Web, only the GIF format provides a fixed palette of colors that remains a part of the file.

Here are two things to watch out for, if a transparent background is your goal: Picking the right color to be transparent, and anti-aliasing — eliminating jagged pixels — at an image's edge. First, you have to be careful that the color you're making transparent isn't a major element in your animated object. Otherwise, whatever you're using as a background color for your Web page will show through. If you know what the background color of your animation is going to be, try not to use it in your characters.

This may be easy to do if your background is a glowing green. It may not be so easy if your background is black or white. You can get around this by using a color one step away from these extremes:

- **For white, try R = 255, G = 255, B = 204.** This color is the pale yellow that is usually displayed next to white in most Netscape CLUTs (color look-up tables). We discuss CLUTS and this RGB notation in Chapter 5.

- **For black, R = 0, G = 0, B = 51 will usually do.** This color is midnight blue.

The other bane of transparency makers is anti-aliasing at the edges of an image. As we discuss in more detail in Chapters 6 and 10, when you use a paint tool, mix an image, or feather, you create a blend between your background and your image. You don't even notice this little edge if you never make the background transparent. Imagine what happens, however, if your Web page background color is dark blue and you have just *flattened* (deleted layers and program-specific information) a Photoshop image to turn it into a GIF. You'll have a nasty light-colored halo of pixels surrounding your object and contrasting with the dark background. You have two choices:

- **Touch up the file manually.** A truly thankless task, editing a file pixel-by-pixel is time-consuming, frustrating, and a likely contributor to repetitive stress injuries.

- **Plan ahead.** Keep a layer of background at the same RGB combination as your Web page's background to anti-alias correctly with your image.

The Incredible Shrinking GIF

Bet you thought you were done! This is the point where the guy on TV says, "But wait, there's more!" A 12K file is good, but not good enough. Most people in the know will tell you that an entire Web page shouldn't be larger than about 30–40K. You can find many Web pages that violate these guidelines, but they tend to fall into two groups. Either they're deliberately graphic-heavy sites geared unapologetically to high-end users, or their designer is clueless. Because telling which is which when you visit these Web sites isn't hard, we feel obliged to make sure that no one thinks you're in group two.

Before you sign up for what is admittedly a time-consuming process, be aware that not all animation frames are good candidates for this kind of hands-on compression. The delicate tweaking you get in a dedicated program like Equilibrium Debabelizer is only worth the extra effort if you have many frames, images with several colors, or are converting from photographic images. Have you been careful to avoid photographs, blends, filters, and anti-aliasing? Have you created your artwork by using only colors drawn from the Netscape non-dithering palette? If so, many Web animation programs will create an excellent global palette for you (a *global palette* is one that is used by your entire animation, not just an individual frame), using only those colors you really need. Alchemy Mindworks GIF Construction Set for Windows and BoxTop Software GIFmation for Macintosh (both of which are covered in Chapter 14) are in this group.

On the other hand, if you want the smallest possible frames, you need more control over your palette-shrinking strategies. This is true whether you are staying simple with GIF animations, or are working with Java applets or in-line plug-in animation packages. In most cases, the file size of the original art you import determines the file size of your finished work. That suggests a move to a dedicated, full featured program — Debabelizer by Equilibrium. Demo copies of this program (Debabelizer Pro for Windows wizards and Debabelizer Toolbox for Macintosh mavens) are on the CD-ROM that accompanies this book.

The steps that follow were created with Debabelizer Toolbox 1.65, the Macintosh version of the Equilibrium graphics processor tools. Although the basic functions are the same on both platforms, the menus and their organization do vary. In particular, all Save and Save As functions, including those for saving palettes, are done from the File Menu in Debabelizer Pro. Debabelizer Pro also has a dialog box called Palette Properties, in which colors in a palette can be flagged for deletion (see Steps 7 and 8 below) or set as transparent. Because of this, if you are a Windows 95 or NT user, your mileage may vary.

Chapter 11: Mondo Conversion: Rehabbing Your Files

Open the PhotoGIF file `PumpPgif.gif` in Debabelizer and see what you can do to strip the file down to its bones. Your mission is to shrink this palette down until the only colors left in it are the ones you really need for the image.

The palette you create when you shrink one GIF in your animation will be used for the rest of the frames. Always create this palette from the frame that has the most variety of color, even if it isn't the first frame.

When you open Debabelizer with a new file, a small Image Infowindow, a window with the open file, and a small representation of the palette belonging to the file appear.

1. **Choose the Magnifier tool in the Image Info window and click inside the image.**

   Every time you click, the image doubles in magnification. You are zooming up the image to make it easier to see which colors in the palette window are important to the image.

2. **Go to the Image Info window and choose the Eyedropper tool.**

   Move the Eyedropper over a color in the image and you notice that the color is highlighted by a marquee in the palette window. Note also that some colors (like the purples) never seem to get highlighted. Because they aren't critical to the picture, these colors are our first candidates for elimination.

3. **Choose Palette⇨Remove Unused and Duplicates from the menu.**

   The palette window shrinks to the real colors in the file. Now you can look at these individual colors more carefully.

4. **Choose Palette⇨Palette⇨Save.**

   The Add Palette To List dialog box appears, as shown in Figure 11-8.

5. **In the dialog box's New palette name for menu text box, type a descriptive name for your palette, and then click the Add button.**

   We chose `pumpkingroup` as the name for our palette.

6. **Choose Palette⇨Set Palette & Remap Pixels, choose your palette's name from the drop-down menu, and check all of the check boxes in this dialog box.**

   By checking all the check boxes, you make sure that colors really do get replaced with the colors in your new palette, that colors that don't exist in the palette get made by dithering, and that the colors you mark as "off-limits" get deleted from the image and replaced with other colors in the palette.

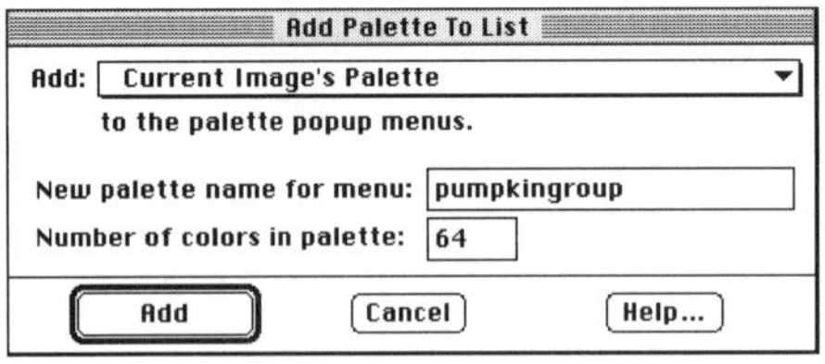

Figure 11-8:
Adding a palette into the Debabelizer database.

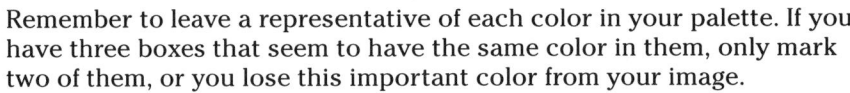

Notice that some colors are very close to each other in shade and hue. By marking these as "off-limits," you tell Debabelizer that you're going to apply a slightly different version of this palette to your image, and that none of the checked colors are invited to the party.

 7. **Look for colors that seem to be identical or very close in color to each other, click on these similar colors to mark them as "off-limits" and, when you're finished, click OK.**

Remember to leave a representative of each color in your palette. If you have three boxes that seem to have the same color in them, only mark two of them, or you lose this important color from your image.

As Figure 11-9 shows, when you click colors, they appear cut at the diagonal, with only the bottom half of the color still showing.

After you click OK, take a look at your image at 100 percent and magnified until you can see individual pixels. You should see little, if any, change. If the change is major and not what you had expected, simply return to the Set Palette & Remap Pixels dialog box, click the Uncheck All button, and try again.

Figure 11-9:
A palette in the process of being remapped.

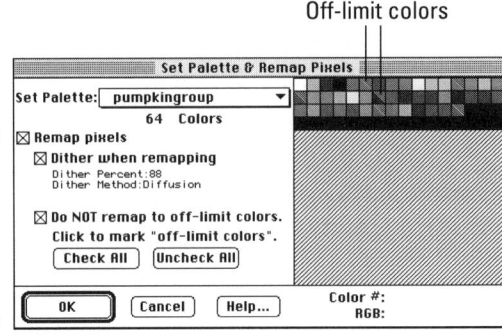

 8. **Return to Palette➪Remove Unused and Duplicates.**

Doing so eliminates the unmapped colors from your palette.

Chapter 11: Mondo Conversion: Rehabbing Your Files

9. **Repeat Steps 6 and 7 until you're certain that every color left in the palette is absolutely necessary to the look of the image.**

   Remember to repeat Step 8 between each time through.

10. **Choose Palette⇨Palette⇨Save and name the newest version of your palette as something that will jog your memory.**

    Now that the palette is saved, you'll want to do a special kind of saving that makes the palette available for your batch conversion of frames.

11. **Choose Palette⇨Palette⇨Stash from the menu.**

    Doing so puts your palette in Debabelizer's memory as a palette you will use for other purposes.

    Our pumpkin is looking fairly skinny, so it's time to save.

12. **Choose Edit⇨Selection Transparency⇨Background Color.**

    This choice identifies the background color of the image as the transparent color for the file.

13. **Now choose File⇨Save As.**

    The Save As dialog box, shown in Figure 11-10, appears. You're going to make several decisions in this dialog box.

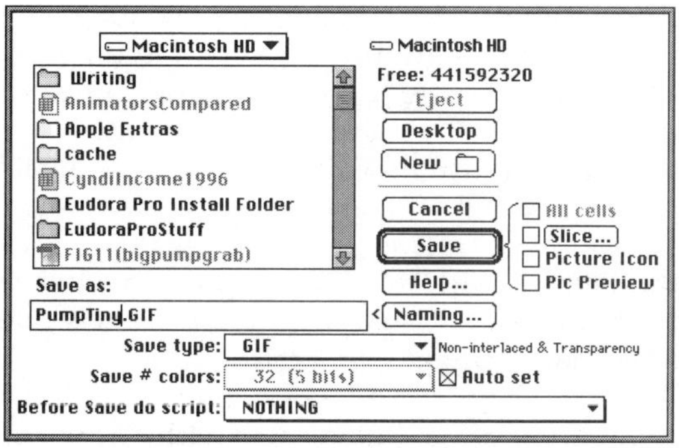

Figure 11-10: Debabelizer's Save As dialog box.

14. **In the Save type drop-down box, choose GIF from the truly massive list of file formats.**

    After you do so, you see the small submenu in Figure 11-11. Make sure that you choose the combination of Non-interlaced & Transparency.

    Don't forget to give the file a new name in the text box named Save as.

    Now this is what we call a menu choice! It's like going to the world's largest Chinese restaurant.

Figure 11-11: GIF options of every flavor can be set in the Save As dialog box.

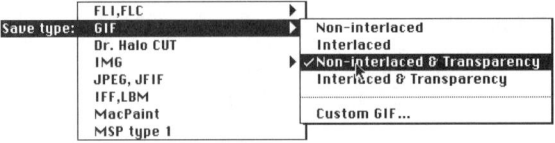

15. **Click the Save button.**

    Check out the file that you just created. A copy of ours called `PumpDeB.gif` is on the CD-ROM. It's a mere 2.8K in size.

Vive la Différence!

If you've followed the steps in the preceding section of this chapter, you've gotten your feet wet in Debabelizer and you're ready to dive into the deep water.

One of the most wonderful things about this program is its ability to do several things at once for you, through the power of batching. When you *batch process* a group of images, you set up an assembly line of functions that you ask Debabelizer to do to all your frames. In this case, you're going to duplicate your frames as GIFs with new names, index them all to the same palette, and make them impressively tiny — all in one breathtaking moment.

There is no free lunch, however. With this kind of power comes more complexity than you probably want. Trust us, though: This is really worth it! You need to do a little file management preparation first. We have a folder called `\chap11\pumpkins` on the CD-ROM, containing eight frames that are waiting to become an animation. If you're working with your own files instead of ours, make sure that all your frames are named alphabetically and numerically, like this:

- `pumpkin00`
- `pumpkin01`
- `pumpkin02`

Notice that these files don't have an extension. That's because these files don't have to be in GIF format for Debabelizer to work with them. As long as they can all share the same color palette, they can be transformed into GIF files as part of the batching process.

Chapter 11: Mondo Conversion: Rehabbing Your Files

Put a zero in front of the frame number because you may have more than nine frames. Doing so insures that frame two really does get processed before frame ten! This is good practice for all animation programs and all forms of animation. Most good programs have a function that enables you to import an entire group of frames at the same time and in the right order. This feature saves you more than the time it takes you to rename your files, right?

After you've named your files in order, put them in their very own file folder/directory. Give the folder a descriptive name, and then put it someplace easy to find. You also want to create another file folder/directory to put your files in after you've made changes to them.

1. **Open your first frame in the sequence in Debabelizer, go to Palette⇨ Set Palette & Remap Pixels, and apply your stashed palette to this image.**

   If you aren't familiar with how to set a palette in Debabelizer, or if you haven't created a palette for this series of animations, go to the section "The Incredible Shrinking GIF" earlier in this chapter for help.

2. **Save the file as a transparent and interlaced GIF with whatever name you'll use for this animation.**

   We use `pumps00` for our new name. Don't forget that `00` after the name to keep your frames in order!

   Make sure that this file is not saved in the same folder that your original files are in. This can cause problems with batching later. Now it's time to set up for the big event.

3. **Choose Misc⇨Compare⇨Compare Options from the menu bar.**

   You are confronted with the Compare Options dialog box, shown in Figure 11-12.

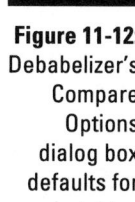

Figure 11-12: Debabelizer's Compare Options dialog box defaults for batching operations.

Part III: Heavy Lifting: Making Technology Work for You

4. **Select the check box marked Set pixel to; then choose the RGB Color value radio button.**

   You want the color in the box next to this radio button to be the same as your transparent color. Ours is white, so the box in Figure 11-12 looks empty. If your transparent color is something else, you'll need to choose it from the color picker.

5. **Select the RGB Color value radio button and set it to your transparent color.**

   You can choose the color you need from the Color Picker button if the color in the box is not already what you need.

6. **Make sure to select the check box for Automatically clear "Compare's Max Bounding Box" at start of Batch Compare, and then click OK.**

   Do this step or you could end up with very strangely trimmed files, because Debabelizer remembers previous settings and applies them to new batches if the settings are not cleared.

7. **Choose File⇨Batch⇨ Compare from the menu.**

   Whether you're following along in Debabelizer or just looking at Figure 11-13, you're confronted with one of the largest and most complicated dialog boxes you've probably ever seen. No worries! You have a guide.

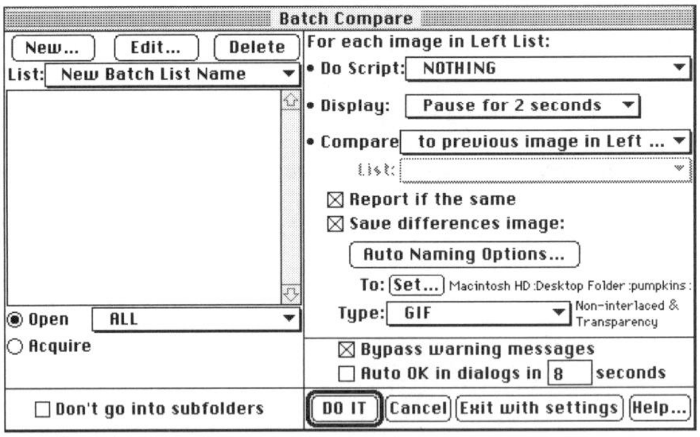

Figure 11-13: Debabelizer's monstrous Batch Compare dialog box lies in waiting for you.

8. **Click the New button.**

   Another dialog box jumps out at you, as shown in Figure 11-14. This box is really just a complex Open dialog box.

9. **Locate your folder using the drop-down menu, and then open it so that you can see all your frames.**

   Remember that empty folder we suggested you make to hold the results of your batched process? Now you get to use it.

Chapter 11: Mondo Conversion: Rehabbing Your Files   217

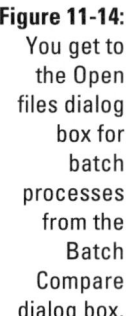

Figure 11-14:
You get to the Open files dialog box for batch processes from the Batch Compare dialog box.

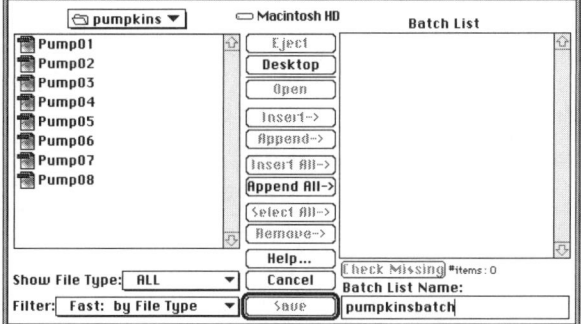

10. **Type a batch name in the Batch List Name text box.**

    We use `pumpkinsbatch` for our batch name.

11. **Click the Append All button.**

    All the files from the left now appear in the Batch List box on the right.

12. **Click Save, and the wonders of the Batch Compare dialog box reappear.**

13. **Choose your batch name from the New Batch List Name drop-down menu on the left.**

14. **Make sure that the Open radio button is selected, and that ALL appears in the drop-down menu.**

    This step tells Debabelizer to process everything in your folder, which is why you wanted to use a clean, empty folder for this process. Imagine the awful results if you compare a group of flaming pumpkins with a group of smiling Mona Lisas!

    Move to the right side of the dialog box, where you set up what Debabelizer will be doing for you in the batch process.

15. **In the Do Script drop-down list box, choose Dither to Stashed Palette.**

16. **In the Display drop-down list box, choose Pause for 2 seconds.**

    This step gives you two seconds to check each frame so that you can see what's happening, and maybe catch your breath!

17. **In the Compare drop-down list box, choose To previous image in Left.**

    Doing so compares an image with the one before it so minor changes in color and position can be documented.

Part III: Heavy Lifting: Making Technology Work for You

18. Select the Save differences image check box.

Enabling this check box saves a new set of files that only contain the pixels that have changed from frame to frame (the "differences" referenced in the name of the check box). The result will be a series of animation frames that have very small file sizes.

19. Click the Auto Naming Options button.

Yes, a brand new dialog box! This is the Auto Namer dialog box. It can be a little tricky, so follow our lead shown in Figure 11-15.

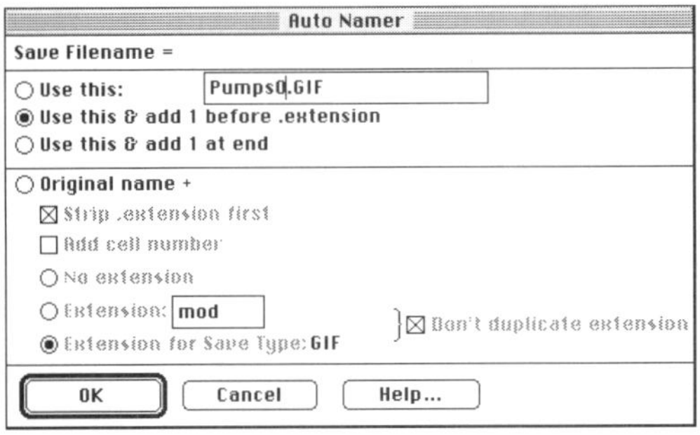

Figure 11-15: The best set of choices for renaming your frames in the Auto Namer dialog box.

20. In the Save Filename = section, choose the Use this & add 1 before .extension button.

This step tells Debabelizer that you will give your frames a name, but it should number them consecutively as it processes them. That way, you have a series of frames with names that increment up by 1 number.

21. Type your file naming setup in the text box of the Save Filename = section and click OK.

The Batch Compare dialog box appears again.

In the Save Filename = text box, we recommend that you type in the first zero and let the program add the other numbers in sequence. If you have more than nine frames, you may have to delete a couple of zeros. Make your decision based on how many files you may have to rename.

22. Click the To: Set button in the Batch Compare dialog box and define the folder or directory in which you want these new files to be placed.

You are now presented with a standard file dialog box for specifying a folder to put the new files into.

Chapter 11: Mondo Conversion: Rehabbing Your Files

23. **Choose GIF from the Type drop-down list box, and make sure that Non-interlaced & Transparency appears to the right of the list box.**

    Whew! Now you know why the button that sets this all in motion is called DO IT!

24. **Click the DO IT! button and watch the show.**

    Debabelizer looks at each file, compares it to the one before, and saves files that contain only those pixels that have changed from frame to frame. Watch the process unfold at about two seconds per frame. Our frames ended up between 600 and 700 bytes each — yes, bytes, not kilobytes. We told you this would be worth it! Now you're ready to bring these files to your animation program of choice, knowing that your Web site will still download like greased lightning.

This may have seemed like a tremendous amount of work, but here's the silver lining: Many of the settings you've put into Debabelizer are things you only have to do once, because the program keeps your choices in its preferences. As long as you continue to use the program, you can take advantage of most of these settings.

Chapter 12
Getting Browser Ready

In This Chapter
- Becoming a Web site tour guide
- Field-testing your animations
- Using HTML to put your animation on the Web page
- Viewing your animation via various browsers

This chapter contains helpful hints for you to remember when preparing your animation for the Web. These items can't make you an instant expert, but we hope that they can guide you as you move beyond the static Web page.

Planning Events

If you want to move beyond a static Web page, think of everything that happens at your Web site as an event. Become a tour guide and plan out your visitor's experience. It's easier to add interactivity and motion graphics if you have this contextual reference. This site-plan becomes the basis for determining which browser standard to support and what HTML coding to write.

Appreciating the Value of Testing

Testing is important and is something you can't ignore. If you really need to be convinced, here's a checklist to shake your complacency:

- Did your animation cause a system crash?
- Did the file download completely?

✔ What was the transfer rate from server to client browser? Any bandwidth problems? *Bandwidth,* incidentally, is the Internet's capacity to handle user traffic: e-mail, Web sites, downloads, animations — everything that shares a common set of cables, wires, and computers.

✔ How fast or slow did the animation run under different computer and browser configurations?

✔ Did all that *looping* drive you to distraction? Looping defines how many times your animation will cycle through from beginning to end when your Web page is accessed by an individual surfer.

✔ Does the animation work with other page content?

✔ Do you like what you created?

To further illustrate our point, we reference the Acme Digital Lab home page, shown in Figure 12-1. You can find this home page on the Web at:

```
www.acmedigital.net
```

Here you view the company's name animated as a series of flipping cards. We picked the flipping cards because we want to reinforce the idea that you don't need a lot of elaborate drawings to create a complex animation. With a little imagination and a dash of daring, you'll discover that you can transform bits and pieces of things that you have on your desktop into Web animations.

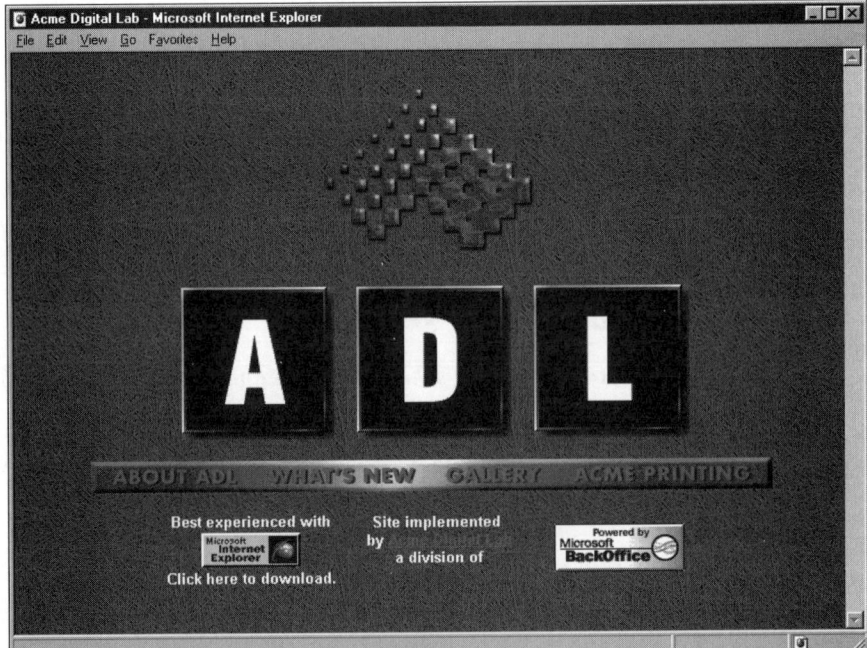

Figure 12-1: The Acme Digital Lab home page, showing an animated title opener.

Chapter 12: Getting Browser Ready 223

We offer the following short history lesson to describe how this animation from Acme was built, and to support our point about the value of testing. To create his company's home page animation, Norbert Florendo, director of Acme Digital Lab, followed these steps:

1. Norbert made each letter graphic in Adobe Photoshop.

2. To add visual interest, he used a Fractal Painter special effects tool to create a shiny metal edge.

3. Then it was back to Adobe Photoshop, where Norbert combined the metal edge with each letter graphic.

4. He then exported each letter graphic to the Photoshop GIF89a module. (Refer to Chapter 1 for more information about GIF89a.)

5. After completing the file conversion to the GIF89a file format, Norbert used Equilibrium Debabelizer Toolbox (Mac version) to batch-process all 14 letter graphics, and then he assigned the same super palette to each GIF file. (You can read more about conversions in Chapter 11.)

6. Norbert animated the artwork by using the Mac software GifBuilder. (Check out Chapter 13, in which we talk about working with GifBuilder.)

7. The three animations were tested to work as one, and adjustments were made in frame counts and timing delays. As shown in Figure 12-2, notice how Norbert varied the delays for each frame. He did this to allow for each word to be spelled out — Acme first, then Digital, then Lab — in sequence. Letters were repeated because of the different word lengths. He added a brief time-delay to Frame 2 and the last frame to allow for elapsed time of display for each GIF animation.

Without a testing phase, these three animations could not have been orchestrated to work as one. Add ample time for testing in your production cycle and you, too, can build your own complex animations.

Macintosh users take note that GIFmation by BoxTop Software offers a browser-compatibility warning as part of its animation package. The warning appears as a standard exclamation-point sign in the Frames window. If you make a choice about an animation, and your choice would mean that certain browsers wouldn't support viewing your animation, the GIFmation warning appears. The warning also tells you exactly which browser will have the problem, and what your viewer will see when using that browser. This feature enables you to make an informed decision about whether to go forward with your planned change.

Another useful Macintosh software tool can be found at the Totally Hip Web site:

www.totallyhip.com/Products/Giffy.html

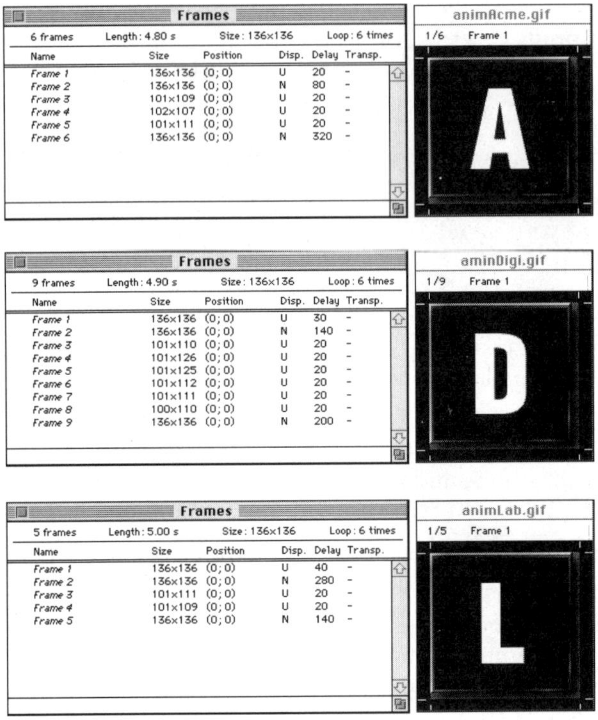

Figure 12-2: Evaluating the animation frames created in GifBuilder.

Look for GiffyView, an animated GIF previewer. You use it to display basic information about GIF89a files, such as transfer rate (baud rate or speed of transfer for data) and the percentage of the animated GIF file loaded.

Attaching Your Animation to Your HTML Page

A detailed review of *hyper-text markup language* (HTML) is not within the scope of this book, but we wanted to pass along two tips. For a more detailed discussion about HTML, check out *Creating Web Pages For Dummies*, by Bud Smith and Arthur Bebak, or *HTML For Dummies*, 2nd Edition, by Ed Tittel and Steve James.

Before you read our tips, first refer to Figures 12-3 and 12-4 to put our comments in the context of a real Web page. Figure 12-3 shows all the image maps included on the Acme Digital Lab home page. Figure 12-4 shows the HTML coding for those image maps. To explain our tips, we reference HTML coding from this home page.

Chapter 12: Getting Browser Ready 225

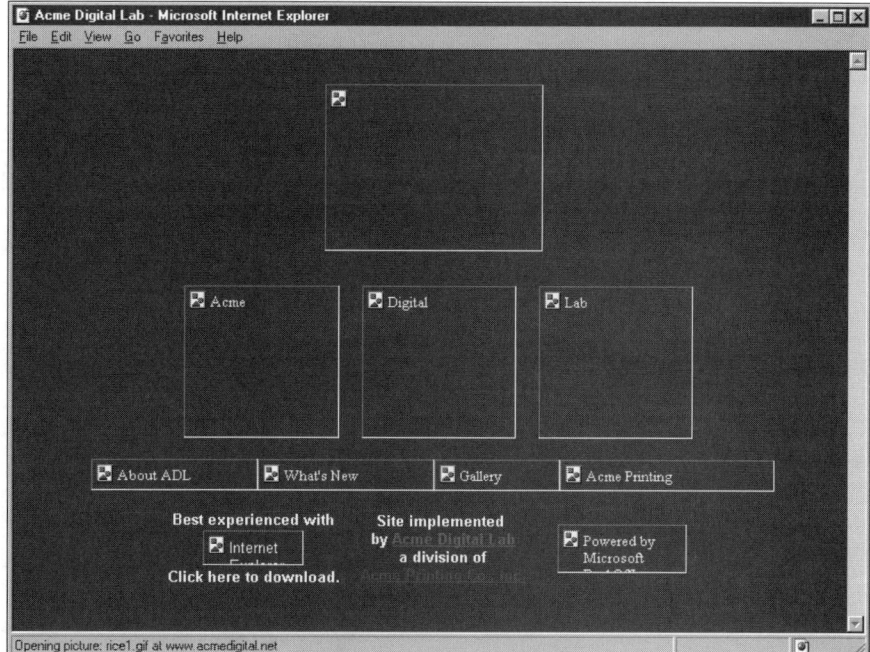

Figure 12-3: Laying out the Acme Digital Lab home page.

For this tip, find the HTML tags for Image Size in the following line of code for the first Acme Lab animation:

```
IMG WIDTH=136 HEIGHT=136.
```

Always include Image Width and Height tags (for static or animated images) in your HTML coding. By including these dimensions in pixels, you eliminate the need for the browser to return to the server to find the size of each image. In the Acme Digital Lab home page example, the browser could have returned to the server ten times! The bottom line is that your page will download faster with fewer trips to the server.

```
!-- Anim. Acme --&gt;&lt;IMG WIDTH=136 HEIGHT=136 VSPACE=15
        HSPACE=10 BORDER=0 ALT=&quot;Acme&quot;
        ALIGN=TOP SRC=&quot;Aimages/
        animAcme.gif&quot;&gt;2&lt;
```

Look at the following HTML code for displaying the Acme Digital Lab's Navigation bar; note the VSPACE and HSPACE tags:

```
VSPACE=0 HSPACE=0
```

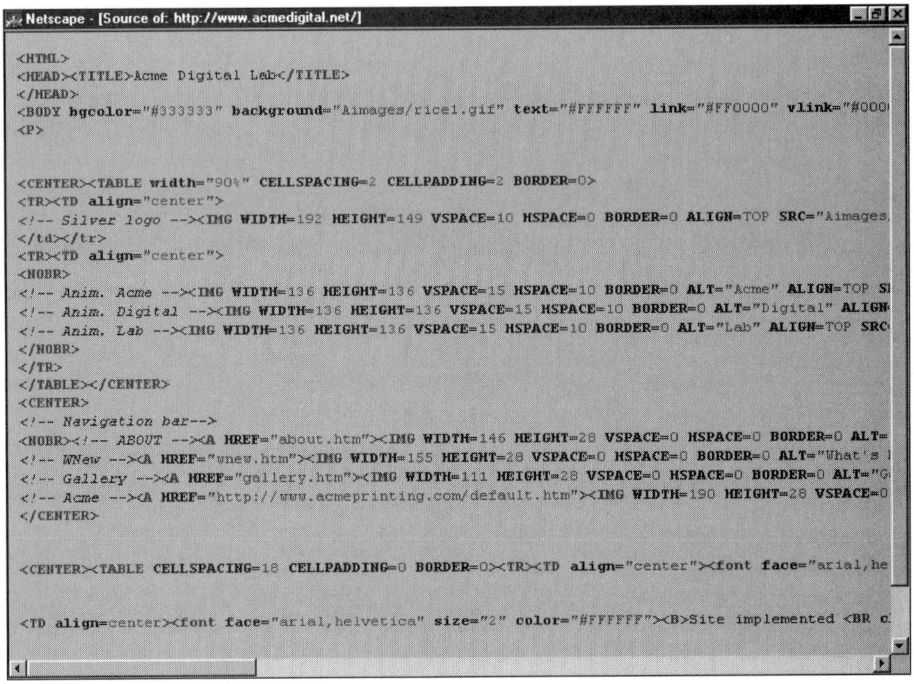

```
Netscape - [Source of: http://www.acmedigital.net/]
<HTML>
<HEAD><TITLE>Acme Digital Lab</TITLE>
</HEAD>
<BODY bgcolor="#333333" background="Aimages/rice1.gif" text="#FFFFFF" link="#FF0000" vlink="#000
<P>

<CENTER><TABLE width="90%" CELLSPACING=2 CELLPADDING=2 BORDER=0>
<TR><TD align="center">
<!-- Silver logo --><IMG WIDTH=192 HEIGHT=149 VSPACE=10 HSPACE=0 BORDER=0 ALIGN=TOP SRC="Aimages
</td></tr>
<TR><TD align="center">
<NOBR>
<!-- Anim. Acme --><IMG WIDTH=136 HEIGHT=136 VSPACE=15 HSPACE=10 BORDER=0 ALT="Acme" ALIGN=TOP S
<!-- Anim. Digital --><IMG WIDTH=136 HEIGHT=136 VSPACE=15 HSPACE=10 BORDER=0 ALT="Digital" ALIGN
<!-- Anim. Lab --><IMG WIDTH=136 HEIGHT=136 VSPACE=15 HSPACE=10 BORDER=0 ALT="Lab" ALIGN=TOP SRC
</NOBR>
</TR>
</TABLE></CENTER>
<CENTER>
<!-- Navigation bar-->
<NOBR><!-- ABOUT --><A HREF="about.htm"><IMG WIDTH=146 HEIGHT=28 VSPACE=0 HSPACE=0 BORDER=0 ALT=
<!-- WNew --><A HREF="wnew.htm"><IMG WIDTH=155 HEIGHT=28 VSPACE=0 HSPACE=0 BORDER=0 ALT="What's
<!-- Gallery --><A HREF="gallery.htm"><IMG WIDTH=111 HEIGHT=28 VSPACE=0 HSPACE=0 BORDER=0 ALT="G
<!-- Acme --><A HREF="http://www.acmeprinting.com/default.htm"><IMG WIDTH=190 HEIGHT=28 VSPACE=0
</CENTER>

<CENTER><TABLE CELLSPACING=18 CELLPADDING=0 BORDER=0><TR><TD align="center"><font face="arial,he

<TD align=center><font face="arial,helvetica" size="2" color="#FFFFFF"><B>Site implemented <BR c
```

Figure 12-4: Looking at the HTML source code.

Always declaring these tags — even if the value equals zero — helps your Web page cross the boundaries between browsers. Never assume that if the browser can't find the tag, the browser understands you're defaulting the value to zero.

```
!-- Navigation bar--&gt;&lt;NOBR&gt;&lt;!-- ABOUT --
          &gt;&lt;A HREF=&quot;about.htm&quot;&gt;&lt;IMG
          WIDTH=146 HEIGHT=28 VSPACE=0 HSPACE=0 BORDER=0
          ALT=&quot;About ADL&quot; ALIGN=TOP
          SRC=&quot;Aimages/baboutr.GIF&quot;&gt;&lt;/
          A&gt;&lt;
```

Quo Vadis? Seeing Your Animation Through Browsing Eyes

Guessing which browser the next visitor to your site is using can be as unpredictable as picking a lottery winner. Just as in the Acme Digital Lab Web site, include a banner at the bottom of the home page proclaiming which browser (or plug-in) is recommended for the best viewing experience.

Chapter 12: Getting Browser Ready 227

To reinforce this message and head off nasty complaints from other browser users, the site encourages you to immediately download their advertised preference. If your site doesn't have this option, then you have no choice but to test your animation with different browser formats. It's a good thing to do anyway.

Demonstrating, in this book format, the differences in animation viewing experience between Microsoft Internet Explorer and Netscape Navigator 3.0, for example, is difficult. As a substitute, look instead at the Acme Digital Lab Navigation bar seen with Explorer in Figure 12-1, and compare it to the Netscape Navigator view of the same bar in Figure 12-5.

In Internet Explorer, you can create a continuous single bar from multiple GIF files, which is graphically more attractive. An added benefit is faster downloads when any words change color on another Web page (the difference is changing a small button versus downloading a larger bar). Viewed using the Netscape browser, this same Navigation bar shows four separate buttons — they're not joined. This is a subtle difference between the two browsers, but enough of a change to impact the look and feel of the Web page.

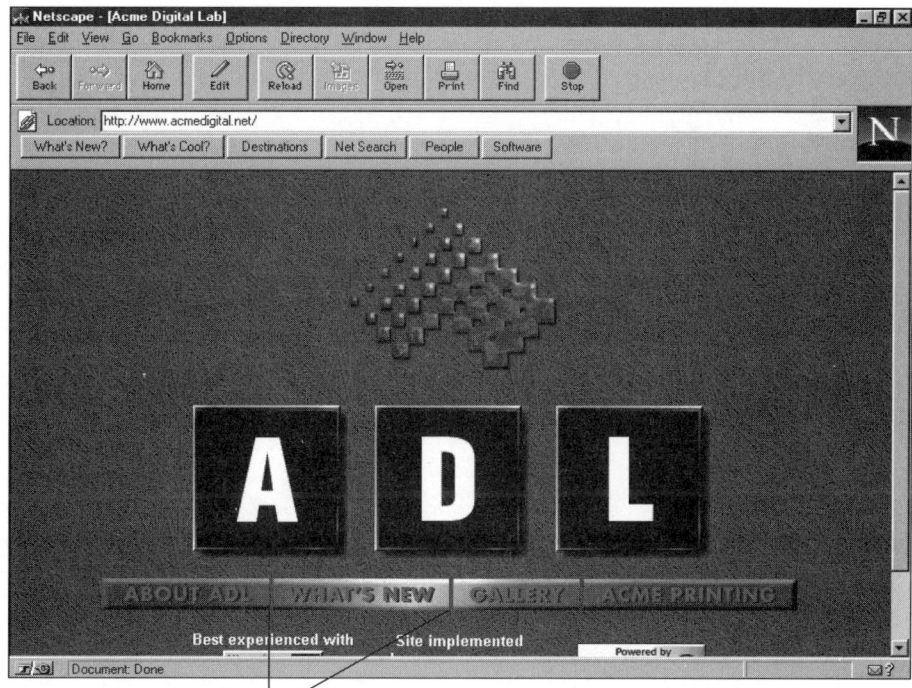

Figure 12-5: Viewing the site with a Netscape browser.

Compare to navigation bar in Figure 12-1

> ### Learning more about the differences between browsers
>
> Here's a Web site for you to check out, if you want to track the browser wars:
>
> www.internet.com
>
> This site is the Mecklermedia Internet news and resources Web site, where you can find the company's Browser Watch. Mecklermedia offers breaking news in the browser and plug-ins industry and a list of browsers and plug-ins available to use with different operating systems: Amiga, Mac, OS/2, UNIX, Windows, and so on.

If you are serious about moving beyond a static Web site, take the time to learn about the idiosyncrasies of different browsers. Until the competing companies fully support a common standard (don't hold your breath on this one!), this extra work is added to your to-do list.

Here are good titles from the *...For Dummies* series that you can read for more information on browsers: *Internet Explorer 4 For Windows For Dummies,* 2nd Edition, by Ned Snell; *Netscape Communicator For Dummies,* by Paul Hoffman; *America Online For Dummies,* 4th Edition, by John Kaufeld; and *Netscape and the World Wide Web For Dummies,* 2nd Edition, by Paul Hoffman.

Part IV
Getting Moving: Animating GIFs & Plug-Ins on Parade

The 5th Wave — By Rich Tennant

"I failed her in Algebra but was impressed with the way she animated her equations to dance across the screen, scream like hyenas and then dissolve into a clip art image of the La Brea Tar Pits."

In this part . . .

You have a tremendous variety of options when you're ready to bring your materials into a Web animation program. This section provides an in-depth guide to the most cost-effective and simplest options. The section also steps you through the animation software while explaining how to make the most of your program. We end with a survey of where you want to go and what tools you can find if you're ready to tackle a little more complexity.

Chapter 13
Free Ride: Web Animation on a Shoestring

In This Chapter
- Discovering the differences between freeware, shareware, and commercial ware
- Finding out basic options in GIF animations
- Using GifBuilder for Macintosh
- Using Microsoft Gif Animator for Windows

*B*y now, your disk is filled with teeny tiny image files, your heart is full of love for all moving things, and your pockets are full of money to spend on Web animation software. Excuse us? Sorry, can't hear you. We're buried under all this animation software.

Although the commercial options for animation software are spilling into the marketplace like paper out of a crazed copier, you can compile your Web work in an astonishing number of inexpensive or totally free ways. If you can download files from the World Wide Web, then the animation world's your virtual oyster. So many options exist that it would be impossible to try to cover even a good percentage of them here. We highlight some of our favorites from the bargain-bin category, to give you a little taste of the banquet that awaits you.

Our tour starts with a couple of the most popular freebies: GifBuilder for the Macintosh and Microsoft Gif Animator for Windows. We show two other programs in Chapter 14 — to show you what you can expect if you shell out a little more of the green stuff.

Common Ground

Every GIF animation program should offer basic image-editing options in case you don't have a graphics-creation program that saves to the GIF89a format. Use these options to choose a color palette, set the bit depth of your files, and decide whether to use dithering to display your colors.

Learning how to be "...ware"

Not too long ago, there was such a gap in price between shareware and commercial products that no one ever confused the two — including the people who wrote the code. These days, shareware-writing code warriors are singing a different tune. "Software for nothing and my pix for free" has been replaced by, "If it makes me money, it can't be that bad." Freeware products get redesigned as feature-rich siblings with a commercial price tag. Bookware (buy the author's favorite book and they throw in the software for free) and shareware are quickly becoming payware. This is an acknowledgement that things have changed, and that even programmers can't live on Jolt Cola and candy alone.

Commercial software, on the other hand, is beginning to look a lot like shareware. Lots of downloadable working demos and beta software are keeping the *try before you buy* ethos of shareware alive. How do you know what's what, if it's all downloadable from the Web?

First, there's *freeware*. Freeware is exactly what it says, within certain limitations: It means that if you download the software, you can use it forever — as long as you abide by the programmer's stated rules. These are usually limited to giving credit where it's due, not pretending that you wrote these cool tools yourself, and sometimes sending postcards so the software author doesn't feel like no one cares. Occasionally, the software is free, but the documentation costs money. It's up to you to decide how much help you need.

Then there's *shareware*. Shareware is one way for programmers to get their names around (freeware is too), and maybe pick up a little money on the side. Shareware is a very civilized concept. It means that the customer can download a fully functional program for a free trial before they shell out money to an unknown source. Unlike other forms of software, it operates on the honor system — depending on the downloader to pay up when the trial period expires.

Unfortunately, not everyone is willing to pay for software that they download. We think this is a moral failing just one level short of stealing cash from Mom's purse and then blaming your best friend. Shareware is created by people who care deeply about affordable software and are still kind and gentle enough to trust their fellow humans. When programmers find their work being treated like freeware, they frequently get tempted to graduate to commercial software.

Telling the difference between shareware and commercial software can sometimes be difficult at first glance, especially because the software costs for shareware and many commercial programs can be very close. When Joe Programmer's shareware program is available for $25, and JosephMade Software's program runs around $39.99, no one is going to miss rent because they bought either one. On the Web, the most obvious way to tell these two types of software apart is how the software is provided.

Unlike shareware, commercial software trial periods are not open-ended, nor do they come with gentle, unenforceable requests that goad you into doing the right thing. Downloadable commercial software comes with strings attached. You can download demos of commercial software, for example, that enable you to see how the program works, but won't let you save a file. Or a demo may only enable you to save a file too small to be of any consequence. For animation software, these demos are fairly useless, because often you don't know how

Chapter 13: Free Ride: Web Animation on a Shoestring

well a program has been written until you can see the file sizes it creates and that the animations work well under fire. Other *strings* are more creative (like splashing the words *Not a* *registered copy* over the finished work), or look similar to shareware but with limits (like giving you a full-featured program with an expiration date).

Remember that the decisions you make about your image can be critical to how big your animations get and how good they look on-screen. Therefore, we strongly recommend that you not rely exclusively on these options unless the animation program gives you control over these decisions, or automates them so well that it's a no-brainer.

Frankly, we haven't seen an animation program yet that always makes the right decisions automatically, but we plead guilty to being nitpickers and control freaks. If you want to know our yardstick for control, check out Chapters 10 and 11 to find out how to change file formats and make your frames as small as possible.

All GIF animation programs should also let you set or change the standard GIF file options. As we discuss in Chapter 11, you should be able to resize your frames, turn interlacing off, and assign or change a transparent color, either frame by frame or for the animation as a whole. These options enable you to fix a minor error that you may have made when you converted the frames, or to reuse GIF images that you created without having to reconvert them.

You don't have many choices in compiling a basic animation, and it is probably just as well. Even the simple choices can take time to sort through. If you're working with a GIF animation program, you deal with four basic elements: position, delay, disposal, and loop. The following sections cover these elements so that you can discover what we're doing — and why — in the programs we cover in this chapter. These four elements are also common to the GIF animation programs we discuss in Chapter 14, although we do not cover the elements in that chapter.

Some browsers handle GIF animation implementation differently than others. In most cases these differences are minimal. In issues of file disposal, at what point an animation begins, and what frame in the sequence is displayed when the animation stops, browser differences can cause problems. Check out Chapter 12 for ways to check your animation before sending out the press releases.

Position

One of the easiest ways to animate an object is to take a single still frame, delete all the background to make it transparent, and then move it around inside the frame area. Doing so saves a lot of time when you make your frames initially, because you only have to make one frame.

Of course, not all image objects work well this way. For example, you can roll a car from one end of a banner to another just by changing the car's position, and the result will probably look fine. If you try this with a dog image, the results could be unintentionally hilarious. See Spot. See Spot stand in cement. Run, Spot, run! Too bad. See Spot play statue-on-wheels — over and over.

Delay

Delay determines how long a frame stays on the screen before the next frame is shown. Any animation program should allow you to set the delay for each individual frame, as well as for the animation as a whole. This enables you to vary the speed of any action, smooth out minor mistakes you may have made in creating your frames, and emphasize actions by freezing them on the screen longer. Delay is usually measured in hundredths of a second, which should give you ample control.

Different systems operate at different speeds. The first time your animation plays, it will be affected by the speed of the viewer's modem line. After that, how fast or slow it moves is determined by the individual computer processor. If you are working on a slow processor, you should be very careful about using the option to run your animation as fast as possible. The animation may look fine on your Pentium or Performa, but on someone else's Pentium II or Power PC it will look like the Three Stooges on amphetamines. Refer to Chapter 12 for tools to help you test your work before you show it to the world.

Disposal

No, this is not about sending your animation down the drain — at least, we hope it isn't. *Disposal* defines what the browser is supposed to do with a frame after it's been displayed the specified amount of time. Disposal is the most misunderstood of the GIF animation options, and is complicated by how different browsers and browser versions handle disposal differently.

Here are three viable choices for file disposal:

- **Unspecified, or No disposal specified.** These mean that the frame simply takes the place of the prior frame, and yields its place to the next frame. Simple, straightforward, and the right thing to use if you're using opaque frames that take up the whole frame image area. This is usually the default setting for an animation program.

- **Do not dispose.** This leaves the image on the screen, even while the next image or images are playing. Use this option if you are using transparency, and particularly if you've been using the Equilibrium Debabelizer process for making very small files as described in Chapter 11. In addition, if you are working with an animation program that optimizes frames by trimming away any pixels that don't change from frame to frame, this is the option to use.

- **Restore to background, or Restore to background color.** This element makes your browser background visible through your animation. This choice differs from just setting up a transparent GIF animation because it flushes the previous image from the browser memory. Use this option if you intend to move one image around in a larger frame.

Every GIF animation software gives you a *restore to previous* option, but think twice (or more!) before you use the option. In theory, this option gives you extra possibilities by letting you *repaint* a file that you have previously shown after disposing of several others. As of this writing, however, this option is only supported in Internet Explorer 3.01 and above. Other browsers categorize the file as Unspecified, or as Do not dispose.

Looping

You set looping to define how many times your animation will cycle through from beginning to end whenever your Web page is accessed by an individual surfer. You get three options here:

- **Never or none.** This means exactly what it says. Your animation plays once, leaving either the first or the last (depending on the browser) animation frame on the screen.

- **Forever.** This keeps your animation running as long as the viewer has your Web page on the screen.

- **X number of times.** You can choose any number between one and 65535, which is fairly close to forever. Older browsers can't handle this setting, and will default to one of the other two options.

Using GifBuilder — Moving in Place

We believe in using the easiest, best tool to fit a task. If you are making GIF animation on a Macintosh platform and you want it small, clean, and simple, you couldn't ask for a better program to do it with than GifBuilder. The fact that Yves Piguet has done all this work for a freeware program makes it even better. The program offers a surprising amount of extras, too.

- **Program:** GifBuilder, by Yves Piguet
- **Category:** Freeware
- **Platform(s):** Macintosh
- **Where to find it:** www.download.com or www.pascal.com

In Chapter 11, we created a series of frames for a small, stationary animation of a Halloween pumpkin. In this section we compile these frames, which can be found on the CD-ROM in a folder called \Chap13\pumpkins — if you'd like to follow along with us. The finished pumpkin animation is also on the CD-ROM. If you have your own frames ready to go, you can use those instead.

Bringing in the files

First, of course, you need to download GifBuilder from the Web and install it onto your hard drive. Next, bring the files from the \Chap13\pumpkins folder into GifBuilder. If you have Mac System 7.5 or above, all you have to do is use its drag-and-drop abilities.

1. **Launch GifBuilder, and choose Window➪Frames.**

   Doing so opens a large, empty Frames window.

2. **Go to your desktop and open the folder that contains your animation frames.**

3. **Select all the files you want to use for your animation in the open window.**

Although GifBuilder enables you to drag any frame in the Frame Window into a different position, your files import according to the order in which they're displayed in your desktop window. We recommend that you follow the naming conventions that we suggest in Chapter 11 and display them by name. As we show in Figure 13-1, doing so enables you to display the frames by name and to import them in the order you intended. Rearranging everything because your window displayed files by date or icon is no fun.

Chapter 13: Free Ride: Web Animation on a Shoestring 237

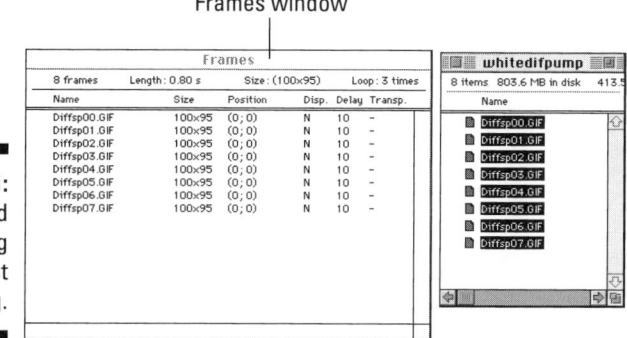

Figure 13-1: Good naming means fast importing.

4. **Drag the files from the open desktop window to the open Frames window.**

   If you're working with a Macintosh operating system older than Version 7.5, you need to open your files one by one through the GifBuilder file menu. Doing so does the job, but is not nearly as efficient.

   The Frame window gives you a status report that tells you exactly how large your frame is, its horizontal and vertical coordinates in the animation space, its method of disposal, interframe delay, and whether the frame is transparent.

   In our pumpkin animation, we used the Equilibrium Debabelizer Batch Difference function to save only the pixels that changed from frame to frame. (Refer to Chapter 11 if you're curious about the process that we followed.) This explains why the dimensions for all the frames except the first one are so much smaller, and why their coordinates do not start at 0;0.

Transparency obscura

If you followed the steps in the preceding section, you now have the sample animation files in place within GifBuilder, but if you are using transparency (which we used in building the animation frames), you need to reset the transparency settings.

GifBuilder doesn't read anybody else's transparency settings except its own. This is meant to be a feature, we think, because there are many different ways to create a GIF file and many different programs that do so. Making you start from scratch is easier than trying to figure out the coding behind every possibility. Doing so can be a real pain, however, if you've got more than a handful of frames. To start the transparency process in GifBuilder after you've loaded your frames into the program, do the following:

1. **Select all the frames in your animation in the Frame Window.**

   You can do this by pressing ⌘+A from your keyboard, or by clicking and dragging down the list of frames in the Frame Window.

2. **Choose Options⇨Transparent Background from the menu, and then choose your transparent color.**

   You see a menu selection like the one in Figure 13-2. We selected White as our transparent color, because this is the background we used when we created our individual frames. If we had selected "Based on First Pixel", transparency would have been set to whatever color was the first one in the color palette used by the frame. "Other" would have allowed us to specify any other color that we had in the palette.

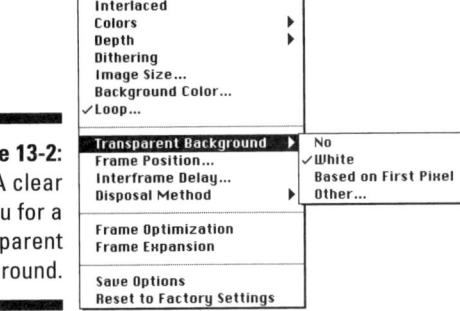

Figure 13-2:
A clear menu for a transparent background.

If you want to ensure that you only specify a background color that's in your file, load the palette used by your animation. To do this, choose Options⇨Colors⇨Load Palette. A File menu dialog box appears, enabling you to select one of your files for use as a palette source.

You may want to use the same transparent color designation for all of your frames, which makes this process much easier.

Be sure to choose No from this list if all the backgrounds in your files are opaque. Otherwise you may end up replacing an important color with a clear area.

3. **If your browser background color is white, or if it's the first color in your color palette, choose the correct option from the menu; if the background color is neither, specify it by choosing Options⇨Transparent Background⇨Other.**

   The GifBuilder color wheel appears, as shown in Figure 13-3.

Figure 13-3: The HSL color wheel for setting a transparent background color other than white.

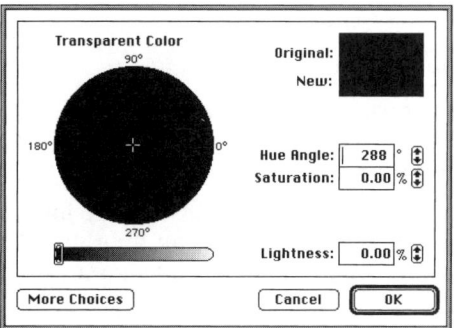

4. **Choose your background color from GifBuilder's color wheel.**

   Things get a little tricky here. If your background is black, no worries. Just move the slider bar at the bottom of the dialog box all the way to the left. If you need a specific color, you'll probably have to return to the software in which you made your frames, to get the Hue degree angle, and the percentages of Saturation and Luminance of your chosen color (the *HSL* numbers).

You'd think that, as a Web animation tool, GifBuilder would have a way of assigning a color by its RGB value, rather than the HSL numbers. If you click the More Choices button, your spirits will lift: On the left of the dialog box you'll find the option to change from Apple HSL to Apple RGB. Select this option, but your elation will probably be short lived. Unlike Adobe Photoshop and most other imaging software, GifBuilder wants its RGB values input as percentages, not as fixed numbers from 0 to 255. If you input 255, you get 100 percent (this will happen if you input any number above 100). We think this is a failing in an otherwise elegantly designed program, but complaining is hard to do when you get your tools for free.

Setting universal animation options in GifBuilder

Fortunately, with GifBuilder the agony of transparency is followed by the ecstasy of simple and straightforward choices for all the standard animation options. You can step through these basic choices now.

Changing frame size

GifBuilder brings in your files at the dimensions in which you created the largest one. If all your frames were created at the same time and with the same specifications, you shouldn't need to make any changes. We don't change our animation's position in our sample, but you may want to. The process of setting up the image frame so that it can move around your Web page is very easy. Do the following:

240 Part IV: Getting Moving: Animating GIFs & Plug-Ins on Parade

1. **Choose Option⇨Image Size from the menu.**

   The Image Size dialog box appears.

2. **Select the Minimum Size radio button to make your window as small as your image will allow, or select the Fixed Size radio button to input the width and height of your working area.**

   In Figure 13-4, notice the relation of the settings in the Image Size dialog box on the left to the preview window image on the right. We plan for the minimum size that the image requires because our pumpkin isn't making travel plans.

Figure 13-4: Minimizing animation size keeps the download short and sweet.

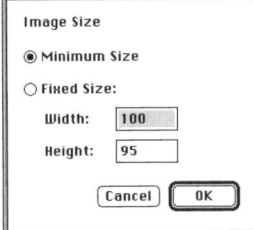 

To show you what changing the Image Size can do, we doubled the working area in Figure 13-5 by choosing the Fixed Size radio button and changing the Width to 200 and the Height to 190. Notice that the pumpkin has not changed size. The active animation area has been expanded to give him room to move.

Figure 13-5: Setting a fixed size means creating a larger active area.

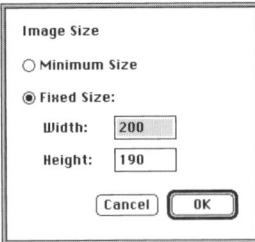 

Setting a larger image area can be a work-around solution to creating an open space around an animation on a Web page. The browser will reserve the fixed space when it displays the page.

The delights of delay

You can set the delay in a purely mechanical way by simply selecting all the frames and giving them the same interframe delay setting. This is a good place to start, but you'll probably want to fine-tune your decisions after you see the result. To set the interframe delay, make sure the Frames window is open and follow these steps:

1. **Select all the frames in the Frame window, and choose Options⇨ Interframe Delay from the menu.**

   You are presented with the Interframe delay dialog box, shown in Figure 13-6.

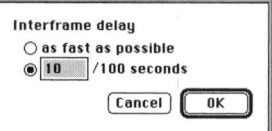

Figure 13-6: Setting an interframe delay in hundredths of a second.

2. **Select the /100 seconds radio button.**

   Unless your animation takes up a lot of space, you almost never want to select the as fast as possible radio button. After the files download to a client computer, they'll be off and running so quickly that you'll beg for an instant replay.

3. **Input a number between 10 and 20, and then click OK.**

   We used 10 for our pumpkins. From experience, we've noticed that most small animations play at a good pace — not too fast, not too slow. In any case, you do have to start somewhere!

   Now it's time to check out the results of your labor.

4. **Press ⌘+R, or choose Animation⇨Start from the menu.**

   If you want to stop at any time, press ⌘+Period.

   If you're happy with the results, you're finished with Delay — at least temporarily.

Even if the animation seems to play well with all frames at the same speed, you may want to set certain motions to start just a little slower, and then build up speed. Doing so can be very useful to simulate a car or similar linear action that demands acceleration. To set certains frame at a slower speed, highlight the frame you want to change and follow the Delay steps again, but this time choose a higher number in the Interframe delay dialog box.

A good disposal method

Earlier in this chapter, we made suggestions about how to decide what disposal form you want for your frames. Although you don't have to dispose of all your frames in the same way, it will probably be an unusual case when you need to vary the settings in an animation.

To find the Disposal function in GifBuilder, choose Options⇨Disposal Method. As you can see in Figure 13-7, you get the four choices that we discussed earlier in the chapter, in the "Disposal" section. Choose the method that best suits your animation. We've chosen Do Not Dispose for our frames.

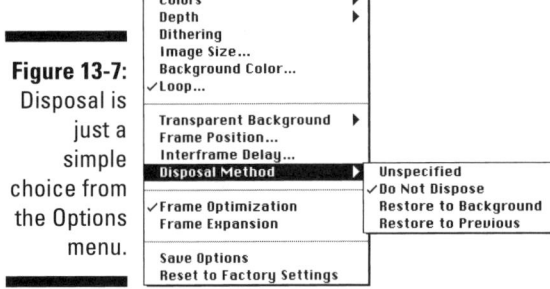

Figure 13-7: Disposal is just a simple choice from the Options menu.

Getting a little loopy

Last but not least, you'll want to decide how many times your animation will cycle through. Very few people choose to run a GIF animation only once. GIF animations are so very short that most viewers will miss your work unless you use looping. Many people also find a large, infinitely looping Web animation to be a curse. Even people who like Web animations can find them an enormous distraction, as they hear their hard drives grind through the cycle over and over and over. You may want to do a middle-ground loop by following these steps:

1. **Choose Options⇨Loop from the menu.**

    The Looping dialog box appears, as shown in Figure 13-8.

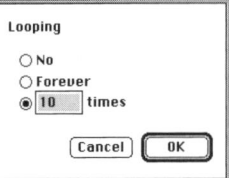

Figure 13-8: The Looping dialog box.

Chapter 13: Free Ride: Web Animation on a Shoestring

2. **Select the times radio button, type a number between 10 and 30 in the text box, and click OK.**

   Doing so gives a visitor ample time to admire your cleverness and artistry without condemning them to a perpetual loop.

Looping is the final segment in our coverage of basic animation settings for GifBuilder. The result of these settings can be found in `PumpAnim1.gif` on the CD-ROM. That file is very small for an animation — only 5.6K — so it loads and plays very quickly. It can be viewed by using your browser to view `pumpkin.html` from the `Chap13` folder on the CD.

Using the special features of GifBuilder

In previous sections of this chapter, we deal with the basic settings you need to create an animation. Even if you are not using GifBuilder, you will find that these basic features exist in any GIF animation program you may use on the Macintosh. GifBuilder has a few extra tricks, however, that you can use to keep your animation files slim and still add a little extra pizzazz to your animations. Here's a brief look at these features.

Using transitioning effects

Transitions are most frequently used in video and animation to create a graceful change between one scene and the next. Transitions can be directional, which means that they start in one position in the frame (for instance, the left side) and then move across or around the frame until the old scene has been replaced with the new one. Transitions can also be random, nondirectional changes in the quality of the image. The old image blurs, breaks into small bits, or somehow gets replaced in small stages with the new image.

For GIF animation, transitions are most useful in smoothing out the loop between the last frame of the cycle and the return to the first frame. Imagine that you're rolling Jack and Jill down a hill to illustrate proper water-carrying techniques. There they are, lying in a heap at the end of the animation. Then in half a blink, Jack and Jill are at the top of the hill. If you use a transition between the last frame and the first one, you minimize the mechanical feel of the loop.

Transitions can be useful for stationary animations, too. Take a good look at the pumpkin animation you created from our frames, and notice that the change between the first pumpkin frame and the second feels a little abrupt. You can change the delay speed on these frames, but you have a better way to curb the abruptness. Just follow these steps:

1. **In the Frames window, select the second of the two frames between which you want to add a transition.**

   In our pumpkin animation, we chose Frame 2.

2. **From the menu, select Effects⇨Transitions⇨Dissolve.**

   See Figure 13-9. If you're familiar with QuickTime software, like Adobe Premiere, you notice that the Transition and Filter options in GifBuilder are very limited. You can create a transition in dozens of ways, and hundreds of variations of these dozens of options exist. Very elaborate transitions can take up significant disk space, however. The GifBuilder transitions are classics and are the cleanest and easiest to apply.

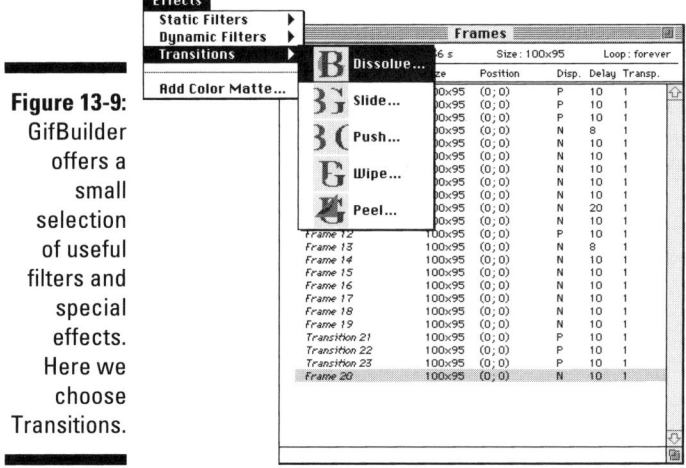

Figure 13-9: GifBuilder offers a small selection of useful filters and special effects. Here we choose Transitions.

The Dissolve transition compares the pixels of two frames, and randomly replaces the pixels of the first with the pixels of the second. If a big difference between the frames exists, the result will look like a curtain of noise as it plays. In our case, our frames are very similar, so the result is very subtle.

3. **In the Dissolve dialog box, type the number of steps you want the dissolve to take.**

   The Dissolve dialog box is shown in Figure 13-10. We used four steps, which means that three new frames are inserted between Frame 1 and Frame 2. GifBuilder simply renames the frames, so now Frames 2, 3, and 4 are the transitions, and Frame 5 is the original Frame 2.

Step through these frames and you see that we have basically used Dissolve to in-between from Frame 1 to Frame 5. Refer to Chapters 3 and 4 for an explanation of in-betweening.

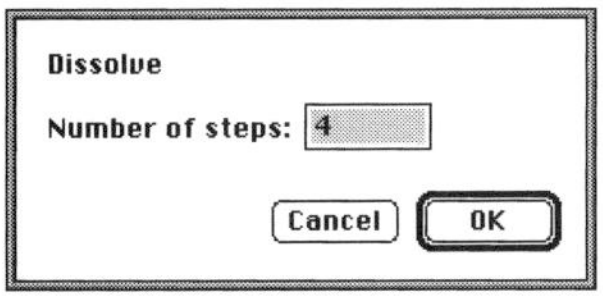

Figure 13-10: Dissolve allows you to apply a simple transition to your frames.

Shrinking after we dissolve

Using transitions will enlarge the animation's file size. GifBuilder offers a way to minimize this problem, as well as help you trim your individual frame sizes, even if you haven't had access to a program like Debabelizer (which we use extensively and plug shamelessly in Chapter 11).

1. **In the Frames window, select all your files.**
2. **Choose Options▷Frame Optimization from the menu bar.**

This function, which is a slightly cruder version of the Compare option in Debabelizer, looks for pixels that change and then draws a bounding box around them. Then it eliminates any pixels that stay the same from the frame.

Highlight one of the Transition frames in our pumpkin animation, and you'll see that only the center portion of the pumpkin — where the flames show through the eyes, nose, and mouth — is selected.

Our final animation, which includes additional frames and a second transition, can be found on the CD-ROM as `PumpAnim2.gif`.

Using Microsoft Gif Animator — Seeing Stars

Microsoft doesn't provide technical support for Gif Animator, but don't worry; the software's very easy to use. Gif Animator has a toolbar, an animation (frames) display column, a scroll bar, and three tabs to open dialog boxes for setting Options (managing your files), Animation (set parameters like frame size and looping controls) and Image (set parameters for individual frames like transparency and position).

- **Program:** Microsoft Gif Animator
- **Category:** Freeware
- **Platform(s):** Windows 95, Windows NT
- **Where to find it:** www.microsoft.com/imagecomposer/gifanimator/gifanin.htm

For our example we used five stars from the typeface Zapf Dingbats as our source artwork. This font offers variations of stars and other graphic elements that can be incorporated into an animation, and is a quick way to get attention for *hot* topics on your Web page. Our stars were saved first in our graphic program's native file format and then exported to GIF:

- **File dimensions:** 36-x-36 pixels
- **Color mode:** RGB
- **Resolution:** 72 dpi
- **Background:** White
- **Font:** Zapf Dingbats
- **Font size:** 36 points
- **Anti-aliasing:** OFF
- **Star colors:** red (R = 255, G = 0, B = 0), yellow (R = 255, G = 255, B = 0)
- **GIF89a specs:** Exact palette, non-interlaced

To build your animation, follow these steps:

1. **If it's not already open, start the graphics program in which you created your artwork.**

2. **Open all the star images files, as shown in Figure 13-11.**

   The file names are `Star1.gif`, `Star2.gif`, `Star3.gif`, `Star4.gif`, and `Star5.gif`.

3. **Start Microsoft Gif Animator.**

   As shown in Figure 13-12, you see the Gif Animator toolbar at the top of the window, the animation frame display column on the left, and the Options tab menu on the right.

4. **Activate drag-and-drop by selecting the Main Dialog Window Always on Top check box.**

   This software offers a drag-and-drop option, which you'll use to move each star from your graphics program to a different Microsoft Gif Animator frame.

Chapter 13: Free Ride: Web Animation on a Shoestring   247

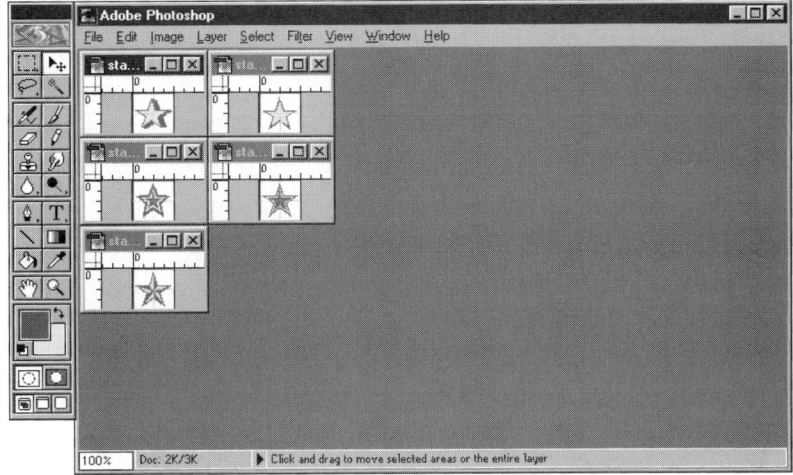

Figure 13-11: The Zapf Dingbat stars.

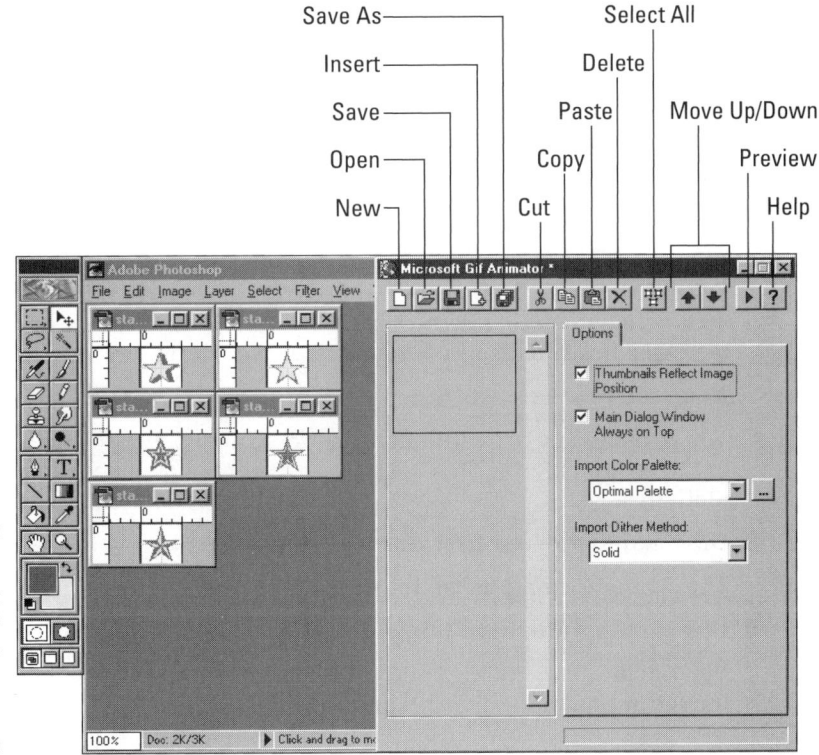

Figure 13-12: Microsoft Gif Animator main window.

Part IV: Getting Moving: Animating GIFs & Plug-Ins on Parade

5. **Select the Thumbnails Reflect Image Position check box.**

   Now you can see your artwork in position relative to the animation frame.

6. **Before you import any images into Gif Animator, set your Import Color Palette (Figure 13-13).**

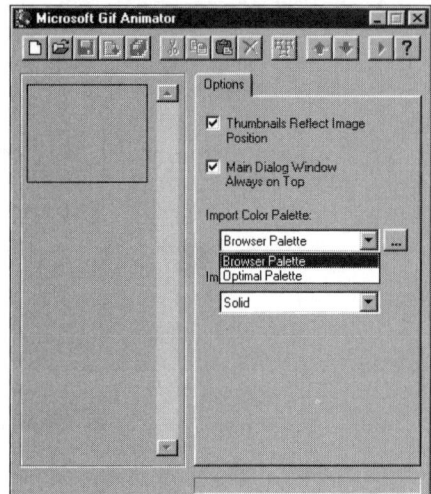

Figure 13-13: Choosing your Import Color Palette.

Because you're working with the same palette colors in each frame, select Browser palette as your Import Color Palette option. This option sets a single palette for the whole animation, and is your best choice for quick downloads of your animated Web graphic.

7. **Next, set your Import Dither Method (Figure 13-14).**

   You're using line art with only two Netscape compatible browser colors in the entire palette. That's why you select Solid as your Import Dither Method.

8. **Drag-and-drop your first star into Frame 1.**

   The Animation and Image tabs are now visible.

9. **Choose the Animation tab.**

   The tab is shown in Figure 13-15. Locate the first two options, which are for setting Animation Width and Height.

Chapter 13: Free Ride: Web Animation on a Shoestring 249

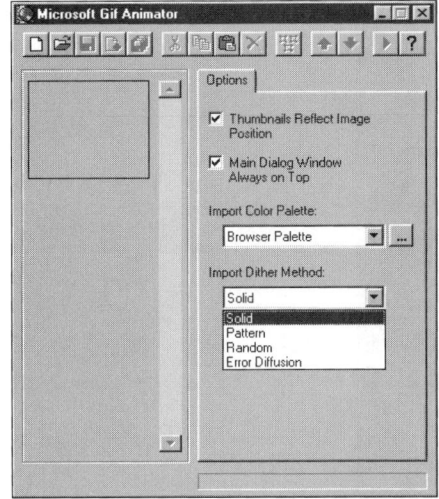

Figure 13-14: Picking an Import Dither Method.

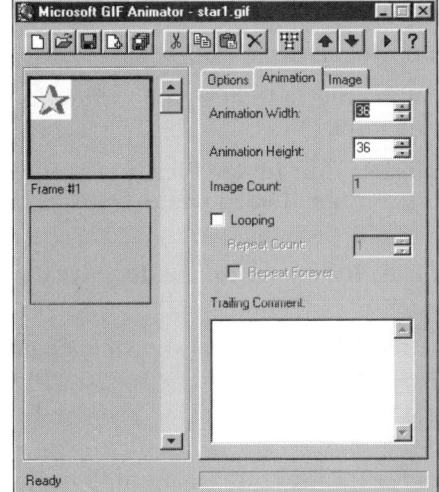

Figure 13-15: Setting the width and height of the animation frame.

10. **Set both Animation Width and Animation Height to 36 pixels.**

    The image size is also 36 pixels. You use these settings because the stars are not changing position in the frame. If you want to move your stars vertically, horizontally, or diagonally along a line of action, set the animation width and height to a number larger than the dimensions of your image file.

11. **Choose the Image tab.**

12. **Make the image file's white background transparent by first selecting the Transparency check box, as shown in Figure 13-16.**

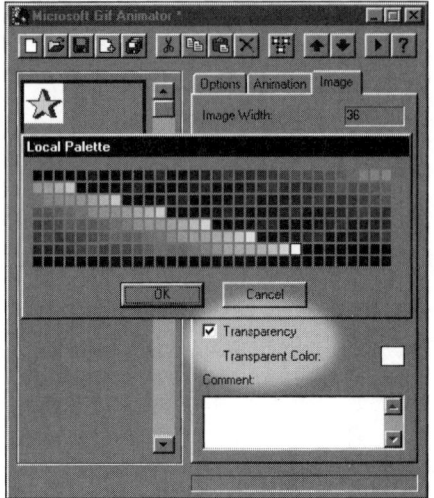

Figure 13-16: Making the white background transparent.

13. **Click the colored square to the right of the words Transparent Color.**

    The Local Palette dialog box appears.

14. **Click the white square in the palette to designate white as your transparent color, and then click OK.**

15. **Drag-and-drop one of the other four image files into Frames 2, 3, 4 and 5, and make the backgrounds of each frame transparent by repeating Steps 11-14.**

16. **In the Image tab, specify how long your image displays during the animation.**

    For this example, set Duration [$^1/_{100}$ s] to 2, as shown in Figure 13-17. Now you need to set the last image specification for your animation — how each frame displays in relationship to the previous and next frames.

17. **Select Restore Background from the Undraw Method drop-down list box, shown in Figure 13-18.**

    This choice removes the previous frame as the next frame is displayed.

18. **If you want to make your animation longer, repeat the placement of your stars as described in Steps 11-14.**

19. **To keep the flow of action smooth, reverse the order of placement, and use the star in Frame 5 only once to create a 9-frame animation.**

    See Figure 13-19 to see the placement of the stars in Frames 5-7.

Chapter 13: Free Ride: Web Animation on a Shoestring 251

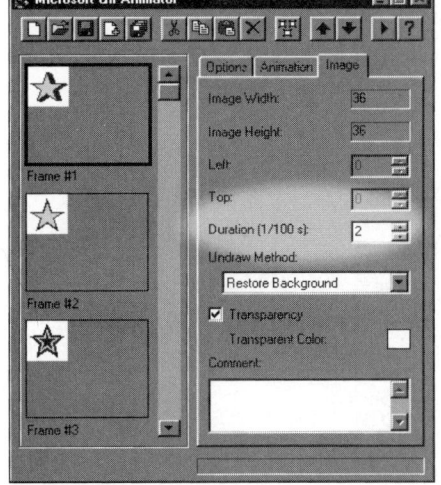

Figure 13-17: Setting how long each frame displays during the animation.

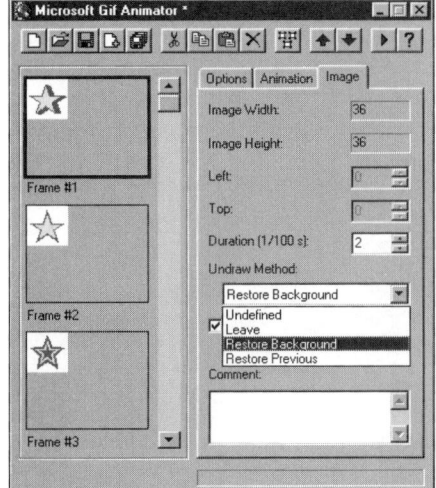

Figure 13-18: Specifying how frames display.

   20. **If you want your animation to loop, choose the Animation tab and select the Looping check box.**

       The Animation tab is shown in Figure 13-20. Below the check box, you can set a Repeat Count or Repeat Forever playback.

   21. **To preview your animation, click the Play button on the toolbar.**

       The Play button is to the immediate left of the Help button, as shown in Figure 13-20.

       Doing so opens the Preview dialog box.

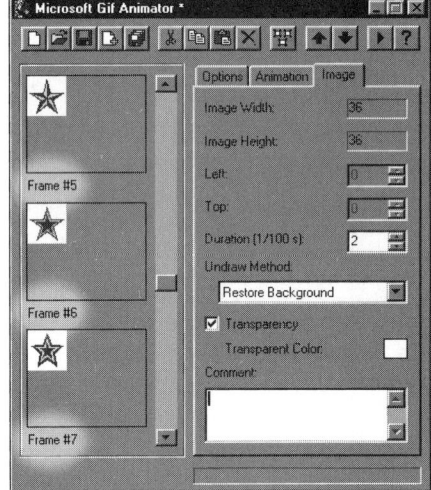

Figure 13-19: Lengthening an animation by reusing artwork.

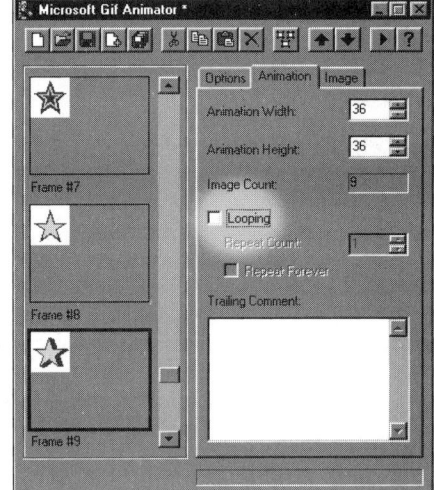

Figure 13-20: Looping your animation.

22. **To play the animation, move the slider bar to the right or press the Play button.**

23. **Click the Save button to save your animation.**

Remember to use a name different from your GIF image files to avoid an *oops* — overwriting one of the animation's image files.

Chapter 14
Cheap Tricks: Inexpensive Web Animation Software

In This Chapter

▶ Using GIFmation for Macintosh and Windows 95
▶ Using GIF Construction Set for Windows

What do we mean by cheap? The answer you get to this question depends on whom you ask. To Donald Trump, there is probably no such thing as expensive software. Of course, the day he decides to put up his own Web page, you can bet we'll be standing in line to take the job off his busy hands. This may be a long shot, but we're betting that — unfortunately for us — you and The Donald are not even third cousins.

Where's our cutoff point? Well, free is really cheap. $99.99 is not cheap, even if you may consider it reasonable. We batted this topic around and decided that anything that falls below a list price of $50 is a tool that most people connected to the Web would find affordable. Besides the two programs we cover in depth in this chapter, you can find other *cheap tricks* at these Web sites: Yahoo! ZDNet Software Library at `headlines.yahoo.com/zddownload/software/`; and CNET site Download.com at `download.com`.

In organizing this chapter, our goal was to give you a sense of what to expect if your goal is to sweeten your Web site — not to go into business as a Web animation guru. The programs we picked stand out not only as cheap dates but as good values for the price. In Chapter 15, we visit the higher-rent district, where we survey easy-to-handle software options with powerful capabilities.

Animating with GIFmation Special Features

GIFmation by BoxTop Software is something like GifBuilder on steroids. If it just did what a free program does a little more elegantly, however, we wouldn't waste your time previewing it here.

- **Program:** BoxTop GIFmation
- **Category:** Commercial software
- **Platform(s):** Macintosh and Windows 95
- **Where to find it:** www.boxtopsoft.com

GIFmation is a program where you definitely get more than you pay for. Besides doing all the basic animation techniques very well, the program pumps up capabilities that can be indispensable to efficient Web animation construction. You can open several animations at a time, make changes and see them in real time, and build global palettes from several images. In addition, GIFmation offers lovely controls for transparency, halo control, and onion-skinning. Take a leisurely walk through these goodies.

Opening multiple animations

Ever wish you could look at two versions of an animation or set up an animation that picks up where another one leaves off? Doing either of these processes is a mega-royal pain if you can open only one animation file at a time. GIFmation lets you open multiple animations simultaneously. All graphic software should have this capability.

Making real-time edits

We're really into immediate gratification. We hate to make a change in frame disposal (see Chapter 13 for more on frame disposal and other basic GIF animation functions) and be unable to see whether we've made the right choice until we run the animation. GIFmation lets you start the animation and add changes as the animation plays, which saves a lot of time and prevents us from having to slow down and show maturity.

Building global palettes automatically

If you don't have a program like Debabelizer by Equilibrium (which you may not have if you don't do a lot of graphics work), optimizing your palettes for an animation is very hard to do. If you're working only with a bunch of *local* palettes, meaning that you have a different palette for each frame, your file is likely to be big — large files make your animation slow. Buying a nifty GIF animation program and having a palette massager thrown in for free is nice.

Here's a quick step-by-step to see how GIFmation handles building palettes. On the CD-ROM that comes with this book, find the folder called `Chap14\Pictwindows` and then find the GIFmation demo. (See Appendix B for more about the CD-ROM.) The demo allows you to import only three frames at a time, but if you visit the BoxTop Software Web site, you can get a temporary license number that enables you to batch-import all the frames in the folder. Now load GIFmation on your hard drive and follow these steps:

1. **Start GIFmation.**

    The program opens with four palettes: Tools, Frames, Palette, and Browser Background.

2. **Choose File⇨New or use the ⌘+N keyboard shortcut.**

    When you begin a new animation, GIFmation opens a document window with a blank rectangle, which represents the image size of the animation. If you know what the dimensions of your animation are, you can set them in advance. We let our dimensions be determined automatically by the frames.

3. **Choose File⇨Import⇨Multiple.**

    After you choose Multiple, the dialog box shown in Figure 14-1 appears. Using this dialog box, you can directly import QuickTime movies and native Photoshop files as well as GIFs and most standard Macintosh image file formats.

4. **Open the PictureWindows (`Chap14\Pictwindows`) folder in the resulting dialog box and click the Add All button.**

    All the images in the folder are added to the Select files to import box on the bottom left.

5. **Click Done to return to the program.**

    The program tells you that it is `creating palette` and `quantizing`. This weird word comes from the world of physics. In GIFmation, it means that the program is throwing out duplicates and is creating a limited color palette based on the images you told it to import. (We're big on trivia.)

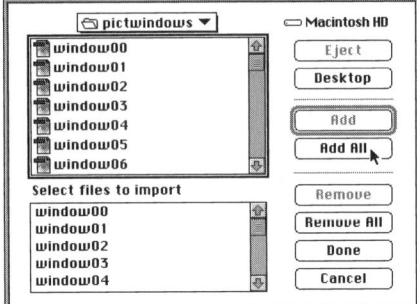

Figure 14-1: The Import Multiple dialog box allows you to import selected files or the contents of an entire folder.

When the program is finished, your files appear as a list in the Frames palette. (If you use Photoshop, notice how familiar this palette looks.) The first frame is displayed in the document window.

As you can see in Figure 14-2, GIFmation has created a *global palette* — a palette that can be used by all the images in your animation — from the files that you have imported. This global palette is a little large, however. We probably introduced some anti-aliasing when we created our files originally. More red colors than we remember creating seem to be in this palette. Now you want to shrink the global palette a little.

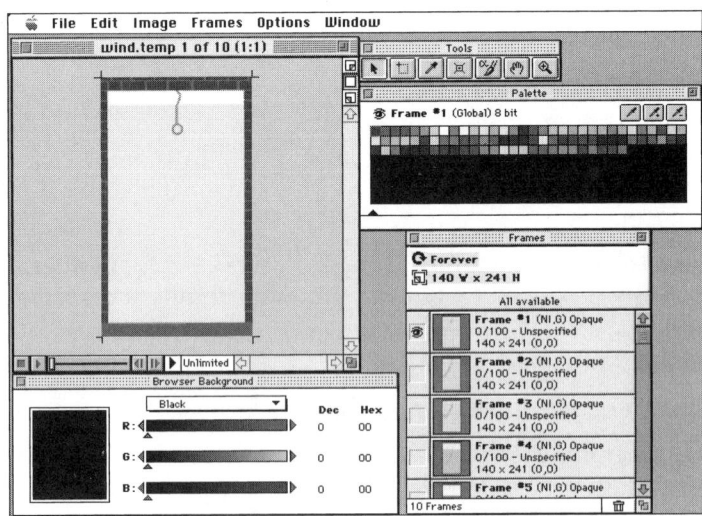

Figure 14-2: GIFmation's work space. Notice the global palette created automatically when you import animation frames.

Chapter 14: Cheap Tricks: Inexpensive Web Animation Software

6. **Select the last image in the Frames palette and then choose Options⇨Palette⇨Use Local Palettes.**

   GIFmation quickly displays a progress bar telling you that it is changing from the global to local palettes. This bar means that any changes you make will be specific to the frame you have selected, not the entire animation.

7. **Choose Options⇨Palette⇨Reduce Bit Depth.**

   You see the Reduce Bit Depth dialog box, shown in Figure 14-3.

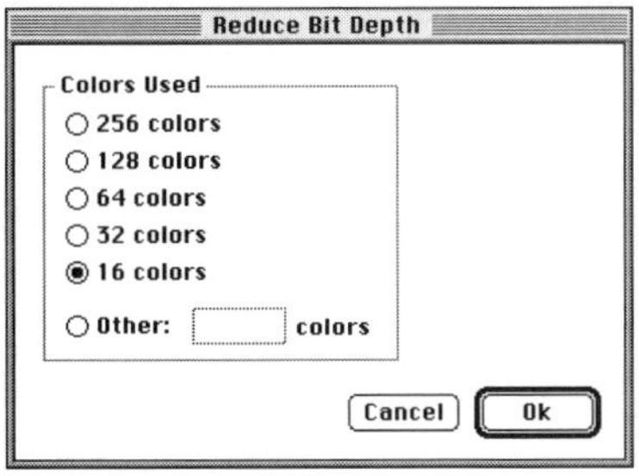

Figure 14-3: Changing the bit depth of one frame in GIFmation.

8. **Select the 16 colors radio button and click on OK.**

   You want to work with the smallest number of colors the frame actually needs. You'll know that you've hit the jackpot when your palette colors shrink but the image on the screen doesn't seem to change. If the program strips away important colors, you can always choose Edit⇨Undo and try again with a larger number.

   Take a look at the Palette window. Several color boxes are filled with what looks like the same shade of red, and other color boxes are filled with a pink that was probably produced through anti-aliasing. Our mission is to eliminate these duplicates.

9. **Click the black triangle at the bottom of the Palette window.**

   The window opens to show you the RGB sliders, shown in Figure 14-4. Notice the three versions of the Eyedropper tool for setting a color as transparent. The first chooses a color from the palette. The second adds another color to the list of transparent shades. The third allows you to make a color, which had previously been designated transparent, opaque.

10. **Click the last red box.**

    Notice that its RGB values are 255 - 0 - 51, which tells you it's the original undithering color we started with and the one we want to keep in the palette.

Part IV: Getting Moving: Animating GIFs & Plug-Ins on Parade

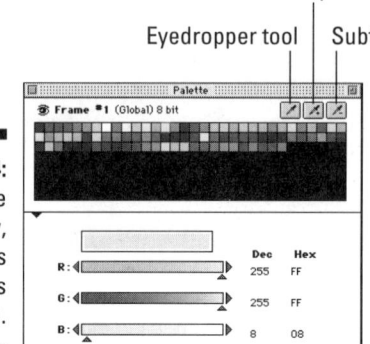

Figure 14-4: The Palette window, with all its options identified.

11. **Click inside the previous red box, change its RGB values to 255 - 0 - 51, and repeat this step for the pink boxes.**

12. **Repeat Steps 7 through 11, choosing the bottom radio button and inserting progressively lower numbers until the extra reds and pinks disappear.**

    We also followed these steps to eliminate the extra black boxes that GIFmation creates to represent the background color, so our final number is ten.

13. **In the menu bar, choose Options➪Palette➪Adjust into Global Palette.**

    This step takes the shrunken local palette and uses it to trim the colors from the global palette. Notice how most of the duplicate reds have been eliminated.

This process is somewhat more time consuming and allows less control than Debabelizer, but it does do the job, and at an unbeatable price.

Controlling transparency

Unlike GifBuilder (which is covered in Chapter 13), GIFmation recognizes transparency settings in existing GIF files, which is an added benefit. In addition, GIFmation enables you to set more than one color in an animation as transparent. If you want to eliminate the color cycle in the Picture Windows animation with GIFmation, do the following:

1. **Go to the Frames window and highlight the frame that contains the color.**

2. **Find that color in the Palette window and click its color box.**

3. **Click the Add Color Eyedropper tool (refer to Figure 14-4) to add this color to the list of transparent colors.**

The incredible shrinking file

Watch your resolutions when you bring files other than GIF files into your animation program. One of the standard procedures followed by Web animation programs in transferring a file to GIF format is to decrease the file to screen resolution. Doing so changes the display size of the file on the screen.

For example, our original PICT files were 250 pixels wide, at 266 dpi. If we imported these files into GIFmation, it would make this conversion, leaving you frames that are 67 pixels wide. We like small, but these files would look like refugees from Disney's *Honey, I Shrunk the Kids.* Even worse, if you mix files of different types and resolutions, they can end up displaying at different sizes, even though they appeared to be the same image size in your original program.

Here's the sad moral of this story: Save everything at 72 dpi in your image-editing program before you animate. GIFmation enables you to resize your images, but only one at a time. This isn't too bad if you've only got three or four images, but it can try your patience if you have to resize more than just a few images.

Editing anti-aliased edges

Back in the not-so-golden age of TV, a thoroughly obnoxious commercial was shown in which a chorus of harpies would taunt, "Ring around the collar! Ring around the collar!" The poor housewife, clearly a loser of the first order, had used the wrong laundry detergent. This mistake was guaranteed to ruin her husband's chance at a promotion. All the people who ought to have something better to do would stare at that stubborn ring of dirt inside his shirt instead of reading his report. We guess it never occurred to anyone to wonder what weird ability would give them the opportunity to see this ring — but that's advertising.

We get to see unsightly rings on the Web almost every day. Of course, we use the nice word *halos* to describe that bunch of anti-aliased pixels that can ruin the look of a perfectly good graphic.

Return to the pumpkin we animated using GifBuilder in Chapter 13. (What, you didn't read Chapter 13? You passed up the chance to play with free software? What would your mother say?) We created it by using a white background and set the background browser color to match. But what would have happened if we decided to change our Web page's background color to black?

1. **Find the file** `PumpStd.gif` **in the folder** `Chap14\GIFimage` **on the CD-ROM.**

2. **In GIFmation, choose File**➪**Import**➪**GIF from the menu.**

3. **In the Browser Background palette, set the RGB value to 0 - 0 - 0 (black).**

   A glance at the Document window in Figure 14-5 confirms your worst fears: An ugly light border around the edge of your pumpkin appears. In most cases, your only option is to return to your image creation software to edit this unsightly ring.

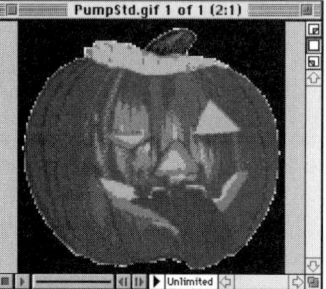

Figure 14-5: Our pumpkin, zoomed up to show the not-so-angelic halo.

Fortunately, GIFmation has halo-killing tools that send those edge pixels to the nether regions, where they belong. Figure 14-6 identifies the options on the toolbar.

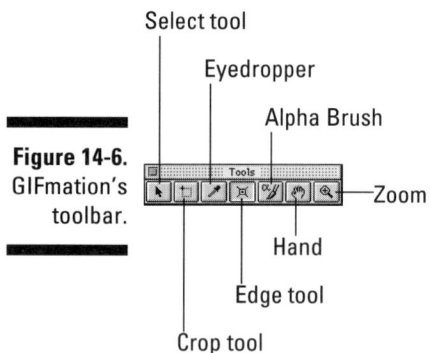

Figure 14-6. GIFmation's toolbar.

4. **Click on the Zoom tool and enlarge the image until you can see the individual pixels clearly.**

   We like 4:1, but then, we're nearsighted!

5. **Click on the Edge tool, move to the Document window, and run the tool lightly around the edges of the pumpkin.**

BoxTop also offers a similar tool in PhotoGIF, but that program doesn't give you a Zoom tool. If you have bothPhotoGIF and GIFmation, do your pixel editing for halos in GIFmation, where you have considerably more control.

You've probably noticed that GIFmation makes assumptions about what is an edge pixel and what isn't. Most of the time, the program's assumptions are fairly good. When GIFmation insists on taking too many pixels or making the edge too jagged, you have another option from the toolbar: the Alpha Brush tool. This tool is for fine-tuning; it turns any pixel it touches transparent, regardless of color.

6. **Click on the Alpha Brush tool and then click on individual pixels to clean up halo stragglers.**

You see the results of this touch-up in Figure 14-7.

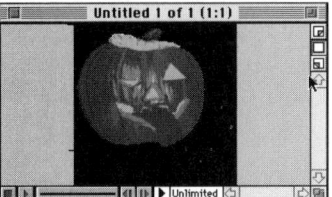

Figure 14-7: Our pumpkin, shorn of its devilish halo by the Edge and Alpha Brush tools.

Onion-skinning

If you read through Part I of this book, you probably know why onion-skinning is so attractive. But even if you didn't, we can show you quickly how this feature works and why you'd want it. Follow these steps to see what we mean:

1. **Follow Steps 1 and 2 in the section "Editing anti-aliased edges," using the same file.**

2. **Import this file three times so that you have the same image as three different frames.**

3. **Choose Options➪Logical Size from the menu.**

The Logical Screen Size dialog box appears, as shown in Figure 14-8. The *logical size* is the actual canvas area, as opposed to the amount of space the image of the pumpkin currently occupies.

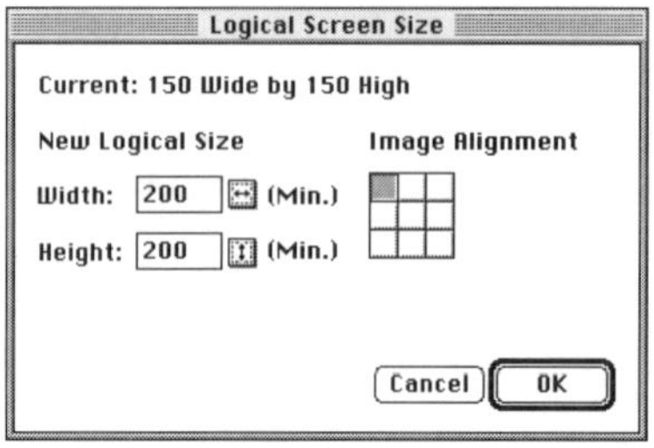

Figure 14-8:
Setting the logical size of your animation is similar to changing the Canvas Size in Photoshop.

4. **Change the logical size dimensions to 200 × 200.**

5. **Select the second frame in the Frame window and choose Options⇨Position⇨Set Position.**

   You see the Image Position in Logical Window dialog box, shown in Figure 14-9.

6. **Type** 15 **in both the horizontal and vertical boxes.**

   Doing this step offsets your image by 15 pixels from the left and top of your image area.

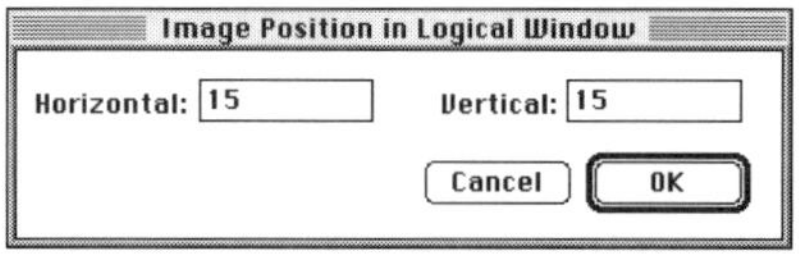

Figure 14-9:
Changing horizontal and vertical coordinates of your animation.

7. **Repeat Steps 5 and 6 for the third frame but type** 30 **in both boxes.**

   Now you're ready to onion-skin.

8. **Highlight the first frame and then click on the Onion-Skin Next and Onion-Skin Previous buttons.**

   These buttons, shown in Figure 14-10, are on the side of the Document window.

Chapter 14: Cheap Tricks: Inexpensive Web Animation Software

We chose the Onion-Skin Next button, which allows the next frame in the animation to be visible through the one you're currently working on. In Figure 14-10, you see the active frame and the *ghost* of the frames before and after the active frame. This really eliminates the guesswork in positioning.

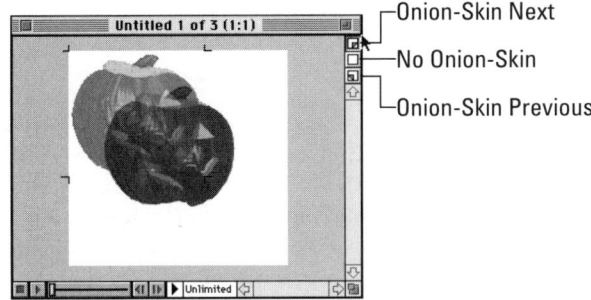

Figure 14-10: The onion-skin buttons on the side of the Document window.

Using GIF Construction Set

If you're looking for an easy-to-learn animation tool for creating looping and rolling text, GIF Construction Set is the solution to your problem.

- **Program:** GIF Construction Set for Windows
- **Category:** Commercial software
- **Platform(s):** Windows 3.1 and 3.11 (16-bit version), Windows 95 and NT (32-bit version)
- **Where to find it:** www.mindworkshop.com/alchemy/gifcon.html

You can download a shareware version from the company's Web site. The software has a preset expiration date, so send in the registration fee (plus the shipping charges). Unregistered copies add a comment block to any GIF file you save. This comment block disappears after you register the program.

GIF Construction Set by Alchemy Mindworks steps you through the process for building animated GIF files. Using the program's well-designed dialog boxes, you take only a few minutes to build, test, and edit transitions, animated banners, and special-effect text titles (like LED signs and soft-shadow animated headlines). Other features that make this program attractive include

- Support for drag-and-drop
- Palette compression

Part IV: Getting Moving: Animating GIFs & Plug-Ins on Parade

- Control and image block editing
- Editing tools to flip, rotate, scale, and crop
- Support for color-editing animated GIF files
- AVI video clip conversion to animated GIF

Using the Animation Wizard

Abracadabra. The Animation Wizard tool makes life simple for even a first-time user of the program. You don't need a to-do list to remember all the production steps. Just click on Animation Wizard's Next button and let the software guide you through the process. The Back and Cancel buttons also help you get around. To see what we mean, follow these steps:

1. **Launch GIF Construction Set.**

    Don't panic when the main window opens. No, you don't see an image window, but that's okay — at this stage, it's not needed. Notice the grayed-out buttons in Figure 14-11. GIF Construction Set lets you know at a quick glance what your possible next option is.

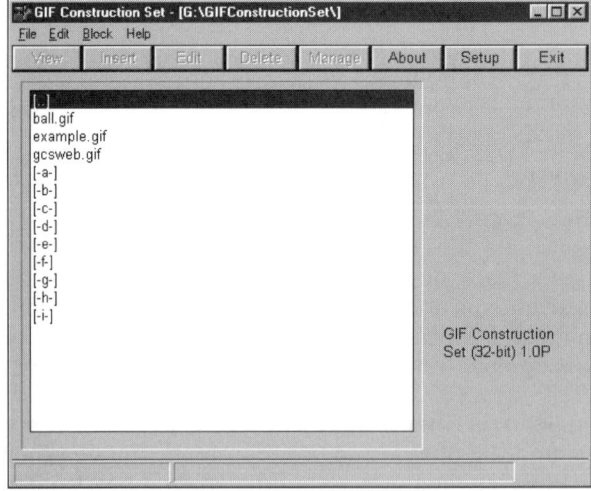

Figure 14-11: The main window showing the menu and file list.

2. **Choose File⇨Animation Wizard or press Ctrl+A, as shown in Figure 14-12.**

    The Welcome screen appears. Click on the Next button to continue to the following screen. The wizard asks you a question: Do you want to create an animated GIF file for use with a World Wide Web Page?

Chapter 14: Cheap Tricks: Inexpensive Web Animation Software 265

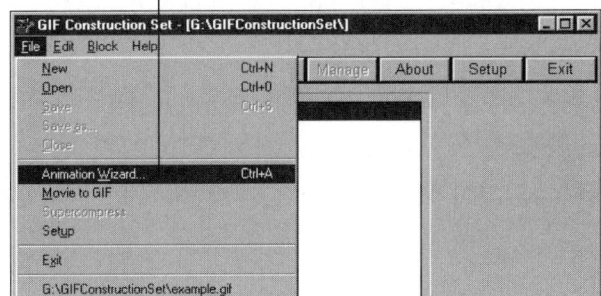

Figure 14-12: Opening the Animation Wizard feature.

3. **Select the radio button marked Yes, for use with a Web page, and then click on the Next button to move along to another question.**

   You can see this wizard screen in Figure 14-13. Too bad other things can't be as simple as this is for optimizing your Web palette to Netscape Navigator.

   You go to another wizard screen that again asks you to choose: Do you want your animation to loop indefinitely or animate once and then stop? Either one is correct. This isn't a make-or-break situation; you always have the option to change your mind later. We talk about editing later on in this chapter.

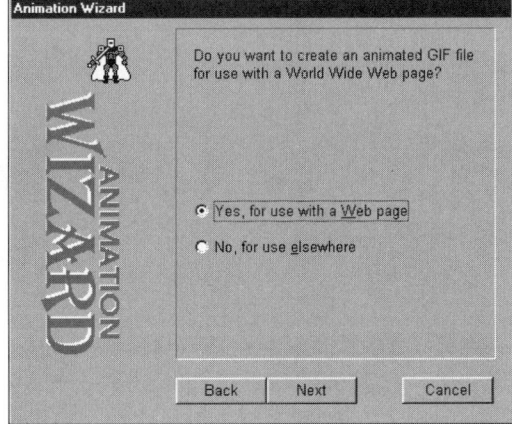

Figure 14-13: An example of the Animation Wizard question-and-answer dialog box.

266 Part IV: Getting Moving: Animating GIFs & Plug-Ins on Parade

 4. **Click on Next to continue.**

 The wizard's third question is a multiple choice to determine your image specifications for the animation. Your four options are

- **Photorealistic:** Alchemy Mindworks defines *photorealistic* as scanned pictures and computer-generated art.
- **Drawn images:** Text or line drawings.
- **Drawn in sixteen colors:** Here, the text and line art colors are limited to the default Windows palette.
- **Matched to first palette:** In this option, the first cell, which can be a background, defines the animation palette, and all the other cells use colors from it.

 5. **Set the image specs and click on Next.**

 After you set the image specs, move on to the next screen, in which you pick the timing delay between frames from the scroll-down menu.

 6. **Use the default value, 100 hundredths, if you have no clue what may work for your animation; then click on Next.**

 As Alchemy Mindworks notes in the instructions that appear in the wizard window (see Figure 14-14), you can change this value after you've built your animation and tested it.

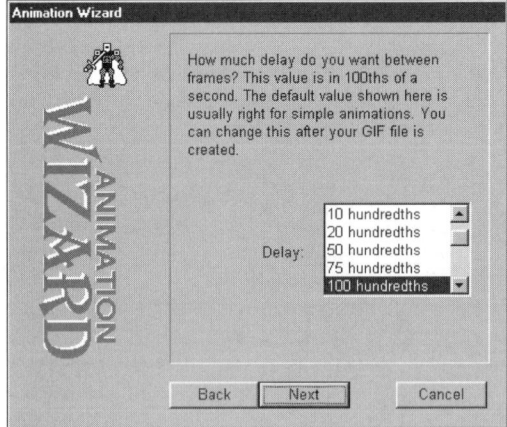

Figure 14-14: You can set the delay between animation frames in this Animation Wizard window.

You now arrive at the final Animation Wizard screen, shown in Figure 14-15. This screen is where you assign your source images to your animated GIF file. For our example, we created a black-and-white text banner using two frames. The second image, Bwaniw.pcx, is the inverse of the first file, Bwanib.pcx. Both files are on the CD-ROM.

Chapter 14: Cheap Tricks: Inexpensive Web Animation Software

7. **In the order in which they animate, highlight one at a time the sample files** `Bwaniw.pcx` **and** `Bwanib.pcx` **and click on Select each image to place in your animated GIF file.**

Alchemy Mindworks recommends importing source images as 24-bit BMP, PCX, PNG, or JPG (also called JPEG) files, rather than GIF files. They also note that Animation Wizard does not include transparency information with the imported file. Use GIF Construction Set to create your transparent animated GIF files.

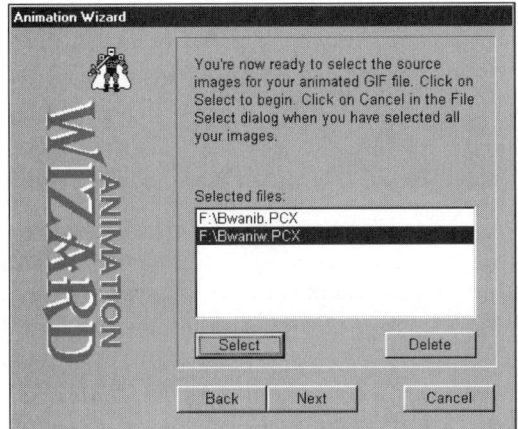

Figure 14-15: Selecting your source images.

8. **Click on the Next button.**

   The GIF animation is generated, and you're returned to the main window, shown in Figure 14-16. On display in the window are the program instructions to run the animation. To preview your creation, click on the View button. Press Escape to exit the View mode.

If you import files as 24-bit images, the program defaults to 256 colors (see the circled entry in Figure 14-16). If your GIF animation has fewer than 256 colors, then compress your palette to minimize file size by using the program's Supercompress feature: File⇨Supercompress. This feature analyzes your animation's palette, displays the status of the compression, and gives you the option of saving or cancelling the results.

To take advantage of other easy-to-use features in GIF Construction Set, go to the text menu at the top of the window (see Figure 14-17). Click Edit and scroll down to reveal four special features:

  ✓ **Banner:** In a dialog box, you enter text and set file specifications to create an animated headline.

268 Part IV: Getting Moving: Animating GIFs & Plug-Ins on Parade

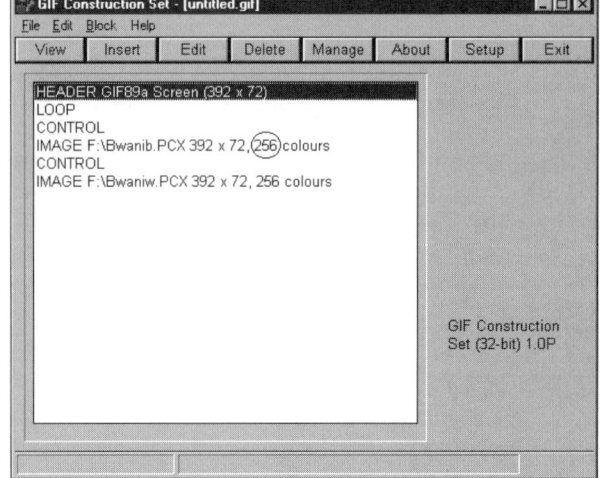

Figure 14-16:
The main window displaying code to run the animation.

- ✔ **Transition:** Edit transitions between cells (frames) by selecting a transition option from a dialog box scroll-down menu. You set display parameters by using the dialog box's check-off list and numeric entry option.

- ✔ **Wide Palette GIF:** With this feature, you construct animated GIF files that can display more than 256 colors.

- ✔ **LED Sign:** Create a scrolling banner that looks like the informational signs you've seen at airports, banks, and subway stations.

Of the four, the one that's the least useful is Wide Palette GIF. The Wide Palette GIF feature is available only in the 32-bit version of GIF Construction Set. Although Wide Palette GIF offers the possibility of working with more than 256 colors, the files are too large and download much too slowly.

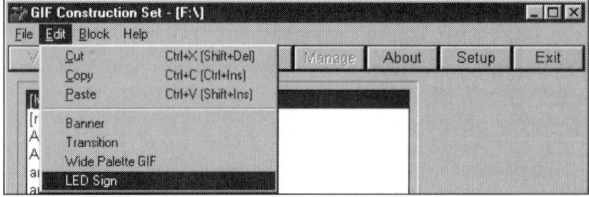

Figure 14-17:
Four editing options.

Making an LED sign

If you're interested in highlighting your latest news item, consider using the LED Sign function. Here's your opportunity to create a scrolling banner that looks like the famous news banner in Times Square. As shown in Figure 14-18, you can assign color, adjust playback speed, and set your sign dimensions. To edit the LED Sign menu, you need to work within the seven-color palette, and you must color-code using the @ sign: @R is red, @G is green, @B is blue, @C is cyan, @M is magenta, @Y is yellow, and @W is white.

The background defaults to black.

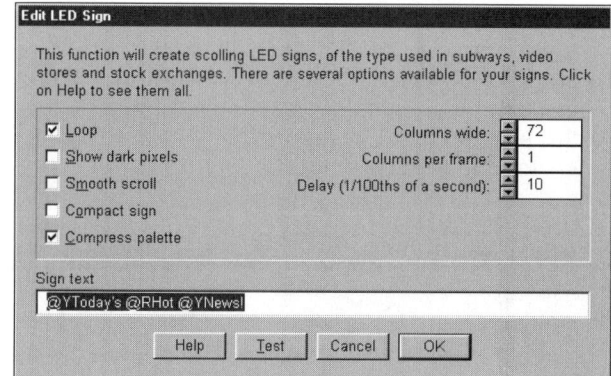

Figure 14-18: Creating an LED sign.

Here's how to code text for an LED banner sign that reads: Today's Hot News! A colored illustration of the LED sign can be found on the CD-ROM in the folder Chap14. The filename is News.pcx.

1. **Go to the text menu at the top of the program's window, click on Edit, and scroll down to select the LED Sign feature.**

   You now see a dialog box.

2. **In the dialog box window located below the label Sign text, type your banner headline text as follows:**

   ```
   @YToday's @RHot @YNews!
   ```

   Notice that no space is added between the color code and the word it's assigned to. Spaces serve their usual function to divide words on a line. The total text length plus color codes can be no greater than 260 characters.

3. **Using the check box list and the numeric entry boxes, set the behavior of your scrolling sign.**

4. **Click on the Test button to preview your LED sign.**

Part IV: Getting Moving: Animating GIFs & Plug-Ins on Parade

 Alchemy Mindworks notes that LED Signs can "generate a large number of individual images, and hence potentially large GIF image." You may want to review the Help listing for Creating LED Signs before building your LED sign. The company provides several hints for maximizing playback and keeping file sizes as small as possible.

Creating soft shadow banners

As shown in Figure 14-19, one of several banner types you can make in GIF Construction Set is Soft Shadow. The software builds the banner with two plain text blocks (repeating the same text) and two control blocks. When you pick the banner Type (right center in dialog box for a scrolling menu of options), only those functions needed remain active. All other menu options are grayed out. For our example, Web Site Under Construction, we chose a script font called Staccato by clicking on the Font button, which brings your list of available fonts into view. From this same menu, you pick your point size (maximum point size is 72). The sample text window displays our 72-point copy. Here are several things to note:

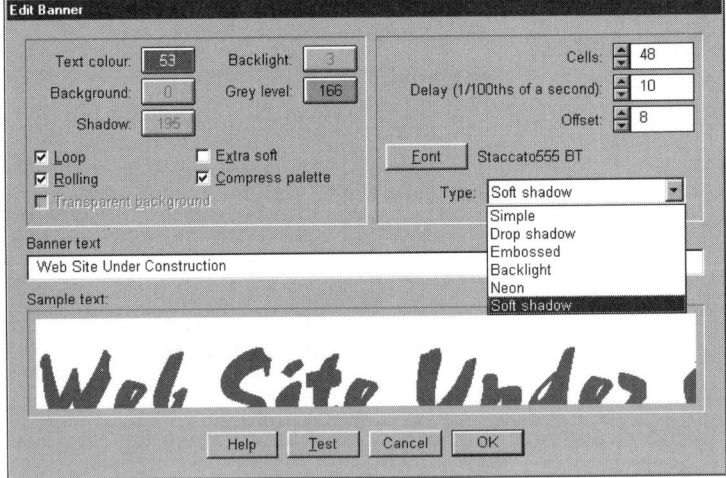

Figure 14-19: You can make a Soft Shadow banner with Gif Construction Set.

- ✔ **Click the Grey level numbered button to assign shadow color:** The number 166 refers to the soft shadow color. The button number changes when you pick a new color.

- ✔ **Use the Offset button to adjust the distance of the shadow from the text:** Click the arrows to change the number.

Chapter 14: Cheap Tricks: Inexpensive Web Animation Software 271

✓ **Font size impacts screen width and height dimensions:** Look at Figure 14-20, and note that when using 72-point type, the width tag is a very large 1,071 pixels. Remember this factor when considering how you may want to use this feature.

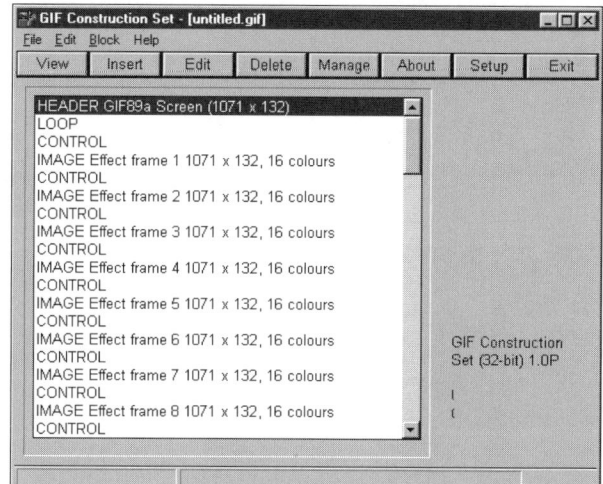

Figure 14-20: Using 72-point type means a huge 1,071-pixel width, as shown by this HTML width tag.

Experiment with the number of *cells* (another name for frames) that you need. The fewer the cells, the faster the banner will scroll across the screen. For our example, we used 48 cells and set delay to 20 ($1/100$ of a second). Always, always test banners on several different machines before using them. Performance is affected by the machine on which they are viewed.

If you decide to edit your animation, click on the line of code to be changed and then select your edit option from the menu. Figures 14-21, 14-22, and 14-23 show where you can change screen dimensions, background color, and palette specs. To change color in your image palette, pick Sorted palette instead of Global palette (Figure 14-21) and then click on the Edit button, which opens a new dialog box (Figure 14-22). Take seriously the program warning about referring to the Help section before changing any colors. If you do decide to modify a color, click on the number to open the palette swatch (Figure 14-23) where you select the color to change. Move the slider bars to set the new color (use Netscape-browser-safe colors only). If you need more help on picking color, refer to Chapter 5.

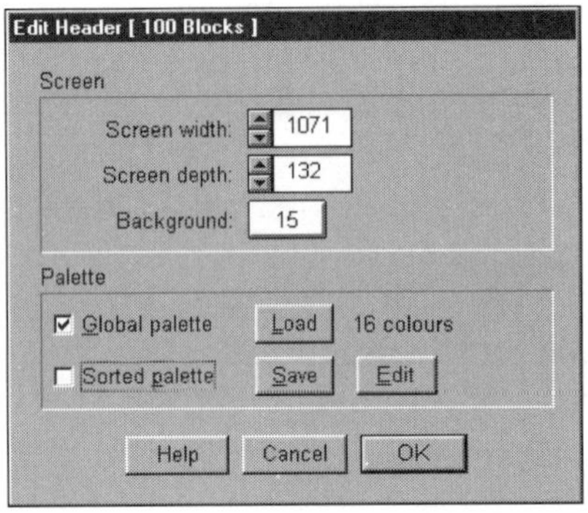

Figure 14-21: Editing your animation's dimensions, background color, and palette.

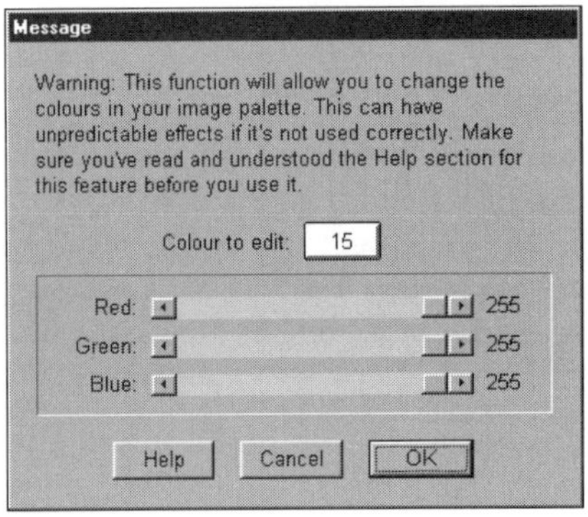

Figure 14-22: Editing a color in your palette.

Unassigned color blocks in the 256-color palette

Colors in animation palette

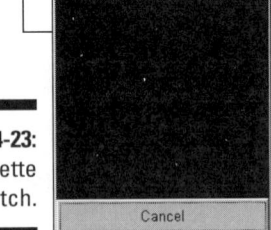

Figure 14-23: The palette swatch.

Editing transitions

GIF Construction Set offers several transition options for your animation. Here's your opportunity to use only one image to create an animated effect. Look at Figure 14-24 and note how you can make an animation appear or disappear, loop, and have a transparent background. Experiment with the different transitions to see which one is the most appropriate for both the image content and Web page placement.

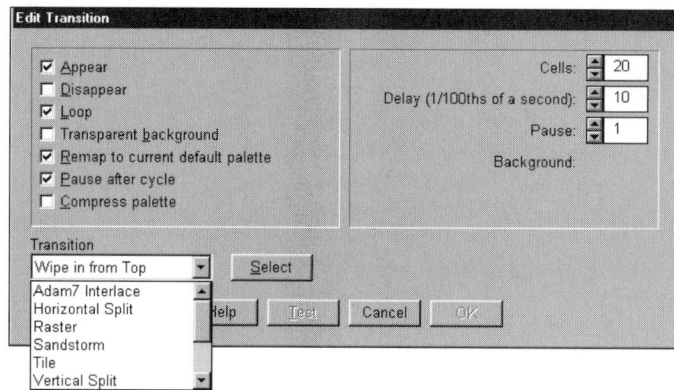

Figure 14-24: The Edit Transition dialog box.

Chapter 15

You Pay, You Play: Commercial Web Animation Software

In This Chapter

▶ Finding out about Web animation software

▶ Discovering WebMotion

▶ Flexing animation muscle using RubberWeb and RubberWeb Composer

▶ Tripping the light fantastic with ObjectDancer

▶ Discovering WebPainter, all in one box

▶ Macromedia Flash 2

One of the neat things about doing a book about Web animation is that new software options keep appearing. In most other areas, software options are mature — which is another way of saying that a big company (no, we won't name names!) has managed to scare away most of its competition. Standardization has its good points, but excitement isn't one of them. In a new and growing field like Web animation, you can still get a new program, which is written by a bunch of unknowns, that knocks your socks off.

The current explosion of Web animation programs has been so knock-your-socks-off overwhelming that we're going to have to start reviewing them in sandals, or doing laundry more frequently! A new program hits the charts almost every week. Fairly soon, just having a great animation program won't be enough. We can see it now: "And, debuting at number 40 with a bullet, it's Web-o-Rama, the first Web animation program that ships with 3-D glasses and a package of microwave popcorn! Free large soda to the first 100 downloaders of our alpha release!" Fortunately, things haven't reached this point yet, although we do love popcorn.

The possible downside of all this variety is that you can't buy just one program that does everything well. Sure, great programs are available, but they have different strengths and weaknesses. Some may not run on the platform you use. Others don't support sound, interaction, or the type of files you want to use. Then there are those programs that do lots of these things, but are more expensive or difficult to learn.

In this chapter, we highlight five programs that have distinctly different features and benefits. We must emphasize that choosing these five wasn't easy, and you're bound to run into someone who's going to complain that we missed their favorite animation program. We're sincerely sorry, but the publisher wasn't receptive to our proposal to bring this book out in three volumes. Maybe next time.

Java Applet of Our Eye: WebMotion

As we write this, there is not a large amount of Java animation applets available, but this will probably change tomorrow. Even when the field broadens, we suspect WebMotion will hold its own.

- **Program:** WebMotion, by Astound
- **Price:** $69.95
- **Platform(s):** Macintosh, Windows 95, Windows NT
- **Where to find it:** www.astound.com

With a price barely over the software discussed in Chapter 14, WebMotion is a good program for someone who is eager to move beyond GIF's comparatively limited options, but can't deal with a long learning curve. This animation program is one that you can use effectively on the same day you break the shrink wrap.

Why use WebMotion?

Using WebMotion and wonderful flower images from PHOTO 24 Texture Resource (see Appendix A for contact information), we created an animation called Flowers.html, which you can view with your Web browser with the file Chap15\flowers.html on the CD-ROM. You also find a WebMotion demo on the CD-ROM. We chose to review this software for the following reasons:

Chapter 15: You Pay, You Play: Commercial Web Animation Software

- **It's a Java applet (see Chapter 1 for a description of Java and Java applets) with a simple and clear interface.** We knew that Flowers would be a fairly large animation, even after we broke it into three separate chunks for quick downloading. (See Figure 15-1 for a look at a single row from a single animation frame.) We wanted the benefits of streaming technology without plug-ins. We were also tremendously impatient, and WebMotion offered the clearest and easiest-to-understand interface we've seen in a program that goes beyond GIF animations.

- **It offers great visual control over object placement.** You can easily drag objects onto the *stage* (WebMotion's animation composition space) and then draw lines or set curves to describe the path of their motion. This means that you choreograph your animation, but WebMotion makes the frames for you from your imported objects. Because WebMotion has special functions for scaling and rotating the object itself, you only have to deal with one motion at a time. The program handles the combination for you. Imagine how easily you can create a flying logo!

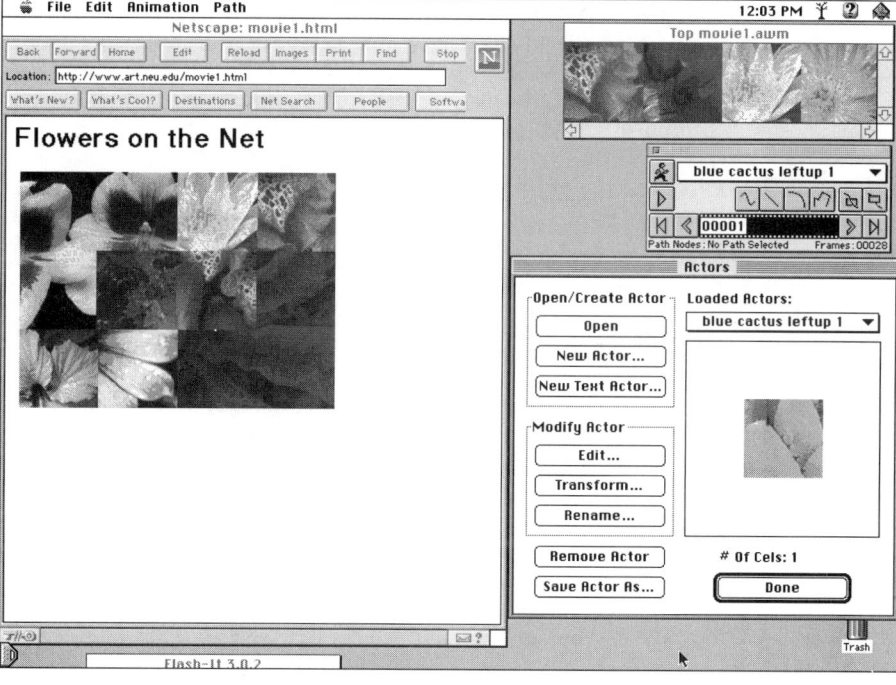

Figure 15-1: One compiled frame in this animation has four actors. We used three separate animations like this to make the completed three-row animation.

- **It makes timing easier to master.** We were working with a large number of images that stay on the screen for different periods of time, and we needed a program with lots of timing control.

    In classic animation, timing is one of the hardest things to get right. If you make a timing change in one frame, you may have to redraw several others. In WebMotion, you can massage your timing frame by frame, or distribute the number of frames you need over the length of your path of motion. Because you can also easily set acceleration into motion and then add deceleration at the end, creating realistic pacing of your action is within your grasp.

- **It automates functions that are very difficult to animate.** Interactions between animated *actors* can be very difficult to develop in most animation programs. In WebMotion, developing interaction between actors can be astonishingly easy. Using the Magnetize function, you can attach two actors to each other so that they maintain their individual motions, but also move together. A good example of how you can use this is when you want one character to chase the other around in a circle.

- **It enables you to add simple interactive elements without the agony of programming.** Most animation programs that offer interactivity give you too many options. WebMotion covers the options you're most likely to use and makes using them easy. The viewer can click your animation and jump to a new URL, click forward or backward in the animation, or play a sound.

If you're into program icons, Astound WebMotion has one of the drop-dead cutest we've ever seen. The little red spider used by Astound for this program probably makes a great animation character.

Drawbacks?

WebMotion by Astound is not for everyone, but if you don't need the things that WebMotion doesn't have, why pay for feature bloat? The following three general drawbacks, however, did stand out to us:

- **WebMotion comes with a mind-bogglingly miniscule manual.** At first this looks like a big benefit. A fat, dense user manual usually means a long learning curve. In this case, however, you're left to figure out important things on your own, such as the different ways to import actors (in a group or as individuals), and how to make actions overlap. We had to deconstruct the samples that came with the package to figure it out. On the other hand, the program is simple enough that this was possible.

Chapter 15: You Pay, You Play: Commercial Web Animation Software

- ✔ **WebMotion lacks guides, or any form of coordinate or pinpoint positioning.** This drawback isn't surprising given the emphasis on keeping the path fluid. However, creating an animation where elements need to butt or animate at precise angles is harder. If you want anything lined up precisely, you'd better have a good eye and a steady mouse hand. The only precise positioning available is the choice of a *registration point* — a point of reference that acts like a pushpin on a bulletin board — to attach a graphic to its path.

- ✔ **WebMotion has no object creation tools, except very simple type functions.** You can make a line of type, but you can't break it apart into individual letters to alter their color or size, or to move them individually.

Flexing Animation Muscle: RubberWeb Composer

Animation is supposed to be fun. Watching animation and thinking up animation ideas is fun. Making these ideas come to life is not always fun. We like RubberWeb because it puts the fun back into the process.

- ✔ **Programs:** RubberWeb Composer, by Rubberflex
- ✔ **Price:** RubberWeb, $99; RubberWeb Composer, $299
- ✔ **Platform(s):** Macintosh
- ✔ **Where to find it:** www.rubberflex.com

RubberWeb approaches the whole concept of new software the way we think it should be approached: looking for stuff that hasn't been done before and making it possible to do the stuff. RubberWeb is a great program for people with active imaginations who are tired of being locked up in the object- and cel-animation world.

Why use RubberWeb?

Actually, RubberWeb is available as two different programs. RubberWeb is actually RubberWeb Composer *Lite*. RubberWeb enables you to work with one imported image and a Photoshop alpha channel. RubberWeb Composer has more distortion functions, supports multiple image layers, and works with key frames.

Using RubberWeb Composer, we created an animation called Calliope, which you can find on the CD-ROM in the Chap15 folder, as well as a RubberWeb demo. Calliope started its life as an oil-refinery photo from Digital Stock (see Appendix A for more information on Digital Stock). Unlike the other animations, we created this one solely because this software exists; it would have been next to impossible with any other program.

RubberWeb is a one-trick pony, but what a trick! We like this program for the following reasons:

- **Photo, not object, oriented.** Very few Web animation programs make working with photographic images easy. You have to create your frames one-by-one and keep any photo based elements as separate cut-out objects. This program lets you do all the fun stuff — work with layers and composite image elements.

- **Incredible morphing functions.** RubberWeb enables you to treat your images as if they were printed on sheets of bubble gum. You can distort, flex, and scale images. These effects not only make for fun images, but gives you the option of making a movie from the process of distortion itself. Imagine a blinking fish-eye, a beating heart, or a flag waving in the wind, and use the program to go from there.

- **Tiny files with big visual interest.** These files don't need streaming technology. Animations are automatically generated from key frames by the browser plug-in — which means that they are incredibly tiny. You can have several of them playing on a Web page at the same time without making your viewers antsy.

- **Very viewer-savvy.** Rubberflex plug-ins automatically read what kind of hardware they're being asked to play on, and adapt the presentation as necessary to ensure that the animation looks the same regardless of the platform. This function eliminates all that time spent in testing the animations on various platforms.

Drawbacks?

Something as new in concept as RubberWeb Composer is bound to have a few speed bumps. Consider for yourself whether these obstacles can get in your way:

- **No sound capability.** We really, really, really wanted to add the sound of a merry-go-round calliope to our animation. As rock philosophers once said, "You can't always get what you want." Maybe sound will be available in the next software revision.

Chapter 15: You Pay, You Play: Commercial Web Animation Software

- **Not a program for a graphics newbie.** Although using RubberWeb Composer can be delightful if you have the right graphics background, without such experience you're in the wilderness with a box of wet matches and no compass. To do anything as exciting as the RubberWeb sample animations, you must have an image-creation program that supports alpha channels. Having prior experience with a video or animation program also helps, because the interface is somewhat complex (see Figure 15-2). Most seriously — we're beginning to sound like a broken record — the manual appears to have been written by a true believer in "No pain, no gain." The folks at Rubberflex do, on the other hand, have among the most responsive and accurate tech support staff we've ever experienced.

- **Non-standard interface.** Macintosh programs are usually distinguished by having a certain similarity of look, feel, and vocabulary, which tends to make it easy for an experienced user to orient themselves in a new package. Rubberflex has created a colorful, but strikingly non-standard, environment.

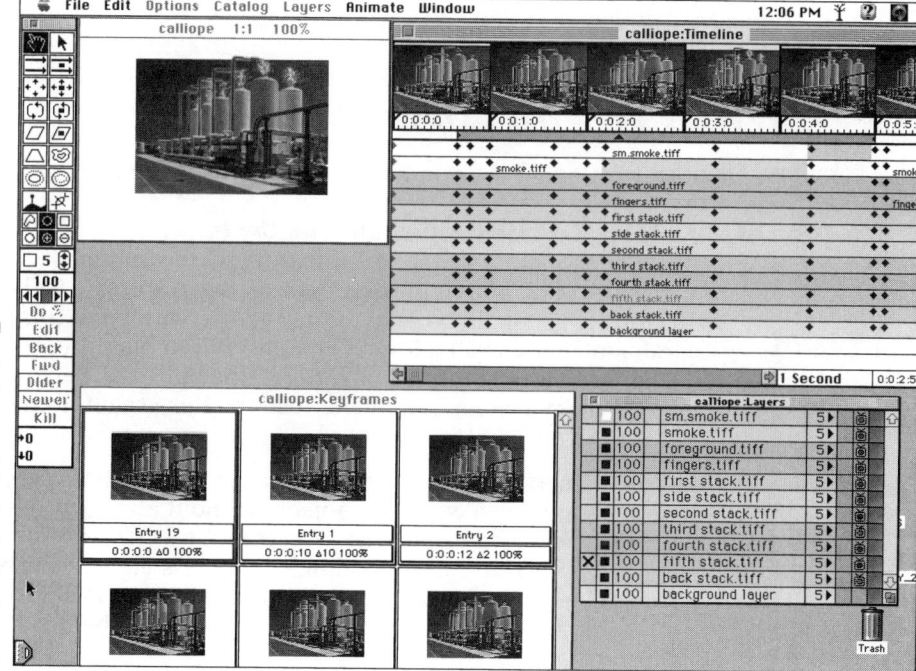

Figure 15-2: The Rubber-Web Composer interface with some of its important windows.

Tripping the Light Fantastic: ObjectDancer

With ObjectDancer, you take a giant step into professional graphics software. Although this program shares features with WebMotion (it focuses on objects and paths), the difference between using these two programs is enormous — kind of like moving from disco to professional ballet. If you've ever worked with Macromedia Director, Adobe Premiere, or Adobe After Effects, you'll feel very comfortable with ObjectDancer.

- ✔ **Program:** ObjectDancer, by Paceworks
- ✔ **Price:** $299
- ✔ **Platform(s):** Macintosh Power PC
- ✔ **Where to find it:** www.paceworks.com

The Paceworks folder on the CD-ROM has a demo version of the program, along with animations that can make you feel like Gene Kelly.

Why use ObjectDancer?

We think ObjectDancer is a winner because it offers the following:

- ✔ **The best typographic capabilities on the Internet.** Typography is the Achilles heel of most animation software. After you type in your word or phrase, you're limited in what you can do to animate it. This is not so in ObjectDancer. If you long to play games with type, this is the only program currently available that enables you to play chess, not tic-tac-toe. Change colors in individual letters. Change sizes. Separate letters and move them around. And never lose the links that tell the program these characters started life in a group.

- ✔ **Good object-manipulation tools.** If you want to rotate a logo, attach sound to action, even anti-alias objects without all the problems that usually make smooth edges a fantasy, then ObjectDancer is the answer to your prayers. You can use built-in transitions and special effects to add immediate interest to your files without looking false or slowing up playback. ObjectDancer can handle all changes can be handled with absolute precision.

- **Lots of import and export options.** ObjectDancer imports a wide variety of formats, including sound and QuickTime movies. But what's equally important for people who hate to redo existing work is that ObjectDancer also exports files that can be used outside the confines of the Web.

- **Enables you to open multiple windows and share objects across animations.** Because ObjectDancer has a library function, anything you import into the program or make within it can be saved and reused in other animations. Being able to work on more than one file at once makes matching alignments, sizes, and movies that relate in a sequence easier.

- **Professional quality timing tools.** ObjectDancer, like traditional video production tools, has a complex, multi-layered time line that gives you easy drag-and-drop control of all timing elements.

Drawbacks?

If you're on the verge of asking, "Shall we dance?" then we know how you feel. We need to give you just a tiny warning about ObjectDancer. This program is really nifty, but it still stumbles a little on the fast steps. You need to consider that ObjectDancer:

- **Is a serious investment.** Whether you pay in time or money, ObjectDancer doesn't come cheaply. It is one of the most expensive Web animation options, but the financial drain is only part of the package. Unless you have extensive prior experience with a similar high-end program, you will burn the midnight oil mastering its ins and outs. Check out Figure 15-3 for a sense of ObjectDancer's rich, but complex, interface.

- **Can't create non-text objects inside the program.** With such a superlative text generation function, ObjectDancer surprisingly doesn't offer any tools to create other elements. Having to import even simple geometric objects from other programs can add a lot of time to the animation process.

- **Lacks interactivity.** Type-based animations are a great basis for dynamic links. The fact that ObjectDancer does not have even the simplest interactive functions when other, less complex programs do seems a pity.

Figure 15-3: Learning how to navigate through the extensive menus of Object Dancer can offer many rewards to those with patience.

All in One Box: WebPainter

- **Program:** WebPainter, by Totally Hip
- **Price:** $169.95
- **Platform(s):** Macintosh, Windows 95, Windows NT
- **Where to find it:** www.totallyhip.com

If you love to draw and cartooning has always been a favorite way for you to pass the time, then consider WebPainter, Totally Hip's cel-based paint and Web animation program. In WebPainter you have the option of creating either GIF animations or Sizzler sprites (stream-based animations on Web pages). Sizzler is a competitive multimedia player to Macromedia Shockwave technology. With the Totally Hip SizzEdit program, the Sizzler multimedia player can be edited to add sound and interactivity. If you want to view animations that support either Sizzler or Shockwave, go to Totally Hip's and Macromedia's Web site to download, and then install, the appropriate plug-in for your browser. You can also find plug-ins at the Netscape Navigator Inline Plug-ins: 3D and Animation Web Page:

```
home.netscape.com/comprod/products/navigator/version_2.0/
plugins/3d_and_animation.html
```

Why use WebPainter?

Check out the Totally Hip folder on the CD-ROM, in which sample animations are available for viewing. We also include for your viewing pleasure the first animated Rich Tennant cartoon! It's located in the folder Chap15\Tennant on the CD-ROM. In the folder you find three variations of the animation (three different file saves), the GIF89a frames saved in WebPainter and Photoshop (compare file sizes — the WebPainter version is compressed), a palette CLUT, and a readme file with details about the animation files. We also provide TIFF and PCT versions if you want to see how these frames work in other programs.

You can use these files for your personal use only but cannot distribute or resell them in any form to third parties. Contact Rich Tennant if you wish to use the files for other applications via fax at 508-546-7747 or e-mail Rich at the5wave@tiac.net.

We feature WebPainter software because the program:

- **Is a professional-quality cel-based animator.** The programmers at Totally Hip understand the animator's world by providing editable cel windows. Because Totally Hip includes drawing tools that you can use to modify each individual cel, it isn't necessary for you to reopen the files in your graphics program to edit them. You can fine-tune artwork, layout, transitions and timing all under one roof.

- **Supports onion-skinning.** In cel animation, you need an onion-skinning tool to do sequence planning and to control the flow of movement and momentum. Seeing previous and following action from one cel to the next is easy in this program. You can turn this feature on and off as needed.

- **Offers a registration tool.** If you're serious about creating smooth action, then you need a registration point to stay constant throughout the animation. You can easily access the WebPainter registration point from the toolbar and place it in the document window with the click of the mouse. Repositioning is no problem; just click the point and drag it to its new position.

- **Features all the standard painting tools.** We didn't need to leave the program to create our drawings. All the familiar graphics program tools are here: Marquee Selection, Lasso Selection, Magic Wand, Eye Dropper, Move, Eraser, Paint Brush, Pencil, Paint Bucket, Air Brush, Magnifier, Registration, Text, Line, Shape, and Smudge.

  The Paint Tools Palette toolbar icon functions are clearly understood, and the toolbar can be dragged to wherever you want on your screen. Submenus exist for selecting brush shapes, line widths, and pattern

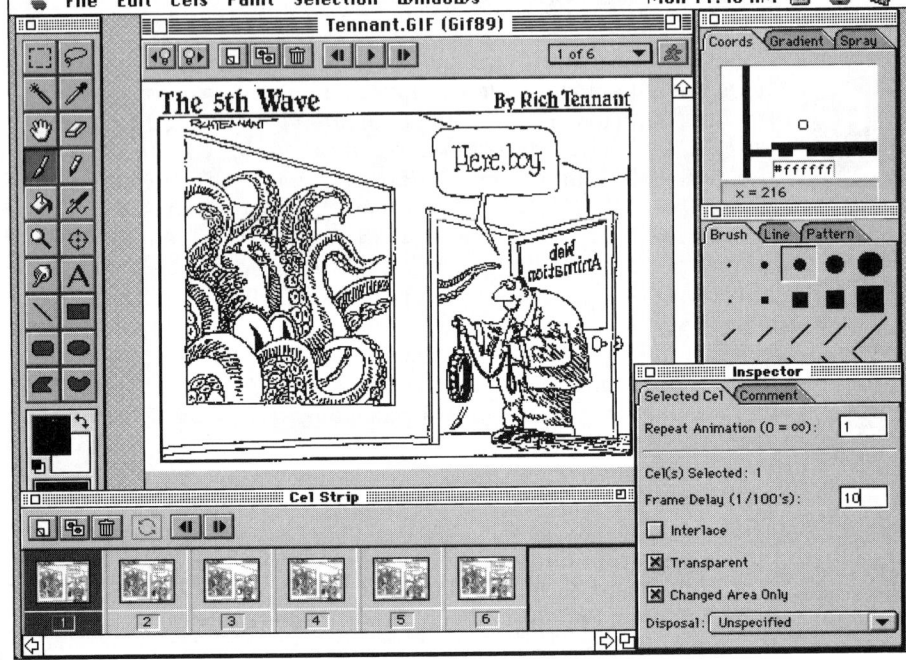

Figure 15-4: The WebPainter work area shows toolbox windows for displaying information about individual cels.

fills. Brush shapes can be edited with the click of the mouse to select or deselect and turn pixels on or off. The Coords, Gradient, and Spray windows enable accurate navigational positioning of the cursor, fine tuning of coloring functions, and nozzle control of the Air Brush tool.

✔ **You can edit an object to create new versions of a cel.** One thing that attracted us to WebPainter version 2.0 is the potential for building animated headlines and/or logos. With the Text tool you can enter your headline copy into a cel or import a piece of clip art. The cel can then be duplicated, and individual cels can be manipulated and transformed by scaling, rotating, slanting, flipping perspective, and cropping.

Drawbacks?

For all of the strengths that WebPainter has, some problems are also present in version 2.0. Consider the following as you develop your animation storyboard.

✔ **Not enough animation-specific distortion tools.** You can use transform tools such as slanting and perspective, but to achieve a fully believable squash and stretch effect with WebPainter, you must do some of your own drawing.

- ✓ **You need to understand the essentials of animation before you can get the most out of this program.** The company provides advanced tutorials to discuss, for example, how to create secondary action in your animation. The tutorial's focus, however, is on which software tools to select. An assumption is made that you have an understanding of animation basics and can draw what is described in the tutorial. Even so, Totally Hip does provide several hundred animation samples on their CD-ROM, each of which you can open in the software.

- ✓ **Does not do in-betweening.** Look at Figure 15-4, in which we illustrate the WebPainter user interface and some of the most important features of the program. The animation we show is based upon a Rich Tennant cartoon. Because WebPainter has no *in-betweening* feature (the capability to generate new animation cels by interpolating between two key frames), Rich had to draw each variation by hand. To save production time we used the Duplicate Cel button to reuse cels and the Cel Strip to reorder some cels. These features simplify the copy and paste function for building cels with composite image files.

If you have teenagers at home who love animation and drawing, give them WebPainter and turn them loose. Your teens will be whipping out animations for you, while creating an impressive portfolio for college.

No Flash in the Pan: Macromedia Flash 2

If you already have some animation experience, particularly with Macromedia Director, you may find yourself cooking up a storm with Flash. This program got its start as FutureSplash Animator, and it doesn't look or function like Director, but the basic principles and animation frame interface are sure to feel like comfort food to you.

- ✓ **Program:** Flash 2, by Macromedia
- ✓ **Price:** $199 (as of August 1, 1997)
- ✓ **Platform(s):** Macintosh, Windows 95, Windows NT
- ✓ **Where to find it:** www.macromedia.com

You find a fully-functional but time-limited demo version of Macromedia Flash 2 on the CD. Figure 15-5 introduces you to the uncluttered Flash interface.

Why use Flash?

Flash is a complex and fascinating tool that's particularly well-suited for creating interactive animations. You can import elements from paint or illustration programs into Flash, and it offers a very nice tracing tool to turn bitmapped graphics into objects. However, if you only import elements from outside, you're missing a lot. Flash is a truly cool place to create object-based illustrations. We know this program will become the favorite tool for many of the animation addicted because it contains:

- **Innovative painting tools.** It's unusual to find a new way to organize paint and draw tools, and Flash makes some things that are frequently difficult remarkably easy. For example, blends are finally done right. You can paint with a gradient blend using a paintbrush and "lock" the blend so that different strokes match up correctly in an image. You can paint inside, outside, or over an object at any time without generating another cumbersome layer or dealing with masks or alpha channels.

- **Easy tweening and key framing.** You can work frame by frame, enable the program to create in-between frames, or mix the two in an animation. You don't have to figure out how many frames or how much time an action should take — Flash handles these aspects of tweening (or *in-betweening*) for you. (If you need to know more about tweening, visit Chapter 4.) It's easy to see which frame sequences are tweened versus drawn, because they display differently in the time line.

- **Objects are infinitely reusable.** All elements you make can be saved as *symbols* (cast members or objects) and accessed multiple times in an animation without adding to the animation size. Even better, symbols live in a library, from where you can take them out and share them among as many animations as you'd like.

- **No programming needed for interactivity.** Unlike using Macromedia Director and then Shocking the files for the Web (see *Shockwave For Director 5 For Dummies* by Greg Harvey if you want to learn how to do this), *interactivity* (assigning and animating buttons) is a dream. You don't need to learn a programming language like Lingo. For example, buttons are saved in all their possible states as one symbol, which means that you don't have to program button interactivity. If your button has an up and down state, both will be saved as part of the symbol file and are activated correctly when clicked.

Drawbacks?

Alas, no program is perfect, even when it's been created by a company as well-established in interactivity as Macromedia. If you're weighing the options, you might want to consider the following:

Chapter 15: You Pay, You Play: Commercial Web Animation Software

Figure 15-5: The Flash working area hides a wealth of complex features in the toolbar and pull-down menus.

- **Learning curve on painting tools.** Wait! Didn't we say we loved the painting tools? You bet, but we had to learn to love them. Although the options they offer are tantalizing, these tools are tough going if you use other illustration programs. A simple example: colors don't transfer between all tools, so you must get used to reestablishing the same color to go from the paintbrush to the pencil tool.

- **Interface logic can take some getting used to.** Macromedia offers some very good lessons to get you started — and believe us, you need them! Some standard functions, such as changing the background color, are surprisingly hard to find. This shortcoming is because the program relies heavily on pull-down and pop-up menus instead of floating palettes. If you're an animation beginner, or you're very production-oriented and need to master a program quickly for your job, you may find Flash a little hard to navigate through.

- **Not easily organized for cel animation.** Flash is an object-oriented program, but it's painting-based, which means that it's hard to build and animate objects with many individual moving parts. Although some simple alignment tools are available, no guides or easy-to-see overlays enable you to select and move a discrete portion of an image.

Chapter 16
Making the Final Cut

In This Chapter
▶ Types of animation problems
▶ A deal breaker of a problem?
▶ Animation files that are too big
▶ Animations that are too long
▶ Animations that are too slow
▶ Animations that are too rough
▶ Viewer-based problems

*B*reak out the champagne! Invite your friends! Put your animation work of art on your Web server! You're finally done and ready to show your work to the world, which is waiting breathlessly for your opus. You envision fame, fortune, or at least admiring looks from your significant other. So (fanfare please) here it is!

Oh. Well, after all, it's only your first Web animation. Anyone can make a little mistake. The animation just needs a little tweaking. No, really! We don't think it looks like your animated cat was stuffed with big, caffeine-laced mothballs and chained to a treadmill! Maybe small mothballs.

What do you do if your animation doesn't live up to your expectations? Do you have to start from scratch? Well, that depends. In this chapter, we talk about frequently experienced problems with animations and how to deal with them.

The Wisdom to Tell the Difference

Problems exist that you can fix with relative ease at the final stages of your animation, and problems exist that force you to go back, back, way back. Nothing compares, however, to misjudging into which of the two categories your difficulty falls. Agonizing over a problem that looks tough but is really a quick fix is pretty bad. Discovering — after lots of playing at the animation stage — that your problems date back to your animation's Jurassic (planning) era is much worse.

Of course, we'd like to think that if you've used this book as a reference and guide, you won't fall prey to any of the problems that will take you back to your original frames or — heaven forbid — to your original idea. If for some reason you've missed critical information, the rest of the chapter gives you yardsticks for measuring the depth of your problem.

Major Problems — Can This Movie Be Saved?

Not too many of these major problems appear in the animation process, which is just as well, because they require returning to an earlier stage in the process. Rather than duplicate information, in the following list we reference the problem and the place in this book where you're most likely to find a solution.

- **Constant, unexpected color shifts.** You have a problem with file color indexing, either with your original source materials or with the animation frames when you converted them.

  Solution: Read Chapter 5 on color and Chapter 11 on file conversion.

- **Viewers complain that they can't follow the action.** People who don't know what you've been up to seem puzzled when they view your animation. Viewers may ask you to stop and run it more slowly so they can *see* it, but then they still have problems, unless the animation is viewed frame by frame.

  Solution: Read Chapters 3 and 4 on planning your animation and characters.

- **Your character shimmers or flutters.** When you created your frames, you probably didn't manage to line up your character's action on a visual *baseline*. Being even one pixel off can make a big difference in the animation's appearance.

  Solution: Read Chapter 9 on imaging tools.

- **The animation is over 30K in size, and your software doesn't stream.** The optimum size for a Web page is commonly quoted as being 30K. If your animation is that large and it isn't the only item on your Web page, your viewers will have download problems. If you're using a plug-in animator that streams your files, this is less of a problem.

  Solution: Read Chapter 1 for a discussion on streaming and Chapters 10 and 11 on file conversion and compression.

✔ **Your animated type is fuzzy and hard to read or looks too rough.** This can be caused by inappropriate use of anti-aliasing when you made your frames. It can also be the result of scaling up bitmapped type.

Solution: Read Chapter 6 on using type in animations and Chapter 9 on imaging tools.

Minor Headaches — Take Two Aspirin And . . .

Most other problems can look fairly bad, but so does poison ivy. For most animations, virtual poison ivy is not life threatening, although it can make you tremendously irritated and uncomfortable for a little while. Here, we throw over-the-counter remedies on your most likely problems at the end of the animation process.

The file is too big

Files that are too big really fall into the gray area between major crises and minor headaches. Much of the division depends on what's making these files so large and how much of the size issue is basic to the animation. Is the problem the physical dimension of the file, or the detail that it requires?

Animation as football field

It's awfully tempting to let frames take up serious screen real estate. Maybe you've laid out a Web page and left a specific amount of space in your layout for this animation. Shrinking it down for something as pedestrian as bandwidth doesn't seem right. Maybe you've got an animation that you made for something else, and all you want to do is import the QuickTime file and post it on the Web. Go back and redo? Suuuuuure.

Unfortunately, you can't solve the problem by just shrinking the animation's browser viewing size, because load time will be the same. An animation with a large file size is always a large, slow-to-download animation, no matter what size it is depicted at in the browser window. You'll have to decide which is more important: a beautifully large animation that almost no one will watch, or a pint-sized version that gets lots of traffic.

If you are going to change previously existing animations for use on the Web, consider importing the animations into an in-line plug-in animation program (see Chapter 1 for a discussion of in-line plug-ins) that uses streaming technology. Frame size will no longer be the determining factor. If this isn't an option, see whether your animation lends itself to being broken into smaller pieces. If clear divisions exist, like a flashing collage of images, you can chop the animation into smaller segments and run each image on the page at the same time. The animation may load in pieces initially, but eventually all the images will play together.

Animation deep as a well

Although in most cases the best solution to the size issue is to bite the bullet and shrink the file size, in certain occasions this just doesn't work. You may have a good animation idea, but the animation may be too detailed. Some of that detail may just be frosting — textures and shading, for example. If this is the case, sacrificing the frosting will be noticed mostly by you, not by your audience. Or you may run into problems with different amounts of details blurring and remaining from frame to frame. If so, your file falls under the "Major Problems" heading from earlier in this chapter. You must remake your frames to simplify them.

The most frequent reason for an animation file being too big is that it has too many colors. Nothing fattens up an animation faster than multiple palettes. You can end up with multiple palettes if you import non-GIF–formatted files into your animation program and you trust the program to cut the extra palettes from the file. Trusting the program is a game of Russian roulette. Sometimes it works and saves you mega-time — but those times it doesn't are heartbreakers. If your file problem is with color depth, however, you probably won't have to remake the files. You just need to invest the time — and maybe money — in a program to create a shrunken global palette for your animation.

The file is too long

Web animation is not the best medium for animating *War and Peace*. Okay, whether the right medium for animating anything by Tolstoy exists is questionable, but that's a little off our topic. What we mean is that *War and Peace* is a very dense book with many parallel plots and complexities. You would need more than a streaming video — you would need a Niagara Falls video. We're not suggesting that you tried something as ambitious as that, but if your animation is running long despite the feeling that you've handled your idea well, you're probably trying to do too much.

The solution for this problem is concept-related, not technical. You have basically two ways you can approach the problem: Limit yourself to a single action or break up your animation.

Limiting yourself to one simple action

Look at your animation and decide for yourself what's the most clever and interesting part. Maybe you have a dog sitting up and begging, catching a bone, and running across a banner. Break these actions into their major parts and you have four chunks:

- Dog sits up.
- Dog begs for bone.
- Dog catches bone.
- Dog runs across banner with bone.

Certain chunks can stand alone; others depend on other actions. You can have the dog sit up, but this is very short indeed. Sitting up and begging, however, doesn't have to result in flying T-bones. This can be an action on its own, compact and complete. The same goes for the combination of begging and catching. The dog running across the banner is also self-contained.

After you isolate these subactions, you can decide which ones are the most successful or the most important for what you're trying to show. For example, if you're running an ad for a dog obedience school, sitting up and begging may be a better way to show your success rate than having Fido run wildly across a banner.

Delete the frames that show action you don't need, and your animation is sure to slim down. Individual frame deletion should be a simple task in most animation programs.

Breaking up your animation

This solution is a variation on the first solution. You still need to break down your animation's action to find where things start and stop and where actions must be seen together. What you do with this knowledge, however, is somewhat different. Instead of tossing away those extra frames, you set up each group of actions as its own animation. In our dog example, you can have up to three animations:

- Dog sits up and begs.
- Begging dog catches thrown bone.
- Dog takes off across the page with the bone in its jaws.

Put each portion of the original animation on a different page on your Web site but in the same relative position on the page, and you have a doggie serial. Even if you show each animation consecutively on the same Web page, the animations load separately and more quickly. Placement on the page helps give the sense that they are linked actions.

The file is too slow

Confusing animations that are too slow with ones that are too long is easy to do. The difference is one of content. Animations that are too long have a natural pacing when they play on your disk drive. They look smooth and contain much action, which lends itself to the kind of action breakdown we discussed in the previous section.

For example, think about a little doggie in the animation window example. Sitting up and begging on a Web page shouldn't need more than six or seven frames. If it's taking 12 frames, your animation is moving too slowly. "What, are you crazy? I needed 15 frames just to get him to sit up!" a student of ours once complained. Well, he was right, but his animation wasn't doing a simple sit up and beg. His dog woke from sleep, arched its back, wagged its tail, and *then* sat up. These are separate subactions and belong under the *too long,* not *too slow,* category.

Animations that are too slow break into fewer subactions. In fact, you may discover that they are not easily broken out at all. Just too little is happening over too long of a time period. To be brutally frank, an animation that's too slow is just *booooring.* And boring is particularly deadly on the Web, when the piece may loop forever — at least until someone flees your page for one with more action.

An animation that's too slow can be a major pain to fix. This situation can happen if the original idea isn't strong enough, which means a trek to Chapter 2 for brainstorming and development information. Assuming that your idea is good, delaying reaction and eliminating frame creep are two basic ways to clean up the execution in the animation program.

Delaying reaction

The simplest way to deal with a dragging animation is just to pick up the delay speed. For your animation, our recommended $^{10}/_{100}$ delay between frames may just be too long. Try the animation once with no delay, to see whether the action smooths out. You may discover that part of the animation now runs too fast, which is easy to solve. No rule says that every frame must spend exactly the same amount of time on the screen. If you need more information about using delay, visit Chapter 13.

Beware! If you are working on a fairly old and tired system, your processor may not be up to the challenge of displaying your work at the right speed. If you're using pre-Pentium or pre-Power Mac hardware, this is almost guaranteed to be the case. Before you make a radical speed change, try to preview your work on a faster system, or put your work on the Web and ask a friend with a zippier processor to view it for you.

Eliminating frame creep

If you are new to animation, you may have fallen prey to one of the most frequent animation problems — *frame creep*. This happens when you try to make your work perfect and smooth, saving every two-pixel movement of an image as a separate frame. The frames keep piling up.

The trick to fix frame creep is knowing how and where to trim. Begin by returning to your storyboard and your key frames. See Chapters 2 and 3 if these terms ring no bells for you. Ask yourself: What were you trying to do? How many key frames did you have? Did you accomplish what you were trying to do in the first place, or did you get sidetracked? Not following your storyboard while creating your frames can cause you to lose sight of your goals.

Assuming that you don't have a storyboard problem, launch your animation program and follow these general steps:

1. **Delete all frames except your key frames and save this animation under another name.**

2. **Run this animation several times, just slowly enough that you can see every frame change.**

    Your stripped-down animation should be very jerky and choppy. If it isn't, you really *have* added too many frames!

3. **Add one in-between frame between each key frame.**

    Ask yourself whether the action is evenly spaced between the key frames. If not, go to the next step.

4. **Add an extra frame where the key frames are too widely spaced.**

5. **Run this animation again.**

Repeat Steps 3, 4, and 5 until you have the absolute minimum number of frames necessary for your sequence to read as an animation. If any areas are clearly missing action, you can cautiously add one frame at a time. You may discover, after you strip most of the frames out and add a few back, that you can solve the rest of your problem simply by varying the individual frame rates.

If most of the animation looks good at this point but you now have a couple of jumps in the animation, address only those places. Either add a frame or, if absolutely necessary, return to your image creation program and make a frame specifically to fill the gap.

The file runs rough

The opposite of *smooth and boring* is *rough and distracting*. Like a car engine with the same jittery symptoms, a rough animation ride has many possible reasons. And just like an engine, isolating the problem can take a little time. Unlike with a car, however, no grease-covered mechanics will solve the problem for you and then hit you with the bill.

First try to figure out what about your animation feels rough. Start by slowing the whole thing down and watching for a telltale sign. Sometimes this will make the problem jump out and grab you. Not obvious? Well, as the great Sherlock Holmes used to say, "Eliminate the impossible. Then whatever is left, however improbable, must be the truth." Time to put on the stalking clothes and examine the evidence.

The case of the missing frames

You know that you tested all your frames when you made them, so why do you have this sense that something isn't right?

Maybe you really did make all the frames you needed, but one has lost its way. This can happen if you are working with a program that imports files consecutively by number and name. Incorrectly typing a character when naming the frame and not catching the mistake is easy to do. Deleting to rename files can often introduce invisible, extra spaces in long Macintosh and Windows 95 filenames. Such minor errors can lead to a dropped file, a file imported out of order, or one file replacing another. Maybe when you drag-and-dropped, you really did drop — a file, that is. Always check your original frames against those that you have in your animation program if a quick jump in the animation frames exists.

The case of the incomplete edit

When you're on the road to a finished animation, you often make several changes. Maybe you experimented with different delay times. Perhaps you tried different ways of disposing of the frames, or you changed the coordinates of a moving object at different intervals. Any of these changes can leave ghosts to ruin an otherwise perfect animation. All it takes is one global edit while incorrect frames were selected, or a change made to one frame instead of many. Retrace your steps. Select everything and redo your global settings. Doing so can catch any number of hard-to-find problems without forcing you to examine every frame individually.

The case of the mixed messages

Sometimes a flash or jump in an animation isn't caused by a missing frame but by a bad case of mix-and-match. If you brought files into your animation from different sources or had to stop work in the middle and return later, you may find that you have not changed transparency settings in all your frames. In a fast-moving animation, mixing transparent and opaque files can lead to flickering and occasional flashes of unwanted color. If you eliminate the other options and you still suffer from frame flicker, examine the individual frames in the problem area for a mix of transparent and opaque elements.

Post-animation blues

After you finish the animation, you naturally assume that the process is over. The animation works nicely and looks good. Then you put the animation on your Web page, browse over to your site, and see whether it's playing. Hmm. . . . Sometimes you find more problems with the animation, as the next few sections explain.

Please make it stop!

Because of inconsistent browser implementation, most people choose to set their animations on a *loop forever* cycle. (For more on looping, see Chapter 13.) Much heat can be generated about the endless loop. Certain people will argue that you'll get complaints only if your animation isn't good, which is not necessarily true. Many people find the constant grinding of their hard drives distracting, not to mention the performance problems that hit their systems with a lot of fast-moving, endless loops taking up RAM. Most viewers won't take the trouble to complain. The noise simply adds to their acquired Attention Deficit Disorder and prevents them from lingering at your Web site.

Making everyone happy is impossible. If you set your animation to loop only a specified number of times (our personal recommendation, when the target audience allows this), you'll run into people whose browsers don't support this option. If you don't loop, you run the risk of the animation not being seen and appreciated.

Eventually, all browsers should accept the *wait for user input* option, which gives the viewer control over this issue. Your only other options are to work with plug-in or Java-applet software that doesn't depend on HTML interpretation to set your repetitions, or to use a CGI script that allows the viewer to turn off the animation.

The file worked fine on my system!

The most frustrating problems are those that show up where everyone can see them. Chapter 12 deals with the value of testing your animation under different browsers, but this may not always be possible. Downloading the latest version of Microsoft Internet Explorer or Netscape Navigator is relatively easy, but finding older versions can be more difficult. No way exists for normal people to check out their animation on a wide variety of platforms and processor speeds.

If your animation looked fine on your local machine but is causing problems on your Web site do the following:

- ✔ **Check for broken links.** When you set up your Web page links, were you careful to use relative, rather than absolute, addresses? If you're getting `file not found` errors, this is probably your problem. If you don't know about setting anchor addresses, we recommend *Creating Web Pages For Dummies* by Bud Smith and Arthur Bebak (IDG Books Worldwide, Inc.).

- ✔ **Check your <IMG SRC> settings in your page's HTML.** It's awfully easy to mistype a Height or Width tag. If your animation runs but looks distorted, you probably just plugged in the wrong character.

- ✔ **Check your MIME type.** If your plug-in animation works beautifully when you load it locally but doesn't work at all when you transfer it to your Web site, your problem may be MIME type. No, this is not the time to make elegant hand gestures while wearing white makeup. *MIME* (Multipurpose Internet Mail Extension) is the matchmaker between a file type and its plug-in. Without a MIME definition, your server acts like it can't find and play your animation. If you're using in-line plug-in software, it's possible that your service provider has not added your plug-in's MIME type to its system. Use those white-gloved fingers to send e-mail to your Webmaster!

- ✔ **Make sure your own browser is up-to-date, is Java enabled, and is loaded with the right plug-ins.** This may seem obvious, but you'd be surprised. We once got a phone call from a panic-stricken person who went to visit a friend and wanted to show off his animation. When they got to the Web site, the animation just sat there, stuck on the first frame. Of course, the friend hadn't seen any reason to download a newer browser version and hadn't realized that a whole world of moving image is out there!

Non-playing animations can also happen because of bugs in *current* browser software. For example, try checking your page with Netscape Navigator 3.0 or Internet Explorer 3.1 if you've been working with Netscape Communicator. If the animation plays, your problem is the specific browser — something you can warn your viewers about with a note on your Web page.

Part V
The Part of Tens

In this part . . .

No *...For Dummies* book is complete without the Part of Tens. In the next chapters, we offer a three-course meal of tasty Tens — a checklist for animation packages, a list of do's and don'ts for image conversion, and a meaty sampler to spark your brainstorming creativity.

Chapter 17
The Checklist — Ten Software Gotta Haves

In This Chapter
- Gotta have layers
- Gotta have scale, skew, rotate, flip, and flop
- Gotta have transparent background
- Gotta have palette optimization
- Gotta have placing coordinates
- Gotta have Netscape and Microsoft browser compliance
- Gotta have editing for text, image, header, and comment blocks
- Gotta have a viewer
- Gotta have a download test
- Gotta have good documentation

Gotta animate, gotta make it dance, and then gotta take a note from Gene Kelly and always be prepared. Identify what's missing from your grab bag of tricks to minimize the glitches and maximize the *wow* factor in your animations. Not only will this increase your production efficiency, but also the added fun factor benefit — your creative juices will be flowing.

Gotta Have Layers

First things first: If your graphics program doesn't support layers, then upgrade. Think of layers as the digital substitute for the clear sheets of acetate that traditional cel animators used to plan out their animations. Layering makes building the necessary parts of your animation easier, by enabling quick duplication of art elements. Afterwards, you can view and edit each layered element in context to each other for positioning, scale, and line of action. Because all the drawing layers are in one file, they also share a common palette, which reduces potential playback problems. When the artwork is completed, each layer is saved as its own file.

Gotta Have Scale, Skew, Rotate, Flip, and Flop

Introduce these software tools into your repertoire, and learn to exploit their potential for building a quick series of animation frames. Using these tools, you magically transform a single piece of artwork into an unlimited number of variations and keep tight deadline jitters at bay. Don't be afraid to experiment by applying more than one tool to the same object. This way you can develop a more complex animated movement. Always remember to make a backup, with a new filename, before modifying anything. Doing so ensures that you can return to the original if you don't like changes you've made.

Gotta Have Transparent Background

You need a transparent background option if you want to use irregularly shaped artwork. Look for this feature in both your graphics and animation programs, because not all animation programs can import image files with their transparent background data. Such programs only recognize the image file. In this case, the transparent color must be assigned in the animation program.

Not all browsers properly display transparent GIF files, so always test transparent GIF animations with multiple browsers and computer platforms. If this becomes a real headache, substitute your Web page's background color (no dithered color) as the assigned transparent color.

Gotta Have Palette Optimization

It's quite simple and straightforward. If you want to shrink your animation to its smallest possible size, look for color-compression features in your animation program. Keep an eye out for global palette options also, so that you can remap (without dithering for non-photorealistic images) the same palette to all your animation frames, regardless of where they were made. Doing so enables you to avoid strange color shifts when the animation is viewed.

Gotta Have Placing Coordinates

When you see an animation on a Web page, three attributes have been assigned: the HTML vertical and horizontal space tags for layout position on the page; the height and width dimensions of the animation frame; and the position of the moving object within each animation frame. Because you want to keep image-size dimensions as small as possible, your animation program should enable you to set an animation frame size larger than the imported image size. Once the frame size is specified, you use the placing coordinates feature to position the artwork within each animation frame to set the position of the moving object within each animation frame.

Gotta Have Netscape and Microsoft Browser Compliance

We won't mince words here: If the animation program you're considering can't create animations that are fully compliant with current big-fish browser standards — or are playable using a Netscape plug-in — find something else to use. Nothing is more upsetting than spending hours building an animation, only to see it turn into an unintended online horror show. Make a habit out of asking around, or checking out newsgroups, to keep abreast of ongoing corporate battles in this arena.

Gotta Have Editing for Text, Image, Header, and Comment Blocks

If you want to fine-tune your GIF animation, look for easy-to-use animation program editing features for specifying revised block parameters, including instructions for controlling image display, graphic rendering, and special features. For example, editing a control block like the header means you can adjust fields, such as the dimensions of the screen area where the GIF file is displayed, its background color, and its global palette.

Gotta Have a Viewer

An absolute must for your animation program is a preview mode. Without this mode, you can't test and finalize such factors as the total number of cels, timing delays, transitions, and whether you want to play it once or to loop your animation. The viewer has a screen for display and buttons to play the animation, stop it, or move it forward and backward on frame. If possible, test your animation on more than one computer, particularly if you're using a fast machine loaded with lots of RAM. What may be perfectly fine on your system may slow to a snail's pace on an older model.

Gotta Have a Download Test

You think you're in the clear; after all, you did follow our advice about previewing and fine-tuning your animation in your software program. Taking these steps is a good start, but unless you have a download test, you may be in for a rude awakening. Now is the time to check for application software and HTML coding bugs. Until you do a series of download tests, you won't know for sure how fast your animation downloads, or if it even loads. You won't know if it plays within different browser environments or fits within the design of your Web page. Skip this step if you want, but be prepared for nasty e-mail.

Gotta Have Good Documentation

This *gotta have* falls into two categories. The first category impacts your learning curve. Before buying a program, check the magazine and online reviews of the program to find out how the manual, Help features, and technical support are rated. Below-average or poor ratings lead to hair-pulling and to tossing the program out the window! Pay a visit to the software company's corporate Web site and see how the program is supported online. Does the company offer tips and tricks, newsgroups, a gallery, and demos to try? If your program is backed by good customer support, your learning curve will improve. You'll enjoy the experience much more as you explore this new territory.

The second category is your housekeeping chores — building a well-organized image database library. The better you document and organize your own stuff, the higher your productivity will be. Take this simple test: If you can describe in detail (quantities and sequence order, please!) what you were eating a month ago on a Tuesday afternoon, forget about this warning. Otherwise, do yourself a favor and get into the habit of keeping track of your work. In six months, you'll thank yourself that you did.

Chapter 18
Ten Commandments of Image Conversion

In This Chapter
- Consider bandwidth
- Crop your files to their minimum image size
- Work at screen resolution
- Scale files before indexing
- Edit before JPEG conversion
- Index to the Netscape palette
- Optimize your palette
- Don't dither flat art
- Don't anti-alias moving objects
- Don't interlace animation frames

You don't get too many opportunities in this life to play God — or even Charlton Heston, come to think of it. You have to grab such opportunities before they slip through your fingers.

Of course, you have to be careful not to grab too hard. Because this looked like one of those chances, we asked our publisher if we could bundle stone tablets with each book. They told us this would be fine if we picked up the shipping costs. That's why we're reduced to paper and a few pages in the Part of Tens. Godhood is not easy.

One note before we hand down the law: if thou haveth problems with the language of us would-be gods, readeth Chapter 11, Verse: Mondo Conversion, for transcendent illumination.

Thou shalt consider bandwidth and keep it holy

This is the World Wide Web Golden Rule. Keep it. Live by it. Write it on walls in bathrooms — with washable ink, of course.

Until we're all connected to the Internet with direct cable or T1 connections — and may that day come soon — keeping bandwidth at the forefront of your mind is the ultimate requirement. Be considerate of those people on a tight budget who can't upgrade their modems each time a new standard hits the streets. Even if you are not the considerate type by nature, watching out for bandwidth violations works to your own selfish best interests. More people will stick around your Web site to see what you have to offer if you serve up your site quickly.

Never do anything to make your images larger than necessary. If your files have to be enormous, invest in a plug-in streaming technology. If you have the knowledge and experience to do something this cutting edge, be willing to shell out the money to ensure that you deliver it under optimum conditions.

Thou shalt crop thy files to their minimum

Whenever possible, your working image frames should be the same size as your final animation. If this isn't possible, constantly zoom out to approximate what your images will look like when they are at their true size. Doing so will prevent you from adding unnecessary detail or making elements too small to appear on the screen. Your files' edges should be trimmed and should not contain pixels that are unnecessary to display your moving objects. If stray pixels are left from unexpected anti-aliasing or moving objects, the pixels should be hunted down and mercilessly deleted.

Thou shalt work at screen resolution

Because your files will never be seen at anything better than screen resolution, keeping all that extra pixel information a high-rez file contains is pointless, unless you like to torture your hard drive. If you really think you'll need to print these files later, save them as a separate document, which may be worth the extra file space. After all, this is why the heavens gave us removable media. Working at screen resolution gives you an accurate sense of how many pixels your file will actually use when it is imported into an animation program. Doing so avoids tedious reimporting that can happen when you mix resolutions in an animation.

Thou shalt scale files before indexing

Nasty, ugly things happen to files that are indexed and then scaled. The animation software can compensate for resampling fairly well when you're still in RGB mode, but life gets tougher when you take away its options. When software resamples an indexed image, the process can introduce blurring, pixelation, and a host of evil artifacts. Even worse, each indexed file in your series can be interpreted in a different way by the software, which leads to objects being off by a fractional pixel. This situation causes your animation to shimmy and shake when it runs.

Thou shalt edit before JPEG conversion

JPEG is a *lossy* compression format. In English, that means that good data gets thrown away, never to reappear if you need it. This situation worsens with an increase in the amount of compression that you use in a JPEG file. Always completely edit photographs before you squeeze them down for Web use. When we talk about editing, we mean cropping out or fixing anything that can cause the information in your file to be reinterpreted. This includes applying filters, scaling, and shifting colors, brightness, and contrast.

Thou shalt index to the Netscape palette

You never know who will be looking at your animation work, or what kind of system they may have. Your safest bet to ensure that an animation will look the way you expect it to look is to use the Web-safe non-dithering (Netscape) palette. This used to be a more difficult commandment to follow than it is now. You once had to convert hex code to RGB numbers and to make palettes from scratch. Now you have no excuse, and we'll send down a plague of ugly dither dots if you try to squeeze out of this one. Web CLUTs (*color look-up tables*) abound. They're downloadable from the Web, available on CD-ROMs accompanying Web graphics books, and included in lots of software.

Thou shalt optimize thy palette

Indexing your palette to the 216-color Netscape palette is not enough, although doing so certainly sets you walking down the righteous image conversion path. Your goal should be to trim down your animation palette until it holds only those colors that you really need to display your images effectively. Extra colors can add weight to your images. Your completed animation will be heavier with the more images you use — which means a slower load time. We know what happens in slow loading Web pages: Those click-happy viewers move on.

Thou shalt not dither flat art

Except for illustration files that make heavy use of color blends, no good reason exists to use dithering when you convert a flat color file to GIF format. What was Mr. Badanimator thinking of when he used lots of blends for an animation that he knew he'd be showing on the Web? As punishment, he must go to Chapter 5 and read all about color.

Dithering should be used only for continuous tone images (photography or photographic-quality computer graphics). For these images, dithering is a requirement if you want them to look even marginally like they did before you processed them.

Thou shalt not anti-alias moving objects

You may think this one belongs in another set of stone tablets, but the issue of anti-aliasing has a lot to do with image conversion. Anti-aliased moving objects violate more than one conversion rule. These objects add unnecessary pixel information to your images, unacceptably enlarging your animation's file size. The objects make it hard to assign transparency to backgrounds because they create a blended buffer zone. Anti-aliased moving type also results in decreased legibility.

Those stair-stepping pixels known as *jaggies* are not pretty, but you experience them differently when they're moving on the screen. Because of motion blur, our eyes fill in the gaps somewhat, thus softening a slightly jagged edge. We don't have any visual mechanism that works to the reverse.

By the way, we've got nothing against anti-aliasing any imagery that stays in place on a Web page. Use anti-aliased backgrounds and static type to your heart's content.

Thou shalt not interlace animation frames

Interlacing is an excellent strategy for a standalone GIF image. Interlacing gives people something to look at while they wait and provides the important sense that something really is happening. If you're showing an animation, however, viewers ought to already know that something is happening. Interlacing wreaks havoc with a GIF animation because it makes each frame display in stages rather than all at once. This profiteth you nothing, if you catch our drift.

Chapter 19
Ten Ways to Make the Earth Move

In This Chapter
- Turning the earth
- Closing in on the earth
- Watching the earth circle the sun
- Making a rock 'n' roll earth
- Walking the earth
- Playing soccer with the earth
- Lifting the earth
- Riding the earth express
- Moving earth
- Rising with the earth

*A*nimations are part planning, part technique, and part tools. The biggest part — and the hardest to give a percentage to — comes down to the *c* word: *creativity.* Everyone is capable of thinking outside the box, but sometimes you need a little push and encouragement. This chapter outlines several different ways to make a simple image of the globe move in a Web animation.

The *key frames* (those that describe critical action points) that follow are the result of the brainstorming process that we discuss in Chapter 2. We've kept them rough — almost exactly as they were originally sketched — so that you can see how little detail you need to develop an animation concept in a brainstorming session. If we can do it, so can you. We've given you ten sketches. Send us e-mail or URLs with the mega-possibilities for a travelling earth that we know you have bottled up inside. We'll post them with credit on our Web site (see the Introduction for addresses).

Earth Turning

Begin at the beginning, as the White King once said to Alice. A tour through the downloadable GIF animation sites on the Web produces at least a dozen variations on the turning-earth idea. Small, medium, and large earths are everywhere. There are flat-color earths and high-resolution blue marbles. Some turn east, and a few turn back time by moving west; we start with Africa and Europe, but because this animation will loop forever, you can start anywhere. All of them operate on the same basic idea shown in Figure 19-1. Our thumbnails show three *snapshots* of the turning process. For a little more research, take a good look at a spinning globe and an atlas, also.

Figure 19-1: Thumbnails of our spinning globe.

Earth Closing In

Figure 19-2 illustrates one of the simplest and most straightforward of our moving earths. You can use this series as is with the animation running once, which leaves the viewer with a close-up of the earth. You can also make a loop, with the close-up earth as the mid-point of the animation. You can duplicate the frames and set them up in reverse order, for an earth that comes forward, and then recedes. A third alternative is to combine a zoom with the earth turning. Zoom the earth to the foreground, and then set the world spinning. Yet another combination, although a bit more complex, would be to spin the globe as the zoom takes place.

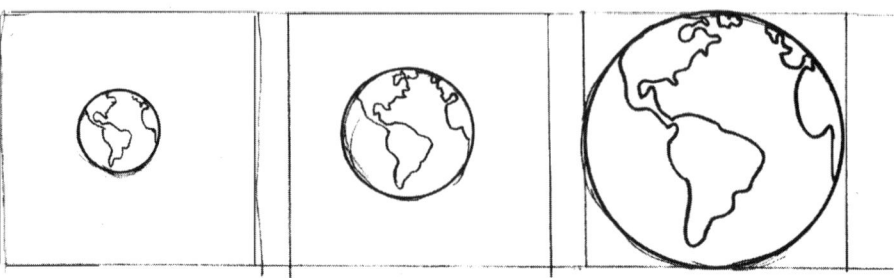

Figure 19-2: This earth can zoom in reverse or be combined with a comet.

Earth Circling Sun

After you make the world turn and zoom into view, taking these actions one step further and putting them into their *real world* context is not a big step. In the case of the earth revolving around the sun, you have several options for how much image to show and where to *stop* the animation. You can keep the sun a flat, bright color, or use the flicker/shimmer effect of fire (as we did in the Pumpkin animation (`Chap13\PumpAnim.gif` on the CD-ROM) to give this stationary object more life. We start our rotation, shown in Figure 19-3, as a foreground to background motion, but it is just as easy to flip the frames horizontally and then run them in reverse order. Astronomy buffs will point out that our sketch of the earth circling the sun shows the earth out of proportion and revolving too close to the sun. This is not a mistake. It's called Artistic License, and we renewed ours recently.

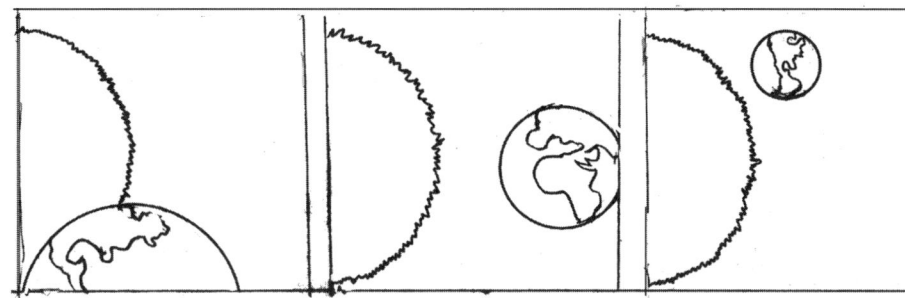

Figure 19-3: Sketch the earth revolving around the sun. Feeling brave? Add the moon circling the earth.

Rock 'n' Roll Earth

This animation takes the techniques of the spinning earth and practically turns them on their ear. In Figure 19-4, our earth *rocks* through the first three key frames. This animation is a simple rotation of one frame, and is easy in a Web animation program that handles elements as objects, like Paceworks Object Dancer. The last frame is envisioned as a banner, where the earth *rolls* from its original position to the other end of the screen. We drew musical notes to make our point more explicit, but the notes could easily be replaced — or augmented — with the right license-free music. Just remember to time your earth's rockin' and rollin' to the beat.

Figure 19-4:
These rock 'n' roll frames are flat objects, but this animation lends itself to shading and 3-D effects.

Earth Walk

With Figure 19-5 begins the kind of animation concept that you seldom develop as a first thought, but you can get to such ideas by letting your mind make associations. Puns can be very good ways of letting yourself see weird juxtapositions of images that may work well in a Web animation.

Figure 19-5:
Tiny details can be useful. Notice how we tip the globe forward a little as the feet poke out.

The earth-walk animation is best made in a program with layers. You initally draw the feet poking out of the globe, but after that you mostly work with variations on two cartoon feet. If you read about the walk cycle in Chapter 4, you see that this animation is an example of putting the concept to good use. If you need to shorten the animation for file size issues, you can begin the animation with the earth's feet already in place. Doing so maintains the visual pun, although you lose the surprise factor.

Earth: Soccer It to Me

This animation is another foot-and-ball interaction similar to "Earth Walk" (described prior to this section). If you've ever wanted to kick the world around, this animation gives you the chance. We decided on soccer because the ball stays low to the ground as the players travel toward the goal. Compare Figure 19-6 with Figures 19-4 and 19-5. We basically recombined elements and actions. Right now, the feet for the Earth Walk animation are very soft and unformed. If we dress them up in sneakers, creating Figure 19-6 becomes mostly a job of virtual cut-and-paste. Always look for opportunities to avoid creating new work for yourself.

Figure 19-6: Soccer-ing it to the earth. You'd change the scale to show a goal kick.

As you get the hang of developing Web animations, you may discover that you can churn them out at a surprisingly fast rate if you only have to collage existing objects. Web sites with a specific theme are particularly good places to explore this approach. If you're fairly good with drawing software, you can change the orientation of this animation to have the foot kick the Earth toward the viewer — thereby creating a variation on the "Earth Closing In" idea.

Earth Lifting

Animations are more interesting if you have a main character interacting with another character in the right context. In the case of an Earth Lifting animation, the Earth is a purely passive element. All of the real action is centered around the forklift, shown in Figure 19-7.

This kind of animation is particularly nice if your drawing skills are stuck somewhere earlier than the Neanderthal era (remember that some cave paintings were fairly good primitive art). The two elements can almost definitely be found in clip-art form, either for free or as commercial products. The action of a mechanical object, especially one on wheels, is extremely easy to animate. You're also not limited to any one motorized device. If you can't find a forklift, try a bulldozer or a dump truck.

Figure 19-7: Making the earth move against its will is truly heavy lifting.

Trivia lovers take note that we came up with this idea while free associating on Douglas Adams's *Hitchhiker's Guide to the Galaxy*. We didn't want to destroy our Earth, but we really liked the idea of a galactic construction company.

Earth Express

Sometimes the idea of moving can be implied rather than explicitly shown. We use the Earth Express animation key frames shown in Figure 19-8 to capture a portion of a longer action. We end the animation before the express courier actually shows up to take the package away. You can add this bit of business at the end if you like or if you happen to be designing a Web site for one of the major carriers (you know who they are). The order of the frames is reasonably important. You want to leave the front panel for last for the punch line. The lid isn't absolutely necessary, but adds a touch of believability and gives the animation a three-dimensional effect.

If you have the time and interest, you can make this animation more of a *story* by giving the globe a personality. Have it react to being packed away. Maybe it tries to push against the lid closing, or moves back and forth as the side panels come up.

This pack-it-and-ship-it animation is most easily created using an illustration program (or even better, a 3-D program that can export images into raster formats).

Chapter 19: Ten Ways to Make the Earth Move **317**

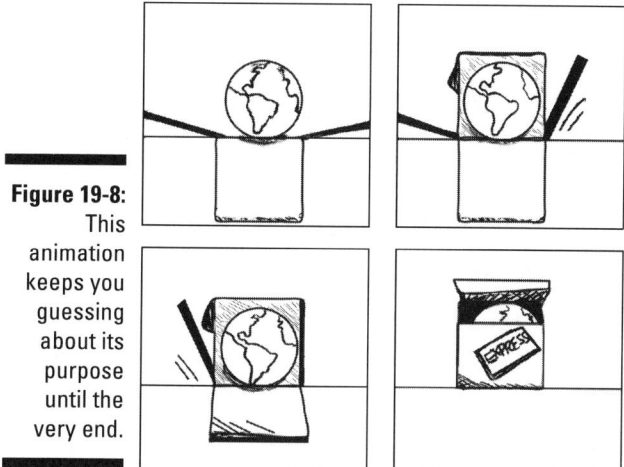

Figure 19-8: This animation keeps you guessing about its purpose until the very end.

Earth Moving

You knew this one was coming, right? We just couldn't resist taking the assignment literally. Like the "Earth Lifting" animation that we discuss earlier in this chapter, Earth Moving is another great animation for the artistically challenged. The rolling earth can be done as a mathematical rotation of the object from frame to frame. Even if you can't find clip art of a moving van — although we suspect you can — this truck is one of the simplest objects to draw from scratch. As you can see in Figure 19-9, all it needs is one rectangle, a few circles and lines, and sans serif type. (And if you keep this moving animation relatively small, this is a good opportunity to create a formal framed rectangle with a background image.)

Remember that you can anti-alias the *signage* (text on the truck) if you end the animation with the Earth in the closed truck, but you should reconsider if you plan to move the truck off the screen.

Figure 19-9: Earth Moving is great for the artistically challenged.

Earth Rising

Unlike other animations in this brainstorming session, Earth Rising is usable when Web page real estate is definitely at a premium. The action is slow, it floats, and it's gentle. It requires very few elements. Because the action is so slow and simple, this animation is also very easy to visualize, which makes it a good introduction to image distortion and frame-by-frame animation. We designed this piece specifically to be created in RubberWeb Composer, because of the software's powerful and relatively simple image-morphing capabilities.

As you can see in Figure 19-10, this animation does not lend itself to looping as it currently stands. If you complete the balloon's rise out of the frame and add an empty frame — for a one- or two-second pause at the end — the effect will be of a new balloon taking shape, rather than an abrupt jump back to the original. Up, up, and away!

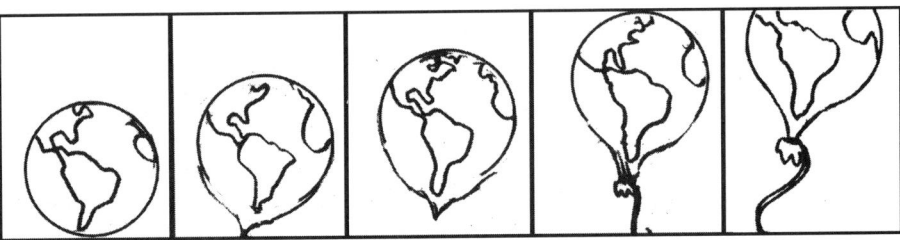

Figure 19-10: Don't let this animation balloon out of proportion. Keep it simple and elegant.

Part VI
Appendixes

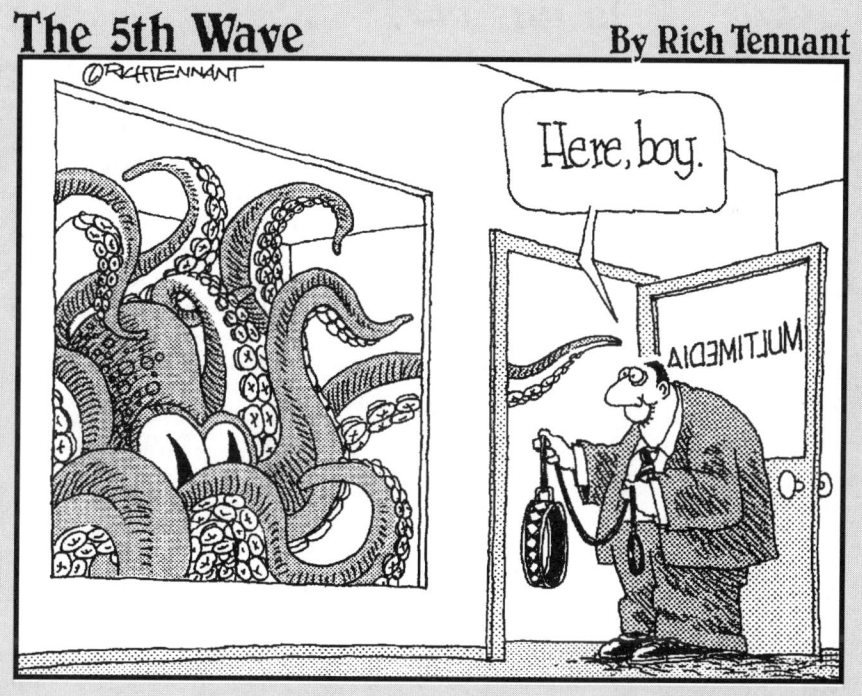

In this part . . .

The Appendixes in this book are very valuable resources for you as a Web animator. The first appendix is a list of resources available to you both on the Web and through the mail. Here you find sources for clip art, photos, software, fonts — many big and small companies that can help you in your quest for the perfect animation. We also include an appendix to explain how and why you want to access the CD-ROM that's attached to the back cover of this book.

Appendix A
Places to Visit Online

This appendix lists some great online resources that you can use as you develop your Web animations.

Global resources

Use these sites to find more information about animation, and even some animation toys!

Searching Yahoo!

Here's a list of URLs where you can search for the who, what, where, how and why of animation. The search results provide lots to choose from to satisfy your curiosity — from well-known Hollywood giants like Disney to freelance animators working on their own.

```
www.yahoo.com/Business_and_Economy/Companies/Entertainment/
       Production/Animation_Special_Effects/
www.yahoo.com/Entertainment/Movies_and_Films/Genres/Anima-
       tion/
www.yahoo.com/Entertainment/Comics_and_Animation/Animation/
```

Web sites that go somewhere

The following listings offer links to related categories and sites, including animators and animation companies, animation news, galleries and exhibitions, forums and chats, calendars of events, career connections, and educational programs.

Animation World Network: www.awn.com

New York University, Tisch School of the Arts Animation Program: Animation Station: found.cs.nyu.edu/animation/station.html

All about GIF animation

Royal Frazier's Web site is a well-known stopping place for anyone interested in animated GIFs.

Royal Frazier's GIF Animation on the WWW: `members.aol.com/royalef/gifanim.htm`

Freeware and shareware to download

At the following sites, you'll find a grab bag of software resources to try, including those we mentioned in this book. Definitely take the time to visit these sites.

Yahoo! ZDNet Software Library: `headlines.yahoo.com/zddownload/software`

CNET Download.Com site: `download.com`

Resources

Cruise through the sites we list here to find the latest animation and graphics software tools and plug-ins, fonts, clip-art, stock photography, and textures collections, and royalty-free music and sound. We also included the URLs for companies that make digital cameras or write about them. Check out some of the digital camera sites even if you're not in the market right now to purchase one. There are great pictures to look at, taken by some of the best photographers from around the world.

Software and Filters

Adobe Systems, Inc.; 345 Park Avenue; San Jose, CA 95110-2704; voice: 408-536-6000; 800-833-6687; fax: 408-537-6000; `www.adobe.com`

Alien Skin Software, LLC; 800 St. Mary's St., Suite 100; Raleigh, NC 27605; voice: 919-832-4124; fax: 919-832-4065; `www.alienskin.com/alienskin`

Astound Incorporated; 3160 West Bayshore Road; Palo Alto, CA 94303; voice: 415-845-6200; fax: 415-845-6201; `www.astound.com`

BoxTop Software, Inc.; P.O. Box 2347; Starkville, MS 39760; voice: 601-324-1800; fax: 601-324-7352; `www.boxtopsoft.com`

Corel Corporation; 1600 Carling Avenue; Ottawa, Ontario K1Z 8R7, CANADA; voice: 613-728-8200; fax: 613-728-9790; `www.corel.com`

Deneba Software; 7400 S.W. 87th Avenue; Miami, FL 33173; voice: 305-596-5644; fax: 305-273-9069; `www.deneba.com`

Equilibrium; Three Harbor Drive, Suite 111; Sausalito, CA 94965; voice: 415-332-4343; 800-524-8651; fax: 415-332-4433; www.equilibrium.com

Jasc Incorporated; P.O. Box 44997; Eden Prairie, MN 55344-2697; voice: 800-622-2793; fax: 612-930-9172; www.jasc.com

Macromedia, Inc.; 600 Townsend Street; San Francisco, CA 94103; voice: 415-252-2000; fax: 415-626-0554; www.macromedia.com

MetaCreations Corporation; 6303 Carpinteria Avenue; Carpinteria, CA 93013; voice: 805-566-6200; 800-472-9025; fax: 805-566-6385; www.metacreations.com

Microsoft; One Microsoft Way; Redmond, WA 98052-6399; www.microsoft.com

PaceWorks, Inc.; 558 Brewster Avenue, Suite 100; Redwood City, CA 94063; voice: 415-261-6180; fax: 415-261-0412; www.paceworks.com

Pantone, Inc.; 590 Commerce Boulevard; Carlstadt, NJ 07072-3098; voice: 201-935-5500; fax: 201-896-0242; www.pantone.com

Quark, Inc.; 1800 Grant Street; Denver, CO 80203; voice: 303-894-8888; 800-676-4575 (customer service); for calls outside of the US: 303-364-5735; fax: 303-343-2086 (customer service); www.quark.com

RubberFlex Software; P.O. Box 50341; Colorado Springs, CO 80949-0341; voice: 719-265-9509; fax: 719-533-0905; www.rubberflex.com

Silicon Graphics, Inc.; 2011 N. Shoreline Blvd.; Mountain View, CA 94043; voice: 800-800-7441; sgi.com or vrml.sgi.com

Sun Microsystems, Inc.; 2550 Garcia Avenue; Mountain View, CA 94043-1100; sun.com

Totally Hip Software, Inc.; P.O. Box 4160, VMPO; Vancouver, British Columbia V6B 3Z6; voice: 604-685-6525; fax: 604-685-4057; www.totallyhip.com

Xaos Tools Inc.; 600 Townsend Street, Suite 270 East; San Francisco, CA 94103; voice: 415-487-7000; 800-289-9267; fax: 415-558-9886; www.xaostools.com

Fonts

Adobe Systems, Inc. (See listing under the preceding section on "Software")

Agfa Division, Bayer Inc.; 200 Ballardvale Street; Wilmington, MA 01887; voice: 508-658-5600; 800-424-TYPE; fax: 508-658-8982; www.agfahome.com/agfatype

Bitstream, Inc.; 215 First Street; Cambridge, MA 02142; voice: 617-497-6222; 800-522-3668; fax: 617-868-0784; www.bitstream.com

Emigre, Inc.; 4475 D Street; Sacramento, CA 95819; voice: 916-451-4344; 800-944-9021; fax: 916-451-4351; www.emigre.com

The Font Bureau, Inc.; 175 Newbury Street; Boston, MA 02116; voice: 617-423-8772; fax: 617-423-8771; www.fontbureau.com

Image Club Graphics (See listing under the section on "Clip Art, Stock Photo, and Textures CD-ROM Collections")

ITC, International Typeface Corporation; 228 East 45th Street, 12th floor; New York, NY 10017; voice: 212-949-8072; fax: 212-949-8485; www.esselte.com/itc/index.html

Monotype Typography, Inc.; 985 Busse Road; Elk Grove Village, IL 60007-2400; voice: 847-718-0400; 800-803-6964; fax: 847-718-0500; www.monotype.com

Publisher's Toolbox (See listing under the section on "Clip Art, Stock Photo, and Textures CD-ROM Collections")

URW (U.S. office); P.O. Box 700, Barrington, NH 03825; voice: 603-664-2130; fax: 603-664-2295; www.urwpp.de

Stock Photography Agencies

PHOTO 24; 7948 Faust Avenue; West Hills, CA 91304; voice: 818-999-4184; 800-582-9492 outside CA; fax: 818-999-5704; www.photo24.com

Tony Stone Images; 800-234-7880 (USA); tonystone.com

Clip Art, Stock Photo, and Textures CD-ROM Collections

Corel Corporation (See listing in the section on "Software")

Digital Stock; 750 Second Street; Encinitas, CA 92075-2262; voice: 760-634-6500; 800-545-4514; fax: 760-634-6510; www.digitalstock.com

D'pix, A Division of Amber Productions, Inc.; 85 North Walnut Street, P.O. Box 572; Lithopolis, OH 43136-0308; voice: 614-834-8834; fax: 614-833-6440; e-mail: amber@infinet.com

Dynamic Graphics, Inc.; 6000 N. Forest Park Drive; Peoria, IL 61614-3592; voice: 800-255-8800; fax: 800-488-3492; www.dgusa.com

Image Club Graphics, A Division of Adobe Systems Inc.; 729 Twenty-Fourth Avenue SE; Calgary, Alberta T2G 5K8; voice: 403-262-8008; 800-661-9410; fax: 403-261-7013; www.imageclub.com

Letraset Digital Products (See ITC listing in the section on "Fonts")

MetaCreations Corporation (See listing in the section on "Software")

PhotoDisc, Inc.; 2013 Fourth Avenue, 4th floor; Seattle, WA 98121; voice: 206-441-9355; 800-528-3472; fax: 206-441-9379; www.photodisc.com

Publisher's Toolbox; 2310 Darwin Road; Madison, WI 53704; voice: 608-243-5900; 800-390-0461 (USA only); fax: 608-243-1253; www.pubtool.com

Royalty-Free Sound and Music CD-ROMs

Corel Corporation (See listing in the section on "Software")

Jawai Interactive; 401 East Fourth Street #443; Austin, TX 78701-3745; voice: 512-469-0502; fax: 512-469-7850; www.jawai.com

Digital Cameras

Here are the Web sites for some manufacturers of digital cameras.

Agfa: www.agfahome.com

Apple Computer: www.apple.com

Canon: www.usa.canon.com/cameras/index.html

Casio: www.casio.com

Chinon: www.chinon.co.jp/index-e.htm

Epson: www.epson.com/graphicarts

Kodak: www.kodak.com

Minolta: www.minolta.com

Nikon: nikonusa.com

Olympus: www.olympus.com

Phase One: www.phaseone.com

Polaroid: www.polaroid.com/digi-world/index.html

Ricoh: www.ricohcpg.com/home.html

Sony: www.sony.com

Here are two sites for more general information about photography:

PDN Photo District News- PIX: pdn-pix.com

PEI PHOTO>Electronic Imaging: www.peimag.com

Appendix B
About the CD

*H*ere's some of what you can find on the *Web Animation For Dummies* CD-ROM:

- Animation tools and viewers
- Authoring and imaging tools
- Image and sound samplers
- Sample files from the authors

System requirements

Make sure that your computer meets the minimum system requirements listed below. If your computer doesn't match up to most of these requirements, you may have problems using the CD. Some programs require a PowerPC processor for Macintosh.

- A PC with a 486 or faster processor, or a Mac OS computer with a 68030 or faster processor. We recommend Pentium or Pentium Pro processors for Windows and PowerPC processors for Macintosh.
- Microsoft Windows 95 or NT version 4.0 or later, or Mac OS System 7.5 or later.
- At least 16MB of total RAM installed on your computer. For best performance, we recommend that Windows 95-equipped PCs and Mac OS computers with PowerPC processors have at least 32MB of RAM installed. You need at least 40MB of total RAM if you want to open and run the Adobe Photoshop 4.0 demo while other programs are open. To minimize the potential for system or program crashing, read program instructions for allocation of memory requirements. Some programs' features require resetting minimum memory size higher than default setting.
- A CD-ROM drive — quad-speed (4x) or faster.
- A sound card for PCs. (Mac OS computers have built-in sound support.)

- A monitor capable of displaying at least 256 colors or grayscale.
- A modem with a speed of at least 14.4 Kbps (we recommend 28.8 Kbps).
- Internet and World Wide Web access.

If you need more information on the basics, check out *PCs For Dummies,* 4th Edition, by Dan Gookin; *Macs For Dummies,* 5th Edition, by David Pogue, and *Windows 95 For Dummies,* 2nd Edition, by Andy Rathbone (all published by IDG Books Worldwide, Inc.).

How to use the CD using Microsoft Windows

To install the items from the CD to your hard drive, follow these steps:

1. **Insert the CD into your computer's CD-ROM drive and close the drive door.**

2. **Click the Start button and click Run.**

3. **In the dialog box that appears, type** D:\SETUP.EXE.

   Most computers have the CD-ROM drive listed as drive D under My Computer in Windows 95. Type in the proper drive letter if your CD-ROM drive uses a different letter.

4. **Click OK.**

   A license agreement window appears.

5. **I'm sure you want to use the CD, so read through the license agreement, nod your head, and then click on the Accept button.**

   After you click on Accept, you'll never be bothered by the License Agreement window again.

   From here, the CD interface appears. The CD interface lets you install the programs on the CD without typing in cryptic commands or using yet another finger-twisting hot key in Windows. The software on the CD is divided into the categories listed in the interface.

6. **To view the items within a category, just click the category's name.**

   A list of programs in the category appears.

7. **For more information about a program, click on the program's name.**

   Be sure to read the information that's displayed. Sometimes a program may require you to do a few tricks on your computer first, and this screen tells you where to go for that information, if necessary.

8. **To install the program, click the appropriate Install button; if you don't want to install the program, click on the Go back button to return to the previous category screen.**

   After you click on an install button, the CD interface drops to the background while the CD begins installation of the program you chose.

   When installation is finished, the interface usually reappears in front of other opened windows. Sometimes the installation will confuse Windows and leave the interface in the background. To bring the interface forward, just click once anywhere in the interface's window.

9. **To install other items, repeat Steps 6, 7, and 8.**

10. **After you finish installing programs, click on the Quit button to close the interface.**

    You can eject the CD now. Carefully place it back in the plastic jacket of the book for safekeeping.

To run some of the programs, you may need to keep the CD inside your CD-ROM drive. This is a Good Thing. Otherwise, the installed program would require you to install a very large chunk of the program or tutorial files to your hard drive, which would keep you from installing other software.

You can press Alt+F4 to exit the CD-ROM interface at any time.

How to use the CD using a Mac OS computer

To install the items from the CD to your hard drive, follow these steps:

1. **Insert the CD into your computer's CD-ROM drive and close the drive door.**

   In a moment, an icon representing the CD you just inserted appears on your Mac desktop. Chances are that the icon looks like a CD-ROM. A window automatically opens.

2. **Double-click on the Read Me First icon.**

   This text file contains information about the CD's programs and any last-minute installation instructions that we don't cover in this appendix.

3. **Double-click each of the category folders to show the CD's contents in that folder.**

4. **To install most programs, just drag the program's folder from the CD window and drop it on your hard drive icon.**

5. **To install Adobe PageMill and other larger programs, open the program's folder on the CD and/or double-click the icon with the words "Install" or "Installer."**

   After you have installed the programs that you want, you can eject the CD. Carefully place it back in the plastic jacket of the book for safekeeping.

To run some of the programs, you may need to keep the CD inside your CD-ROM drive. This is a Good Thing. Otherwise, the installed program would require you to install a very large chunk of the program or tutorial files to your hard drive, which would keep you from installing other software.

What you find

Here's a summary of the software on this CD. For a more in-depth review, refer to the documentation in the program's or sampler's file folder on the CD-ROM. A listing of Web sites and other contact information is in Appendix A.

If you use Windows, the CD interface helps you install software easily. (If you have no idea what I'm talking about when I say "CD interface," see the section, "How to use the CD using Microsoft Windows.")

If you use a Mac OS computer, you can enjoy the ease of the Mac interface to quickly install the programs. (See the section, "How to use the CD using a Mac OS computer" if the last sentence leaves you clueless.)

Most of the programs on the CD are shareware, freeware, or trial versions of commercially available software. *Shareware* means that you can try out a program before paying for it. *Freeware* programs can be used for as long as you want. Companies that distribute *trial* (or *demo*) programs limit the software's usefulness by disabling certain features, such as saving or printing, or may have a set time limit on how long the program is fully functional. Be sure to read the program's `Readme` files or manuals for more information.

Animation tools and viewers

The CD-ROM has several neat programs to help you develop your animations.

- **Adobe Acrobat Reader:** Acrobat Reader is a free program that lets you view and print Portable Document Format, or PDF, files. (Windows and Macintosh)

- **Astound WebMotion:** WebMotion can create animations for use on Web pages. (Windows and Macintosh)

- **Astound Web Player:** Web Player is freeware and assists in the playback of Web animations created with Astound WebMotion program. (Windows 3.1, 95)

- **BoxTop Software GIFmation demo:** GIFmation is a powerful tool for creating animated GIF images for use on a Web page. (Windows 95 and Macintosh)

- **Macromedia Flash trial:** Flash 2 is a tool that generates small, fast animations for use on Web pages and can support sounds as well. (Windows 95, NT, and Macintosh)

- **Macromedia Shockwave:** Shockwave is a tool that can take applications created with Director, Flash, Authorware, and Freehand, and convert the application so that it runs within a Web browser. Netscape Navigator or Microsoft Internet Explorer plug-in. (Windows and Macintosh)

- **PaceWorks ObjectDancer:** ObjectDancer allows you to create multimedia animations and to either display them directly on the Internet or integrate them into a multimedia title using your favorite authoring environment. (Macintosh PPC)

- **RubberFlex AnimaFlex:** AnimaFlex is a Netscape plug-in player for AnimaFlex animations created using RubberWeb or RubberWeb Composer software. (Windows and Macintosh)

    To install AnimaFlex, start your Web browser and open the file `readme.htm` in the AnimaFlex folder.

- **RubberFlex RubberWeb and RubberWeb Composer demo:** RubberWeb and RubberWeb Composer create Web animations in two forms: GIF and AnimaFlex. RubberWeb and RubberWeb Composer can produce full-screen, highly compact, true color animations as QuickTime movies for your multimedia projects. (Macintosh PPC, download 68K versions from Web site)

- **Totally Hip Software WebPainter demo:** WebPainter can build interlaced, transparent, and animated GIF files for use on a Web page. Supports other formats, including AVI movies and Sizzler formats. (Windows 95, NT, and Macintosh)

Authoring and imaging tools

We included on the CD some really useful tools to create Web pages and images. Take a look at these:

- **Adobe PageMill tryout:** PageMill 2.0 helps you create Web pages without using HTML, the language for designing Web pages. (Windows 95 and Macintosh)

- **Adobe Photoshop tryout:** Photoshop 4.0 is a powerful graphic design tool with which you can create or modify images. (Windows 95 and Macintosh)

- **Alien Skin Eye Candy demo:** Eye Candy is a collection of filters for Photoshop. Place in the Photoshop plug-ins folder. (Windows and Macintosh PPC)
- **Astound demo:** Astound is a powerful presentation creation program in which you can add sound, movement, animation, interaction, and video to your presentations. (Windows 3.1, 95, and Macintosh)
- **Equilibrium DeBabelizer Pro & DeBabelizer Toolbox demos:** DeBabelizer Pro (Windows) and DeBabelizer Toolbox (Macintosh) are powerful conversion programs in which you can clean up and convert images and movies from many platforms and formats.
- **Macromedia Backstage Internet Studio trial:** Backstage Internet Studio is a collection of programs that can help create sophisticated database-driven Web sites. (Windows 95)
- **Panimation Nodester demo:** Nodester is a software program that creates and edits QuickTime Virtual Reality (QTVR) panoramas for educational, commercial, and non-commercial applications. (Macintosh PPC)
- **Xaos Tools Fresco sampler:** Fresco is the Organic Image Collection, created using a unique new artificial intelligence technology under development by Xaos Tools. (Macintosh)
- **Xaos Tools Paint Alchemy demo:** Paint Alchemy, a Photoshop-compatible plug-in, is the painterly and organic effects engine that provides access to 101 preset brushing styles. (Macintosh)
- **Xaos Tools Terrazzo demo:** Terrazzo is an Adobe Photoshop standard plug-in for creating seamless tileable patterns from any source imagery. (Macintosh)
- **Xaos Tools TubeTime demo:** TubeTime is an Adobe Photoshop standard plug-in that allows you to add video interference to images, making them look as if they are captured from a television set. (Macintosh)
- **Xaos Tools TypeCaster demo:** TypeCaster allows users to create 3-D text in any application that accepts Photoshop plug-ins. (Macintosh)

Image and sound samplers

Try some of these sample graphics and sound files on for size.

- **Digital Stock sampler:** Digital Stock is a leading provider of high-quality, royalty-free stock photography on CD-ROM. The files are in TIFF format. (Windows and Macintosh)
- **D'pix sampler:** Image samples from D'pix, a division of Amber Productions. The images are in JPEG format. (Windows and Macintosh)

- **Dynamic Graphics sampler:** Image samples from Dynamic Graphics, a Midwest graphic design company. Images are in GIF and EPS formats. (Windows and Macintosh)
- **ITC demo:** Sample Postscript 1 and True Type fonts from the Fontek collection, and sample Postscript 1 and True Type fonts and utilities from the DesignFont collection. (Macintosh)
- **ITC demo, Letraset web.STIR Art Kit:** web.STIR is a collection of high-quality graphic images designed specifically for use on the World Wide Web. (Macintosh)
- **Jawai Interactive Screen Caffeine sampler:** The Screen Caffeine Pro sampler is a collection of textures, examples, buttons, sounds, and other items for multimedia and Web pages. Images are JPEG files; sounds are WAV format. (Windows and Macintosh)
- **Photo24 sampler:** A photographic collection of flowers and plants from Photo24, a provider of high-quality stock photos and art. The images are in TIFF format. (Windows and Macintosh)

If you have problems (of the CD kind)

We tried to compile programs that work on most computers with the minimum system requirements. Alas, your computer may differ, and some programs may not work properly for some reason.

The two likeliest problems are that you don't have enough memory (RAM) for the programs you want to use, or you have other programs running that are affecting installation or running of a program. If you get error messages like `Not enough memory` or `Setup cannot continue,` try one or more of these methods and then try using the software again:

- Turn off any anti-virus software that you have on your computer. Installers sometimes mimic virus activity and may make your computer incorrectly believe that it is being infected by a virus.
- Close all running programs. The more programs you're running, the less memory is available to other programs. Installers also typically update files and programs. So if you keep other programs running, installation may not work properly.
- Have your local computer store add more RAM to your computer. This is, admittedly, a drastic and somewhat expensive step. However, if you have a Windows 95 PC or a Mac OS computer with a PowerPC chip, adding more memory can really help the speed of your computer and allow more programs to run at the same time.

If you still have trouble with installing the items from the CD, please call the IDG Books Worldwide Customer Service phone number: 800-762-2974 (outside the U.S.: 317-596-5261).

Glossary

Anti-aliasing: Anti-aliasing adds pixels to the edge to minimize the jagged look of bitmapped text and graphics. It creates a subtle transition between the foreground object and the background. Use with caution for Web animation.

Applet: Applets are little applications that are activated from the server. They enable people without programming skills, or even scripting skills, to create cross-platform, browser ready material.

ASCII (American Standard Code for Information Interchange): In word processing, it is used to refer to the Text Only file format, and is the most universal method for importing and exporting text between software programs.

AVI (Audio Visual Interleaf): To compete with Apple Computer's QuickTime for Windows, Microsoft created this standard digital video format. AVI is for Windows only, and QuickTime is released for both the Macintosh and Windows platforms.

Bandwidth: Bandwidth refers to the Internet's capacity to handle user traffic: e-mail, Web sites, downloads, animations — everything that shares a common set of cables, wires, and computers. Data is received faster by the client (user's) computer from the server with a higher bandwidth. A 28.8 baud modem and a standard telephone line have a slower bandwidth than a dedicated T1 line. The older 14.4 and earlier modem models take even longer to download animated files. Solving bandwidth problems is critical for distributing video and multimedia on the Web.

Banner: A large image map area set aside, usually at the top or bottom of a Web page. This space can be used for advertising.

Bit depth: The number of colors a bitmap can contain. For example, 8-bit color can have up to 256 colors.

Bitmapped image: An image built from a series of pixels. Each pixel is arranged in a series of rows and columns, like a needlepoint canvas. If the pixel represents one bit, the image is black and white. If the pixel represents 32 bits, the image can have millions of colors and will appear photorealistic.

CGI (Common Gateway Interface): CGI scripting has been around for a long time in Internet terms. When a Web user's computer (the client) contacts a server by typing in a URL, the server must respond in a standard way. This means that all servers must share a common language. If you can communicate with the server in that common language, CGI enables you to run programs, or offer access to images or information that are not part of its own programming.

CMYK (Cyan, Magenta, Yellow, Black): The four colors used in process printing and desktop color printers. To create cyan, magenta, or yellow on the screen, mix equal amounts of two primary RGB colors: green + blue, red + blue, or red + green. Convert CMYK images to RGB if you want to use them for the Web.

Crop tool: This has nothing to do with agriculture. You use the Crop tool to reduce the size of an image by removing those parts you don't want anymore. Keep a copy of the original on file, just in case you change your mind later.

Dithering: Dithering creates colors you don't actually have in your palette, by building a pattern from many different, adjacent colors. Because the pattern is not easily visible to your eyes, the pattern looks like a solid color on the screen or in print.

DPI (Dots Per Inch): This acronym relates to the number of dots a printer, or other output device, can print or display per square inch. An image will appear more realistic when printed with a higher density of dots. A monitor displays an image at 72 or 96 dpi. Keep this in mind when repurposing print graphics for the Web.

Flipbook: Originally a real book that you would flip from front to back to see an animation in rough form. The flipbook is the basic idea behind GIF animation. A *GIF animation* is a group of individual GIF images with some coding that tells a browser which frames to display, how much time should elapse between each frame, and what to do with the frame after it's been shown.

Font: Another name for a single typeface style, such as Helvetica Bold or Times New Roman Italic. Several fonts can be part of a typeface family.

Freeware: Software you can download from the Web or FTP (File Transfer Protocol) site that doesn't require registration. Check the Read Me file with the application for more details about usage restrictions.

GIF: A picture file compressed for fast downloading and uploading on the Internet. GIF (Graphics Interface Format) was developed by the pioneering online service CompuServe as a cross-platform method of displaying high-quality images.

GIF89a: The GIF89a file format, which is based on GIF 87, supports several very important elements we need for Web animation: delay settings in $1/100$ of a second, transparent color, multiple images encoded in a single file, and the ability to code application-specific extensions inside the GIF file.

HSL (Hue, Saturation, Luminance) or HSB (Brightness): A color mode for displaying an RGB image as values of Hue, Saturation and Luminance (Brightness).

HTML (HyperText Markup Language): The acronym for HyperText Markup Language. HTML is a text coding language for tagging text and graphics on a Web page. It identifies what's on the Web page and how it will be rendered.

Hue: Hue is another word for describing a color name. For example, red, green and blue are hues.

Icon: An icon is a picture symbol used to represent a software application or tool on your computer desktop.

Indexed color: This is color mode in which you cannot have more than 256 palette colors. Converting a 24- or 32-bit photorealistic image to indexed color helps to reduce file size. In Adobe Photoshop 4.0, eight palette types for converting an image to indexed color exist: Exact, System (Macintosh), System (Windows), Web (216 colors), Uniform, Adaptive, Custom, and Previous.

Inline plug-in: A plug-in is software that adds something functional to another program, but can't stand alone as an application. It is external to your browser's own code, and is written by the companies that want their software readable on many platforms. A plug-in displays the work inside the browser, rather than in a separate viewer window.

ISP (Internet Service Provider): ISPs offer connections and services to the Internet and the World Wide Web. Many providers offer free disk space on their servers, and you can use this storage option to upload your own Web site to the Internet. Check with your ISP for details.

Intranet: Intranets are set up by companies or organizations for their own internal use, and aren't open to the public. Intranets operate like the Internet and World Wide Web, but the content is specific to, and controlled by, the company that runs it.

Jaggies: Jaggies appear in bitmapped graphics and text when you use curved or diagonal lines. Because bitmaps are created from pixels, an object's edge resembles a flight of stairs. Anti-aliasing helps to minimize the rough, jagged look.

Java: Java, developed by Sun Microsystems, is an interpreted object-oriented programming language. To a programmer, this means that Java is one example of a new type of programming language and that it bears some relationship to C++, except Java is more streamlined. Many programs we use daily on our PCs are written in C++, but we never interact with the language directly ourselves. You don't have to expect any more contact than that with Java itself.

JavaScript: JavaScript, unlike Java itself, is actually something called an API (Application Programming Interface). APIs are like negotiators in diplomacy. They provide a means for unruly applications to play together in harmony. Netscape developed JavaScript specifically to enable people on different platforms to take advantage of their browsers' capacities to deliver information.

JPEG (Joint Photographic Experts Group): This is a file format for storing compressed images, and is used for the display of photographs on the Web.

Key frame: The major action frames of an animation from which the in-betweening frames are developed.

Luminance (Brightness): This term describes how light a color is. For example, because yellow is closer to white light than blue, it has a higher luminance or brightness factor. A color's luminance increases when you add more white light to it.

MIDI: MIDI is basically a form of artificial sound generation. You make MIDI sound and music completely in the computer, or with complicated connections between digital instruments and the computer.

Morphing: This software technique makes it possible to build new images by combining two source pictures. If you ask the software to create three new variations, the first variation will be most closely like the first source image, the second will be equally merged, and the third will look more like the second source image.

MPEG (Motion Picture Experts Group): MPEG (Motion Picture Experts Group) is the high quality video compression format that most professional digital video artists prefer.

Multiple Image: An animated GIF contains multiple image frames in a single file.

Onion-skinning: This is an animation technique in which you can see a dimmed version of the preceding or following cel as you are working on the current image. Onion-skinning makes positioning all the cels to each other easier.

Glossary

Optimizing (palette): This is the ability to minimize a palette to the fewest possible colors in a single file or animated GIF. Optimizing a palette can speed up download times.

QuickTime: Apple's QuickTime plug-in is one of the must-haves in the Web world, especially now that Apple has released its new *fast-start* version, which puts animations directly on the Web page — sound and all. QuickTime for Windows is a competitive format to Microsoft's AVI for Windows.

RGB (Red, Green, Blue): RGB is the acronym for the additive primary colors red, green, and blue (RGB) — which you've seen in paint or graphics programs. On a computer capable of displaying 24-bit color, you get 255 different levels for each primary color. White is 0,0,0 and black is 255,255,255.

Repurposing: A term used to describe the transformation of existing content, from print and other sources, into Web material.

Resolution: Resolution is how you describe the level of detail in an image as it appears on the screen or in print. With a higher image resolution, the number of pixels within a file is greater, and the file is larger. Screen images are considered to be low resolution.

Saturation: Also called *chroma*, it's a color term for describing the purity of a color hue. 100 percent saturation is pure color. When you increase a color's transparency value, you reduce its saturation.

Scripting: Here's a word that can have two meanings because of the convergence of industries: 1. The written action plan for an animation, which is represented by the storyboard. In sound animation, it can also refer to character dialogue. 2. A programming language like Lingo that is built into Macromedia Director, and is used to control frames, sprites, or scores.

Shareware: Low-cost software applications that you can download from the Web and FTP (File Transfer Protocol) sites. These time limited demos require registration and payment of fees for long-term use.

Streaming: The process of creating and delivering a streamed file. A Web server is contacted, and locates a large file that has been compressed using a current format. This file begins to send a stream of data to the Web surfer's machine. Instead of waiting for the entire file to show up, a plug-in that understands the format begins to collect the streaming information into a buffer — kind of like a virtual bucket with a pour spout. As the buffer begins to fill, the plug-in starts playing the file, pouring it out of the buffer spout, and onto the screen — collecting more at the same time. Once played, the streamed video is dumped out of the computer memory.

T1 connection: A high speed, dedicated digital telephone line used by corporations to send data over their networks to and from remote locations. This costs a lot more to install and use than your standard telephone line and modem.

Transition (animation): The way in which one animation frame changes into the next frame. Dissolve, wipe from the right, and split screen are some examples of animation transitions. What timing delay you set for frame display controls the speed of the transition. With a smaller delay (in $1/100$ of a second), the transition will occur faster.

Transparency: This term refers to those pixels in the background that aren't visible. An application needs to support transparency, otherwise you can't create or use irregularly shaped graphics on your Web page.

URL (Uniform Resource Locator): The format for specifying the address of an Internet document. The URL is made up of three parts: the protocol (`http` for Web addresses), the server name (`www.company.com`), and the path of the document (`/example/doc.html`).

VRML (Virtual Reality Modeling Language): If you see this term, think 3-D. It's the Web standard for displaying 3-D computer graphics.

Index

• A •

Acme Digital Lab home page, 222–223
  best browser or plug-in to use, 227
  image maps, 225
  Navigation bar, 226
  VSPACE and HSPACE tags, 226
action
  overlapping, 77
  speeding up and slowing down, 77–78
ActiveX, 28
additive color, 86–87
additive color wheel, 88
Adobe Acrobat Reader, 330
Adobe Dimensions, 38
Adobe Illustrator 6.0.2, 14
  Filters⇨Roughen Filter in Distort
      command, 61
Adobe PageMill, 331
Adobe Photoshop 4.0, 14, 331
  .ACO files, 93
  .ACT files, 92–93
  adding weight to typeface, 121–122
  anti-aliasing, 194
  changing image resolution, 189–191
  Channel window, 180
  CLUT (color look-up table), 92–93
  Color Picker dialog box, 87
  Color/Swatches/Brushes palette dialog box
      (F6) function key, 87
  Color Table dialog box, 92–93
  common reference point for frames or cels,
      171–172
  Crop tool, 187
  cropping images, 186–188
  custom palette swatch, 92–93
  Cutout dialog box, 164
  cutout drawing, 164
  demo version, 167
  Dodge and Burn tool, 194
  Duplicate Layer command, 188
  Duplicate Layer dialog box, 186, 188
  Edit⇨Fill command, 180
  Edit⇨Stroke command, 121
  extra layers, 169
  Eye icon, 170

feathering photograph edges, 161–163
File⇨Export⇨Export to GIF89a
    command, 179
File⇨New command, 92
File⇨Save A Copy command, 179, 200
File⇨Save As command, 205
Filter⇨Artistic⇨Cutout command, 164
Filter⇨Noise⇨Dust and Scratches
    command, 152
Filter⇨Pixelate⇨Fragment command, 141
Filter⇨Stylize⇨Wind command, 140
Foreground or Background color icon, 87
Fragment filter, 140–141
frames, 167–171
Image Size dialog box, 189–190
Image⇨Crop command, 188
Image⇨Image Size command, 189–190, 204
Image⇨Mode⇨Color Table command, 92
Image⇨Mode⇨Indexed Color command, 92
Indexed Color dialog box, 193
JPEG conversion, 200–202
JPEG Options dialog box, 200–201
Layer window, 168–169, 186–188
Marquee Options dialog box, 162
Marquee tool, 161
metamorphosing photos into clip art,
    179–180
Move tool, 170
PhotoGIF color reduction dialog box,
    205–208
Photoshop Layers palette, 168
Save A Copy dialog box, 170, 200
Save A Copy function, 170
saving files in 2.5/3.0 version, 197
Selection tool palette, 194
Smudge tool, 194
Spray Paint tool, 194
Stroke dialog box, 121
Swatches dialog box, 93
tools, 194
View⇨Show Grid command, 170
View⇨Show Guides command, 170
Wind filter, 140–141
Window⇨Show Channels command, 179
Window⇨Show Layers (F7) command, 168
Window⇨Show Swatches command, 92

Web Animation For Dummies

advertising banners, 11, 125
Agfa ActionCam, 155
Alchemy Mindworks Animation Wizard, 198
Alchemy MindWorks Web site, 263
aliasing, 193
alpha channels, 134, 179
An Illustrated Index of Web Colors
    Web site, 91
AnimaFlex, 331
animated advertising, 11
animated
  buttons, 38
  icons and logos, 37–38, 126
  type, 108
animation. *See also* Web animation
  anti-aliasing, 193–194
  anticipation, 74–75
  arcs, 71–73
  attaching to HTML page, 224–226
  body parts responding to other parts
    movement, 69–73
  breaking up, 295–296
  broken links, 300
  browser problems, 300
  causing problems after working fine, 300
  color cycle, 167
  Color Model Sketch, 95–96
  common reference points, 171–172
  cropping images, 186–188
  curve, 71
  definition of, 10
  developing story and, 130
  dividing into smaller pieces, 294
  Earth-moving, 311–318
  eliminating frame creep, 297–298
  enlarging small frames, 185
  exaggeration and, 70
  filters, 193
  frame as part of, 52–53
  gravity, 71
  image sizes, 183–186
  incomplete edit, 298
  intellectual property, 142–145
  keeping users in place with, 130
  large files and bandwidth, 184
  limiting action, 295
  logical size, 261–262
  loop forever cycle, 299
  looping, 222, 235
  losing resolution, 188–191
  making images move, 69–79
  MIME type, 300
  missing frames, 298
  missing point of, 80
  mixing transparent and opaque files, 299
  moving down Web page with, 129
  naming frames, 215
  no transitions between frames, 80
  optimizing palettes, 255
  overlapping action, 77–78
  photographs, 147–154
  picking up delay speed, 296–297
  portion of photograph, 174–179
  poses telegraphing information to user, 56
  positioning in storyboard, 46–53
  running in slow motion, 80
  scale to speed equation, 81–82
  scaling down before conversion, 185
  selecting clip art for, 128–135
  simplicity of, 94, 192–193
  small size of, 185–186
  speeding up and slowing down, 78
  squash and stretch, 75–77
  testing, 54, 221–224
  timing, 80–82
  too fast, 80
  too large, 293–294
  too many colors, 294
  transitions, 243–244
  uneven pacing, 81
  unnecessary background detail, 191
  updated browsers, 300
  viewing through Web browsers, 227–228
  visual cues, 129
  walking, 79
  window size, 185
animation cycle, 78–79
animation software, 231, 233–234
  commercial, 275–276
  delay, 234
  demos, 232–233
  disposal, 234–235
  Flash 2, 287–289
  GIF, 231, 233–235
  GIF Construction Set, 263–273
  GifBuilder, 236–245
  GIFmation, 254–263
  inexpensive, 253
  looping, 235
  Microsoft Gif Animator, 239, 245–252
  ObjectDancer, 282–283
  PhotoGIF, 261
  position, 234
  resolution of files brought into, 259
  RubberWeb Composer, 279–281
  WebMotion, 276–279
  WebPainter, 284–287

Index 343

animation software requirements
  comment block editing, 305
  download test, 306
  flip and flop, 304
  good documentation, 306
  header editing, 305
  image editing, 305
  Internet Explorer compliance, 305
  layers, 303
  Netscape Navigator compliance, 305
  palette optimization, 304
  placing coordinates, 305
  rotating, 304
  scaling, 304
  skewing, 304
  text editing, 305
  transparent background, 304
  viewer, 306
animation troubleshooting
  animated type fuzzy, 293
  animation too large, 293–294
  animation too large and software doesn't stream, 292
  character shimmers or flutters, 292
  color shifts, 292
  existing problems, 291–292
  files run rough, 298–299
  files too big, 293–294
  files too long, 294–296
  files too slow, 296–298
  major problems, 292–293
  minor problems, 293–300
  post-animation blues, 299–300
  unable to shrink size, 294
  viewers can't follow action, 292
animation window and frames, 44–45
Animation World Network Web site, 321
anti-aliasing, 122–123, 193–194, 209, 335
  moving objects, 310
  Web animation, 123
anticipation, 74–75
API (Application Programming Interface), 18
applets, 18, 335
arcs, 71–73
ARTROOM, 128
ASCII (American Standard Code for Information Interchange), 335
aspect ratio, 44
Astound, 16, 19, 330, 332
  Web site, 276
asymmetry, 56–59
AVI (Audio Visual Interleaf), 23, 335

• B •

background
  color, 103–105, 209
  high contrast, 105–106
  not equal in importance with foreground, 104
  overemphasizing, 104–105
  patterns, 105
  simplicity, 105
  transparent, 209
  unnecessary detail, 191
Backstage Internet Studio, 332
bandwidth, 184, 199, 222, 308, 335
banners, 335
batch processing, 214–219
Benday screen, 132
Bettmann Collection, 158
bit depth, 335
bitmapped images, 335
bitmapped text, anti-aliasing, 122–123
blends, 101–103
  potential problems with, 101
BMP file format, 196
body copy, 124
body language, 64–65
Bounce file, 75
BoxTop Software Web site, 254–255
brainstorming, 32
  accessibility, 34–35
  checking out other Web sites, 33
  clarity of idea, 35
  clarity to others, 35
  difficulty in animating, 35
  idea-generating tools, 33–34
  lots of ideas, 33
  simple research, 33
  striving for multiplicity, 33
  technical know how, 35
  tired or distracted, 34
  visual possibilities, 35
  writing down every idea, 34
browser-safe palette, 90–91, 94
  neutral colors, 100
browsers for clip art, 131
buffers, 24–25
business Web sites, 11
buttons, 38
Bwanib.pcx file, 266, 267
Bwaniw.pcx file, 266, 267

• C •

caesar.pcx file, 66
calligraphic letters, 108
Calliope animation, 280
CD-ROM animation contents
  Chap04 folder
    Bounce file, 75
    caesar.pcx file, 66
    puppet.pcx file, 58, 64
    snowtmp1.gif file, 76
    snowtmp2.gif file, 76
    squash.html file, 77
    Squash1.gif through Squash9.gif, 77
  Chap05 folder
    mntcon.gif file, 106
    mntcoolr.gif file, 99
    mntwarm.gif file, 97
    mntwmcl.gif file, 99
    mount.gif file, 96, 98, 106
    vistease.pcx file, 103
  Chap07 folder, 0080030.tif file, 134
  Chap08 folder, RmanFin1.PCX file, 161
  Chap09 folder, RmanFing.PCX file, 174
  Chap11 folder
    Pumpkin.pcx file, 204
    PumpStd.gif file, 205
    wndmll.tif file, 200
  Chap13 folder
    pumpkin.html file, 243
    pumpkins file, 236
  Chap14 folder, 167
    News.pcx file, 269
    Pictwindows file, 255
  Chap14\GIFimage folder, PumpStd.gif file, 259
  Chap15 folder, 280
  Chap15\Tennant folder, 285
CD-ROM photo collections
  file formats, 159–160
  file sizes, 159–160
  licensing and usage fees, 158–159
  MetaPhotos, 160
  number of images on, 159
  what is available, 160–161
cel animation, 79
cels, 79
  common reference points, 171–172
CGI (Common Gateway Interface), 336
  scripts, 26–27
cgi-bin directory, 27
characters
  constructive laziness, 66
  dissecting moving parts, 65–67
  in-betweening, 68
  key poses, 55
  onion-skinning, 67
  posing, 55–65
  simple objects, 56
  technological techniques, 67–68
  turning head, 72–73
clip art, 127–128
  ARTROOM, 128
  average dimensions, 131
  Benday screen, 132
  black and white or color options, 131
  browser, 131
  browsing World Wide Web for, 128
  CD-ROM collection resources, 324–325
  clipping paths or built-in alpha channels, 134
  color changes to, 139–140
  comping, 145
  customizing, 136–141
  developing story and, 130
  drawing programs, 128
  Dynamic Graphics ArtWorks, 128
  endlessly editing, 130
  file dimensions, 132
  file formats, 132
  Image Club Graphics, 128
  intellectual property, 142–145
  keeping users in place with, 130
  metamorphosing photographs into, 179–180
  modifying silhouette to suggest action, 140–141
  moving down Web page with, 129
  originally designed for print, 132–135
  painting programs, 128
  Publisher's Toolbox, 128
  ready-to-use GIF or JPEG files, 131
  reproduction criteria, 132–133
  resale uses, 145
  RGB, indexed color images, 131
  royalty-free, 145
  selecting for animation, 128–135
  too many anchor points, 134
  transparent backgrounds, 131
  value-added assets, 134
  vector-based drawings, 134

very small file sizes, 131
visual cues, 129
Web-ready images, 130–131
clipping paths, 134
CLUT (color look-up table), 91–93
CMYK (cyan, magenta, yellow, and black), 60, 88, 336
CNET Web site, 322
 Download.com, 253
color, 85–87
 additive, 86–87
 attention grabbers, 97–98
 background, 103–105, 209
 background and foreground not equal in importance, 104
 blends, 101–103
 browser-safe palette, 90–91
 buttons, 38
 changes to clip art, 139–140
 closer to pure, 97
 CLUT (color look-up table), 91–93
 CMYK (cyan, magenta, yellow, and black), 60, 88
 Color Model Sketch, 95–96
 cool, 98–99
 custom palettes, 93–94
 depressing, 100
 group of related, 100–101
 hexadecimal values for, 91
 high contrast, 105–106
 neutral, 99–100
 personality, 60–61
 primary, 85–86
 quiet, 98–99
 reactions to, 96–100
 RGB (red, green, and blue), 60, 88–90
 saturation, 99
 subtractive, 86
 warm, 97–99
Color Computer Displays for the World Wide Web site, 91
color cycle, 167
Color Model Sketch, 95–96
Color Picker, finding, 87
color wheel, 88
comment blocks, editing, 305
commercial animation software, 275–276
commercial software, 232
 demos, 232–233
comp, 145
compositing, 168

compressing files, 199
 difference in file size, 202
 GIF conversion, 203–219
 JPEG conversion, 200–202
concepts, 31
connecting ideas to Web sites, 37
constructive laziness, 66
contents, 40
contrapposto, 59
cool colors, 98–99
Copyright FAQ Web site, 144
Copyright Myths FAQ Web site, 144
copyrights, 144
 scanning photographs, 154
Corbis Web site, 158
Corel PHOTO-PAINT 6.0, 14
 artistic vignette photographic effect, 163
 changing image resolution, 189–191
 Color Picker (Ctrl+F2) keyboard shortcut, 87
 Color Picker dialog box, 87
 demo version, 167
 Effects⇨Artistic⇨Vignette command, 163
 Effects⇨Noise⇨Dust and Scratch command, 152
 Mask⇨Save⇨Save to Disk command, 180
 metamorphosing photos into clip art, 180
 Resample command, 189–190
 Resample dialog box, 189–190
 Save to Disk dialog box, 180
 View⇨Roll-Ups⇨Color command, 87
 Vignette dialog box, 163
Corel Web site, 128
CorelDRAW!, 14
Crop tool, 336
cropping
 files, 308
 images, 186–188
 images to fit action, 51–52
custom
 color palettes, 93–94
 palette swatch, 91–93
customizing clip art
 color changes to, 139–140
 modifying silhouette to suggest action, 140–141
 star dingbat, 136–138
customizing photographs, 161–166
cutout drawing, 163–166
cycles, 78–79

• D •

D'pix sampler, 332
Dabbler, 14
Debabelizer, 186, 235
Debabelizer Pro, 15, 210, 332
Debabelizer Toolbox, 332
  Add Palette To List dialog box, 211
  Auto Namer dialog box, 218
  Batch Compare dialog box, 216–219
  batch processing, 214–219
  Compare Options dialog box, 215–216
  Edit⇨Selection Transparency⇨
    Background Color command, 213
  Eyedropper tool, 211
  File⇨Batch⇨Compare command, 216
  File⇨Save As command, 213
  Image Infowindow, 211
  Magnifier tool, 211
  Misc⇨Compare⇨Compare Options
    command, 215
  Palette⇨Palette⇨Save command, 211, 213
  Palette⇨Palette⇨Stash command, 213
  Palette⇨Remove Unused and Duplicates
    command, 211–212
  Palette⇨Set Palette & Remap Pixels
    command, 211, 215
  pumpkingroup palette, 211
  Save As dialog box, 213
  Set Palette & Remap Pixels dialog box, 212
decorative
  numbers and letters, 125
  typefaces, 116
delay, 234
digital audio sound plug-ins, 23
digital cameras, 154
  Agfa ActionCam, 155
  high resolution, 156
  high-end, 155
  low resolution, 155–156
  mid-range, 155
  point and click, 155
  resources, 325–326
digital contact sheet, 155
digital photos. *See also* photographs
  digital contact sheet, 155
  getting ready for World Wide Web, 154–158
  high-resolution preparation, 156–158
Digital Stock collection, 159
Digital Stock sampler, 332
disposal, 234–235
dissecting moving parts, 65–67
Distortion tools, 173
dithering, 203, 336
  flat art, 310
documentation, 306
down-sampling images, 191
download test, 306
DPI (dots per inch), 152, 336
drawing programs and clip art, 128
Dynamic Graphics ArtWorks, 128
Dynamic Graphics clip art folder, 171
  035X0697 file, 132
  059GL01.eps file, 129
Dynamic Graphics sampler, 333

##

Earth-moving animations
  Earth circling sun, 313
  Earth closing in, 312
  Earth express, 316–317
  Earth lifting, 315–316
  Earth moving, 317
  Earth rising, 318
  Earth turning, 312
  Earth walk, 314
  Earth: soccer to me, 315
  key frames, 311
  rock 'n' roll Earth, 313
editorial animation, 11
emphasis with animation, 39
enlarging small frames, 185
EPS (Encapsulated PostScript) file format, 132
Equilibrium Debabelizer, 15, 210–219, 332
exaggeration and animation, 70
Eye Candy, 332
eyebrows, 63
eyes and expression in animation, 62–63

• F •

feathering, 194
file format converters and GIF animation, 14
file formats, 195
  BMP, 196
  choosing, 196–198
  GIF, 196, 198
  JPEG, 197–198

miscellaneous, 197
necessity of changing images, 199
PCX, 196
Photoshop, 197
PICT, 196
PNG, 196
preferred, 197–198
system picture, 196
TIFF, 196
files
  compressing, 200–219
  cropping, 308
  running rough, 298–299
  scaling before indexing, 309
  too big, 293–294
  too long, 294–296
  too slow, 296–298
filters
  animation and, 193
  resources, 322–323
Flash 2, 23, 287, 331
  cel animation difficulties, 289
  drawbacks, 288–289
  easy tweening and key framing, 288
  innovative painting tools, 288
  interactivity ease, 288
  interface logic, 289
  learning curve on pointing tools, 289
  objects infinitely usable, 288
  reasons to use, 288
flat color filled vase, 102–103
flip and flop, 304
Flip and Flop tool, 173
flipbooks, 54, 336
Florendo, Norbert, 223
Flowers.html file, 276
font family
  italic, 113
  proportional ratio, 111–112
  Roman, 113
  script, 113
  stroke thickness, 112–113
fonts, 108, 336
  adding typefaces, 114–116
  bolder and Web animation, 115
  building font family, 111–113
  capital letter heights, 119
  capitals versus lowercase, 120
  CD-ROM collections, 117
  combining serif with sans serif, 118–119
  evaluating, 115
  font manufacturers, 117
  italic, 113
  lightweight, 115
  listing your, 114–115
  mixing and matching, 117–122
  obtaining, 116–117
  opposites, 120–122
  organizing, 115
  outline versus filled shapes, 120
  printing out sample, 115
  proportional ratio, 111–112
  proportions, 119
  resources, 323–324
  Roman, 113
  sans serif, 118–119
  scale extremes, 120
  script, 113
  script curves versus angular geometry, 120
  serif, 118–119
  stem weights, 119
  stroke thickness, 112–113
  texture extremes, 120
  Upright, 113
  value-added bundles, 116
  World Wide Web, 117
  x-heights, 119
foreground
  high contrast, 105–106
  not equal in importance with background, 104
frame creep, 297–298
frames, 44–45, 124
  Adobe Photoshop, 167–171
  breaking out of, 48
  common reference points, 171–172
  delay, 234
  disposal, 234–235
  enlarging small, 185
  interlacing, 310
  missing, 298
  no transitions between, 80
  as part of animation, 52–53
  placing characters, 46–48
  too many, 297
  viewing old while creating new, 170
  Windowshade animation, 167–171
freeware, 232, 336
Fresco, 332
FTP (File Transfer Protocol) files, 142

• G •

GIF (Graphics Interface Format) files, 336
GIF 87 files, 14
GIF animation
  adapting presentations, 16
  compression, 199
  dependability, 13
  ease of creation, 13
  file format converters, 14
  GIF 87 files, 14
  GIF animation programs, 15
  GIF optimizers, 15
  GIF89a files, 13–14
  image creation software, 14
  low cost, 13
  minimum tools for, 14
  painting programs, 14
  plug-ins, 13
  programs, 14
  repurposing presentation software, 15
  small file size, 13
  text editor, 15
  time required to make frames, 13
  transitions, 243
  version not supported by plug-ins, 21
  Web browser support of, 13
  Web browsers handling differently, 233
GIF animation software, 231–235
Gif Construction Set, 15, 210, 263
  Animation Wizard, 264–267
  banner, 267
  color-coding, 269
  editing animation, 271–272
  editing transitions, 273
  File➪Animation Wizard (Ctrl+Q) command, 264
  File➪Supercompress command, 267
  font sizes, 271
  image specifications for animation, 266
  importing source images, 267
  LED sign, 268–270
  number of cells, 271
  offsetting shadow, 270
  shadow color, 270
  soft shadow banners, 270–271
  special features, 267–268
  Supercompress feature, 267
  timing delay between frames, 266
  transitions, 268
  Welcome screen, 264
  wide palette GIFs, 268
GIF conversion, 203–208
  batch processing, 214–219
  reducing images further, 210–213
GIF file format, 14, 196, 198
  custom color palettes as, 94
  indexed color, 203–205
GIF images, 12
GIF optimizers for GIF animation, 15
GIF89a files, 13–14, 337
GifBuilder, 15
  Animation➪Start (⌘+R) command, 241
  background color, 238
  Cancel (⌘+period) keyboard shortcut, 241
  changing frame size, 239–240
  color wheel, 238–239
  delay, 241
  disposal method, 242–243
  Dissolve dialog box, 244
  Dissolve transition, 244
  Effects➪Transitions➪Dissolve command, 244
  Frames window, 236–238, 244–245
  HSL (Hue, Saturation, and Luminance) numbers, 239
  Image Size dialog box, 240
  Interframe delay dialog box, 241
  loading palette used by animation, 238
  looping, 242
  Looping dialog box, 242–243
  Option➪Image Size command, 240
  Options➪Colors➪Load Palette command, 238
  Options➪Disposal Method command, 242
  Options➪Frame Optimization command, 245
  Options➪Interframe Delay command, 241
  Options➪Loop command, 242
  Options➪Transparent Background command, 238
  Options➪Transparent Background➪Other command, 238
  resetting transparency settings, 237–239
  RGB (red, green, and blue) colors, 239
  Select All (⌘+A) keyboard shortcut, 238
  selecting files for animation, 236–237
  shrinking after dissolve, 245
  special features, 243–245
  transitioning effects, 243–244
  universal animation options, 239–243
  Window➪Frames command, 236
GiffyView, 224

Index

GIFmation, 15, 67, 254, 331
  Add Color eyedropper tool, 258
  Alpha Brush tool, 261
  automatically building global palettes, 255–258
  Browser Background palette, 260
  browser-compatibility warning, 223
  controlling transparency, 258
  Document window, 260, 262
  Edge tool, 260
  editing anti-aliased pixels, 259–261
  File⇨Import⇨GIF command, 259
  File⇨Import⇨Multiple command, 255
  File⇨New (⌘+N) command, 255
  Frame window, 258, 262
  local palettes, 257
  Logical Screen Size dialog box, 261–262
  Onion-Skin Next and Onion-Skin Previous buttons, 262
  onion-skinning, 261–263
  opening multiple animations, 254
  Options⇨Logical Size command, 261
  Options⇨Palette⇨Adjust to Global Palette command, 258
  Options⇨Palette⇨Reduce Bit Depth command, 257
  Options⇨Palette⇨Use Local Palettes command, 257
  Options⇨Position⇨Set Position command, 262
  palette creation, 255
  Palette window, 257–258
  Position in Logical Window dialog box, 262
  quantizing, 255
  real-time edits, 254
  Reduce Bit Depth dialog box, 257
  trimming colors from global palette, 258
  Zoom tool, 260
GIFmation for Macintosh, 210
global palette, 210, 256
gradient tool, 101
gradient-filled vase, 101–103
graphic widgets, 167–171
  animating portion of photograph, 174–179
  common reference point for frames or cels, 171–172
  grids, 171–172
  layers, 167–171
  metamorphosing photos into clip art, 179–180
  transforming multiple objects from one source, 173

graphics programs and transform tools, 173
gravity, 71, 74–79
graying down pattern, 105
grayscal.gif file, 100
grids, 171–172
Gutenberg, Johannes, 108

• H •

halftone screens, 151–152
Harcourt, John, 148
headers, editing, 305
headlines, 124
hexadecimal color values, 91
high contrast, 105–106
high-end digital cameras, 155
Hoffman, Ivan, 144
HSB (hue, saturation, brightness), 337
HSL (hue, saturation, luminance), 239, 337
HTML (HyperText Markup Language), 224, 337
HTML code
  IMG SRC tag, 300
  integrating Java applets, 19
HTML pages
  attaching animation, 224–226
  Image Width and Height tags, 225
hue, 337
humor, 36

• I •

icons, 126, 337
Image Club Graphics, 128
image conversion, 307
  anti-aliasing moving objects, 310
  bandwidth, 308
  cropping files, 308
  dithering flat art, 310
  editing before JPEG conversion, 309
  interlacing animation frames, 310
  Netscape non-dithering palette, 309
  optimizing palette, 309
  scaling before indexing, 309
  screen resolution, 308
image creation software and GIF animation, 14
image maps on Acme Digital Lab home page, 225
image sizes
  economy of, 183
  small, 185–186

images
  anti-aliasing, 209
  batch processing, 214–219
  compositing, 168
  compression, 199
  cropping, 51–52, 186–188
  down-sampling, 191
  editing, 305
  losing resolution, 188–191
  making move, 69–79
  resampling, 190
  screen resolution and, 189
  silhouetting, 209
  white space, 52
imaginary 3-D, 49–50
imaging programs and transform tools, 173
in-betweeners, 79
in-betweening, 68
index cards and storyboard, 53–54
indexed color, 203–205, 337
inertia, 78
inexpensive animation software, 253
inline plug-ins, 337. *See also* plug-ins
  ease of music and sound integration, 22
  interactivity, 22
  minimum tools, 25
  multipurpose, 22
  QuickTime plug-in, 22–23
  Shockwave plug-in, 23
  small file size, 22
  sound, 23
  stability, 22
insider knowledge, 36–37
intellectual property
  copyrights, 143–144
  personal use, 144–145
  persons in pictures, 143
  right to use, 144
  royalty-free, 144
  U.S. Copyright Office Web site, 143
  written permissions, 143
interlacing frames, 310
international audience, 36
Internet
  bandwidth, 199
  large files and bandwidth, 184
Internet Explorer
  Acme Digital Lab home page, 227–228
  animation software compliance, 305
intranets, 337
IrfanView32, 15
ISPs (Internet Service Providers), 337

CGI (Common Gateway Interface) scripts policies, 27
Web browsers, 19
italic fonts, 113
ITC demo, 333
ITC Web site, 138
Ivan Hoffman, B.A., J.D. Attorney At Law Web site, 144

• J •

jaggies, 193, 337
Java, 17–18, 21, 338
Java applets, 17–18
  advantages, 19
  different file formats and, 19
  GIF animation version, 21
  integrating into HTML code, 19
  Java applet creation software, 19
  larger and more sophisticated animation, 19
  learning curve, 19
  minimum tools, 19
  non-Java-enabled browsers and, 19
  plug-ins and, 19
  speed, 17
  WebMotion, 276–277
JavaScript, 18, 338
JPEG (Joint Photographic Experts Group) files, 197–198, 338
  compression, 199–202
  editing before conversion, 309
  potential problems with, 198

• K •

key frames, 68, 338
  cel animation, 79
  earth-moving animations, 311
key poses, 55
Kodak Photo CD-ROM format, 160

• L •

layers, 167–171, 303
  extra, 169
  naming, 169
  onion-skinning correct new positions, 169–170
  as tracing paper, 170
  turning off unnecessary elements, 170
Letraset web.STIR Art Kit, 333
lightweight typefaces, 115

Index 351

Lingo, 23
local palettes, 255
logical size, 261–262
logos
  animated, 126
  animating, 37–38
  building from elements, 38
  converting 2-D to 3-D, 126
  design standards, 126
  enhancing original, 38
  permissions, 126
  position variations, 38
  size variations, 38
  three-dimensional, 38
looping, 222, 235
luminance, 338
Lynda Weinman's Web site, 91

• M •

Macintosh OS
  Get Info dialog box, 202
  Web Animation For Dummies CD-ROM usage, 329–330
Macromedia Director, 23
Macromedia Web site, 23, 284, 287
main titles, 124–125
making images move
  animation cycle, 78–79
  anticipation, 74–75
  body parts responding to other parts movement, 69–73
  gravity, 74–79
  mass with volume, 74–79
  overlapping action, 77–78
  speeding up and slowing down, 78
  squash and stretch, 75–77
  turning character's head, 72–73
  walking, 79
  weight, 74–79
manipulating shapes, 62–63
mass with volume, 74–79
Mecklermedia Internet news and resources Web site, 228
menu lists, 124
MetaCreations PowerPhotos Bugs and Butterflies series, 134
MetaPhotos, 160
Microsoft GIF Animator, 15
  animation height and width, 249
  Animation tab, 248–249, 251
  building animation, 246
  duration, 250
  Image tab, 249–250
  Import Color Palette, 248
  Import Dither method, 248
  Local Palette dialog box, 250
  looping, 251
  main window, 245–247
  Options tab menu, 246, 248
  playing animation, 252
  Preview dialog box, 251
  previewing animation, 251
  saving animation, 252
  transparent background, 249
  Zapf Dingbat stars, 246–247
Microsoft Image Composer 1.0
  Art Effects dialog box, 165–166
  Color Picker dialog box, 87
  Color Swatch icon, 87
  cutout drawing, 164–166
  Edit⇨Copy Channel⇨Alpha command, 180
  Edit⇨Paste command, 180
  metamorphosing photos into clip art, 180
  resolution, 189
  Tools⇨Art Effects (Alt+7) command, 164
  Tools⇨Patterns and Fills command, 180
Microsoft PowerPoint, 16
Microsoft Web site, 246
mid-range digital cameras, 155
MIDI, 338
Midi sound plug-ins, 23
miscellaneous file formats, 197
mixing and matching fonts, 117–122
mntcon.gif file, 106
mntcoolr.gif file, 99
mntwarm.gif file, 97
mntwmcl.gif file, 99
modifying silhouette to suggest action, 140–141
moiré, 152
monitor
  calibrating scanner to, 152
  resolution, 189
moody hues, 60–61
morphing, 338
mount.gif file, 96–98, 106
movement. *See* making images move
moving down Web page with clip art, 129
MPEG (Motion Pictures Experts Group) format, 22, 338
multimedia files, 24–25
multiple images, 14, 338
music, 29

N

naming layers, 169
Netscape Navigator
  Acme Digital Lab home page, 227–228
  animation software compliance, 305
  browser-safe palette, 90
  version 2.0 and GIF89a files, 14
  version 3.0 and QuickTime plug-in, 23
Netscape non-dithering palette, 60–61, 309
Netscape Web site, 284
  plug-ins, 20
neutral colors, 99–100
New York University Web site, 321
News.pcx file, 269
Nodester, 332
noise, 152
non-Java-enabled Web browsers, 19
Not enough memory error message, 333
Nova Development Web site, 128

O

ObjectDancer, 69, 282, 331
  difficulties in use of, 283
  good object-manipulation tools, 282
  high cost, 283
  import and export options, 283
  lack of interactivity, 283
  multiple windows, 283
  non-text objects, 283
  professional quality timing tools, 283
  reasons to use, 282–283
  sharing objects across animations, 283
  typographic capabilities, 282
object-oriented programming language, 18
objects
  position, 234
  transforming multiple from one source, 173
objects feature. *See* layers
OLE (Object Linking and Embedding) controls, 28
onion-skinning, 67, 79, 338
optimizing palette, 309, 339
originally designed for print clip art
  CD-ROM catalog sampler, 132
  checking out Web sites, 132
  file dimensions, 132
  file formats, 132
  reproduction criteria, 132–133
  too many anchor points, 134
  value-added assets, 134
overemphasizing background, 104–105
overlapping action, 77–78

P

Paceworks Web site, 282
Paint Alchemy, 332
Painter, 14
painting programs, 14
  clip art, 128
palettes
  local, 255
  optimizing, 255, 304, 309
patterns, 105
PCX file format, 196
pencil test, 79
personal Web sites, 10
personality, 59
  body language, 64–65
  color, 60–61
  eyes, 62–63
  eyebrows, 63
  manipulating shapes, 62–63
  moody hues, 60–61
Perspective tool, 173
Photo24 sampler, 333
PhotoGIF plug-in, 171, 203, 205–208, 261
photographs. *See also* digital photos
  animating portion, 174–179
  artistic vignette effect in Corel PHOTO-PAINT 6.0, 163
  Bettmann Collection, 158
  CD-ROM collections, 158–161
  customizing, 161–166
  cutout drawing, 164–166
  Digital Stock collection, 159
  effects and filters, 161–166
  feathering edges in Photoshop 4.0, 161–163
  file formats, 159–160
  file sizes, 159–160
  GIF compression, 199
  good for scanning, 148
  halftone screens, 151–152
  handling, 152
  Kodak Photo CD-ROM format, 160
  licensing and usage fees, 158–159
  metamorphosing into clip art, 179–180
  model-release form, 148
  noise, 152
  number of images available, 158
  positioning on scanner, 152
  scanning, 151–154

Index

Tony Stone Images, 159
unnecessary background detail, 191
your own, 147–151
Photoshop file format, 197
PICT file format, 196
Picture Agency Council of America, 159
Pictwindows file, 255
Piquet, Yves, 236
placing
  characters, 46–48
  coordinates, 305
planning Web animation with storyboard, 41–54
plug-ins, 13. *See also* inline plug-ins
  advantages, 22
  constantly downloading, 20
  definition of, 21
  inline, 20
  Java applets and, 19
  Java versus, 21
  PhotoGIF, 171, 203, 205–208
  QuickTime, 22–23
  Shockwave, 23
  sizes of, 20
  work arounds, 21
  WorldView for Netscape Navigator, 26
PNG file format, 196
point and click digital cameras, 155
pose, definition of, 55
posing characters
  asymmetry, 56–59
  contrapposto, 59
  exaggerating reality, 59
  information about character, 56
  personality, 59–65
  simple changes for effect, 56
  symmetry, 57
  where they bend, 58
position, 234
preferred file formats, 197–198
presentation software, repurposing, 15
presentations, adapting, 16
preview scan, 153
primary colors, 85–86
printing font sample, 115
programming, 25–26
  ActiveX, 28
  CGI (Common Gateway Interface) scripts, 26–27
  VRML (Virtual Reality Modeling Language), 26
programs
  Adobe Acrobat Reader, 330
  Adobe Dimensions, 38
  Adobe Illustrator 6.0.2, 14
  Adobe PageMill, 331
  Adobe Photoshop 4.0, 14, 87, 331
  Alchemy Mindworks Animation Wizard, 198
  AnimaFlex, 331
  Astound, 16, 332
  Astound WebMotion, 69
  Backstage Internet Studio, 332
  CLUT (color look-up table), 91–93
  Corel PHOTO-PAINT 6.0, 14, 87
  CorelDRAW!, 14
  custom palette swatch, 91–93
  Dabbler, 14
  Debabelizer, 186, 235
  Debabelizer Pro, 15, 210, 332
  Debabelizer Toolbox, 15, 210–219, 332
  Eye Candy, 332
  finding Color Picker in, 87
  Flash 2, 23, 331
  Fresco, 332
  Gif Construction Set, 15, 210
  GifBuilder, 15
  GiffyView, 224
  GIFmation, 15, 67, 210, 223, 331
  IrfanView32, 15
  layers, 167
  Macromedia Director, 23
  Microsoft GIF Animation, 15
  Microsoft Image Composer 1.0, 87
  Microsoft PowerPoint, 16
  Nodester, 332
  ObjectDancer, 69, 331
  Paint Alchemy, 332
  Painter, 14
  resampling images, 190
  RubberWeb, 331
  RubberWeb Composer, 331
  Shockwave Flash, 23
  SizzEdit, 284
  Terrazzo, 332
  transform tools, 173
  TubeTime, 332
  TypeCaster, 332
  Web Player, 331
  WebMotion, 16, 19, 69, 330
  WebPainter, 15, 67, 69, 331
PSD (Photoshop) files, 134, 197

Publisher's Toolbox, 128
PumpAnim1.gif file, 243
PumpAnim2.gif file, 245
PumpDeB.gif file, 214
Pumpkin.GIF file, 205
pumpkin.html file, 243
Pumpkin.pcx file, 204
pumpkin00 file, 214
pumpkin02 file, 214
pumpkin03 file, 214
pumpkins file, 236
pumpkins folder, 214
PumpPGIF.gif file, 208, 211
pumps00 file, 215
PumpStd.gif file, 205, 208, 259
puppet.pcx file, 58, 64
puppet2.pcx file, 64
puppet3.pcx file, 64

• Q •

QuickTime plug-in, 15, 22–23, 339

• R •

ready-to-use GIF or JPEG files, 131
related colors, 100–101
repurposing, 339
  presentation software, 15
resale uses of clip art, 145
resampling images, 190
resolution, 339
  definition of, 188
  losing image's, 188–191
resources
  clip art CD-ROM collections, 324–325
  digital cameras, 325–326
  fonts, 323–324
  royalty-free sound and music CD-ROMs, 325
  software and filters, 322–323
  stock photo and texture CD-ROM collections, 324–325
  stock photography agencies, 324
RGB (red, green, and blue), 60, 88, 339
  GifBuilder, 239
  image channels, 179
  numeric values for, 89–90
RGB, indexed color images, 131
right to use, 144
RmanFin1.PCX file, 161
RmanFing.PCX file, 174

rock 'n' roll Earth animation, 313
Roman fonts, 113
Romanf file, 174
Rotate tool, 173
rotating, 304
Royal Frazier's GIF Animation on the WWW Web site, 321
royalty-free
  clip art, 145
  intellectual property, 144
  sound and music CD-ROMs, 325
Rubberflex Web site, 279
RubberWeb, 331
RubberWeb Composer, 331
  drawbacks, 280–281
  morphing functions, 280
  no sound capability, 280
  non-standard interface, 281
  photo instead of object oriented, 280
  prerequisites for use, 281
  reasons to use, 279–280
  sparse documentation, 281
  technical support, 281
  tiny files, 280
  viewer-savvy, 280
running in slow motion, 80

• S •

sans serif fonts, 118–119
saturation, 99, 339
scale to speed equation, 81–82
Scale tool, 173
scaling, 304
  animation, 185
  files before indexing, 309
scanners, 151–153
scanning photographs
  copyrights, 154
  halftone screens, 151–152
  library system for organizing scans, 154
  moiré, 152
  print record, 154
Scott, Flo, 155–156
Screen Caffeine Pro sampler, 333
screen resolution, 308
script fonts, 113
scripting, 339
scrolling banner, 269
searching Yahoo!, 321
sense of direction, 49

serif fonts, 118–119
server push, definition of, 27
servers and cgi-bin directory, 27
Setup cannot continue error message, 333
shapes, manipulating, 62–63
shareware, 232, 339
Shockwave, 331
Shockwave plug-in, 23
silhouetting, 209
Silicon Graphics VRML Web site, 40
simple objects as characters, 56
simplifying animation, 192–193
SizzEdit, 284
Sizzler plug-in, 15, 284
Skew tool, 173
skewing, 304
snowtmp1.gif file, 76–77
snowtmp2.gif file, 76
software resources, 322, 323
sound, 29
  plug-ins, 23
speeding up and slowing down, 78
Springer, Lonnie, 128, 171
squash, 75–77
squash.html file, 77
Squash1.gif file, 77
Squash9.gif file, 77
Star animation, 246
star dingbat, 136–138
stationary animation transitions, 243
stem weights, 119
stock photo CD-ROM collections, 324–325
stock photography agencies, 324
Stone, Summer, 119
story line, 31
storyboard, 42–43
  aspect ratio, 44
  breaking out of frame, 48
  cropping images to fit action, 51–52
  dimensions, 43–44
  frame as part of animation, 52–53
  ignoring background, 44
  imaginary 3-D, 49–50
  index cards and, 53–54
  positioning animation, 46–53
  preparing template, 44–45
  testing animation, 54
  tools, 42–43
storyboards
  history of, 43
  key frames, 68
  numbering, 45

streaming, 24–25, 339
stretch, 75–77
subheads, 124
subtractive color, 86
subtractive color wheel, 88
symmetry, 57
system picture-file formats, 196

• T •

T1 connection, 340
Tennant, Rich, 285
Terrazzo, 332
testing animation and Web sites, 221–224
text, 107–108
  advertising banners, 125
  anti-aliasing, 122–123
  body copy, 124
  combining with titles, 123–125
  consistency, 124
  decorative numbers and letters, 125
  editing, 305
  frames and menu lists, 124
  headlines and subheads, 124
  main titles, 124–125
text editors and GIF animation, 15
texture CD-ROM collections, 324–325
TIFF file format, 196
timing
  missing point of animation, 80
  no transitions between frames, 80
  running in slow motion, 80
  scale to speed equation, 81–82
  too fast, 80
  uneven pacing, 81
titles, combining with text, 123–125
Tony Stone Images, 159
Totally Hip Web Painter, 15, 67, 69, 331
Totally Hip Web site, 284
transform tools, 173
transforming multiple objects from one source, 173
transitions, 243–244, 340
transparencies, 14, 340
transparent backgrounds, 131, 209, 304
TubeTime, 332
turning character's head, 72–73
type, animated, 108
TypeCaster, 332

typefaces
  adding, 114–116
  adding weight to, 121–122
  basic geometric shapes, 109
  creation of, 108–110
  decorative, 116
  lightweight, 115
  lowercase letters, 110
  uppercase letters, 109–110

• U •

U.S. Copyright Office Web site, 143
uneven pacing, 81
universal graphic widgets, 167–180
Upright fonts, 113
URL (Uniform Resource Locator), 340

• V •

vase01.pcx file, 101
vase02.pcx file, 102
vase03.gif file, 101
vase04.gif file, 102
vases
  flat color filled, 102–103
  gradient-filled, 101–103
vector-based drawings, 134
viewer, 306
Visual Teaser animation, 103–105
visual cues, 129
voice-only sound plug-ins, 23
VRML (Virtual Reality Modeling Language), 26, 340

• W •

walking, 79
warm colors, 97–98
Web animation, 9–10. *See also* animation
  advertising banners, 11
  animated advertising, 11
  anti-aliasing, 123
  bolder fonts and, 115
  brainstorming, 32–35
  business Web sites, 11
  buttons, 38
  concepts, 31–32
  connecting ideas to Web sites, 37
  contents, 40
  definition of, 10
  different technologies, 12–25
  dimensions, 43–44
  easy threshold solutions, 12–16
  easy to upgrade, 29
  editorial, 11
  emphasis with, 39
  freshness, 29
  GIF animation, 12–16
  humor, 36
  inline plug-ins, 20–23, 25
  insider knowledge, 36–37
  international audience, 36
  Java applets, 17, 19
  limitations, 28–30
  logos, 37–38
  midrange solutions, 16–23, 25
  modular files, 29
  multiple images, 14
  no alternative artwork, 30
  overshadowing ideas with, 39
  page location, 39
  peace and quiet, 29
  personal Web sites, 10
  planning, 41–54
  programming, 25–28
  sense of direction, 49
  small files, 29
  story line, 31
  too many on page, 39
  transparency, 14
Web Animation For Dummies CD-ROM
  Adobe Acrobat Reader, 330
  Adobe PageMill, 331
  Adobe Photoshop, 331
  AnimaFlex, 331
  animation tools and viewers, 330–331
  Astound, 332
  authoring and imaging tools, 331–332
  Backstage Internet Studio, 332
  D'pix sampler, 332
  Debabelizer Pro, 332
  Debabelizer Toolbox, 332
  Digital Stock sampler, 332
  Dynamic Graphics sampler, 333
  Eye Candy, 332
  Flash 2, 331
  Fresco, 332
  GIFmation, 331

image and sound samplers, 332–333
ITC demo, 333
Letraset web.STIR Art Kit, 333
Macintosh OS usage, 329–330
Nodester, 332
ObjectDancer, 331
Paint Alchemy, 332
Photo24 sampler, 333
problems, 333
RubberWeb, 331
RubberWeb Composer, 331
Screen Caffeine Pro sampler, 333
Shockwave, 331
system requirements, 327–328
Terrazzo, 332
TubeTime, 332
TypeCaster, 332
Web Player, 331
WebMotion, 330
WebPainter, 331
Windows 95 usage, 328–329
Web browsers
  frame disposal, 234–235
  GIF animation support, 13
  handling GIF animation differently, 233
  ISPs (Internet Service Providers), 19
  Java-enabled, 21
  non-Java-enabled, 19
  viewing animation through, 227–228
WebPainter, 15, 67, 69, 331
Web Player, 331
Web sites
  animated advertising, 11
  business, 11
  checking out other, 33
  connecting ideas to, 37
  music, 29
  personal, 10
  planning events, 221
  reasons for adding animation, 37
  sound, 29
  testing, 221–224
Web-ready clip art images, 130–131
WebMotion, 16, 19, 69, 330
  adding simple interactive elements, 278
  automating difficult functions to animate, 278
  drawbacks, 278–279
  ease of timing, 278
  interaction between actors, 278

lack of precise positioning, 279
object creation tools, 279
reasons to use, 276–278
registration point, 279
sparse documentation, 278
visual control over object placement, 277
WebPainter, 15, 284, 331
  animation prerequisites, 287
  drawbacks, 286–287
  editing object as new version of cel, 286
  GIF animation, 284
  in-betweening, 287
  onion-skinning, 285
  professional-quality cel-based animator, 285
  QuickTime plug-in, 15
  reasons to use, 285–286
  registration tool, 285
  Sizzler plug-in, 15
  Sizzler sprites, 284
  standard painting tools, 285–286
  too few animation-specific distortion tools, 286
weight, 74–79
white space, 52
WindLo.jpg file, 201
WindMax.jpg file, 200–201
window size for animation, 185
Windows 95
  Web Animation For Dummies CD-ROM usage, 328–329
  GIF optimizers, 15
Windows NT GIF optimizers, 15
Windowshade animation
  color cycle, 167
  frames, 167–171
wndmll.tif file, 200–201
wndmllsm.tif file, 202
World Wide Web
  browsing for clip art, 128
  fonts, 117
  getting digital photos ready for, 154–158
  large multimedia files, 24–25
  streaming, 24–25
WorldView for Netscape Navigator plug-in, 26

• X •

x-heights, 119

• Y •

Yahoo!
　searching, 321
　ZDNet Software Library site, 253, 322
yelscale.gif file, 101–102

• Z •

Zapf Dingbats, 136

EYE CANDY 3.0

**Attention owners of this book:
You can buy Eye Candy for only $99!**
SAVE $100.00 off the regular retail price of $199.
Just mention special code: "WAFDEC" when ordering.

"Eye Candy offers a very valuable set of filters that is both very useful and very easy to experiment with. The unique blend of usability and intuitive effects sets the standard for the Photoshop plug-in industry." **-NT Studio, 4/97**

"For Web graphics, Eye Candy provides some of the most useful filters we've seen, allowing you to quickly produce attractive text and 3-D buttons and boxes." **-MacWeek, 3/97**

"Both novices and experts will be thrilled with the outstanding results.... If you have Photoshop, you've got to get Eye Candy 3.0!" **-Bright Ideas, 5/97**

Now there's Eye Candy 3.0 for After Effects. With this new version, Eye Candy's wonders are animated in Adobe After Effects. Eye Candy for After Effects can create lapping fire and billowing smoke on any object. Bevels and glows are quick and easy. With Swirl, Glass, and Jiggle objects ripple and pulse.

Be sure and check out our web page for examples of animations created using Eye Candy.

Eye Candy 3.0 is the answer to Photoshop* users' prayers. It quickly and easily adds special effects to print, Web, and presentation graphics. In seconds, these filters create effects that normally require hours of tweaking. Fur, Smoke, Fire, and Squint, simulate natural phenomena better and more quickly than most users can by hand. Professionals love Eye Candy because it makes commonly needed effects like bevels and drop shadows in one click. Amateurs love it because they can create special effects like the ones in this ad.

*Also works with JASC Paint Shop Pro 4.12, Corel Photo-Paint 7.467 or Photo Paint Plus 7.663

Alien Skin, Eye Candy, and Eye Candy for After Effects are trademarks of Alien Skin Software, LLC.
Adobe, Photoshop and After Effects are registered trademarks of Adobe Systems, Inc.
All other products' names are trademarks of their respective owners. We will never wear suits.

Macworld Magazine
AUGUST 1997 Macworld STAR Rating ★★★★ 7.9
best of show MACWORLD EXPO

ALIEN SKIN SOFTWARE
1100 Wake Forest Rd. Suite 101
Raleigh, NC 27604 USA
www.alienskin.com
(919) 832-4124 fax: (919) 832-4065

IDG Books Worldwide, Inc., End-User License Agreement

READ THIS. You should carefully read these terms and conditions before opening the software packet(s) included with this book ("Book"). This is a license agreement ("Agreement") between you and IDG Books Worldwide, Inc. ("IDGB"). By opening the accompanying software packet(s), you acknowledge that you have read and accept the following terms and conditions. If you do not agree and do not want to be bound by such terms and conditions, promptly return the Book and the unopened software packet(s) to the place you obtained them for a full refund.

1. **License Grant.** IDGB grants to you (either an individual or entity) a nonexclusive license to use one copy of the enclosed software program(s) (collectively, the "Software") solely for your own personal or business purposes on a single computer (whether a standard computer or a workstation component of a multiuser network). The Software is in use on a computer when it is loaded into temporary memory (RAM) or installed into permanent memory (hard disk, CD-ROM, or other storage device). IDGB reserves all rights not expressly granted herein.

2. **Ownership.** IDGB is the owner of all right, title, and interest, including copyright, in and to the compilation of the Software recorded on the disk(s) or CD-ROM ("Software Media"). Copyright to the individual programs recorded on the Software Media is owned by the author or other authorized copyright owner of each program. Ownership of the Software and all proprietary rights relating thereto remain with IDGB and its licensers.

3. **Restrictions on Use and Transfer.**

    (a) You may only (i) make one copy of the Software for backup or archival purposes, or (ii) transfer the Software to a single hard disk, provided that you keep the original for backup or archival purposes. You may not (i) rent or lease the Software, (ii) copy or reproduce the Software through a LAN or other network system or through any computer subscriber system or bulletin-board system, or (iii) modify, adapt, or create derivative works based on the Software.

    (b) You may not reverse engineer, decompile, or disassemble the Software. You may transfer the Software and user documentation on a permanent basis, provided that the transferee agrees to accept the terms and conditions of this Agreement and you retain no copies. If the Software is an update or has been updated, any transfer must include the most recent update and all prior versions.

4. **Restrictions on Use of Individual Programs.** You must follow the individual requirements and restrictions detailed for each individual program in Appendix B: "About the CD" of this Book. These limitations are also contained in the individual license agreements recorded on the Software Media. These limitations may include a requirement that after using the program for a specified period of time, the user must pay a registration fee or discontinue use. By opening the Software packet(s), you will be agreeing to abide by the licenses and restrictions for these individual programs that are detailed in Appendix B: "About the CD" and on the Software Media. None of the material on this Software Media or listed in this Book may ever be redistributed, in original or modified form, for commercial purposes.

5. **Limited Warranty.**

   (a) IDGB warrants that the Software and Software Media are free from defects in materials and workmanship under normal use for a period of sixty (60) days from the date of purchase of this Book. If IDGB receives notification within the warranty period of defects in materials or workmanship, IDGB will replace the defective Software Media.

   (b) IDGB AND THE AUTHORS OF THE BOOK DISCLAIM ALL OTHER WARRANTIES, EXPRESS OR IMPLIED, INCLUDING WITHOUT LIMITATION IMPLIED WARRANTIES OF MERCHANTABILITY AND FITNESS FOR A PARTICULAR PURPOSE, WITH RESPECT TO THE SOFTWARE, THE PROGRAMS, THE SOURCE CODE CONTAINED THEREIN, AND/OR THE TECHNIQUES DESCRIBED IN THIS BOOK. IDGB DOES NOT WARRANT THAT THE FUNCTIONS CONTAINED IN THE SOFTWARE WILL MEET YOUR REQUIREMENTS OR THAT THE OPERATION OF THE SOFTWARE WILL BE ERROR FREE.

   (c) This limited warranty gives you specific legal rights, and you may have other rights that vary from jurisdiction to jurisdiction.

6. **Remedies.**

   (a) IDGB's entire liability and your exclusive remedy for defects in materials and workmanship shall be limited to replacement of the Software Media, which may be returned to IDGB with a copy of your receipt at the following address: Software Media Fulfillment Department, Attn.: *Web Animation For Dummies*, IDG Books Worldwide, Inc., 7260 Shadeland Station, Ste. 100, Indianapolis, IN 46256, or call 800-762-2974. Please allow three to four weeks for delivery. This Limited Warranty is void if failure of the Software Media has resulted from accident, abuse, or misapplication. Any replacement Software Media will be warranted for the remainder of the original warranty period or thirty (30) days, whichever is longer.

   (b) In no event shall IDGB or the authors be liable for any damages whatsoever (including without limitation damages for loss of business profits, business interruption, loss of business information, or any other pecuniary loss) arising from the use of or inability to use the Book or the Software, even if IDGB has been advised of the possibility of such damages.

   (c) Because some jurisdictions do not allow the exclusion or limitation of liability for consequential or incidental damages, the above limitation or exclusion may not apply to you.

7. **U.S. Government Restricted Rights.** Use, duplication, or disclosure of the Software by the U.S. Government is subject to restrictions stated in paragraph (c)(1)(ii) of the Rights in Technical Data and Computer Software clause of DFARS 252.227-7013, and in subparagraphs (a) through (d) of the Commercial Computer–Restricted Rights clause at FAR 52.227-19, and in similar clauses in the NASA FAR supplement, when applicable.

8. **General.** This Agreement constitutes the entire understanding of the parties and revokes and supersedes all prior agreements, oral or written, between them and may not be modified or amended except in a writing signed by both parties hereto that specifically refers to this Agreement. This Agreement shall take precedence over any other documents that may be in conflict herewith. If any one or more provisions contained in this Agreement are held by any court or tribunal to be invalid, illegal, or otherwise unenforceable, each and every other provision shall remain in full force and effect.

Installation Instructions

The *Web Animation For Dummies* CD-ROM contains a variety of programs and sample files, either free or try-before-you-buy, for both Windows and Macintosh users. When you access the CD via your computer's CD-ROM drive, you see only those programs and sample files that are available to your computer platform. Please note that some Macintosh OS computer programs require a PowerPC processor. Refer to the individual program folders for more details and/or visit the company's Web site to confirm system requirements.

To install the CD in Windows 95 or Windows NT 4.0 or later, do the following:

1. **Insert the CD into your computer's CD-ROM drive, close the drive door, click the Start button, and click Run.**

2. **In the dialog box that appears, type** D:\SETUP.EXE **and click OK.**

   If your CD-ROM drive is listed as a drive other than D (under My Computer in Windows 95), type the proper drive letter in place of *D*.

   After you click OK, a license agreement window appears.

3. **Read through the license agreement and, if you agree with the terms, click the Accept button.**

   (After you click Accept, you'll never be bothered by the License Agreement window again.) The CD interface appears; use it to install the programs on the CD. The software on the CD is divided into categories as shown on the interface. Turn to Appendix B in this book for more information about what's on the CD.

If you use a Mac OS computer, you install the items from the CD to your hard drive by following these steps:

1. **Insert the CD into your computer's CD-ROM drive and close the drive door.**

   In a moment, an icon representing the CD you just inserted appears on your Mac desktop. Chances are that the icon looks like a CD-ROM. A window automatically opens.

2. **Double-click the Read Me First icon.**

   This text file contains information about the CD's programs and any last-minute instructions that you need to know about installing the programs on the CD.

3. **Double-click each of the category folders to show the CD's contents in that folder.**

4. **To install most programs, drag the program's folder from the CD window and drop it on your hard drive icon.**

5. **To install Adobe PageMill and other larger programs, open the program's folder on the CD and/or double-click the icon with the words "Install" or "Installer."**

   Turn to Appendix B in this book for more information about what's on the CD.

You are welcome to make copies of the sample files and modify them for your own use. You may not publish the files in any form or claim copyright to them. If, after following the instructions in Appendix B, you still have problems installing the programs from the CD attached to this book, please call the IDG Books Worldwide Customer Service phone number: 800-762-2974 (outside the U.S.: 317-596-5261).

IDG BOOKS WORLDWIDE REGISTRATION CARD

Visit our Web site at http://www.idgbooks.com

ISBN Number: 0-7645-0195-X
Title of this book: Web Animation For Dummies®
My overall rating of this book: ❏ Very good [1] ❏ Good [2] ❏ Satisfactory [3] ❏ Fair [4] ❏ Poor [5]
How I first heard about this book:
❏ Found in bookstore; name: [6] ❏ Book review: [7]
❏ Advertisement: [8] ❏ Catalog: [9]
❏ Word of mouth; heard about book from friend, co-worker, etc.: [10] ❏ Other: [11]

What I liked most about this book:

What I would change, add, delete, etc., in future editions of this book:

Other comments:

Number of computer books I purchase in a year: ❏ 1 [12] ❏ 2-5 [13] ❏ 6-10 [14] ❏ More than 10 [15]
I would characterize my computer skills as: ❏ Beginner [16] ❏ Intermediate [17] ❏ Advanced [18] ❏ Professional [19]
I use ❏ DOS [20] ❏ Windows [21] ❏ OS/2 [22] ❏ Unix [23] ❏ Macintosh [24] ❏ Other: [25]
(please specify)
I would be interested in new books on the following subjects:
(please check all that apply, and use the spaces provided to identify specific software)
❏ Word processing: [26] ❏ Spreadsheets: [27]
❏ Data bases: [28] ❏ Desktop publishing: [29]
❏ File Utilities: [30] ❏ Money management: [31]
❏ Networking: [32] ❏ Programming languages: [33]
❏ Other: [34]

I use a PC at (please check all that apply): ❏ home [35] ❏ work [36] ❏ school [37] ❏ other: [38]
The disks I prefer to use are ❏ 5.25 [39] ❏ 3.5 [40] ❏ other: [41]
I have a CD ROM: ❏ yes [42] ❏ no [43]
I plan to buy or upgrade computer hardware this year: ❏ yes [44] ❏ no [45]
I plan to buy or upgrade computer software this year: ❏ yes [46] ❏ no [47]
Name: **Business title:** [48] **Type of Business:** [49]
Address (❏ home [50] ❏ work [51]/**Company name:**)
Street/Suite#
City [52]/**State** [53]/**Zip code** [54]: **Country** [55]

❏ **I liked this book!** You may quote me by name in future IDG Books Worldwide promotional materials.

My daytime phone number is _____

IDG BOOKS WORLDWIDE
THE WORLD OF COMPUTER KNOWLEDGE®

☐ **YES!**
Please keep me informed about IDG Books Worldwide's World of Computer Knowledge. Send me your latest catalog.

NO POSTAGE
NECESSARY
IF MAILED
IN THE
UNITED STATES

BUSINESS REPLY MAIL
FIRST CLASS MAIL   PERMIT NO. 2605   FOSTER CITY, CALIFORNIA

IDG Books Worldwide
919 E Hillsdale Blvd, Ste 400
Foster City, CA 94404-9691